THE COMPANION GUIDE TO
KENT AND SUSSEX

THE COMPANION GUIDES

It is the aim of these guides to provide a Companion
in the person of the author; who knows
intimately the places and people of whom he writes, and is able to
communicate this knowledge and affection to his readers
It is hoped that the text and pictures will aid them
in their preparations and in their travels, and will
help them remember on their return.

BURGUNDY · THE COUNTRY ROUND PARIS
DEVON · EDINBURGH AND THE BORDER COUNTRY
FLORENCE · GASCONY AND THE DORDOGNE
GREEK ISLANDS · ISTANBUL · LAKE DISTRICT
LONDON · MADRID AND CENTRAL SPAIN
NEW YORK · PARIS · ROME
SICILY · TURKEY · VENICE

THE COMPANION GUIDE TO

KENT AND SUSSEX

KEITH SPENCE

COMPANION GUIDES

First published 1973
New edition 1989

Reissued 1996
Companion Guides, Woodbridge
New edition 1999

ISBN 978-1-900639-26-2

*The publishers and author have done their best to ensure
the accuracy and currency of all the information in*
The Companion Guide to Kent and Sussex.
*However, they accept no responsibility for any loss, injury,
or inconvenience sustained by any traveler as a result
of information or advice contained in this guide.*

Companion Guides is an imprint of Boydell & Brewer Ltd
PO Box 9, Woodbridge, Suffolk IP12 3DF, UK
and of Boydell & Brewer Inc.
668 Mt Hope Avenue, Rochester, NY 14620, USA
website: www.boydellandbrewer.com

Transferred to digital printing

This publication is printed on acid-free paper

Contents

TO PENNY

List of Illustrations

The illustrations on pages 103, 173 (top), 247, 267 (top), 293 (top), 323, 337, 345, 353, 373 and 397 were kindly provided by the South East England Tourist Board.

Maps

Preface

In the preface to the second edition of this book, published ten years ago, I commented on the changes that had taken place in the two counties since the first edition came out in 1973. 'Villages have lost their corner shops and been smartened up by prosperous commuters; farmers have grubbed up endless miles of hedges in the pursuit of ever-increasing mountains of grain; there are pedestrian precincts in the major centres; and smaller towns have been rescued by bypasses from traffic strangulation. Industrial estates, leisure centres, superstores and private housing have proliferated on the outskirts of the larger towns; while in the smaller ones estate agents and building societies now outnumber the butchers, greengrocers and ironmongers.'

This process has continued during the past decade, and in many ways things have got worse. An increasing number of churches are closed because of theft or vandalism; vast juggernauts lurch along once-peaceful country lanes; and all over the countryside clusters of 'executive houses' have been dotted about, architecturally banal, guarded by security gates, remote from shops, schools, stations and pubs, and reliant on two or more cars per family to keep them in touch with the amenities of civilisation. Covered shopping malls in such comparatively small towns as Tunbridge Wells and Horsham have contributed further to the decline in old-style town centres. However, the opening of the huge Bluewater shopping complex outside Dartford in 1999 may eventually prove just as lethal to the superstores and malls of the past decade as these have been to the traditional High Street shops. Old-style country pubs have been bought up by consortiums, restyled to suit a trendy non-rural clientele and often given new names.

Ten years ago the major physical and scenic transformation in the two counties was a recent occurrence – the great storm which swept across the South-East in October 1987, leaving an estimated ten million trees uprooted and shattered. At the time I wrote that 'its scars will not be healed for generations', but fortunately such pessimism has proved unfounded, and the storm's devastation has largely

xiii

vanished, due to enormous efforts made in clearing away the débris and planting new trees and shrubs, in every tended area from major woods and parkland to small private gardens. Nothing so dramatic has since taken place, though two natural disasters, put down to global warming, have affected the South Coast – in January 1998 a tornado swept through the town of Selsey, and exactly a year later hundreds of thousands of tons of chalk fell into the sea from Beachy Head.

In August 1989 the National Trust had its own disaster, when fire gutted the magnificent seventeenth-century mansion of Uppark, on the West Sussex downs. Fortunately the damage was repairable, and after miracles of restoration work throughout most of the 1990s Uppark has returned to its former glory.

Ten years ago the impending opening of the Channel Tunnel was awaited with some dread, but in the event it had far less impact on its surroundings than people had anticipated, apart from the huge marshalling yard at Cheriton outside Folkestone, and the new dual carriageway that runs over the crest of Shakespeare Cliff and links the M20 with Dover. The tunnel has even produced a minor tourist and wildlife bonus in the form of Samphire Hoe – a small country park below the cliff, created on the millions of tons of chalk produced by the tunnel workings. It seems likely that the Tunnel Rail Link, due for completion in 2007, will have far more visual impact, with such major constructions as a new bridge across the Medway outside Rochester, and a tunnel through the North Downs south of Chatham. The main impact of the Channel Tunnel services has been felt by the shipping lines, which no longer run passenger ferries from Ramsgate, Sheerness or Newhaven (though Newhaven has begun a small-scale catamaran service). However, seagoing commerce has greatly expanded, mainly due to the setting up of the Medway Ports consortium at Sheerness, Chatham, and Thamesport on the Isle of Grain.

On the positive side, new long-distance footpaths have been created, giving access to stretches of countryside and coast previously untrodden by the general public. Waymarked and usually well maintained, they make it easy to enjoy the scenery without the constant risk of negotiating a length of barbed wire across a right-of-way, or falling foul of cantankerous farmers. Numerous small country parks have opened, as have artistic amenities such as the open-air sculpture park near Goodwood. Many castles and country houses are no longer just buildings to be tramped round, but have become settings for weddings and conferences, while their grounds are used for re-enactments of jousting tournaments and battles long ago.

In 1989 I wrote that Kent and Sussex in the twenty-first century might become 'a chain of conurbations, interspersed with vestigial patches of Green Belt open country and farmland'. This process is bound to accelerate if the government fulfils its dream of building up to five million new houses in England by 2016, over 50,000 of them on green-field sites in West Sussex alone. All the same, we must continue to hope that those responsible for the remaining beauty of the two counties, whether in national or local government, or as individuals, will have the good sense to keep that dismal vision at bay.

Lamberhurst, 1999

Acknowledgments

As with the two earlier editions, I am greatly indebted to the many tourist information officers, librarians, museum curators and local historians who have made helpful additions and pointed out errors in the text. I would specially like to thank the following: Janet Adamson (Folkestone Library), Kevan Atkins (Margate Library), Rosemary Baird (Goodwood House), Margaret Bird (Rye Castle Museum), Ann Bishop (Leeds Castle), Carol Blackwell (Christ's Hospital), Christoph Bull (Dartford Library), Andrew Clay (Newtimber Place), P. A. Close (Cranbrook School), John Coleman (Knole), M. R. A. Constantine (Ashdown Forest Centre), Julianne Davis (Nymans Garden), Ruth Eldridge (Chiddingstone Castle), Sister Helen Forshaw (St Leonards–Mayfield School), Susan Fullwood (Chichester Museum), Bernadette Gillow (Ightham Mote), C. Goddard (Battle Abbey), Stephanie Green and Hannilore Lixenberg (Royal Pavilion, Brighton), Georgie Hammond (Gravesend Library), Guy Hart Dyke (Lullingstone Castle), Karen Hawkins (Lullingstone Roman Villa), Dr Mary Hobbs (Chichester Cathedral), Mansell Jagger (Canterbury City Council), Amelia Jameson (Dover Museum), Marice Kendrick (Boughton Monchelsea Place), Pat Kennedy (Parham Park), Jeremy Knight (Horsham Museum), Christopher Lloyd (Great Dixter), John Loudwell (Upnor Castle), Claire Mason (Maidstone Museum), Sylvia McKean (Herne Bay Library), Peter Miall (Charleston), Leila Moore (Uppark), Anthony Morse (Chatham Historic Dockyard Trust), Nigel Nicolson (Sissinghurst Castle), Diana Owen (Petworth House), Arthur Percival (Faversham Society), Katy Pitt-Williams (St Augustine's Abbey, Canterbury), R. A. Pullin (Hever Castle), Sara Rodger (Arundel Castle), David Rudkin (Fishbourne Roman Palace), Sue Samson (Sittingbourne Library), Brother Simon (St Hugh's Charterhouse), Peter Sowerby (Deal Tourist Information Centre), Margaret Sparks (Canterbury Cathedral), Tim Tatton-Brown (Rochester Cathedral), Stefan van Raay (Pallant House Gallery, Chichester), Bonnie Vernon (Penshurst Place), Franklyn Welsh (Chilham Castle Estate), Sally White (Worthing Museum), Sue Yates (University of Sussex).

xvi

1

The Darent Valley, Dartford and Gravesend

A S YOU HEAD east from London along the A296 from Greenwich through Bexley and into Kent, you are following the ancient Watling Street, the Roman highway from London to Canterbury. Down the centuries this corner of Kent has been steadily eaten away and given to London; the most recent encroachment took place in the 1960s, when Erith, Bromley, Bexley, Chislehurst and Orpington lost their Kentish status – though they preserve it nostalgically in their addresses. Greater London now ends half way across **Crayford Marshes**, which still have cattle grazing on them in a quite unmetropolitan way.

Watling Street runs straight as the surveyor's art could make it down a hill to the River Darent and up the other side into **Dartford**. This was the start of the Roman Derenti Vadum and the Saxon Derentford. What is left of the old town, among the chemical, engineering and paper-making works, clusters down by the river – the parish church, a few timbered buildings, the High Street with the Royal Victoria and Bull coaching inn. The Darent seems a small stream to have given rise to so much growth. You can follow its course southwards through the park behind the public library, by way of the nineteen-mile Darent Valley Path, which takes you upriver as far as Sevenoaks. To the north you can walk to the Thames past Dartford's industries and across the salt marshes, crisscrossed by drainage dykes and haunted by redshank, heron and snipe. A couple of miles downstream the huge spans of the Dartford Bridge carry the southbound M25 traffic across the river.

The library, or rather the museum which forms part of it, is a good place to start from, as it takes the story of the Thames Valley back a quarter of a million years ago, when Swanscombe Man chipped his flints and hunted elephant among the marshes. Built largely of sandstone with plenty of cupolas and carved swags, the library was given to the town in 1916 by the Scottish-born tycoon Andrew

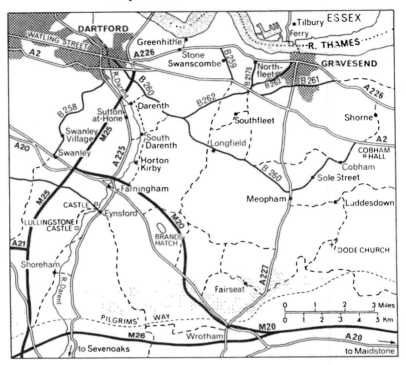

Carnegie (of the Carnegie Trust). It contains an impressive local history collection. Behind it in the park are some paving stones from the Roman Watling Street, and a reconstruction of a few feet of masonry which formed the entrance to the Roman villa at Farningham, five miles up the Darent valley.

The church is a massive flint and stone building, with a square tower jammed in the corner between north aisle and chancel. There was probably a Saxon church on the site; the lower sections of the tower were built about 1080, perhaps by Bishop Gundulf of Rochester. The Norman church was added to in later centuries, including a chapel to St Thomas Becket (the North Chapel), and in the fourteenth century the nave and aisles were rebuilt in their present form. A new chancel arch was built in 1862 to replace an unusually low medieval arch.

The most impressive monument is to Sir John Spilman and his wife, below the arch between north chapel and chancel. Spilman, who was a goldsmith and jeweller to Queen Elizabeth I, came from Lindau in Germany. Apart from his other skills, he was a paper-

2

maker, and in 1586 started a paper-mill in Dartford, presumably about where the Arjo Wiggins mill now stands. It is said to have been the first commercially successful paper-mill in the country. Sir John, who died in 1626, is also said to have introduced lime trees to this country. The arms of his wife, incorporating a man in a jester's cap, appear on the tomb; the use of this device as a watermark may be the origin of the term 'foolscap'.

By the church, on the corner of Bullace Lane, is the Wat Tyler, a half-timbered pub where Tyler and his men are reputed to have stopped for a drink on their way to London during the rebellion of 1381. The revolt was part of the general unrest felt throughout the country after the Black Death, aggravated by the dislike felt for new taxes. Tyler's followers released prisoners and destroyed manorial records; the meeting at Mile End between 100,000 rebels and the young King Richard II, who promised to honour their grievances but went back on his word, is one of the most dramatic episodes of English history.

Dartford's industries lie to the north towards the Thames. Behind the station is the Glaxo Wellcome works, a headquarters of insulin production, with the Darent widened out into a lagoon in front of it; and down Priory Road is the Arjo Wiggins mill, successor to Spilman's Elizabethan enterprise.

Heading south from Dartford up the Darent valley along the A225, the first village of any distinct character you come to is **Sutton-at-Hone**, with the country just about holding its own against the town. The church lies down a lane west of the main road. In Victorian times it was ruthlessly altered by Ewan Christian, architect to the Ecclesiastical Commissioners. The entrance was cut downwards about three feet, so that the door handle in the south porch is now nearly six feet off the ground.

Inside Christian inserted an arcade of dumpy grey marble columns, topped with yellowish curlicued capitals – things to wonder at in a simple medieval church. Against the south wall stands the noble tomb of Sir Thomas Smith (or Smythe), who died in 1625. An inscription gives the career of a true merchant adventurer, who was among other things 'late Governour of ye East-Indian, Moscovia, French and Sommer-Iland Companies: Treasurer for the Virginian Plantation: Prime Undertaker (in the year 1612) for that noble Designe, the Discoverie of the North-West Passage'. Smith was knighted by James I in 1603, and sent as ambassador to Russia the following year. He retired to Sutton in 1620, after accusations that he

3

had enriched himself from the funds of the Virginia Company. Sutton Place, where he lived, has been pulled down; but its brick Tudor wall survives across the main road from the church.

St John's Jerusalem (National Trust) at Sutton is one of the gems of this valley. It was a Commandery of the Knights Hospitallers, a half-military, half-religious order founded after the first Crusade. Henry VIII dissolved the Order in 1540; now all that remains of the Commandery is the east end of the chapel, with its three lancet windows, and the massive flint walls, hidden by later brickwork. Abraham Hill, who was one of the founders of the Royal Society, and introduced cider-making from Devon to Kent, bought St John's in 1665; and a century later Edward Hasted, whose monumental history of Kent has never been superseded, lived there for twenty years and broke himself with the money he spent on improvements. The garden is as perfect in its way as the house, with a moat all round it fed by and forming part of the Darent, a formal flower garden, and magnificent trees – copper beech, cedar, horse chestnut and weeping willow. The whole place has an astonishing serenity within a stone's throw of a busy main road and only a couple of miles from Dartford's swarming industries.

Across the river from Sutton are the villages of **Darenth** and **South Darenth**, linked by a narrow road with open views along the valley. Darenth church is built on three different levels, rising towards the altar; the east end gives a curious grotto-like effect, with crude vaulting and deeply cut window splays. The tub-shaped stone font dates from the first half of the twelfth century, and has a frieze of animal and human figures; one panel shows a baby being completely immersed in a font.

The main landmark of this stretch of the valley is industrial – the enormous Victorian brick chimney of the **Horton Kirby** Paper Mills. Over 200 feet high, it is square at the base and round for the top sixty or so feet. The first paper mill was built here in 1820 on the site of an old flour mill beside the Darent, and the village still clusters round it as in the early days of industry. Opposite is the well-named Jolly Millers pub. Horton Kirby has another splendid example of Victorian brickwork, in the grand railway viaduct which strides across the valley. In 1972 the foundations of a large Roman villa were uncovered near the village, including a vast granary 130 feet long.

Though **Farningham** stands at the junction of two trunk roads, it manages to avoid them both. The wide main street crosses the

4

Darent by an eighteenth-century bridge, and downstream is a weird brick and flint folly, a kind of two-dimensional bridge which could never carry anything. The gardens of the grand eighteenth-century Lion Hotel run down to the river, across the road from the tall white weather-boarded Mill House.

Opposite is the church, mainly thirteenth- and fourteenth-century, with a square battlemented tower. The splendid fifteenth-century font illustrates a different sacrament (ordination, baptism, confirmation etc.) on each of the eight sides. The figures are carved with tremendous vigour. A stylishly dressed bride and groom clasp hands, a demon grabs a penitent by the shoulder, a priest anoints the breast of a dying man. In the churchyard at the back is a square-domed mausoleum to Thomas Nash, who died in 1778 and was the uncle of John Nash, the architect of Brighton's Royal Pavilion. In the old days the girls of the village used to try and throw a pin through the hole in the wall above the inscription, hoping (or fearing) that the devil would peer out if they succeeded.

West of Farningham the A20 brings you up Farningham Hill to the sprawl of **Swanley**, which nevertheless has its rustic side. This is **Swanley Village**, a mile to the north, which consists of a narrow street of old houses and an odd little Victorian church down a byroad. On the other side of Farningham the A20 (largely duplicated by the M20) swings south-east across the Downs, past the giant transmitter mast at the top of Wrotham Hill. The chief lure hereabouts is the Brands Hatch motor racing circuit.

Continuing along the A225, a mile south of Farningham is **Eynsford**, a picture-postcard village, with timbered houses, a narrow stone bridge with a ford beside it across the Darent, and the stone walls of a ruined Norman castle. As the centre of Eynsford lies off the main road, the banks of the Darent can be used for general relaxation, and on a fine summer afternoon the whole village seems to be paddling, fishing, or lazing about by the stream.

The church has a spindly wood-shingled spire, with a brightly painted clock face on the tower dated 1904. The inside is lopsided, as in Tudor times a chapel replaced the north transept, and the north wall was rebuilt to give the whole place an asymmetrical effect. The east end is a rounded Norman apse. There are few monuments, apart from a moving seventeenth-century memorial slab on the floor of the south transept. 'In this silent dormitorie' lies Mary Bosvile, who died in 1659 aged seventeen, and who 'like a jewell taken out of a box was shewen to the world and put up againe'. Her mother, Lady Sarah

5

Bosvile, died the following year: 'thus in a short space death tooke away root & branch, mother & daughter'.

When its high flint wall was unbroken, **Eynsford Castle** (English Heritage) must have brought a harsh military note into the peaceful valley. It was built about 1100, by a Norman family who called themselves de Eynsford after the place where they settled. A good deal of the curtain wall still stands, some of it to its full height of nearly thirty feet. In the fourteenth century the castle seems to have become largely derelict, though it was later patched up from time to time. In the eighteenth century it was used as kennels for hunting dogs by the Hart Dykes of Lullingstone. Now the austere walls are lightened by plants which have colonized the flint. One rarity from Nepal (*Leycesteria formosa*), with brilliant green leaves, white spring flowers and mauve autumn berries, finds it a perfect substitute for a Himalayan cliff.

The byroad to **Lullingstone** runs from Eynsford for about a mile beside the quiet meanderings of the Darent, passing under a handsome striding brick viaduct of the Swanley–Sevenoaks branch line. The magnificent **Roman villa** (English Heritage) lies about half a mile north of Lullingstone Castle, and is protected against the weather by a large wooden hangar, with glass cases displaying small objects found on the site. The villa was first discovered in the mid eighteenth century, when workmen digging post holes for a park fence brought up fragments of mosaic. Systematic excavation has resulted in a comprehensive picture of life in the Romano-British countryside.

The site is a natural one for a farm, with the Darent supplying water transport and grazing, and the hills on either side providing both ploughland for corn and timber for building and fuel. The land was farmed in pre-Roman times; the first flint and mortar house was built by a native farmer eager to become Romanized, and adopting the ideas of comfort brought north by the new masters of Britain. Towards the end of the second century the house was occupied by a Roman, possibly an important government official who used it as a country retreat. It was probably this magnate who brought with him the two bearded ancestral busts, now in the British Museum, of which casts are shown at Lullingstone.

For most of the third century the house was abandoned, and the next occupant found these busts and set them up as cult objects. The two mosaic floors were added about the middle of the fourth century. In the Reception Room, Bellerophon riding the winged horse

Roman mosaic from the villa at Lullingstone, showing Jupiter transformed
into a bull, carrying off Europa.

Pegasus spears a diminutive Chimaera, the whole thing looking like
a prototype for a medieval St George and the Dragon. Four cheerful
dolphins surround the figures, and in the four corners of the design
are the four seasons, one of them (Summer) obliterated by the
eighteenth-century post hole. On the floor of the apsidal dining-room
leading off the reception room Europa rides unconcernedly to her
fate on the back of Jupiter disguised as a bull.

While plenty of other villas have baths and mosaics, one feature is
unique to Lullingstone. This is the Christian chapel, founded about
AD 385 when the owner was converted. Its plaster walls were
painted with the Christian Chi-Rho monogram (the original is now in
the British Museum), and six half-lifesize figures standing with arms
outstretched in the early Christian attitude of prayer. Towards the
end of the fourth century the farm was abandoned, and only the
chapel remained in use. Then early in the fifth century a fire burnt
the whole thing to the ground; soil washed down from the hills
above covered the ruins; and they remained hidden for 1,500 years.

7

Like the villa, **Lullingstone Castle** is a product of centuries of change. You approach the house (not really a castle at all) through a massive brick-built gatehouse, built about 1497. In front of you, across an enormous lawn, stands what appears to be a wide three-storey eighteenth-century house, with lakes formed by damming the Darent stretching away to the south; and on the north side of the lawn a small church, with flint walls, miniature cupola, classical porch, and medieval windows.

In the middle of the fourteenth century the Manor of Lullingstone passed to the Peche family. A descendant, Sir John Peche, was responsible for much of what we see today – the gatehouse, and the Tudor mansion behind the Georgian façade. He was something of a prodigy. In 1494, aged twenty-one, he won the prize in the Royal Jousts before King Henry VII. The following year he was Sheriff of Kent and brought Perkin Warbeck, the pretender to the throne, prisoner to London. He was knighted in 1497, and was later Lord Deputy of Calais. After the death of Henry VII in 1509, he became a trusted adviser of the young Henry VIII, and accompanied him to the Field of the Cloth of Gold in 1520. He died in 1522, and his youthful-looking effigy lies in the church beneath a sumptuously carved stone canopy, with peach stones (a rebus or visual pun on the name Peche) among the foliage. His jousting helmet is above the dining-room fireplace in Lullingstone Castle.

Sir John left no direct descendants, and Lullingstone passed to his nephew, Sir Percyvall Hart, whose vast painted tomb, with effigies of him and his wife, is on the south side of the chancel. The inscription above gives a flattering portrait of the old man, who died in 1580 aged eighty-four, and managed to hold on to his court offices through the reigns of Henry VIII, Edward VI, Mary and Elizabeth. As 'Chief Sewer' he supervised the arrangements of the royal table, the seating of guests, and the tasting and serving of dishes (the title has nothing to do with drainage, but comes from the French *asseoir*, to seat). As 'Knight Harbinger' he was responsible for arranging lodgings when the king was on tour with his retinue (the literal meaning of a harbinger).

The west wall of the north chapel is filled by an elaborate monument to the last of the Lullingstone Harts, another Percyvall, who died in 1738. He built the present front to the house, and made considerable internal alterations. The male Hart line died out with him. His daughter, Anne, married Sir Thomas Dyke, descended from a family of Wealden ironmasters, and from then on successive Hart Dykes have inherited Lullingstone.

In spite of its Queen Anne façade, much of the interior of Lullingstone Castle is little altered since Tudor times. The Great Hall is still a Tudor hall, though with Queen Anne panelling. One wall of the hall is dominated by a triptych of old Sir Percyvall, painted in 1575, and his two sons. He looks much as Henry VIII might have been expected to look had he reached white-haired and healthy old age. In his waistband is the silver-hilted knife which went with the office of Chief Sewer.

A wide staircase leads up to the apartments prepared by Mr Percyvall Hart for Queen Anne's visits. It is lit by a ten-candle lantern, reputedly the only lantern to survive from Whitehall Palace, which was burnt down in Anne's reign. At the foot of the stairs hangs a portrait of Sir William Hart Dyke, who was a friend of Disraeli, and who when young worked out with his friends the rules of lawn tennis on the Lullingstone grass. The staircase treads were made deliberately shallow to help the overweight queen, who had great difficulty in climbing stairs. Upstairs, Queen Anne's state drawing-room has a remarkable barrel-vaulted plaster ceiling, decorated with pendants, and medallions of Romulus, Tarquin and other illustrious or notorious Romans. At one end is a portrait of Queen Anne; at the other her nail-studded travelling chest, with her favourite doll beside it, strikes an oddly pathetic note.

Though it is only a few miles from Bromley and Orpington, **Shoreham**, two miles south of Lullingstone, remains astonishingly remote. No main roads pass through it, and it is still very much the quiet riverside village where Samuel Palmer painted his visionary pictures of the Kentish countryside. The focal point of Shoreham is the little bridge over the Darent, with a watersplash ford beside it; the river runs beside the road for a short way. Near the bridge is Palmer's white Water House. He lived here with his father and old nurse from 1827 to 1833, fired by William Blake's mystical fervour and visited by a group of young fellow-disciples. Blake himself came down to Shoreham at least once before his death in 1827.

The church is at the eastern entrance to the village, with a long avenue of trimmed yews running parallel to it. It is built of flint, with a tiled roof, and has a brick and flint eighteenth-century tower, with a brick pinnacle at each corner. The massive entrance to the south porch is said to be carved from a single piece of oak. Inside the most magnificent feature is the fifteenth-century carved oak rood screen right across the nave, with a door behind the pulpit for access. Inside the door is a brilliantly coloured Victorian painting showing one of the highlights of nineteenth-century Shoreham history. This was the homecoming in 1875 of Verney Cameron, son of the vicar of Shoreham and a naval lieutenant, who led the second Livingstone relief expedition, sent out to Africa by the Royal Geographical Society. When Cameron met Livingstone's men at Tabora, in what is now Tanzania, the great explorer was already dead; but members of the expedition pushed on and were the first Europeans to cross Africa from one side to the other.

In the King's Arms, across the river from the church is an 'ostler's box', a kind of sentry box where the ostler would wait to look after customers' horses. On the inside of the box a window opens directly into the bar, and through it can be seen a waxwork ostler ready for action.

Returning to Dartford, and heading east along the Gravesend road (A226), you come to a landscape of giant cement-works' chimneys and huge areas gouged out of the ground by chalk quarries and stone and gravel workings. One of the most spectacular of these is at the suitably named village of **Stone**. A chalk outcrop has been left sticking up from the quarry, with grass and trees on the top, marking the former land level and rising at a rough estimate about eighty feet above the quarry floor; and much of Stone is perched above a man-made cliff. Stone church lies down a little side road, with views over the chimneys of Greenhithe to the Thames and across to the Essex shore. Inside much of the stone tracery is so fine that it is believed to have been carved about 1260 by the masons responsible for Westminster Abbey.

It is worth making a detour round **Greenhithe**, with glimpses of the Thames, deepwater jetties, and a narrow street of houses and pubs typical of all old sailing towns.

Huge quarries form the background to **Swanscombe**, which lies half a mile south of the main road. The blackened, flint-built church had a spire on its squat tower until 1902, when lightning destroyed the tower and did much internal damage. The lower part of the tower is Saxon. In Palaeolithic times Swanscombe Man lived and hunted on the gravel levels to the north; and it was at Swanscombe in 1066 that the people of Kent defied William the Conqueror and won the right to continue their ancient privileges. Chief of these was the custom of gavelkind, whereby land was divided equally among all the sons of the family instead of going to the eldest. According to a picturesque legend, each man carried a green branch over his head, and Duke William, like Macbeth, found a forest marching towards him. When he came within earshot, the Kentish army threw away their branches and revealed themselves as fully armed and ready to fight if their demands were not met. William prudently granted their terms, and received Dover Castle in return.

Between Watling Street (A296) and Stone, one of the mightiest of the chalk quarries – more than half a mile across – has been turned into the new **Bluewater** shopping complex, the largest such venture in Britain and one of the largest in Europe. The floor of the quarry has been sculpted with roads and small lakes, and filled with the impermanent-looking shopping arcades to be seen on a lesser scale on the outskirts of many towns. What gives Bluewater its special flavour is the contrast between its setting in a towering chalk amphitheatre created by generations of heavy industry, and the ephemeral appearance of buildings inspired by late twentieth-century consumerism.

You know you are in **Northfleet** by the looming brick tower of Sir Giles Gilbert Scott's Roman Catholic church, built in 1914. Northfleet has the remnants of a green, now covered by tarmac, south of the road, with the parish church behind it. Its fourteenth-century carved oak screen is said to be the oldest in Kent. In the churchyard are tombs to local worthies, including the Rosher family, one of whom (Jeremiah) tried in the 1830s to turn Northfleet into a resort, to be called Rosherville. Hidden away in a quarry north of the road are the enormous Bowater paper works.

Northfleet merges imperceptibly into **Gravesend**, which has an unmistakable smell of the sea, mixed with a whiff of mudflats. In past centuries whole fleets used to anchor off Gravesend, and the river still has shipping of all shapes and sizes, from sailing dinghies to container ships making for Tilbury Docks on the north side of the river. Gravesend is the headquarters of the Port of London Authority's Thames Navigation Service, which operates from a modern waterside building with a roof sprouting aerials and radar scanners. Below it is the pretty little Royal Terrace Pier, built in the 1840s.

In earlier times, before the railway took over the traffic, Gravesend owed its importance to its monopoly of passenger traffic by water to London – the so-called 'long ferry'. In 1380 Gravesend was sacked by the French, and the ferry privilege was granted to the town as a means of raising money to repair the damage. Once their right was established, the Gravesend men stuck to it for over four centuries. On the whole they seem to have given good value for money: the fare remained at twopence from 1515 until 1737, when it was raised to sixpence. The long ferry evolved its own special transport, the tilt-boat, so named not because it was liable to turn over (though that was known to happen) but because the forty or so passengers were covered with a 'tilt' or awning. The 'short ferry' still carries foot passengers across the river to Tilbury.

Old Gravesend is a small rectangle bounded on the south by the main road and on the north by the Thames. Much of this area is now a shopping centre. The parish church (**St George's**) was built after a disastrous fire in 1727 which destroyed most of the town; it is a brick barn, with a tower topped by a white pinnacle, and was rebuilt largely by a grant from George II.

St George's is a place of pilgrimage to Americans, as Princess Pocahontas was buried in the chancel of the old church in 1617; there is a bronze statue of her in the churchyard. Pocahontas, daughter of a powerful American Indian chief, was only thirteen in 1608 when she saved Captain John Smith, one of the early Virginia colonists, from execution at her father's hands. The story goes that she fell in love with Smith, but on hearing that he was dead eventually married another settler, John Rolfe, after being baptised under the name Rebecca. Rolfe brought her to England in 1616, where she was fêted at the court of James I; but the following year she died of fever on her way down the Thames back to Virginia. The 1995 Walt Disney film *Pocahontas* gave a tremendous boost to Gravesend's tourism, in spite of (or perhaps because of) its dubious historical accuracy.

Though much of Pocahontas's story is disputed, there is no doubt at all about the contribution of another epic figure to Gravesend. General Gordon was in command of the Royal Engineers there from 1865 to 1871, and was responsible for the forts that guard the Thames downstream from Gravesend – Shornmead on the south bank and Coalhouse on the north. You can walk to the remains of Shornmead along the river embankment. In addition, Gordon did a lot of work for the Ragged School and other local institutions. Tilbury's restored seventeenth-century fort can be seen from Gravesend straight across the Thames; the Gravesend earthworks, of a similar date, are now a public garden, with the Gordon Promenade along the river and a statue of the general among the paths and flower beds. At about the time that Gordon was building his forts, the composer Rimsky-Korsakov was an officer in the Russian navy and was posted to Gravesend. While there he wrote part of his first symphony – the first-ever symphony by a Russian composer.

Gravesend High Street leads straight down the hill to the Town Pier, and still has some weatherboarded houses left. Half way down are the massive Doric columns of the Town Hall, with a way through them to the Borough Market, looking like a miniature Covent Garden; 'Chartered 1268' is inscribed over the entrance. At the end of the eighteenth century, Hasted tells us, Gravesend was famous for its market gardens, and especially its asparagus, which was known as 'Gravesend grass'.

At Gravesend, long-distance walkers put on their boots to begin the Saxon Shore Way, which circumnavigates the Kent coast round to Rye, or the Weald Way, which crosses Kent and Sussex to end at Eastbourne.

Inland across the A2 from the Northfleet and Gravesend, a haphazard collection of North Downs villages are starting to coalesce into one huge suburban sprawl. **Southfleet** is an old village in orchard country, built round a crossroads, with a big stone and flint church. Roman tiles used here and there in the walls came from the Roman settlement at Springhead (Vagniacae) on Watling Street near by. Unusually, the church has never had any major structural alterations since it was built in the fourteenth century. Inside it is spacious, with enormous chancel and wide aisles. The octagonal font is carved on all sides; among the carvings are St Michael, winged and in armour, weighing souls, and a yale – a goatlike heraldic beast, with grinning mouth and serrated horns.

Two of these villages must be among the most straggling in the whole country: **Longfield**, about three miles end to end, and **Meopham** (pronounced Meppam) about four. The centre of Meopham is the green, with a wide triangle of turf complete with neat cricket pavilion on one side of the road, and the suitably named Cricketers pub on the other. Back from the road is a well preserved black-painted smock windmill. Only two miles from Meopham, yet in utter remoteness, is **Luddesdown** – a manor house, church and a few houses sheltered and hidden by enveloping folds of the downs. Luddesdown Court is said to be the oldest house in continuous occupation in England, if not in the world; the occupants go back to William the Conqueror's half-brother, Odo, Bishop of Bayeux, who features prominently in the Bayeux Tapestry. **Dode** church, two miles south along the narrowest of lanes, is all that remains of a village decimated by the Black Death in 1349. The little flint-walled Norman church, with slit windows, was re-roofed and restored early this century. It is extremely hard to find, as most of the signposts in the area have been smashed off by lorries or vandals (this goes for much of the North Downs).

Though it is so near Rochester, **Cobham** is remarkably self-contained and unspoilt, with its church and almshouses, and **Cobham Hall**, now a girls' boarding school, set in its landscaped park. The framework of Cobham Hall dates from the time of William Brooke, tenth Lord Cobham, a notable figure at Queen Elizabeth's court. He built the long Tudor wings north and south of the old manor house, each wing with a cupolaed tower at either end. His son, Henry Brooke, the eleventh Baron. was the last of the Cobham line. In 1603 he joined Sir Walter Raleigh in the abortive attempt to place Lady Arabella Stuart on the throne instead of James I, and was tried and sentenced to death. Luckier than Raleigh, his sentence was commuted to life imprisonment, but Cobham Hall was forfeited to the Crown.

Ten years later James gave Cobham to his second cousin Ludovic Stuart, the Duke of Lennox (later Lennox and Richmond). The Stuarts were fervent royalists. Two of the third Duke's sons were killed in the Civil War (their double portrait hangs in the Gilt Hall); and the fourth Duke took charge of burying the body of Charles I at Windsor after his execution. In the 1660s Charles Stuart, the sixth and final Duke, built the present central block on the site of the old medieval house.

He was more famous for his marriage than his building activities. In 1667 he married Frances Stuart, one of the greatest beauties of Charles II's court, known as 'La Belle Stuart'. Unlike many of her friends, she was unwilling to become yet another royal mistress; though Charles insisted that she sat to the engraver Roettier for the figure of Britannia, and she has appeared on the coinage ever since (see Goodwood. p. 410). In a splendidly novelettish scene, one stormy night La Belle Stuart crept from Whitehall wrapped in a dark cloak, met the Duke of Richmond at Southwark, drove down with him to Cobham, and lived happily as Duchess until he died five years later. As in all good romances, the king finally forgave her, and she returned to court (perhaps ironically) as Lady of the Bedchamber.

Cobham passed by devious processes of inheritance to the Earls of Darnley, and it was the third and fourth Earls at the end of the eighteenth and beginning of the nineteenth centuries who added the finishing touches. First, of all James Wyatt, and subsequently George and John Repton, adorned, altered, enlarged and rebuilt Cobham inside and out. The Reptons' landscaping father, Humphry, laid out the garden and park, planting the giant cedars which still shade the lawns, and the lime avenue which once stretched away to Cobham village.

A tour round the house is chiefly memorable for the contrast between massive stone Tudor fireplaces and delicate eighteenth-century plasterwork ceilings. The wide granite staircase up to the gallery was built in 1602, as the final feature of the Tudor house. The Darnley state coach (kept on the upper floor) was built about 1715 and is a great showpiece. Glorious in gilding and scarlet, it still rocks gently on strong leather springs. In 1953 the then Lord Darnley wanted to use it at the Queen's coronation, but it was not considered roadworthy by the police.

Downstairs is the Repton library, now the school library. On the mantelpiece is a small photograph of an urn, which links Cobham with the history of English cricket. After the Australians defeated England at the Oval in 1882, a mock obituary appeared in the *Sporting Times* lamenting the death of English cricket, and ending up: 'The body will be cremated and the ashes taken to Australia.' Hence the term 'the Ashes' for a test series between England and Australia. As a sequel, an English team left for Australia to recover the Ashes captained by Ivo Bligh, later Lord Darnley. Bligh's team won two out of three matches. After the second Australian defeat, some of Melbourne's young ladies burnt a bail, put the ashes in an urn and gave it to Bligh. He was so taken with one of the girls that he married her; and she is the Edwardian Countess whose portrait hangs in the long gallery. The urn was kept at Cobham for many years, and is now at Lord's.

Cobham's sumptuous Gilt Hall rises two storeys high to an elaborate gilded plasterwork ceiling, and was the banqueting hall in the seventeenth-century central block. Wyatt or, more probably, Sir William Chambers, converted it into a music room by adding the musicians' gallery and organ gallery.

Wyatt's most extraordinary work at Cobham lies away in the woods to the east of the house. This is the **Mausoleum**, begun in 1783 as the burial place for the Darnleys but never consecrated, because, so the story goes, the Bishop of Rochester refused to have anything to do with a building ill-omened enough to have its

foundation stone laid in a thunderstorm. You get there from Cobham
down a tunnel of trees, then across a field track marked by a line of
gigantic oaks, some of them suitably blasted, then into the thickets
and bracken of the Great Wood. Suddenly, at the top of a rise, you
see a pyramid of stone above the trees – the roof of the mausoleum.
Magnificent in its crumbling desolation, it exudes a brooding
melancholy. Young saplings sprout from the roof; the niches in the
round chapel are defaced with charcoal scrawls; and below ground
rows of recesses wait vainly for generations of dead Darnleys. Plans
to restore it have not yet materialised.

The nineteenth-century artist Richard Dadd is commemorated in
Cobham Park at a spot known as 'Dadd's Hole'. In 1843 Dadd
stabbed his father to death here, in a fit of insanity – a crime for
which he was kept in a mental hospital, where he painted his strange,
hallucinatory visions of fairyland.

The dead lords of Cobham lie in and around the village church.
Cobham church is famous for its memorial brasses. The chancel is
paved with them – fifteen altogether, from 1299 to 1529, with a few
others elsewhere in the church. They lie there in two rows with their
feet pointing towards the east, the lords in armour and the ladies in
high head-dresses with pet dogs at their feet. Most notable in the
story of Cobham was the fourteenth-century Sir John, who in 1367
restored and beautified the church (on his brass he holds a model of
it in his hands). He was a companion of the Black Prince in the wars
against France, built Cooling Castle a few miles to the north in the
Hoo peninsula, and together with Sir Robert Knollys, rebuilt
Rochester bridge. He was tried and condemned to death by Richard
II (commuted to banishment), was restored to favour by Edward IV
and died in 1407.

A few yards south of the church, across a strip of grass, is the
College, built and endowed by Sir John de Cobham in 1362 for five
priests, converted into almshouses in Elizabethan times, and
modernized in 1956. It is a little quadrangle of flint and stonework,
with doors leading off to the pensioners' rooms, each with the name
of his or her village – Hoo, Halling, Shorne. On the south side is the
medieval hall, now a common room, and in the garden at the back
are the ruins of the medieval kitchen. Modern planners could learn
something from this idyllic Elizabethan old people's home.

Across the road from the church is the timbered **Leather
Bottle** pub, mentioned in Dickens's *Pickwick Papers* and full of

Dickensiana; and near by is a gigantic iron village pump. set up in 1848 to mark a Darnley coming-of-age.

Owletts (National Trust), at the western end of the village, was built in Charles II's time by a prosperous farmer, Bonham Hayes. Its ornate plaster ceiling, dated 1684, above the staircase well, incorporates cherries, hops and other sources of Kentish farming wealth. Sir Herbert Baker, the architect with Lutyens of Imperial New Delhi, lived here from 1917 until his death in 1946. Baker also bought and restored **Yeoman's House** (let to a tenant by the National Trust), in Sole Street, round the corner from Cobham; its fourteenth-century great hall may be seen by appointment.

2

Rochester and the Medway

A T **Gads Hill**, a couple of miles west of Rochester up the A226, Shakespeare and Dickens confront each other. On the north side of the road is the Sir John Falstaff, near the spot where the sack-swilling knight lay in wait with Prince Hal to rob the 'pilgrims going to Canterbury with rich offerings, and traders riding to London with fat purses'. Shakespeare made his travellers dismount at the top of the hill, preparing to walk down the other side to stretch their legs, and in the old days it must have been quite a tiring pull-up from the end of Rochester Bridge.

Almost opposite the Falstaff is **Gads Hill Place**, where Dickens lived for the last fourteen years of his life. This is Dickens country, the area where he spent much of his life and the setting for several of his novels. He lived as a boy in Chatham, and would go for long walks with his father, often passing Gads Hill. He coveted the house, and was told by his father 'if you were to be persevering and were to work hard you might some day come to live in it'. By 1856 Dickens had worked hard enough, and bought this undistinguished red brick house, with its bay windows and little white cupola on top. It is now a school, with small brown-uniformed girls running in and out. Directly opposite is a garden with lawn and tall trees, where Dickens worked in a chalet during his last years; the day before he died, in June 1870, he had been working there on his unfinished last novel *Edwin Drood*. It is now in the grounds of the Charles Dickens Centre, Rochester (see below).

The centre of **Higham** village has been drawn southwards by the magnetism of Rochester, but the old nucleus lies two miles away on the edge of the marshes down the dead end of Church Street. The medieval church and hamlet are set in a strange combination of orchards, pylons and industrial chimneys. The church is built in alternating bands of flint and stone, with a little shingled bellcote at the back. The great old door is superbly carved with roses and is said

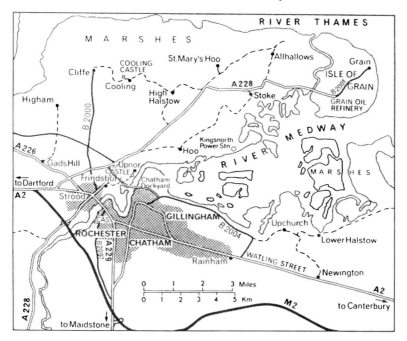

to be fourteenth-century, and there is a traceried rood screen of the same date.

Cliffe-at-Hoo, north up the B2000, has a massive church begun in 1260. In 774 Offa, King of Mercia, built a rough wooden church here and dedicated it to St Helen, a favourite saint of the Mercians, and according to British legend the daughter of Coel ('Old King Cole') of Colchester. No other church in Kent is dedicated to her. In the later Middle Ages Cliffe became an important port, but after a disastrous fire in 1520 it faded away, until the rise of the Kentish cement industry in Victorian times brought new prosperity. It now has a large riverside petrol storage depot. A lane leads down past disused quarries and gravel pits, now used for watersports, to the remains of a massive Victorian fort.

From Cliffe, a narrow road, hardly more than a lane, meanders above the Thames mudflats. Like Gads Hill, the village of **Cooling** links Shakespeare and Dickens. In the churchyard at Cooling is a grave with thirteen small lozenge-like stones round it, which Dickens made the family grave of Pip's relations (though he only allowed them five lozenges), where Pip met the terrifying convict Magwitch with irons on his leg. A little way west is **Cooling Castle,** built by

19

the Cobhams and the home of Sir John Oldcastle, the model for Falstaff. The turreted gatehouse and a good deal of walling can be seen from the road. The fortifications were built in the 1380s, to defend the port of Cliffe from French raiders. On one of the towers John de Cobham prominently fixed an inscription in the form of a copper legal document and seal, congratulating himself in rhyme for his patriotism in fortifying Cooling.

At some time in his life Oldcastle came under the influence of Wycliffe's teachings, chief of which was the need to spread the English translation of the Bible and to fight the corruption of the established church. Of all Wycliffe's followers (contemptuously called Lollards) Oldcastle was the most formidable, entrusted with military command by Henry IV and the confidant of his son Prince Hal; in this at least Shakespeare was correct. When Oldcastle encouraged the spread of Lollard opinions in Kent, and even tried to convert the prince, he was accused of heresy. After some years in hiding on the Welsh Marches, and in spite of the friendship of Prince Hal (by now Henry V), he was captured, tried, condemned and burnt as a heretic in 1417. He was the very opposite of the fat coward portrayed by Shakespeare. In the play *Henry IV* Falstaff was originally called Oldcastle, but Shakespeare is thought to have changed the name in deference to the wishes of the Cobham family. Indeed, in the epilogue to the second part of the play he went so far as to say 'for Oldcastle died a martyr, and this is not the man'.

High Halstow, seven miles from Lower Halstow (see below) as the seagull flies across the Medway, and double the distance by road, is expanding fast along its hilltop. **Northward Hill**, towards the Thames, has one of the largest heronries in Britain, looked after by English Nature and the Royal Society for the Protection of Birds. **St Mary's Hoo**, the most remote of these remote places, is just a small cluster of windswept houses and a bare church high above the marshes.

Allhallows on Sea, down by the Thames, is something of a resort, with a caravan park, and a wide grass expanse behind the shingle foreshore. Head south from here to **Lower Stoke** and take the main road (A228) through the site of a disused oil refinery to the **Isle of Grain** at the eastern end of the peninsula. **Grain** village, at the end of the road, has a small esplanade, with marvellous views of the Thames and Medway shipping, and across the river to the high-rise blocks of Southend. An imaginary line from London Stone, on the north side of Grain, to Southend Pier marks the limit of the jurisdiction of the Port of London Authority.

Returning along the main road, a byroad leads down to **Hoo** (in full, Hoo St Werburgh). This consists largely of modern housing estates, though there are relics of a Georgian village at its centre. The church, on the edge of the marshes, has a tall spire which makes a graceful contrast with the giant chimney of the Kingsnorth power station.

The next side road brings you to **Upnor**, a quiet little backwater consisting of a single street of narrow weather-boarded houses sloping down to a slipway, and the splendid Elizabethan **Upnor Castle** (English Heritage). For over a century Upnor was a key point in the Medway defences. As the navy grew under Henry VIII and his successors, the upper reaches of the Medway below Rochester bridge were used for laying up the fleet. In 1559, the year after she came to the throne, Queen Elizabeth gave orders for a fort to be built at Upnor, well downstream from the embryo dockyards at Chatham. This original fort consisted of the large square stone building overlooking the river, and a wedge-shaped gun bastion built out into the water. Forty years later the castle was enlarged with a gatehouse and outer retaining wall, and this is more or less the form it has kept ever since.

The only time Upnor was put to the test was an ignominious disaster for the navy. In 1667 the Dutch fleet under de Ruyter sailed up the Medway, broke the chain boom stretched across the river below Upnor, defied the castle guns and attacked the British fleet anchored off Chatham. Several ships were burnt, and the *Royal Charles* was captured and sailed back in triumph to Holland. The diarist John Evelyn called it 'a Dreadfull Spectacle as ever any English men saw and a dishonour never to be wiped off'. Thereafter Upnor declined into a powder magazine, a general storehouse, and a museum.

The way into the castle leads past an eighteenth-century barracks, now derelict. The outer wall, stone with brick trimmings on top, still looks good and solid; much of the stone was taken from Rochester Castle. The gatehouse leads into a long courtyard, planted with a pair of Turkey oaks said to have been grown from acorns brought back from the Crimean War. The museum exhibits are in the magazine across the courtyard: guns, a collection of Romano-British pottery, and display cases with diagrams, plans and engravings of the Medway defences down the years. An unusually wide spiral staircase links the magazine to the bastion below; it has a central well for hauling up powder, and a lead-cased handrail to lessen the risk of fire. From the bastion there are wide views up and down the Medway, and across to the Chatham peninsula.

Nowadays Upnor, with its quiet waters and sheltered moorings, is deservedly popular with small-boat sailors. But a century and a half ago more sinister superannuated ships were anchored off Upnor – the prison hulks where convicts rotted away their lives, unless they were lucky enough to escape, like Magwitch in *Great Expectations*. Dickens, with a novelist's licence, shifted the hulks round to the north side of the Hoo peninsula, beyond the Cliffe marshes – 'the dark flat wilderness . . . intersected with dykes and mounds and gates'.

As you approach Rochester from the west, two old villages, long since swallowed up, lie on either side of the A2. **Frindsbury** has a church like an echo of Rochester cathedral, with its square flint tower and shingled spire standing commandingly on a bluff above the Medway. It was reconstructed in 1075 by a certain Paulinus, who appears along with Bishop Gundulf of Rochester in two of the lancet windows in the chancel; and it was much altered by the Victorians.

The only thing worth looking at in **Strood**, across the A2 from Frindsbury, is **Temple Manor** (English Heritage), hidden away among a depressing area of riverside industry. The house, basically a thirteenth-century inner and outer chamber on the first floor, with an undercroft below, was built for the Knights Templar, probably about 1240. When the order was abolished in 1312 it became a prosperous farmhouse. In the seventeenth century it was extended to the east and west, and an old engraving shows it with outbuildings and a grassy field sloping down to the Medway, where today there are factories and the railway. The undercroft has some fine vaulting, and the main floor still has well-carved surrounds to some of the lancet windows.

Rochester has the advantage of compactness, forced on it by the course of the river, which doubles back on itself to form a promontory on which the old town stands. As you approach it across the bridge, you are faced by the twin medieval grandeurs of castle and cathedral, standing side by side as reminders of secular and ecclesiastical power. Mr Jingle's Rochester is still very much the same: 'Ah! fine place – glorious pile – frowning walls – tottering arches – dark nooks – crumbling staircases – Old Cathedral too.' To Dickens Rochester was also Dullborough and Cloisterham; and especially the scene of Pip's pursuit of his great expectations, from Mr Pumblechook's gabled shop in the High Street to the crumbling red brick of Restoration House, the Satis House where Miss

22

Havisham lived in candlelight among her rotting bridal finery. Mr Pickwick's Bull Hotel (now the Royal Victoria and Bull) is thoroughly Dickensified. The upstairs ballroom, with its twin fireplaces and musicians' gallery, can hardly have been altered since the Pickwick Club assembled there.

Rochester's history began long before the Romans. Their name for it, Durobrivae, is derived from the Celtic *dwr* (water) and *briva* (ferry), and there must have been a Belgic stronghold guarding so important a crossing. Watling Street crosses the Medway here; in places the walls of the medieval castle follow the walls of the Roman camp; and the Roman bridge, continuing the High Street, was roughly on the line of the modern bridge.

Christianity came to Rochester in AD 604, when St Augustine consecrated Justus, a missionary monk sent from Rome, as the first Bishop of Rochester; and King Ethelbert built a small stone church there. The modern name for the city derives from 'Hrofe-Caestre', the camp of Hrof or Roffa, a pre-Christian Saxon warlord. During the Anglo-Saxon period Rochester was periodically attacked by marauding Danes, and even as late as 1075 the Saxon church was 'utterly forsaken, miserable and waste, from lack of all things within and without'. Two years later the situation was taken in hand with the consecration of Gundulf, a Norman monk, as bishop. This energetic prelate immediately began work at Rochester, building the castle (though not the massive keep), a monastery, and the **Cathedral**. He also helped to build the White Tower in the Tower of London. **Gundulf's Tower**, embedded in the masonry of the cathedral's north side like a buttressed sentry box, was built as the bell tower in the early twelfth century, well after Gundulf's time, and only got its present name in the eighteenth century. About fifty feet of the tower still stands; its top was removed in about 1800.

The spectacular **West Front** with its great Norman door dates from about 1160. The two inner and two outer pinnacles, with their octagonal roofs and blind arcading, were restored by J. L. Pearson in 1888. Most of the front is taken up with a huge Perpendicular window, inserted in 1470 and renewed in the early nineteenth century, dwarfing the richly-carved Norman door below it. This door, with its row of diminishing arches one inside the other, surrounding a tympanum of the seated Christ in majesty with the symbols of the evangelists, is no doubt the original entrance used when the cathedral was consecrated in 1130, in the presence of King Henry I.

23

The cathedral interior, with its tombs, screens and odd corners, is so full of architectural variety that you could spend days there and still find something new. Much of it is massively Norman, like the south aisle arcade, and the later elaborately moulded arches of the north arcade. Gundulf's work can be seen in the **Crypt**, where his austere round arches give place to springing Early English vaulting. It is worth looking for the medieval graffiti scratched on the crypt piers. The cathedral has some striking examples of architectural ingenuity, like the curious arches below the vaulting in the north transept, with one asymmetrical opening uncomfortably squeezed against the next.

Between the north transept and the choir transept are the worn steps where the pilgrims climbed on their way to the shrine of St William of Perth, long since disappeared. In 1201 William, a charitable Scottish baker who used to give every tenth loaf he baked to the poor, was murdered just after he had spent the night in Rochester at the start of a pilgrimage to the Holy Land. The monks of Rochester seized eagerly on this possible rival to Canterbury's St Thomas, burying him in style and setting up a shrine to him. The choir was complete and in use by 1227.

Most of the memorials of interest are in the south transept. Largest is the memorial with its sleeping effigy of Dean Hole, who died in 1904 aged eighty-five. Samuel Reynolds Hole was the epitome of the Victorian sporting parson – an enthusiastic fox-hunter, a friend of John Leech the cartoonist, and a writer on gardening. A great organiser of rose shows and founder of the National Rose Society (Tennyson called him 'the rose king'), he grew 135 varieties in the Deanery garden at Rochester. The west front of the cathedral was restored under the supervision of this tireless man, who at the age of seventy-five went on a lecture tour of the United States and raised £500 for the work. On the wall behind this monument is a tablet to Dickens. Richard Watts, the sixteenth-century Rochester philanthropist (see below), peers down from the wall like a bearded prophet out of William Blake.

Rochester Cathedral contains a social history of the Middle Ages in the two-hundred-odd heads carved as corbels or ceiling bosses, from dignified monks to grimacing wild men. On the north wall of the choir a fair amount remains of a painting of one of the favourite medieval cautionary tales – the Wheel of Fortune, seen as a treadmill, with the ambitious rising to the top and the man who has made good looking anxiously down the far side of the wheel. The choir walls are bright with golden lions and fleur-de-lys on a red and blue background, repainted during Sir Gilbert Scott's restorations of the 1870s, and based on fragments of fourteenth-century painting found behind some old woodwork. The early thirteenth-century choir stalls, though much restored, are the earliest in Britain.

Typical of the cathedral, in that you may miss it if you do not look out for it, is the elaborately carved fourteenth-century chapter-room door. On the left side is the Church, shown as a female figure holding a staff surmounted by a cross; on the right the Synagogue, a blind-folded figure with a broken staff. Above them, sloping inwards towards the point of the arch, are four Fathers of the early Christian Church.

Though the outer bailey of **Rochester Castle** (English Heritage) is now domesticated, it would be impossible to tame the majestic harshness of its keep. The line of the outer walls is due to Gundulf; the keep, seventy feet square and towering to well over a hundred feet, was built by William de Corbeuil, Archbishop of Canterbury, at the end of the 1120s. In 1215 the rebel barons held the castle for nearly two months against King John's siege weapons, only surrendering when sappers undermined one of the corner towers. A tunnel was dug under the tower, shored up with pit-props. The besiegers then brought 'forty of the fattest pigs of the sort least good for eating', placed them round the pit-props and set fire to them. As the props burnt through, the tower collapsed. After this, wrote a contemporary chronicler, 'few cared to put their trust in castles'; though Rochester Castle was repaired and again besieged, unsuccessfully, by Simon de Montfort in 1264.

As you climb the keep, its structure is very clear, with grand entrance on the first floor, on the second floor a galleried great hall divided down the middle by a tall arcade, and on the top floor living quarters and chapel. From the battlements there is a tremendous view in all directions: up the Medway beyond the leaping ribbon of the M2, across the river to the unlovely sprawl of Strood, and down river over the cathedral roof, past the zigzag cladding of its spire, to the mudflats of Chatham Reach.

Behind the keep is Boley Hill, with two houses worth looking at. **Satis House** has a bust of Richard Watts over the door, a twin to the monument in the cathedral. The name is said to have arisen after Queen Elizabeth spent the night there. In the morning Watts asked her if she had been comfortable, to which she replied 'Satis', the royal equivalent of 'Not bad'. (Dickens transferred the name Satis House to Restoration House, a few minutes' walk away in Maidstone

25

Road.) Next door is the gabled and timbered **Old Hall,** where Henry VIII is said to have met Anne of Cleves, his 'Flanders mare', when she arrived in England.

One of Henry's victims, Bishop John Fisher, lived in the former **Bishop's Palace** south of the cathedral. The friend of Erasmus and Sir Thomas More, he defended Catherine of Aragon against the king and refused to countenance the divorce. In 1535 the Pope made him a cardinal, at which Henry burst out: 'Well, let the Pope send him a hat when he will; but I will so provide that whensoever it cometh, he shall wear it on his shoulders, for head he shall have none to set it on.' Fisher was executed on Tower Green in 1535, and canonised four hundred years later. Also in the Close is **Minor Canon Row,** seven redbrick Georgian houses with neat white-painted windows. The fourteenth-century **Prior's Gate** spans the road just behind.

Behind the cathedral close is one of Rochester's most friendly open spaces, **The Vines,** where the monks had a vineyard, and where now there are lawns and plane trees, decimated by the great storm of 16 October, 1987. Down one of the avenues and across the Maidstone Road is **Restoration House,** from the outside still recognisably Miss Havisham's (open occasionally in the summer). Redbrick and E-shaped, it was built in 1587, and got its name from the tradition that Charles II stayed there on his return to England in 1660. Miss Havisham's room is a large and dignified panelled drawing-room, which it needs a strong effort of the imagination to envisage as Dickens's candlelit abode of scuttling spiders and shattered bridal dreams.

Apart from the Dickensian buildings already mentioned, most of old Rochester lies in the High Street. Dickens called the clock that juts over the street 'inexpressive, moonfaced and weak'; it juts from the front of the **Corn Exchange,** given to the town in 1706 by Sir Cloudesley Shovell, that admiral with the unforgettable name. His portrait hangs below the elaborate plaster ceiling he presented in the council chamber of the splendid seventeenth-century **Guildhall,** now Rochester's main museum. On display are portraits of city worthies, the sumptuous civic plate and regalia of Rochester and Chatham, ship models, dolls and toys.

Farther up the High Street are the three gables of the **Six Poor Travellers' House,** or **Watts Charity,** put up in 1579 by the philanthropist Richard Watts for six travellers 'not being rogues or proctors' (an abbreviation for 'procurator', a religious vagrant of the day). The façade dates from 1771. Set back a few yards away is **La**

Providence, a little precinct of early Victorian houses, the descendants of almshouses founded here in 1718 by Huguenot refugees from France.

The Tudor brick **Eastgate House,** which stands end on to the road, contains the **Charles Dickens Centre,** where a series of galleries and rooms are crammed with lively three-dimensional tableaux illustrating the novelist's villains such as Bill Sykes, along with Little Nell and other members of his gallery of insipid heroines. Portraits, letters and photographs illustrate his development as man and writer. In the garden is the chalet from Gads Hill (see p. 00); you can go up the outside stair to the first-floor room where Dickens worked.

Every summer the streets of Rochester come alive with fully animated Mr Pickwicks, Miss Havishams, Peggottys and David Copperfields – a thousand or more citizens of Rochester in Dickensian costume for the annual Dickens Festival.

Rochester's bridges are still administered by the Bridge Wardens, who operate from the **Bridge Chamber** near the castle. The Bridge Trust for the upkeep of the original bridge was founded in 1391. The Cobhams and other local magnates were often the trustees, and the bridge was considered so important that in 1489 the Archbishop of Canterbury 'remitted from purgatory all manner of sins for forty days' for anyone who contributed to its upkeep. The Bridge Chapel next door can be visited (by request to the Bridge Clerk, Bridge Chamber). It stood at one end of the medieval bridge, slightly upstream from the modern bridge, and was used by travellers wishing to give thanks for a safe arrival in Rochester. Round the walls are plans and paintings of the bridge at various times from the Romans on. The old bridge was demolished in 1856; its stonework went as filling for the Esplanade, and its balustrade now runs along the river bank across the road from the Bridge Chamber.

Even the locals are not quite sure where Rochester ends and **Chatham** begins. It does not really matter, as the importance of Chatham lies in its acres of dockyard and barracks, both naval and military. The imperceptible boundary comes somewhere along Chatham's narrow High Street, which keeps close to the river and is hemmed in by buildings of every period. Where the houses open out, at the foot of Dock Road, is the Town Hall, which has some things worth looking at. Upstairs in the council chamber is an intricately detailed scale model of the *Victory*, and a sedan chair in which the commandants of the Chatham garrison used to be carried about before the days of official cars. The mayor's chain can be seen on request: it is a double chain, of which the inner band, gold decorated with coloured Venetian glass, was worn by the Doges of Venice and is said to be over a thousand years old – a suitable translation from one dockyard centre to another. Also in Chatham is Dickens's childhood home, south of the station at 11 Ordnance Terrace. Dickens's father, John Dickens, moved to the Navy Pay Office at Chatham dockyard in 1816, and spent six years at Chatham, five of them in this three-storey yellow brick house.

Half way up Dock Road the disused St Mary's Church stands in a superb position looking out across the Medway. From near-dereliction it has taken on a new lease of life as the **Medway Heritage Centre**. Its walls are covered with memorials to naval officers killed in action down the centuries, and the exhibits in the nave and aisles tell the story of the Medway as a geographical entity and a busy waterway from prehistoric to modern times.

Across the road from the Heritage Centre, a scrub-covered hillside, honeycombed with tunnels and the remains of fortifications, stretches east towards Gillingham. Known as the **Great Lines** from the eighteenth-century earthworks that crisscross its sides and summit, the hill was subsequently used for military manoeuvres. **Fort Amherst**, a key section of Chatham's eighteenth-century landward defences, has been restored; its acres of bastions, redoubts and hillside burrowings are an impressive reminder of the strategic importance of Chatham in past centuries. The summit of the Great Lines is crowned by a huge naval war memorial consisting of a tall white column supporting a green globe, decorated with figureheads and medieval prows, with pavilions at its foot. From this point the whole Medway panorama can be seen: the slopes of the Isle of Grain, the Kingsnorth power station, clusters of barges and an odd coalescing of Rochester cathedral and castle into a single square-towered building.

As was mentioned earlier, the Medway's importance to the navy began in the mid sixteenth century. The Chatham peninsula was ideal for the winter jobs of refitting, caulking and scraping the ships, as there was shelter, a good rise and fall of tide, and soft rock-free mud for the vessels to rest on. Even in those early days the river covered in shipping must have been an awe-inspiring sight. William Lambarde, in his 1570 *Perambulation of Kent*, wrote lyrically of the Elizabethan 'Navie Royall'. 'No Towne, no Citie, is there (I dare say) in this whole Shire, comparable in right value with this one

28

Fleete: nor shipping any where else in the whole world to be founde, either more artificially moalded under the water, or more gorgeously decked above.' He goes on to list 'these most stately and valiant vessels', of which just a few read like a litany of Elizabethan enterprise: 'Elizabeth Ionas, Tryumph, Whyte Beare, Merhonora, The Victorie, Arke Rawleigh, Dew Repulse, The Garlande'.

The navy's fifth and most famous *Victory* was launched at Chatham in 1765, so she was already elderly by the time of Trafalgar. Her keel was laid in 1759 during the Seven Years War – one of twelve ships of the line laid down at the urging of William Pitt the Elder, who later chose Chatham as the title of his earldom. Building her was slow and expensive: in the 1759 naval estimates £3,500 was allocated for her hull, and subsequent costs ran to about £8,000 a year. The war was over by the time she was launched, and she was laid up at anchor – 'in ordinary', as the eighteenth century called mothballing. By 1771 she was leaking so badly that £4,000 had to be spent on repairs. (Multiply these figures by at least 1,000 to give approximate modern values.)

The **Historic Dockyard** in Chatham, where the shipwrights, quarterboys, caulkers, oakumboys, joiners and sailmen sweated on the *Victory*, evokes the great days of the 'wooden walls' better than anywhere else in the country. Today a gallery called **Wooden Walls** evokes the building of the *Valiant* in 1758, using all the latest display techniques of sight, sound and smell. The dockyard began in 1547 with a storehouse on the wharf, as a part of Henry VIII's naval expansion scheme, and closed down in 1984, having covered more than 400 years of naval construction from the unstable wooden tubs of Tudor times to the sleek submarines of the twentieth century. When the navy moved out, responsibility for its southernmost eighty acres was taken over by the Chatham Historic Dockyard Trust. Nearly a hundred buildings and other structures survive, mainly from the eighteenth century, making Chatham far and away the finest of the old royal dockyards still in existence.

The fortress-like brick **Main Gate**, with two brown towers and a large gilded royal coat-of-arms over the entrance, dates from 1722. Beyond it is the plain square dockyard **Church**, built in 1806–10. Many of the buildings, though utilitarian, are of great elegance, like the **Sail and Colour Loft**, built in 1723. This huge workshop, where the sails for the *Victory* were made, is almost a hundred yards long. Even longer – 1,135 feet, or nearly a quarter of a mile – is the

Ropery, now powered by electricity instead of capstan and muscle but still used for making rope. From a viewing gallery beside the ropewalk you can watch the lumbering machines, one dating from as far back as 1811, twisting the yarn into ropes, and the ropes into still thicker ropes. The old materials such as flax, hemp and sisal still have the edge over man-made fibres, as they can withstand wear and tear better – and, more importantly, do not snap suddenly and without warning, as nylon and similar fibres tend to do.

Oldest and most stylish of the buildings is the **Commissioner's House**, built in 1704, where the dockyard supremo lived. In *Pickwick*, Mr Jingle sums up the Chatham hierarchy as it was during Dickens's childhood: 'Dockyard people of upper rank don't know dock-yard people of lower rank – dockyard people of lower rank don': know small gentry – small gentry don't know tradespeople – Commssioner don't know anybody.' Fine though this house is, by far the most impressive structures in the whole dockyard are the **Covered Slipways** that line the Medway – a sequence of vast roofed spaces built between 1838 and 1855, showing the steadily evolving boldness of their builders. The last naval ship was launched from them in 1966. One of them now houses a magnificent array of old lifeboats.

Visitors to the dockyard will eventually be able to experience life in the Victorian navy when the sloop HMS *Gannet* is fully restored. Built at Sheerness in 1878, she was a hybrid, powered by both sail and steam and built of timber planks on iron frames. She saw service all over the world's oceans, from Valparaiso in Chile to Suakin on the Red Sea, which she defended in 1885 after the fall of Khartoum. The last warship to be built for the Royal Navy at Chatham, the submarine *Ocelot*, has now found moorings in a huge inland dock nearby. Launched in 1962, commissioned in 1964 and taken out of commission in 1991, she saw service until the Falklands campaign. You can now tour her cramped interior from end to end, even peering through the periscope at Upnor Castle across the river – the war technology of Elizabeth II's reign linked to that of Elizabeth I. It is incredible to think that seventy men lived for three months at a stretch in this claustrophobic metal tube, so pressed for space that they could take only one spare pair of socks and one of underpants.

The dock where *Ocelot* is moored is on the edge of the once-bleak expanse of mudflats known as St Mary's Island, at the northern end of the peninsula. The area is being transformed into an ambitious waterside development of modern housing and light industry called **Chatham Maritime**, complete with schools, a marina and a riverside walk. At the time of writing (1999) it is too early to judge of its ultimate impact on the Medway scene, but it can surely only be an improvement on the previous desolation. A new road tunnel has been driven under the river and emerges south of Upnor Castle, bypassing Chatham and Rochester Bridge and linking eventually with the M2.

For centuries Chatham has had barracks as well as a dockyard. The most important of these, **Brompton Barracks**, on the hill above the dockyard, is now the home of the Royal School of Military Engineering. The main entrance to the barracks lies a short way up the hill from the roundabout on Wood Street. The original barracks consists of a continuous range of two-storey buildings built round three sides of an enormous square, with a columned portico at the centre of each side. It was built in 1804–6 for the artillery; in 1812, after the experiences of the Peninsular War, Wellington set up a school there for training engineer officers and soldiers in the arts of sapping, mining, bridging and other military field works. Since then it has branched out into every aspect of the Royal Engineers' work, from military photography to chemical warfare.

Round to the left, in Prince Arthur Road, is the **Royal Engineers Museum**, in the oddly impressive Ravelin Building, formerly the Electrical School, designed by a Major Moore in the first decade of the twentieth century. Its series of bulbous domes, startlingly white above the red brick, originally housed searchlights. Beginning with such early examples of military engineering as an assault bridge built by Julius Caesar, the museum brings the story up to the present by way of William the Conqueror's portable castles, the eighteenth-century fortifications of Gibraltar, and the first-ever guided missile – a wire-controlled torpedo dating from the 1880s. General Gordon, the greatest R.E. of all time, appears in effigy as 'Chinese Gordon', wearing the jewelled and embroidered court robes of a mandarin. He is also commemorated by a statue back in the main barracks, mounted in full uniform on a supercilious Sudanese camel.

Gillingham is a sprawl of barracks, hospitals and nondescript houses, with nothing much to stop it as it spreads along the dead straight line of the A2. It continues uninterrupted to **Rainham**, where suddenly a monumental church tower juts up south of the main road, like an old oak among a mass of scrub. It has a lop-sided ruggedness, emphasized by the ancient roof timbers and kingposts, roughly adzed into shape. East of the church is a reminder of the open country beyond in a string of oasthouses, end on to the road.

31

Gillingham has its own quiet pleasure beach, **The Strand**, at the western end of the Lower Rainham Road. This runs parallel to the main road along the edge of the estuary, with orchards on either side, and little side roads leading down to mudflats with beached boats, and derelict quays. Back roads carry on to **Upchurch**, a crossroads village at the heart of a small peninsula. The church has a spire of 'candle-snuffer' type, consisting of a pyramid base and octagonal top. In 1560 a certain 'Edmund Drakes' became vicar of Upchurch. This was almost certainly Edmund Drake, the father of Sir Francis, who as a Protestant lay-preacher had fled from his native Devon about 1549 to escape persecution. Before coming to Upchurch he had been prayer-reader to the fleet in the Medway, and had himself lived on one of the hulks; no doubt his son learnt much of his sailing skill pottering about the tidal waters of the estuary.

For a riverscape of saltings, beached barges, high winds and hulks, **Lower Halstow** is the place. The Romans gathered oysters and made bricks here, and in the Middle Ages the monks farmed the low-lying fields, building earth walls to keep out the sea. The sheep they bred were the ancestors of the Romney Marsh sheep of today. The church, standing on a low mound above flood level, goes back to early Norman or even Saxon times, and is a jumble both inside and out, with Roman tiles among the stonework, and decaying medieval wall paintings inside.

Newington, inland among the orchards, is a biggish village stretching along the A2. Its church, isolated a little to the north, is a magnificent building, dating mainly from the late thirteenth or early fourteenth century, with a soaring Perpendicular tower built in alternate stripes of flint and ragstone, and a long tiled roof. In the south chancel is an arcaded tomb, known as the shrine of St Robert of Newington; Robert is otherwise unknown, but may have been a pilgrim murdered while on his way to Canterbury. In the Middle Ages cripples used to thrust their legs into the recesses of the shrine, in the hope of a miraculous cure.

At the entrance to the churchyard is the 'Devil's Stone', one of two sarsens which presumably go back to pre-Christian times. According to one legend, the Devil was so annoyed with the ringing of Newington church bells that he decided to remove them. After collecting them one night in a sack he jumped down from the tower but landed on the stones and fell over. The bells rolled out of the sack and down the lane leading to Halstow, where they ended up at the bottom of a stream which has bubbled melodiously ever since.

3

Along the Canterbury Road

THERE ARE NOW two Canterbury roads: Watling Street (A2), still serviceable after almost twenty centuries; and the sinuous sweep of the M2, cutting across the countryside in lordly disdain, and so remote from the villages it passes that you cannot leave it between Sittingbourne and Faversham. Nevertheless, the M2 is, paradoxically, the best way to get a first impression of this stretch of country, as you can enjoy it like some magnificent landscape film, with only minimal worries about the traffic – the endless pattern of apple and cherry orchards, village churches so close it seems as though you could touch them, and in the distance the industrial blur of Sittingbourne, the green slopes of Sheppey, and a glimpse of the muddy waters of the Swale.

A mile or so east of Newington the main road from Maidstone to Sheppey (A249) crosses Watling Street. It is worth making a short southward detour here to **Borden**, not yet swallowed up by Sittingbourne near by. The church, with its low, wide tower, makes a satisfying close to the main street. Beyond the churchyard is a large thatched barn right in the village, and a good half-timbered house beside it. The church tower is late Norman, built about 1160, with a vast round-headed arch into the nave. Inside there is a striking and well preserved mural painting above the arcade showing a bearded St Christopher with staff and Christ-child.

You get from Borden to **Tunstall** along Heart's Delight Road, as pretty as the name. The church tower was Victorianized by the addition of a strange saddle-backed roof (there is another at Ospringe, see below). Inside there are simple, regular fourteenth-century arcades, and a pompous seventeenth-century effigy of Sir Edward Hales, reclining ponderously in full armour, and so dignified that no one has ever dared to scratch initials on him.

Sittingbourne is the easternmost of Kent's Thames-side industrial towns, and for years has been the victim of unplanned piecemeal

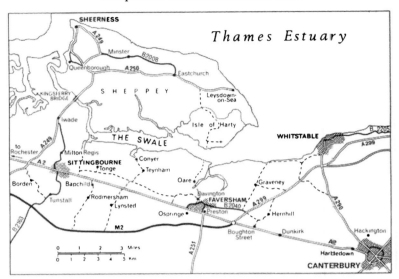

expansion. However, it has recently been receiving something of a facelift. The High Street, with its two extensions West Street and East Street, still has the vestiges of a Georgian thoroughfare about it; it is pedestrianized on Saturdays and semi-pedestrianized the rest of the week. The big flint-built parish church (normally locked because of vandalism) is on the north side of the street, next door to a cinema-cum-bingo hall; its fine traceried windows are set back only a few feet from the pavement. There was an early Norman church on the site, but most of the present building dates from the thirteenth and fourteenth centuries. The massive west tower was completed in the fifteenth century. In 1762 the church roof was destroyed after workmen repairing the leads left a fire burning during their lunch hour; and the nineteenth century brought the usual crop of pious 'restorations'. As it now stands, the wide nave and narrow aisles make it a most graceful building.

South of the High Street is the Avenue of Remembrance, lined on either side with hornbeams, each with a plaque commemorating a Sittingbourne man killed in the First World War; few war memorials anywhere show such a blend of practicality and imagination. North of the High Street you are plunged almost at once into industry, with the vast paper mill in Mill Way. You can get the best idea of this side of the town by going down Crown Quay Lane, which leads to an industrial estate and the wharves along the muddy meanders of

Milton Creek, amid salt flats, streams and inlets, dotted with factories and timber yards. The Milton Creek landscape is best seen from the Sittingbourne Steam Railway – a narrow-gauge line built early this century to service the paper mills between Sittingbourne and the Swale. Trundling over a viaduct, it comes to an end after two miles at the Kemsley Paper Mill.

Far older than Sittingbourne is **Milton Regis**, now relegated to the status of a suburb. The 'Rex' of its name was reputedly King Alfred. Its steep High Street is lined with timber-framed and Georgian houses, until recently battered by lorries carrying gigantic rolls of paper but now relieved by industrial link roads; at its summit is a little green, with a splendidly preserved fifteenth-century court hall at one side of it. The courtroom is on the first floor; on the ground level is the lock-up, with low barred doors. The magnificent church is north of the town, on the edge of the marshes. Its huge black flint tower dominates a bleak outlook of saltings, power lines and housing estates. It was probably built in the early fourteenth century, but incorporates much earlier work, including Roman tiles from settlements near by.

The gateway to **Sheppey** is through the monumental twin archway of **Kingsferry Bridge**, 'like some great megalith', says John Newman, in *West Kent and the Weald*. The central section of the bridge lifts vertically for boats passing up or down the Swale; sail has right of way over road traffic, and the mightiest of container lorries have to wait while yachts pass underneath. (A second bridge to take the ever-increasing traffic load has been promised, but is still some years off.) Once over the bridge, you see why the island got its name: Sheppey means 'sheep island', and the low-lying marsh grasslands are still dotted with sheep. However, in much of Sheppey this is changing, and over on the other side of the island, near Harty, the land is being deep drained and ploughed into prairie-like fields.

In the Middle Ages ships to and from London tended to avoid the north coast of Sheppey and used the Swale instead; and so in the 1360s Edward III built a castle at the northern end of the Swale to guard this important sea passage, naming it **Queenborough** in honour of Queen Philippa. The castle has vanished, but Queenborough still has vestiges of its history as a busy harbour town, notably in the High Street, which looks like a poor relation of old Portsmouth. Though it is ramshackle and run-down, Queenborough has plenty of assets which deserve to be salvaged. The view of the Medway estuary from the quay at the end of the

35

High Street is superb: a wide seascape of boats from Thames barges to tankers, and the inescapable giant chimney of the Kingsnorth power station. South of the High Street a narrow creek brings small boats right into the heart of the town. The eighteenth-century Guildhall, with a fine light council chamber built above an arcade, makes a dignified centrepiece to the battered buildings familiar to Nelson. **Deadmans Island**, a muddy flat across the Swale, was the burial ground of sailors and passengers who died while in quarantine, and also of prisoners in the Medway hulks.

In the spring of 1732 the artist William Hogarth and four of his London drinking cronies visited Queenborough, via Gravesend and Rochester, on a boozy five-day trip down the Thames and back again. When they got home one of these friends, Ebenezer Forrest, wrote a lively account of this 'Peregrination', which Hogarth illustrated with a number of drawings. One of these shows Queenborough, where they stayed with 'a Merry Woman at a private House', befriended a stranded group of sailors, and met the local gravedigger, who told them that 'the Mayor is a Customhouse Officer and the Parson a Sad Dog'. After exploring the town, 'Wee return'd to our quarters Drank to our Freinds as usuall and Emptied Several Cans of Good Flip and all Sung Merrily'. The next day they rolled uphill to Minster (see below), the furthest point on their trip, and returned to London by boat from Sheerness, seasick for much of the journey.

Sheppey's prosperity is concentrated in **Sheerness**, where the Medway joins the Thames. Sheerness is an extraordinary jumble of a place, a mixture of funfair switchbacks, classical harbour buildings, factories and caravans. Though it is not obvious, it is an island beyond an island, as at the southern end of the town an artificial waterway cuts off the triangular tip of Sheppey. As early as 1547 a gun battery was set up on Garrison Point to guard the Medway, but nothing much was done about Sheerness until the defences were destroyed by the Dutch fleet under De Ruyter in 1667. Two years later a strong fortress was built at Garrison Point, and a naval dockyard, surveyed before the Dutch attack by Samuel Pepys, was laid out on the sheltered side of the point.

In 1797 Sheerness and its offshore waters were the scene of the great Nore mutiny (the Nore is an offshore sandbank). The sailors of the Nore Command presented a list of grievances to the commander-in-chief, were rejected, and took the law into their own hands, hoisting the red flag of mutiny and compelling other crews to join

them. At first the inhabitants of Sheerness were sympathetic and supported the mutineers ('carnival with a grim undercurrent' is T. J. Woodthorpe's phrase in his history of Sheppey); but they eventually swung round to the Government, and supplies to the mutineers were cut off. The outcome was inevitable: the mutineers surrendered, four hundred sailors were arrested, and the ringleader, Richard Parker, was court-martialled and executed.

The *Times* of 3 July, 1797, carried a graphic account of the extraordinary composure with which he met his end. Woken at six aboard HMS *L'Espion*, he had breakfast, then at eight thirty he climbed on to the quarter-deck, where he recited the 51st Psalm. At nine a gun was fired, after which he drank a glass of white wine and was prepared for execution. The Provost Marshal 'attempted to put a cap on, which he refused; but on being told it was indispensible, he submitted . . . He then turned round, for the first time, and gave a steady look at his ship-mates on the forecastle, and, with an affectionate kind of smile, nodded his head and said, "Good bye to you!" . . . then the cap being drawn up over his face, walking by firm degrees up to the scaffold, he dropped the handkerchief, put his hands in his coat-pockets with great rapidity, and at the moment he was springing off, the fatal bow-gun fired, and the reeve-rope catching him, run him up, though not with great velocity, to the yard-arm.'

As you come into Sheerness from Queenborough, you drive below the high frowning brick walls of the former naval **Dockyard**, which take up the whole of one side of West Street and continue round the corner into the High Street. The dockyard's administrative buildings, dating from the early nineteenth century, consist of a large classical compound; unfortunately the public can get no farther than the security guard at the main entrance (except by prior arrangement). However, you can get a good idea of the rest of the scheme from Naval Terrace, now private houses, outside the main enclosure, and the large brick dockyard church, now disused. The dockyard is now run as a commercial harbour by Medway Ports.

The High Street still consists mainly of little two-storey early nineteenth-century houses; it peters out before crossing the zigzag moat that formed part of the old fortifications, and then begins again at the comical blue clock tower which is the nearest approach Sheerness has to a town centre. The main public buildings are in Broadway, which begins at the tower; the parish church, built of yellow brick, pinnacles and all, in the 1830s, has little of interest except a strange bronze memorial plaque, covered with Masonic symbols, on the outside of the west wall.

There is no coast road on Sheppey; to get from Sheerness to the island's villages you have to go inland, as far as the aptly named Halfway Houses.

East of Sheerness is the high ground that forms the spine of Sheppey and was the first part of the island to be settled. The beginnings of **Minster**, now a nondescript seaside town, go back to the seventh century, when a nunnery was founded there by St Sexburga. About 670 Sexburga, the widow of Ercombert, a Saxon king of Kent, established a nunnery (*monasterium*, hence Minster) on Sheppey. Destroyed by the Danes in 855 and attacked two hundred years later by Earl Godwin, it was re-established and rebuilt on a grand scale about 1130. The abbey church, which incorporates some of the earlier Saxon building, stands on the crest of a hill above what remains of Minster's old village centre. It is in effect a complete double church. On the north side is the monastic church or 'Nun's Chapel', and on the south the parish church, added in the thirteenth century when the arcade was pierced through the original south wall.

Inside the impression is one of peaceful spaciousness, with the light interior of the parochial church in contrast to the comparative gloom of the Nun's Chapel. There are some magnificent monuments, forming a textbook of medieval clothes and armour. On the south wall is the canopied tomb of Sir Robert de Shurland, who was Baron of Sheppey and Lord Warden of the Cinque Ports, and died about 1310. Behind the armoured effigy is carved a horse's head rising from the waves.

According to one of R. H. Barham's *Ingoldsby Legends*, this is de Shurland's horse Grey Dolphin. After killing a priest the baron had been banished from the court, but hearing that the king was at anchor off Sheppey, he mounted Grey Dolphin, swam out to the ship, was pardoned, and swam back to shore. When he landed, a local witch prophesied that the horse would be his death, where-upon he drew his sword and cut off its head. Months later, walking along the shore, he kicked the skeleton, injured his toe and died as a result, presumably from blood poisoning, thus fulfilling the prophecy. When Hogarth and his friends visited Minster in 1732, they were told that the locals believed this tale so strongly 'that wee did not Dare to Declare our Disbeleif of one Tittle of the Story'.

A more prosaic explanation for the horse's head is that it was placed on the tomb to show that de Shurland, as Lord Warden, had

the privilege of 'wreck of sea' – the right to ride into water at low tide and claim possession of anything washed up on shore by touching it with the tip of his lance.

Eastchurch is still a small country village, with a Perpendicular church hardly altered since it was built in the 1430s. Two lurid windows in the south aisle commemorate the flying pioneers Charles Stewart Rolls (partner of the Rolls-Royce team) and Cecil Grace, both killed in flying accidents in 1910. Across the road is what looks at first glance like a typical inscribed war memorial wall behind a small garden, but in fact commemorates the founders of British aviation – Moore-Brabazon, Rolls, Sopwith. On either side the stone is carved with small replicas of the primitive biplanes and triplanes in which they made their early lurching flights. Many of the flyers operated from Eastchurch aerodrome, down the road that leads south from the village; the buildings are now a prison. In 1909, at **Shell Beach**, near Leysdown, Moore-Brabazon became the first British pilot to carry out a circular flight of one mile, and Charles Rolls at much the same time made a two-mile flight from Eastchurch aerodrome round the church tower and back.

Leysdown-on-Sea is a wilderness of holiday camps, chalets and caravan sites, with the consolation of vast views across the Thames estuary. On one side the dark brown landslides of **Warden Point** show where Sheppey is constantly losing its high ground to the sea, and on the other the marshes join the mudflats, the happy hunting-grounds of bait-diggers and bird-watchers.

A narrow road half way between Leysdown and Eastchurch zigzags down to **Harty**, a forgotten land which is the epitome of Sheppey. It has its own medieval church (at Sayes Court on the 1:50,000 map), a neglected gem of a building along a farm track. At the west end a rough timber framework supports the bellcote, and in the south chapel is a unique fourteenth-century chest, carved on the front panel with a pair of jousting knights and their squires. At the end of the road a long, low-built pub called the Ferry House looks across the Swale to the steeple of Faversham church. When Harty Ferry was open it was less than a mile by water, but it is now twenty-seven miles by road.

A mile north of Kingsferry Bridge, a long track leads down from the A249 to the **Elmley Marshes** reserve, run by the Royal Society for the Protection of Birds. Covering more than 3,000 acres, it is the haunt of thousands of wildfowl and waders, many of which spend the winter there.

East of Sittingbourne, the fruit-growing farmlands are dotted with little villages on either side of the A2. Nearest is **Bapchild**, whose delightful name has nothing to do with baptism, but comes from the Saxon Beccancelde, meaning either 'unhealthy chill water', or 'spring of the brook'. The church is a pretty little building, with a tall broach spire and a cool, white-painted interior. It is mainly Norman and Transitional; the capitals of the chalk pillars are carved with a different design on each. Behind the altar in the Lady Chapel is a long, low mural of the crucifixion, painted about 1300 and much faded. An unusual object to find in a church is a mammoth's tooth, kept in a glass case.

Rodmersham, half a mile south of Bapchild, consists mainly of prosperous Georgian farmhouses. The flint church has a startlingly red roof and a good Perpendicular battlemented west tower. **Tonge**, north of the main road, is hardly a village at all – just a small barn-like church in an overgrown churchyard, and a watermill which was once powered by water from the dammed-up moat of Tonge Castle. Lambarde quotes a rhyme, already old in the sixteenth century, perhaps deriving from the low-lying nature of the country:

> *He that will not live long,*
> *Let him dwell at Muston, Tenham, or Tong.*

Murston is a suburb of Sittingbourne; **Teynham** is a scattered village down the A2, built partly along the main road, and partly round the station half a mile away. In Lambarde's time Teynham was the centre of fruit-growing in Kent, where in the reign of King Henry VIII a certain Richard Harris 'planted by his great coste and rare industrie, the sweet Cherry, the temperate Pipyn, and the golden Renate' (the renate or reinette, 'little queen', was a French variety of apple – perhaps the Golden Delicious of its day). The remote church is north of the railway, hidden behind farm buildings and fruit trees, and over-looking a large hop garden. You get to it down a track and through a thatched lychgate. The cruciform interior, thirteenth-century with fifteenth-century arcades, is brilliantly lit through the huge east window. The road ends at **Conyer**, beside a muddy creek crammed with small boats.

Lynsted, due south across the A2, has the perfect village centre, consisting of a church, pub and a few houses on top of a hill, with a cluster of half-timbered houses below. The church has a tower at the north-west corner with shingled broach spire and boarded belfry; the three gables of the eastern end dominate the village.

It is hard to imagine anyone not liking **Faversham**. It has streets of fine old houses, a creek that brings the sea right into the heart of the town, and enough industry to keep it from becoming just another stagnant beauty-spot. **Faversham Creek** was in use as early as Roman times, and the Romans had a settlement called Durolevum in the vicinity. Today's name first appears in a charter of the Saxon king Coenwulf as 'the King's little town of Fafresham'; and early in the Middle Ages it was important enough to be given status as a 'limb' or associate port of the Cinque Port of Dover. As the importance of its port declined, new industries, notably gunpowder manufacture and brewing, kept Faversham prosperous; and it gives the impression of a town that has kept on a thoroughly even keel.

In its general layout, Faversham has not altered substantially since Edward Jacob, a local historian, described it two centuries ago. 'It principally consists of four long spacious and well paved streets, forming a somewhat irregular cross, in the centre whereof stands a convenient market-place, over which is the guildhall.' Jacob's own solid Georgian-fronted house, with its ground floor now a shop, still stands in Preston Street, on the corner of Cross Lane. Its elegant front masks a medieval structure, part of whose timber frame can be seen along the Lane. The mellow red 'bricks' are actually so-called mathematical tiles, used in the eighteenth century to update timber-framed façades then considered old-fashioned.

Nearly opposite is the medieval **Fleur de Lis Heritage Centre**. For centuries it was an inn, but it now belongs to the Faversham Society, the area's conservation watchdog, which opened it as a heritage centre in 1977. It was the first of its kind in the south of England, and its displays present a vivid evocation of the town's life down the centuries, with exhibits such as a brickworks' barrow, a model sailing barge and an old-time barber-shop. The Centre incorporates the town's tourist information centre and a bookshop which stocks over 60 publications produced by the Faversham Society.

West Street and East Street, at right-angles to Preston Street, run from one side of the town to the other, centring on the big white-painted Ship Hotel, a coaching inn built over an alley. The smartly-painted **Guildhall** is a fascinating hybrid – a Regency council chamber built above an Elizabethan arcade. The arcade, with its sturdy wooden pillars, was built to shelter market stall-holders and customers, and four centuries later still serves the same purpose. Behind the hall is a fancifully ornate cast-iron Victorian pump, picked out in red, white and dark blue. Near by the New Royal cinema, which opened as the Odeon in 1936, is a striking 'Tudorbethan' building which claims to have the largest screen in Kent.

The northern arm of the 'irregular cross' begins here, and consists of Court Street and its continuation Abbey Street. Court Street is wide and dignified, a good mixture of timbered gables and overhangs, Georgian brickwork and Victorian frontages, all harmonizing together. The street is full of the smell of brewing from Faversham's own brewery, Shepherd Neame, on its western side. It has been there since 1698, and keeps its workings discreetly hidden away between Court Street and the creek, though it welcomes visitors. More prominent on the opposite side of the street is the former Whitbread-Fremlin brewery, which has been adapted for a wide range of other uses.

At the top of Court Street, between the cottages of Church Street, you get a sudden close-up view of the most astonishing sight in Faversham – the tall west tower of the **Parish Church**, surmounted by a delicately fretted pinnacle of stone. This soaring steeple, like a spire with its insides cut away, was put up at the end of the eighteenth century, and takes its inspiration from Wren's steeple on the City church of St Dunstan's-in-the-East. In turn, it inspired the Waterloo Tower in Quex Park, Birchington. You can see it from all directions: in the distance from the M2, from the shore of Sheppey, or closer at hand across the saltings towards Oare. Inside, it is just as extraordinary. The nave was completely rebuilt in 1755 by George Dance, at a time when the central tower was found to be unsafe and taken down; Dance's arcades of elephantine Tuscan columns make a grotesque contrast with the chancel and rare double-aisled transepts built four and a half centuries earlier. In the north transept one of the octagonal pillars still has some of its original painted decoration, done at the time of the building about 1305. The choir misericords include a flute player, and various other human, demonic or animal figures. In the south chapel is a Decorated stone tomb canopy, with a plaque that suggests it may be the resting place of King Stephen, who died at Dover in 1154. He was buried in Faversham Abbey church; at the Dissolution, so the story goes, his bones were dug up and thrown into Faversham Creek, but subsequently salvaged and reburied in the parish church.

The **Old Grammar School,** in Church Walk near by, dates from 1587 and has remained largely unspoilt, apart from being turned into

Sailing barges moored in Faversham Creek.

a masonic hall 300 years later. The first-floor schoolroom has changed little since eighteenth-century schoolboys carved their names there. Faversham's great **Abbey**, founded by King Stephen in 1147, stood a little way north of the church, on a site now occupied by playing fields. Excavations have shown that the abbey church was enormous, nearly three hundred feet long. The abbey was approached along Abbey Street, the northern continuation of Court Street and one of the showplaces of Faversham, now that the buildings have been rescued from near-dereliction and impeccably restored.

Among the few abbey buildings that survive is the guesthouse, though not in its entirety. It was a large corner property, of which the north wing (**Arden's House**) and part of the south wing (**Arden Cottage**) still remain; both are timber-framed with jettied upper floors. Arden's House incorporates part of the stone-built outer gateway. Its name perpetuates Faversham's most notorious scandal – the murder of Thomas Arden. After the abbey was dissolved in 1538, Arden (or Arderne, as the name was often spelt) bought some of the abbey lands and set himself up in the guesthouse, eventually becoming mayor of the town. His wife Alice (grand-daughter of the builder of Henry VIII's flagship the *Mary Rose*) and her lover Thomas Mosby decided to murder him. In collusion with two sinister accomplices called Loosebagg and Black Will, they made a number of unsuccessful attempts on his life. On the night of 15 February, 1551, Arden was finally done away with while playing a game of 'tables' (draughts or backgammon) with Mosby in the parlour.

In the words of the *Faversham Wardmote Book*: 'Black Will . . . came with a napkyn in his hand, and sodenlye came behind the said Ardern's back, threw the said napkyn over his hedd and face, and strangled him, and forthwith the said Mosby stept to him, and strake him with a taylor's great pressing Iron upon the scull to the braine, and immediately drew out his dagger, which was great and broad, and therewith cut the said Ardern's throat.' After this butchery the accomplices dragged the body to a field at the back of the house and left it there. They were nearly all arrested and executed. Alice was burned to death at Canterbury, Mosby was hanged at Smithfield, and Black Will was caught and burned at Flushing; only Loosebagg seems to have escaped.

The grim story, told by Holinshed in his *Chronicles*, was taken up by an unknown Elizabethan playwright, who wrote *The Lamentable and True Tragedie of Master Arden of Feversham in Kent*, first published in 1592. This sulphurously lurid melodrama – which has been attributed to both Shakespeare and Marlowe – broke away from the tradition that only great rulers were suitable subjects for tragedy. Not only are the characters drawn from life, but the settings are realistic as well: the playwright brings in Rainham, Sittingbourne and Sheppey, and the streets and inns of Faversham. Every few years it is performed in the courtyard of Arden's House.

At the end of Abbey Street is **Standard Quay**, where Thomas Arden carried on a lucrative business as commissioner of customs. The old brick and timber warehouses, among the oldest still in use in the country, were built in the seventeenth century out of materials mostly salvaged from the old Abbey refectory. Just beyond, and reached by a footpath, is **Iron Wharf**, where several preserved sailing barges are berthed. In Conduit Street, behind the Shepherd Neame brewery, the fifteenth-century timbered town storehouse on the quay has a new lease of life as the headquarters of the local sea cadets, re-christened 'Training Ship *Hazard*'. Its name comes from the ship supplied by the town in 1588 to fight the Spanish Armada.

Until the 1930s Faversham's main industry, apart from beer, was the making of gunpowder, which began there at least as early as Queen Elizabeth's reign. At the **Chart Gunpowder Mills** (off South Road and buried among the houses of Nobel Court) you can get some idea of the manufacturing process; the mills, powered by a large water-wheel, have been restored by the Faversham Society. They date from the late eighteenth century, and are the oldest of their kind in the world to survive intact. Explosions were an ever-present risk. A particularly bad one took place in 1847 with the advent of guncotton (cotton steeped in nitric acid and sulphuric acid), when a new factory out on the marshes to the north blew up. Twenty people were killed, trees within fifty yards were uprooted, and the explosion was heard nearly as far as Maidstone. Even worse was a TNT explosion in 1916, when more than a hundred employees lost their lives. This was the worst disaster in the history of the British explosives industry; the shock-wave was felt as far away as Norwich. The last works were closed in 1934. Near the Gunpowder Mills, in South Road, is a monumental range of gabled almshouses; built in the 1860s, they are a fine example of Victorian philanthropy on the largest scale.

Stonebridge Pond, at the end of West Street and reached by a peaceful riverside walk from Chart Mills, is the town's main beauty spot, complete with traffic signs warning drivers to look out for ducks waddling across the road. This attractive haunt of wildlife was once part of Faversham's oldest gunpowder factory, and reminds us that industrial legacies need not always be ugly.

Back on the A2 is **Ospringe Street** – a conservation area in its own right but desperately in need of a bypass. On opposite corners of Water Lane are the only two buildings to survive from the **Maison Dieu**, one of Faversham's three medieval religious foundations. The building on the east side dates from about 1250 and is a private house; the other, slightly later in date, is now a small museum managed by the Faversham Society for English Heritage. Both were originally the homes of chantry priests. Maison Dieu was a multi-purpose foundation, serving as hospital, pilgrims' hostel and almshouses, but intended mainly as a royal stopover for kings, queens and foreign princes on the road between Dover and London. The main complex, on the other side of the street, included a great hall, dovecote and corn mill; the museum tells its story, features finds from a nearby Roman cemetery and traces the development of the parish of Ospringe.

The Victorian saddle-backed tower of Ospringe church, a landmark as you drive along the M2, lies below the road embankment, half a mile south of the Maison Dieu. The church is worth going into for the splendid reclining alabaster figure of James Master (died 1631) in his shroud. Across the road is the half-timbered Queen Court, on the site of a medieval manor house granted by Henry III to Queen Eleanor.

Faversham's southern suburb, **Preston**, has a nice medieval church among the modern housing estates. Inside there are exceptional fourteenth-century sedilia, with carved faces peering through the holes in the canopy above. There is also a grandiose tomb to Roger and Joan Boyle, grandparents of Robert Boyle, the philosopher and scientist who propounded Boyle's Law. A short way to the south, across the M2, the **Brogdale Horticultural Trust** carries on Faversham's fruit-growing traditions. Its thirty-odd acres contain more than 2,300 varieties of apple, 550 of pear, 350 of plum and 220 of cherry, not to mention bush fruits, nuts and vines – a treasurehouse of colour and flavour preserved for more enlightened generations, though most of these varieties are unfamiliar to fruit-farmers and unknown on supermarket shelves.

On the western side of the town is **Davington**, again mainly modern housing. The pyramid-capped tower of the Norman church stands prominently on a hill; it forms part of Davington Priory, founded in 1153, which looks like a gabled manor house but in fact incorporates part of the monastic buildings. A little west of Davington, by the B2045, are the remains of the **Oare Gunpowder Works**, worked by Huguenot immigrants three hundred years ago; it is now a woodland park crisscrossed by the streams that fed the watermills. Nearby, at the head of Oare Creek, is a small wetland nature reserve with an unusual mixture of fresh- and salt-water plants. **Oare** itself is a trim yachting village on a branch of Faversham Creek. Past Oare church the road ends on the south side of Harty Ferry, with a causeway leading down to the soft mud of the Swale.

Graveney, above the marshes east of Faversham, is hardly more than a hamlet but has a superb church, mainly fourteenth-century, with a low battlemented tower and startlingly red tiled roof. Inside it has the light-flooded look of a Romney Marsh church. In the north aisle is a magnificent fifteenth-century canopied brass to John Martyn and his wife Anne; he is shown in the robes of a High Court judge and holds a heart inscribed 'Jhu mcy' (Jhesu Mercy). At the feet of the figures is an inscription in Latin couplets. The church still has its old box pews.

Hernhill, on the other side of the Whitstable road, is a complete contrast. The village is enclosed by orchards; in front of the tree-filled churchyard is a small green, with neat white houses behind. The church is a Perpendicular building, with battlemented west tower.

The woods between Hernhill and **Dunkirk** saw the last of the Kentish risings against authority. In the 1830s a Cornishman called John Nichols Thom settled in the area, took the name of Sir William Percy Honeywood Courtenay, and in 1832 stood as parliamentary candidate for Canterbury, dressed as a 'Knight of Malta', as he styled himself. He spent some years in a lunatic asylum, and on his release at the end of 1837 proclaimed himself the Messiah and gathered a band of about a hundred disciples, mainly downtrodden farm labourers. In May 1838 a warrant was issued for his arrest, but he shot the constable's brother and retreated into the woods, taking his followers with him. Troops were sent in; Thom shot the officer who called on him to surrender, and was then killed himself, with several of his followers. One reason for the dissatisfaction of the locals was said to be the lack of a church, and so in 1840 Dunkirk church was built.

Boughton Street, back towards Faversham, is a long straight village, with an impressive number of half-timbered and Georgian houses. Boughton (or Boughton under Blean) church is down back roads to the south, at the top of a hill behind a large farm. It has good Early English lancets in the nave, and in the north aisle a magnificent monument to Sir Thomas Hawkins and his wife Ann, by the seventeenth-century sculptor Epiphanius Evesham.

The last village on the pilgrim's journey to Canterbury was **Harbledown**, which Chaucer called '*a litel toun, Which that y-cleped is Bobbe-up-and-doun*'. Nothing could better describe the switchback of Harbledown. Over the brow of the hill past the parish church the pilgrims would have seen the cathedral (though trees now hide it), and would no doubt have speeded up from an amble to a canter, as the gait of horses on the road to Canterbury was called, in abbreviation for 'Canterbury gallop'. A disapproving Lollard, William Thorpe, gave a typically killjoy view of the pilgrims: 'They will ordaine to have with them both men and women that can well sing wanton songs; and some other pilgrimes will have with them bagpipes; so that in everie town that they come through, what with the noise of their singing, and with the sound of their piping, and with the jangling of their Canterburie bels, and with the barking out of dogs after them, they make more noise than if the king came there away.'

St Nicholas's Hospital for lepers at Harbledown was one of the minor attractions of the journey, as it had a relic of Becket – one of his shoes, which the pilgrims kissed as they passed by. Early in the sixteenth century the shoe was still being offered, as it was to Erasmus and Colet, two men of the new age. Erasmus was not openly hostile; but Colet was self-righteously offensive, asking the company, in Lambarde's account of the occasion, 'What mean these beasts, that we should kiss the shoes of all good men? why doe they not by the same reason offer us their spittle, and other excrements of the body to be kissed?' The hospital was founded by Archbishop Lanfranc in 1084. When leprosy died out in the next couple of centuries it became a general hospital, and is now almshouses.

Down the hill below the almshouses is a spring called the **Black Prince's Well**; the three feathers of the Prince of Wales's arms are carved over its arch. The water is said to be medicinal, which may account for the fact that the hospital was built near by.

4

Canterbury

MOST VISITORS TO Canterbury, like Chaucer's pilgrims, make straight for the cathedral, though unlike the pilgrims they can no longer see Becket's jewel-encrusted tomb, destroyed long ago by Thomas Cromwell's men, who took twenty-six cartloads of booty away with them. But in many ways it is best to leave the cathedral until last, though any exploration of Canterbury will take you past it continually, and you are never out of sight of it for long. Canterbury is not a city to be rushed through. It is a place of sudden surprises, of little gardens opening up between buildings, of medieval stonework glimpsed across the river, of plaques on the wall and stones set in the pavement as reminders of things vanished.

Looked at on the map, Canterbury is like a crossbow, with the town walls forming the sharply reflexed arms of the bow and the Stour like a slack bowstring at the walls' two ends. The main street forms the stock of the bow, running north-west to Whitstable and south-east to Dover. For the purpose of exploration, the city falls neatly into three parts: St Peter's Street, the West Gate and all the area north-west of the Stour; the cathedral and the streets immediately round it; and the remaining quadrant, largely blitzed in 1942 and the scene of Canterbury's major rebuilding schemes, on the other side of the High Street. The area beyond the walls is not so easily defined; but apart from the university nothing worth looking at is more than twenty minutes' walk from the town centre.

As you walk round the city walls of Canterbury, you are following the original outline of the Roman town. But though the gates still correspond to the Roman gateways, nothing survives of the original Roman grid plan of streets. When the Romans came for good in the middle of the first century they are unlikely to have found much of a settlement; the Belgic tribes probably had their stronghold at Bigbury, on the hills near Harbledown. After pacification it was natural that an important town should grow where Watling Street (the

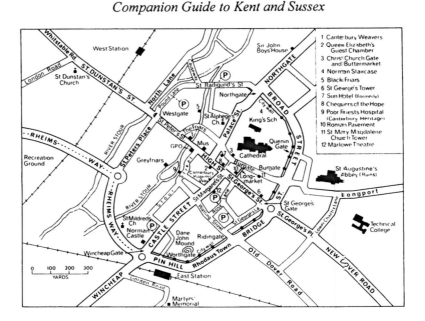

London–Dover road) crossed the Stour (here divided into two arms), with other arteries of the road system radiating to Richborough and Lympne.

Kent was so peaceful that walls were not needed until the end of the third century, when Saxon pirates were becoming a serious menace. Roman Canterbury had the usual baths and forum, an amphitheatre, and large villas. Part of the mosaic pavement of one of them, well below ground level, can be seen below modern shops at the Roman Museum in Butchery Lane. The Roman name for the town, Durovernum Cantiacorum (Durovernum of the Kent men) probably perpetuates the original name, as the Celtic prefix *dwr-* is found where there is water to be crossed (compare Durobrivae for Rochester). The modern name comes straight from the Anglo-Saxon Cantwarabyrig, the burgh or stronghold of the men of Kent.

So the popular picture of Augustine landing in Kent in AD 597 to convert a mob of savages is grotesquely inaccurate. For nearly two centuries since the withdrawal of Roman troops England had split into petty kingdoms; but a civilization as all-embracing as the Roman does not vanish overnight. The king of Kent, Ethelbert, was a pagan, but his wife Bertha, daughter of the Frankish king, was a Christian, and on her marriage had brought Bishop Liudhard with her as her private chaplain. Liudhard had already been in England about twenty years when he asked Pope Gregory for help in the work of conversion, so that Augustine found his work well begun, and Ethelbert no doubt already half-convinced. In his brief seven years as archbishop, Augustine established Christianity as the official religion, set up an efficient church administration, and – most important of all from the point of view of Canterbury – built both a priory in the present cathedral precincts, and the abbey that bears his name outside the walls. The tall stone pillar that stands in a corner of the ruins may have been the phallic pagan monolith worshipped by King Ethelbert in his chapel, while Queen Bertha made her way through the Quenin (or Queen-in) Gate, past the future site of the abbey, to St Martin's church on the side of the hill near by.

The site of **St Augustine's Abbey** (English Heritage) was chosen for two reasons: first, it was more suitable for the life of contemplation outside the bustle of the city; and second, the early Church did not permit burial within a town's walls. This was the burial place of the early archbishops – St Augustine himself, and his successors Sts Lawrence, Mellitus and Justus (the empty tombs are now under a protecting roof); of Ethelbert, Bertha and Liudhard; and of later kings.

The Saxon complex of abbey church, side chapels and ancillary buildings was swept away at the end of the eleventh century, when the great twin-towered abbey church was built almost as large as the cathedral itself. This church was torn down in its turn, along with the cloister and other monastic buildings, at the Dissolution, and the stone was shipped across the Channel for the fortifications of Calais, or sold to local builders. What was left was turned into a royal staging-post on the journey from London to Dover; hence the Tudor brickwork above the blocked up Norman arcading of the north aisle.

The various levels of abbey ruins make them hard to unravel; the little **Church of St Pancras** to the east is simplicity itself by comparison. Built of Roman brick, almost certainly by Augustine, it was at one time thought to have been Ethelbert's idol-chapel before his conversion. The surviving brick window arch at the east end is from a fourteenth-century rebuilding, using Roman bricks.

West of the abbey is St Augustine's College, built in the 1840s to train missionaries for Australia, now part of the King's School. It incorporates the abbey gatehouse, built about 1300 by Abbot Fyndon and known as the Fyndon Gate. Charles I and Queen Henrietta Maria spent their wedding night in the chamber over the gate in 1625, but with the abbey's decline as a staging-post it fell on hard times, ending up as brewery and beer-garden before being salvaged for the missionaries. William Butterfield's flint-built quadrangle is far more austere than the fanciful turrets and decorated stonework of the Fyndon Gate. The medieval refectory, much restored, is still used as the school dining hall; and below the chapel is a vaulted undercroft, with panels recording the generations of missionaries who trained at St Augustine's before going out to Pretoria or Jamaica, Quebec or Zanzibar.

St Martin's Church, where Queen Bertha worshipped, is the oldest church in continuous use in this country. It was founded well before 597, and the chancel certainly goes back to this time. In all probability this was the original Christian church of Roman Durovernum, built in the third or fourth century and surviving the pagan interregnum. Until Ethelbert's conversion Augustine used St Martin's as his base; and it seems likely that the font inside the church was the one used to baptize Ethelbert and his courtiers. The western end of the chancel, built largely of Roman brick, was no doubt Bertha's original chapel. The western wall of the church is even older, and is thought to have been the wall of the original Roman church, restored and reused when a larger building was needed by Augustine. Though the view from the churchyard is largely blocked by the high walls of the prison, you can get magnificent end-on glimpses of the cathedral away in the distance.

In 1997 the abbey got a face-lift to celebrate the 1,400th anniverary of Augustine's arrival in England. A new museum was built, with computer displays outlining the abbey's history from its foundation in the seventh century to its dissolution in 1538, and all sorts of items excavated from the site, including medieval floor tiles and a mitre belonging to one of the last of St Augustine's abbots.

This excursion outside the walls sets the scene for the Canterbury we all know, or feel we know – the Canterbury of narrow crooked streets and timber-framed houses projecting over the pavements, not all that different (if you disregard the shopfronts) from the town familiar to the Knight and the Pardoner, the Miller, the Reeve and the Wife of Bath. Starting at St George's Gate and walking straight through the town to the West Gate, you pass many of the most interesting buildings, besides getting an idea of the small scale of the town (the main street is hardly half a mile from end to end and is pedestrianised for its full length). First, on the right, is the tower of **St George's** – all that was left after the blitz of the church where the

1,500 years of Christianity: Canterbury Cathedral from the ruins of
St. Augustine's Abbey.

Elizabethan playwright Christopher Marlowe was baptized in 1564. On the same side is a shopping precinct, the Longmarket, with the **Roman Museum** already mentioned off Butchery Lane. The mosaic is on display, along with brooches and pottery, and the remains of a hypocaust.

Here St George's Street becomes the **High Street**. On the corner of Mercery Lane are the mighty overhanging beams of a pilgrims' inn, the Chequer of the Hope (now a jeweller's), which once stretched right back to the Buttermarket. A little farther on the left is the half-timbered house known as Queen Elizabeth's Guest Chamber (now a teashop), dated 1573, with a cheerful frieze of painted and moulded cupids, grapes and barrels at second-floor level Opposite is an incongruous piece of redbrick Victorianism, the Beaney Institute, now the **Royal Museum and Art Gallery**. James George Beaney was one of the most colourful characters produced by nineteenth-century Canterbury. Born in 1826, he trained as a doctor, and as a young man went out to Australia. He returned to take part in the Crimean War, and then settled for good in Melbourne, where he had a profitable but chequered medical practice; he was tried twice for manslaughter and once for murder after unsuccessful operations. He never forgot his birthplace, and when he died in 1891 he left Canterbury £11,000 to found the Institute. The museum, above the public library, is small and well laid out, with cases among other things of fine porcelain and works of art.

In the same building is the **Buffs Museum,** crammed with the uniforms, medals and warlike paraphernalia of Canterbury's own regiment. The Buffs lost their separate identity in 1961. and so this museum gives a picture of a finite period of military history, from the regiment's beginnings as the Holland Regiment (formed from mercenaries fighting for the Dutch against Spain) in the 1660s, to its final operations in Aden three centuries later.

A few yards farther on the road rises to King's Bridge over the Stour. On the left is **Eastbridge Hospital,** founded soon after Becket's death as a hostel for poor pilgrims. They paid fourpence a night for the use of the lofty refectory hall, the chapel and the chilly vaults below. When a fireplace was removed in the hall a magnificent tempera painting was uncovered, thought to be contemporary with the building, showing Christ giving his blessing in a gesture of Byzantine remoteness. Across the river the High Street becomes St Peter's Street, taking its name from a medieval church set back behind a small garden. On the right-hand side are the timbered gables of the **Canterbury Weavers** house – one of the many houses taken over by Protestant weavers from the Continent towards the end of the sixteenth century, after the Massacre of St Bartholomew in France and the Spanish persecution in the Low Countries. Beyond the Weavers you can see the town ducking-stool, a joke nowadays but in reality a homely and effective instrument of torture, as anyone who has struggled for breath under water will know.

The splendid **West Gate** loses much of its impressiveness by being isolated as a traffic island and by having traffic continually scraping under its arches. In its day it must have been an effective part of the fortifications. For a long time a room above the gateway was used as the town prison. The Rev. William Gostling, a canon of the cathedral, wrote in his *Walk in and about the City of Canterbury*, with a proper eighteenth-century sense of self-satisfaction: 'The way up is through a grated cage in the gate, level with the street, where the prisoners, who are not more closely confined, may discourse with passengers, receive their alms, and warn them (by their distress) to manage their liberty and property to the best advantage.' Upstairs there is a small museum where you can visit the room over the gateway, with a cell in each corner and the wooden condemned cell against an inside wall, and an odd collection of mantraps and boneshaker bicycles. From the roof there is an excellent view across the red-tiled roofs of the town to the west end of the cathedral.

Walter Jerrold, in his 1907 *Highways and Byways* guide, says that in 1859 a Mr Wombwell, 'the great menagerie man', wanted to pull down the Westgate to allow his elephants through. He petitioned the corporation, who were evenly divided – but luckily the gate was saved by the mayor's casting vote.

Beyond the West Gate is **St Dunstan's Street**, as pretty as anything in Canterbury – at least until the level crossing is reached. Most famous, and photographed, is the House of Agnes Hotel, a gabled building reputedly the home of Agnes Wickfield, in *David Copperfield*. Over the level crossing is **St Dunstan's**, the church where in 1174 King Henry II changed into penitent's clothes before walking barefoot through the streets to the cathedral, to be scourged before Becket's tomb. Another and later Chancellor who came to a violent end is associated with St Dunstan's. When Sir Thomas More was executed on Tower Hill in 1535, his daughter, Margaret Roper, obtained his head; after her death it was buried in the Roper family vault below the church.

On either side of St Peter's Street the city is an inconsequential place, little more than an unplanned island between the two branches of the Stour. Yet it has two of the riverside corners of Canterbury most worth hunting out – the **Black Friars** below the bridge, and the **Grey Friars** above it. The Black Friars (Dominicans) came to Canterbury in 1237, and got their site about twenty years later. The best view of the remaining buildings is from the bridge half way along the Friars; the guest house is on the left bank of the river, and the refectory, now used as the King's School art gallery, on the right. The Grey Friars (Franciscans) had come to Canterbury in 1224, before the Dominicans, but did not have a permanent site until 1267. There is only one relic of their friary, a pretty little stone building built right over a branch of the river, and reached through a beautifully tended kitchen garden (entrance in Stour Street). The building straddles the stream, with dumpy pillars for support at either end; surprisingly, it is said never to get damp. It consists of a large upstairs room, with a smaller room opening off it, and may have been built for the provincial or head of the order. In later years it was used by Flemish weavers, and as a prison.

Before they moved to their island garden, the Franciscans lived at the **Poor Priests' Hospital,** in Stour Street, established about 1200. Beautifully restored and refurbished, it is now the **Canterbury Heritage Museum,** laid out as a time-walk through the city's history from Roman times to the present day. Holograms, models and display cases make this into one of the most imaginative of modern museums. Its treasures range from a spectacular hoard of Roman spoons, to George Stephenson's 1830 locomotive *Invicta*, which once hauled trains on the Canterbury–Whitstable line, long since defunct.

Farther down Stour Street, on the corner of Hospital Lane, is **Maynard and Cotton's Hospital,** a neat little row of single-storey early eighteenth-century almshouses. **St Mildred's,** founded in the eighth century and thus the oldest church inside the walls, is down a cul-de-sac at the end of the street; the early church was rebuilt after a fire in 1246. Nearby is the entrance to a long-established tannery, founded in 1791. A few yards away are the remains of **Canterbury Castle,** the square buttressed keep guarding the ancient Wincheap Gate. It was built at the end of the eleventh century, and in the Middle Ages was used as a royal prison. In 1381 Wat Tyler and his men attacked it and burnt the prison records, and in the Civil War it was temporarily held by the Royalists. Now it is hardly more than a shell, but what survives is impressive enough.

The name 'donjon' for a Norman keep has been transferred, and altered in the process, to **Dane John Mound**. It is now thought in fact to have been a Roman or pre-Roman burial ground, and nothing to do with defence. The mound was tidied up, terraced and surmounted with an obelisk about 1800, and the gardens below, with their lime avenue, neat houses and encircling city wall, are a marvellous example of an urban open space, unplanned but just right. In the gardens is a monument to Marlowe, with a bare-breasted Victorian Muse bewailing the poet. The son of a shoemaker, Marlowe was educated at the King's School, and is reputed to have combined writing with secret service work, until he was murdered in a brawl in Deptford at the age of twenty-nine. It is now thought that the brawl was a put-up job designed to eliminate Marlowe, who was becoming indiscreet. His name is perpetuated in the **Marlowe Theatre**, in The Friars. Nearby, St Margaret's Church now houses the **Canterbury Tales Visitor Attraction** – a reconstruction in tableaux, sound effects, and even the occasional smell, of the medieval world. It cunningly dovetails five of Chaucer's tales with scenes the pilgrims knew, from the Tabard Inn in Southwark to St Thomas's gilded shrine in the cathedral.

Most of the quadrant on the other side of the High Street is taken up by the cathedral and the close, though there are plenty of other things to see: the tower of **St Mary Magdalene's Church** in Burgate, which survived the blitz and is now used as a shelter for a number of murky memorials; the noble timbered buildings of the **Buttermarket**; the extraordinary lopsided door of the gabled **King's School Shop**, round the corner in Palace Street. Also in Palace Street is **St Alphege's**, an Early English church with a strange barn-like top to its tower. It now houses the **Canterbury Environment Centre** – an educational centre aimed largely towards instilling a sense of history in the young people who visit it. Alphege is one of Canterbury's own saints; as archbishop in 1012 he was carried off by the Danes, and finally pelted to death with beef bones during a drunken feast at their camp in Greenwich.

In the **Christ Church Gateway** the cathedral has a glorious approach, 'a very goodly, strong, and beautiful structure, and of excellent artifice', as a seventeenth-century writer, William Somner, called it. Probably started in 1517 and completed about 1520, it was put up as a memorial to Prince Arthur, Henry VII's eldest son, who died in 1502. Though the figure of Christ was removed from the tall central niche in 1643 (not by the Cromwellians, as is usually stated), the front still has its rows of brightly painted shields and heraldic devices. The corner turrets were pulled down about 1803, so that a prosperous Canterbury banker could have an uninterrupted view of the cathedral clock from the door of his premises. They were not replaced until the gateway was restored in the 1930s. In 1990 the empty niche was filled with a statue of Christ by Klaus Ringwald.

Visitors now have to pay an entry charge at the gateway; when this was introduced in 1995 there was a general outcry, but in fact there was plenty of historical precedent. Walter Jerrold in about 1900 was allowed to enjoy the nave in peace, but nowhere else. 'To visit the shrine, the various chapels and tombs, to penetrate the crypt, to go to the Martyrdom, it is not only necessary to pay, but having paid one is led round by an iterating cicerone who confuses where he would enlighten, who gabbles certain archaeological, architectural or other data, and hurries his little flock on to the next viewpoint.'

Canterbury Cathedral – or, to give it its full name, the Cathedral Church of Christ, Canterbury – is a building of supreme poise and splendour. Externally the graceful pinnacles of Bell Harry Tower reconcile the conflicting elements of many architectural styles, and are the first glimpse of the cathedral as you enter Canterbury from any direction. Yet for all its outside beauty the chief glories of the cathedral are internal: the delicate shafts of the nave, which forms a huge vestibule to the cathedral; the powerful columns of the inward-turning choir; the vast windows of medieval stained glass, some of which survived the fanaticism of the Puritans; and the calm solemnity of the crypt.

Since Saxon times Canterbury Cathedral had been the main church of English Christendom; but without the mixture of political squabbling and clashes of personality that led to Becket's murder, and hence to the canonization and the pilgrimages, it would certainly never have grown to its immense size and richness. There was a Saxon cathedral on the site, the successor to a church consecrated by St Augustine; but William the Conqueror's first archbishop, Lanfranc, lost no time in pulling down the building – already badly damaged by fire in 1067 – and replacing it by one of his own. Lanfranc and his successor, Anselm, were typical of the international administrators appointed to high office by the Norman kings. Both were Italians, and both had been priors of the abbey of Bec, in Normandy.

Lanfranc had completed his cathedral in seven years, beginning about 1070; though his work was largely obliterated by later building,

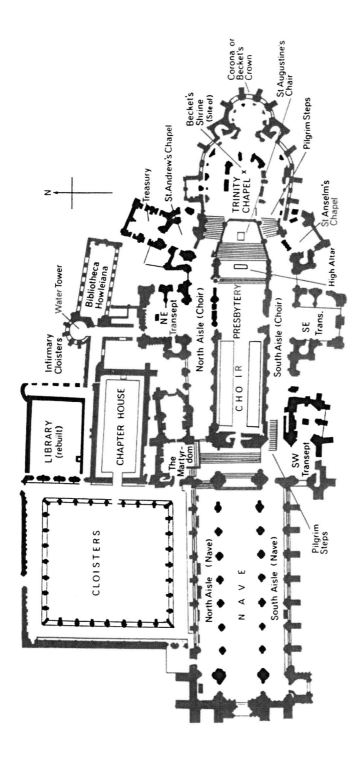

N

Corona or Becket's Crown

St Augustine's Chair

Becket's Shrine (Site of)

Pilgrim Steps

St Andrew's Chapel

Treasury

TRINITY CHAPEL x

St Anselm's Chapel

Water Tower

Bibliotheca Howleiana

High Altar

NE Transept

North Aisle (Choir)

PRESBYTERY

South Aisle (Choir)

SE Trans.

Infirmary Cloisters

CHOIR

LIBRARY (rebuilt)

CHAPTER HOUSE

The Martyr-dom

SW Transept

CLOISTERS

Pilgrim Steps

North Aisle (Nave)

NAVE

South Aisle (Nave)

his north-west tower stood until 1832, when it was pulled down in a misguided desire for symmetry and rebuilt in Perpendicular style. The present Norman parts of the cathedral are mainly the work of Anselm, who pulled down Lanfranc's choir and built a very much larger one of his own. The best idea of the Norman cathedral can be got from outside, on the south side: the south-east transept, with its round-arched Norman windows and blind arcading, in marked contrast to the flourishes of the Perpendicular south-west transept below Bell Harry Tower; and the pretty little side chapel, set at an angle, known as **St Anselm's Chapel** (Anselm was canonized after his death).

The **Crypt** is the most miraculous of the Norman survivals. A forest of Romanesque columns surrounds a little central chapel, and leads on to the solid simplicity of the massive pillars built later to support the weight of the Trinity Chapel overhead. The Romanesque capitals are carved with an uninhibited delight in the sculptor's fancy – a pointed-eared half-human figure struggling with two ferocious beasts, jugglers, grotesque human heads, weird medieval animals, or, when naturalistic inspiration failed, delicately interlacing abstract patterns.

Such was the cathedral that Becket knew. A door leads from the north-west corner of the crypt into the corner, known as the **Martyrdom**, where Becket was cut down. On the wall a jagged cruciform sculpture, designed by Giles Blomfield, casts a sinister shadow. A pair of jagged-edged swords hanging from the arms of the cross symbolize Becket's murder; below their reddened points is a simple slate table altar, with the name THOMAS carved on the floor in front of it. Becket's career exemplified the major conflict of mid twelfth-century England: whether the civil courts should have jurisdiction over the priesthood. And when the two protagonists were men as self-willed as Henry II and his archbishop, and the age was one of violence, then murder was the foreseeable outcome.

Becket was born in London about 1118, of French parents. A contemporary described him as 'slim of growth and pale of hue, dark of hair, with a long nose and straightly featured face; blithe of countenance was he, winning and lovable in all conversation, frank of speech in his discourse, but slightly stuttering in his talk, so keen of discernment and understanding that he could always make difficult questions plain after a wise manner'. He began his career as secretary to Archbishop Theobald of Canterbury, went with him in exile into France in 1152, and returned with him two years later when, on the death of King Stephen, Henry of Anjou succeeded to the English throne as Henry II.

Becket, still well under forty, was made Archdeacon of Canterbury, and in 1155 reached the highest secular post in the kingdom as Chancellor of the Realm. He lived in enormous splendour, whether he was holding court in Canterbury, or campaigning in France in the medieval tradition of the warrior-prelate, accompanied by a huge retinue which included eight wagons, one fitted up as a chapel and two carrying wine and beer. Strangely enough, he had not yet been ordained priest; and when Theobald died in 1161, Becket, the natural choice as his successor, went through the ordination ceremony only a day before being consecrated archbishop.

Now that his power almost rivalled the king's, a clash of policy was inevitable, and the two men's friendship turned to enmity. In 1164 Henry exiled Becket to France, and from his exile he sent out a stream of excommunications as he struggled to keep the clergy immune from civil law, threatening the king himself with the final sanction of the church. After six years of bickering, Henry and Becket had an uneasy reconciliation in France in November, 1170, and Becket was at last allowed to return to Canterbury. In exile he had adopted austerity with all the earlier zeal he had shown for luxury, wearing a hair shirt next to his skin and allowing his body to become lice-ridden and verminous.

Welcomed back in triumph to Canterbury, he at once showed that exile had not taught him caution. Even before crossing the Channel he had excommunicated the bishops of London and Salisbury, and his sermons and general conversation on his return were as outspoken as ever. This was the situation when Henry, listening to rumours that came to him in France, shouted in rage 'Of the caitiffs who eat my bread, are there none to free me of this low-born priest?' So four knights, William de Tracy, Reginald Fitzurse, Richard le Breton and Hugh de Morville, crossed the Channel before the king could take back his words, laid their plans at Saltwood Castle, and on 29 December rode along Stone Street to Canterbury.

In his last days Becket seems to have had a premonition of death. On Christmas Day he preached a sermon which prophesied that there would soon be another Christian martyrdom; and in an audience he gave the four knights on the afternoon of the 29th he told them that he defied them to the death. This was not long coming. That evening, in the dull winter twilight, Becket met his murderers in the cathedral, near the cloister door. The Martyrdom is slightly different today: Becket confronted the knights on a small staircase that no longer exists. When they tried to drag him into the cloister, to avoid the sacrilege of killing him in his cathedral, he threw one of them to the ground. Then all except Hugh de Morville drew their swords and cut him down, slicing off the crown of his head and spattering the pavement with his blood and brains. At the spot where one of the swords shattered on the pavement once stood the Altar of the Sword's Point, one of the goals of pilgrimage. Becket was buried in the crypt, and the cathedral's great epoch began.

Within three days came the first miraculous cure of a woman who appealed to Becket as a saint. By Easter 1171 Canterbury was already a place of pilgrimage; the Pope canonized Becket in 1173; and in July the following year the remorseful king crossed over from France and performed public penance, walking barefoot through the streets and kneeling to be scourged in the crypt before the tomb. That autumn Anselm's choir caught fire; the blazing roof fell in, and the marks of the searing heat can still be seen in the stonework of the wall of the south aisle. With money pouring in from the pilgrims, Canterbury could afford the best possible rebuilding. The great architect William of Sens was brought over from France, and during the next five years the **Choir** was rebuilt, resting on those magnificent columns, alternately round and octagonal, and crowned by capitals of marvellous foliation. In 1178 William of Sens, while superintending work on the vaulting, fell fifty feet from the scaffolding and injured his back, and was forced to return to France.

French William's misfortune was the great opportunity for his successor, William the Englishman, 'small in body, but in workmanship of many kinds acute and honest', a contemporary chronicler called him. English William rounded off the cathedral, literally as well as metaphorically, building the **Trinity Chapel** to house the tomb of Becket and raising it high on the columns of the eastern crypt, which accounts for the final flight of steps up which the pilgrims climbed. **St Augustine's Chair**, a medieval marble throne, constructed in sections for ease of transport and used at the enthronement of Canterbury's archbishops, stands behind the High Altar. At the extreme east end English William built the circular annexe known as the **Corona** or **Becket's Crown**, either because it was shaped like the severed top of the saint's head, or because the piece of skull was kept there as a relic. The Corona has been rededicated as the **Chapel of the Saints and Martyrs of Our Own Time**.

Though the patterned floor of the Trinity Chapel is now bare, the knees of centuries of pilgrims wore a narrow groove across the marble, as they peered through the grille at the marvels of **St Thomas's shrine.** According to the cathedral guide, this consisted of a marble table, which 'carried an oak chest shaped like an ark, strongly bound with iron. The timber-work was covered with golden plates, embossed with golden wires, pearls and precious stones. The painted wooden cover which usually concealed it was drawn up, at a signal from the guide (a monk), by pulleys from the roof.' So for three and a half centuries, until Thomas Cromwell dismantled the gorgeous trappings and carted them away to Henry VIII's coffers, the fervent, the credulous and the holiday-makers came to gaze at the shrine of the 'hooly, blisful martir', to study the windows, of a darker blue than any sky, where his miracles were depicted, and to feel, like modern visitors to Canterbury, the power of great architecture.

After the visual complexities of the eastern end of the cathedral, the **Nave** is all simplicity. Built by Henry Yevele (pronounced 'Yeevely'), the greatest master of the early Perpendicular style, at the end of the fourteenth century, its calm spaciousness provides an open area where the thousands of milling sightseers can get their bearings, peering at their guidebooks or listening in to the prerecorded descriptions of the building. Yevele's trademark is the use of shaft rings to interrupt the unbroken vertical lines, but only 'a mere whispered interruption', as Newman calls it. His probable portrait is on one of the roof bosses in the cloister, near the door into the cathedral; he is shown with curly forked beard, and his eyes closed in death. By the same door are stones that commemorate links between Canterbury and French William's home town of Sens.

The cathedral's final and greatest external adornment, the **Bell Harry Tower**, was not added until the end of the fifteenth century, when the journeys of the pilgrims had only a few decades left to run. The 'Harry' after which it is named is a bell cast in 1635, the successor to a bell called Henry given by Prior Eastry, who built the screens enclosing the choir in about 1304. Below the tower, at the crossing, the ceiling is magnificently fan-vaulted, a final firework-burst of decoration to mark the dying of the Middle Ages, and its blend of aspiration, greed, corruption and saintliness of which Canterbury Cathedral is the embodiment.

It is impossible to do more than scratch the surface of the cathedral in a few pages. Monographs have been written on single aspects like the stained glass, which alone would take months to get to know properly. To study the **Windows** the experts recommend binoculars: nevertheless the main thirteenth-century glass – the 'poor man's bible' in the north aisle of the choir and the miracle windows round the Trinity Chapel – are all near enough to study with the naked eye. These miracle windows were huge advertisements for the effectiveness of St Thomas's shrine, and showed the kind of cures the. sick pilgrims might expect, though only if they fulfilled their side of the bargain. Thus when Sir Jordan Fitzeisulf's household was smitten with the plague, his eldest son was given holy water from Canterbury and recovered; but Sir Jordan did not pay the customary thank-offering and so the plague broke out again, ensuring that the proper sum was offered up at the tomb of St Thomas. The windows convey something of the Lourdes-like attitude that must have prevailed at Canterbury, at least in the early days of the pilgrimages, when St Thomas, if suitably approached, could cure anything from toothache to paralysis or insanity. Thomas himself can be seen, in green-robed majesty, at the bottom of Window 1 (top of steps, north side).

As striking as the glass is the unrivalled series of tombs: the procession of archbishops, glowing darkly in the crypt or resplendent in the aisles; the Black Prince lying in gilded armour below a tester painted with the Trinity; pudgy, shrewd-looking Henry IV and his wife, on the other side of the Trinity Chapel. In the nave are monuments to men as diverse as the composer Orlando Gibbons, who died at Canterbury in 1625 while on his way to Dover with the Chapel Royal musicians to welcome Queen Henrietta Maria; and the Canterbury benefactor James George Beaney, previously mentioned.

All the glamour of medieval publicity makes it easy to forget that the cathedral was also the church of the largest Benedictine monastery in the country. The monastic buildings lie on the north side of the cathedral. The **Great Cloister**, reached from the Martyrdom, is not the cloister that Becket knew, but a later rebuilding of about 1400. The ceiling bosses are a heraldry-lover's delight. Opening off the east side is the **Chapter House**, rebuilt about 1304, where the monks carried on their administration. A huge empty building, with stone seating backed by arcades the whole way round and a big stone throne for the prior, it has an elaborate barrel-vaulted roof of 1405 and is mainly lit by an enormous Perpendicular west window. From a distance it looks curiously like a Victorian market building or railway station; it is now used for exhibitions, lectures and social functions. The library next to it was destroyed by a bomb in 1942 and rebuilt in 1954. Between the chapter house and library a passage leads to what is left of the **Infirmary Cloisters**, where the monks convalesced before returning to the full rigours of monastic life. Half way along is a delightful little building, perched up on columns, which is practical as well as aesthetic – the **Water Tower** built by Prior Wibert in the twelfth century to house the monastery's main cistern. A drawing by the monk Eadwin of about 1165 gives a diagram of the water supply and a rough idea of the appearance of the cathedral in Becket's time.

North of the infirmary cloister you leave the shade of buildings for the sunny spaciousness of the **Green Court**, through a passage known as the **Dark Entry** because of the sudden transition from light to gloom when you go into it. It was in the Dark Entry, according to one of Barham's *Ingoldsby Legends*, that the body of Nell Cook was buried in a vault after she had poisoned a canon and the 'niece' with whom he lived. Every Friday night her ghost walks abroad –

And whoso in that Entry dark doth feel that fatal breath,
He ever dies within the year some dire, untimely death!

Though she is popularly supposed to have existed, in reality she is a figment of Barham's fertile imagination.

On the opposite side of the Green Court are the big arches and tiled roof of the **Norman Staircase**, which led up to a large pilgrims' hall (it now leads to the King's School library); and near by a great Norman gate, its archway elaborately carved, brings you to more **King's School** buildings and the outside world. The school got its name after the old monastic school was granted a new charter by Henry VIII in 1541, but its history goes back very much further than that, possibly to the time of Augustine, who would certainly have founded some kind of academy to train boys for the expanding church. The Rev. Gostling, as a loyal King's Scholar, pushed it back to the Druids – though as he said, 'it will be in vain to continue this search any further'.

If the King's School is groaning under the weight of age, the **University of Kent**, at the top of St Thomas's Hill along the Whitstable Road, only began its career in 1965. A place of wide concrete paths and treeless lawns, it stands on a splendid site, with the whole of Canterbury spread out below. The buildings are spread over a wide area; the individual colleges are inward-looking, built

65

round central quadrangles. In a century or so it will no doubt have got the necessary educational mellowness, like the spiky Victorianism of **St Edmund's School**, built on the same hill.

Below the university is **Hackington**, a village swallowed up by Canterbury, and one of the prettiest corners of the city. The first crude attempts at cricket are said to have been carried out on Hackington green. The home of Kent cricket nowadays lies on the other side of the city, at the **St Lawrence Ground**, a mile or so down the Old Dover Road. It attracts thousands of visitors each August to Canterbury's Cricket Week, first held as long ago as the 1840s. It is the only major ground to incorporate a tree (a huge old lime, thought to be about two centuries old) within its boundaries; in keeping with the tree's venerable uniqueness, if a ball touches any part of it the batsman scores four runs and cannot be out from a ball caught off it. Only twice in its history has anyone lofted a ball clean over it. It was recently found to have a fungal disease, and a new young lime has been planted near it as its eventual replacement.

5

Thanet and the Coast Resorts

HEADING NORTH-EAST FROM Canterbury along the A28 – yet another Roman road – towards the Isle of Thanet, the first place you come to is **Sturry**, which has a curved village street bypassed by the traffic. The name comes from 'Estuari', and a branch of the Stour still flows along its western side. The church is basically Norman, with aisles added later; remains of Norman windows can be seen above the arcades.

In the Middle Ages, when the Stour was wider and deeper than it is today, **Fordwich**, just south of Sturry, was the port of Canterbury, where stone from Caen in Normandy was landed for the cathedral, along with hogsheads of wine for the thirsty monks of Christ Church and St Augustine's abbeys. Fordwich was important enough to be ranked as a 'limb' of the Cinque Port of Sandwich, with its own mayor and jurats, who had the right to carry out such punishments as drowning criminals in the river. It is still very much a riverside place, though dinghies have taken over from the cargo boats of earlier years.

At its centre is the Tudor timbered town hall; the stone ground floor was used as a storeroom and prison, while upstairs is the courtroom where criminals were tried, still with the wooden bar at which they stood to plead their case. The crest of the mayor of Fordwich included a trout on a plate – a reference to the good eating quality of fish from the Stour. The church nearby has traces of Saxon stonework in the tower. Inside it keeps its old box pews (the mayor's pew was the front left-hand one) along with two more ancient objects – a rough-hewn wooden chair, cut from the solid and unique in England, and beside it the 'Fordwich stone', carved in the form of a colonnade with tiled roof above and probably part of a Norman tomb of about 1100.

From Sturry you can continue eastwards to Thanet, or turn north along the A291 for Herne Bay. A couple of miles down the road you pass thick woodland on your left – the remains of the ancient Forest of Blean, which once covered the ridge between the Stour and the sea.

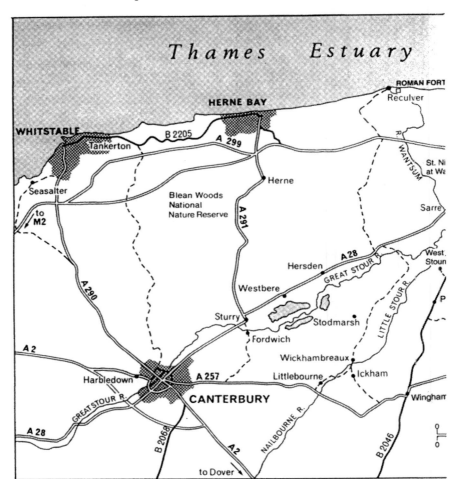

Here almost 200 acres have been designated as the **Blean Woods National Nature Reserve**, where in summer you can (if you know how to recognise it) spot the rare heath fritillary butterfly, and hear nightingales singing among the thickets. A little further north is the original village of **Herne** – a nice curve of brick and weatherboarding climbing the hill, and a medieval church opposite, half hidden by tall horse chestnuts. Most of the church is fourteenth-century; the Perpendicular Lady Chapel, added a century later, is of

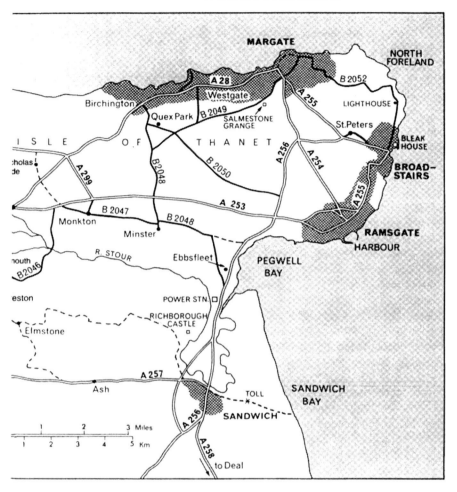

such quality that it has been suggested that the designer was Robert Vertue, Master Mason to Henry VII and builder of Henry VII's Chapel at Westminster, who owned land in Herne. Nicholas Ridley, the Protestant bishop burnt at the stake in 1555, was vicar here in the 1540s, and it was under his direction at Herne that the *Te Deum* was first sung in English. Herne's black smock mill is still standing, and has been restored to working order.

Herne Bay is a quiet, old-fashioned resort which is now enjoying something of a revival with a new small harbour and a summer

69

festival. It was laid out in the 1830s by 'two capitalists', according to a local history, and was visited by Mr Jorrocks, the sporting grocer of R.S.Surtees's novels, on his voyage to Margate in the 1830s. The Dolphin Hotel where he stayed is still there. Herne Bay's main landmark is the clock tower on the front, given in 1837 by Mrs Ann Thwaites, 'the opulent city widow', *Punch* called her in 1842. The tower, says the article, 'seems to have been designed after one of those rolls of brawn for which the adjacent city of Canterbury has for centuries been so famous'. It is thought to be the first-ever free-standing purpose-built clock tower.

The nineteenth-century pier, which once stepped for three-quarters of a mile out to sea on its spindly iron legs, was largely destroyed by a storm in 1978. It was built in 1832, to shorten the time taken to travel to the continent – boats from London were met by stagecoaches that took travellers down to Dover. The pier pavilion was burnt down in 1970 and replaced by a lumbering, modernistic sports centre. A harbour has recently been created between the pier and the clock tower, complete with a harbour arm for strolling along and a launching slipway. St George's Terrace opposite the end of the pier makes some attempt at seafront dignity, and just behind is the quiet (and strictly private) greenery of Oxenden Square. The tourist information centre near the clock tower has a good small local museum telling the story of the town, from the Stone Age to its heyday as a Victorian tourist resort.

Far out at sea, on a clear day, you can make out the gaunt skeletal outlines of a cluster of metal forts constructed during the Second World War to guard the Thames estuary. Standing on concrete legs on the sinisterly named Shivering Sand, these massive boxes were meant to deter German aicraft from flying up the Thames to bomb London; but by the time they were in position the Battle of Britain was long over, and they joined the ranks of such useless and long-superseded South Coast fortifications as the martello towers and the Victorian Thames-side forts.

Three miles east of Herne Bay the twin towers of **Reculver** (English Heritage) stand out in brooding silhouette against the brilliance of sea and sky. The towers mark the Roman fort of Regulbium, one of the Forts of the Saxon Shore built about AD 280 by Carausius, the self-styled Emperor of Britain. Reculver stands at the northern end of the Wantsum channel, once a wide sea lane for shipping; Richborough (see below) guards the southern end. But whereas Richborough is stranded inland and largely survives, Reculver has been half washed away by the sea; and what remains of the ruins is now drowned in a flood of caravans. The foundations of massive Roman masonry can be followed round from the King Ethelbert inn.

Reculver's most splendid ruin is not Roman but Christian, the twin medieval towers that survive from the ancient church built as so often right at the centre of the Roman fortress. A small apsidal Saxon church was built here as early as the seventh century; the towers, known as the Two Sisters, date from a twelfth-century enlargement. For hundreds of years the church at Reculver was a landmark to shipping, but by 1809 erosion had gone so far that it was decided to demolish it. Most of it was blown up by gunpowder. The towers, shorn of their tall spires, were sold to Trinity House, who rebuilt them 'sufficiently conspicuous to be useful to navigation', as an inscription says. Two of the columns were saved and are now in the crypt of Canterbury Cathedral.

At the base of the towers botanists have found a yellow-flowered plant called alexanders. The Romans used to eat its celery-flavoured stems, so perhaps it has been growing there since Regulbium was built seventeen centuries ago. The breezy clifftop between Reculver and Herne Bay is now a country park.

From Herne Bay you come down into **Whitstable** past the wide grassy slopes of **Tankerton**, with a ship's mast marking the highest point; below the beach the long spit of Street Stones runs far out to sea. For centuries 'Whitstable' has been synonymous with 'oysters' – and it still is, though the famous Whitstable Natives (*Ostrea edulis*), which grew wild on the seabed, have now given way to farmed Pacific oysters (*Crassostrea gigas*), which are bred in tanks and reach maturity on oyster beds in the shallows. They tell you at the **Oyster and Fishery Exhibition**, out on the harbour arm, that while you can only eat Natives when there is an R in the month, you can eat the Pacific variety whenever there is a D in the day.

Whitstable's streets are filled with the metallic slap of rigging twanged by the wind, from small boats beached in alleys or backyards, and out on the mudflats bent figures delve about for bait or shellfish. Between the High Street and the sea are the 'Walls' that give Whitstable its character – rows of fishermen's cottages, the weatherboarding often painted in alternate bands of black and white. In earlier centuries Whitstable was the port for Canterbury, and communication between the towns was considered so important that they were linked by the first railway in Kent, opened in 1830, and long since derelict. Nothing survives of medieval Whitstable except for All Saints' Church half a mile inland. **Seasalter, Whitstable's** western suburb, perpetuates in its name the medieval saltpans on the edge of the mudflats.

Back on the A28 and making for Thanet from Sturry, you come to **Westbere**, built above the marshes that fill the Stour estuary. A combination of gravel working and mining subsidence has created an area of large lakes, now surrounded by trees and thoroughly natural-looking, between Westbere and the Stodmarsh promontory to the south. Westbere's fourteenth-century church is hardly more than a chapel, yet it has some fine things in it: corbel figures below the chancel arch, overwhelmed by the weight of stonework above them (a similar figure, in paint not stone, is at Coombes, in Sussex, see p. 362); and exquisitely carved sedilia. **Hersden** nearby is a former mining village; the spoil tips of the Chislet Colliery form a manmade bluff south of the main road. Half covered in saplings, they add something to the flat countryside.

As you approach Sarre, at the entrance to Thanet, there is little to show that you are in effect leaving the mainland of Kent for an offshore island. Yet the **Wantsum** channel, shown on the map as a network of streams and drainage channels, was a sea lane for centuries, for the Romans and Saxons, and right until the late Middle Ages. But the shingle built up, the silt accumulated, and now only the watermeadows mark where merchantmen and warships once sailed in ghostly convoy.

The **Isle of Thanet** is unlike any other part of Kent. Though the coastal strip is Kent's pleasure ground, and the housing estates sprawl from Margate to Ramsgate, inland there are huge windswept fields, and the treeless airy landscape has more in common with Picardy than with the Canterbury orchard country. The history of Thanet begins by rather suspect tradition in AD 449, when King Vortigern of Kent asked the Jutish leaders Hengist and Horsa for help against Pictish raiders, and they brought their warriors across the sea to Ebbsfleet (see below). In return, they were given Thanet; and, having established a foothold, proceeded to conquer the rest of Kent and enslave the Britons who lived there.

Sarre – the gateway to Thanet, where you can fork left for Margate or right for Ramsgate – seems to consist of nothing but hotels and pubs. One of them, the Crown, is known as the Cherry

Brandy Inn because the house still distils its own liqueur from a recipe brought over by a Huguenot refugee who was landlord at the end of the seventeenth century.

St Nicholas at Wade, just off the Margate road, grew up beside a ford across the Wantsum; hence its name. It is a windy village, with a main street in two parts called simply 'The Street' and 'The Length'. Some of the older houses have brick gables of Dutch outline. The church is a really fine place, big, open and flooded with light.

Margate now sprawls along almost the entire north coast of Thanet. **Birchington**, the westernmost of its satellite villages, is the only one to keep any separate character; though **Westgate**, with its wide topiary gardens above the sea and redbrick hotels, breaks the monotony of the seaward side. Birchington has a good medieval church facing a triangle of asphalt that must once have been the village green. There is an incredibly varied collection of monuments in the north chapel, memorials to the Crispes of Quex Park, the Birchington estate named after the medieval Quek or Queke family. Sir Henry, who died in 1663, was nicknamed Bonjour Crispe, because, after being forcibly kidnapped from Quex and held for eight months in Flanders before ransom was paid, as a true Englishman he only picked up the word '*bonjour*' – but thereafter used it whenever he spoke to the villagers. Near the font is a window in memory of the Pre-Raphaelite artist Dante Gabriel Rossetti, who died at Birchington in 1882; a Celtic cross in the churchyard marks his grave.

Adjoining **Quex Park**, a creeper-covered nineteenth-century house, is one of the sights of Thanet, the **Powell-Cotton Museum**. Major Percy Powell-Cotton, who inherited Quex in 1894, spent half a century spreading alarm and death among the mammals of Africa and Asia; but he was far more than a mere trophy-hunter. In a series of enormous rooms he created tableaux showing the animals in their natural habitats – everything from white rhinoceros to tiny antelope standing in stuffed verisimilitude amid jungle or savannah. Since his death in 1940 the collection has expanded into a superb display of weapons, musical instruments and costumes from every primitive region of the world. One of his predecessors, John Powell-Powell, was an enthusiastic bellringer and built the **Waterloo Tower** in the park to practise his hobby. The gracefully curved, white-painted iron spire surmounting the tower can be seen above the trees.

Though Margate is now so large, its centre is still that unsurpassed crescent of sand to which Londoners have flocked for the last two centuries. Round this have grown up the brash trappings of a modern resort: the Dreamland amusement park, which Margate has made its symbol, towering flats by the seafront, a modern shopping centre built on the site of Cecil Square, the first of the eighteenth-century developments, now vanished without trace. For all its prosperity, Margate is lacking in any sense of style. You feel that nobody cares very much what happens to it as long as the bingo tellers are kept busy, the fruit machines and video games are milking the holidaymakers of their cash, and there is enough room between the parked coaches for the odd car to squeeze through. All of which is a pity, as there are still parts of old Margate like Trinity Square and Fort Crescent to show what has been lost, and what still might be salvaged.

Until Benjamin Beale, a Margate Quaker and glover, invented the covered bathing machine about 1753, Margate was just another fishing village. But with the machines, the sands, and easy access from London by boat, Margate could not fail in the early days of the seaside holiday. By 1775 there were thirty machines in use, trundling swimmers decorously from the bathing rooms to the water's edge, and dumping them in the sea protected from cold winds and inquisitive stares by a collapsible umbrella attached to the frame of the machine.

In those days of terrible roads, and before the railway reached Margate, visitors arrived from London by boat – the famous 'Margate hoy'. These clumsy craft wallowed down the Thames and back laden with seasick passengers, until the steam packet ousted them about 1815. A magnificent picture in the hall of the public library shows the steamer arriving at the jetty in 1869, in a confusion of parasols, portmanteaux, shoeshine boys, reunited families and cheerful excursionists. The jetty, built in 1855 and lengthened twenty years later, was severely damaged in a storm in 1978 and subsequently demolished. Margate's **Pier**, built by Rennie between 1810 and 1815, is a rounded stone arm guarding the harbour; at its landward end is the porticoed customs house building, dated 1812.

The old parish church, **St John's**, lies up the hill at the south end of the High Street. It is a big gaunt building, built on the site of a Saxon church of about 1050, with an enormously long nave flanked by twelfth-century Late Norman arcading. An unexpected survival among ramshackle buildings in the middle of the town is the Tudor timber-framed house on the corner of King Street and Trinity Hill. Now a museum, containing bygones and pictures of old Margate, it was totally derelict in 1950 and saved at the eleventh hour. Half a mile inland is **Salmestone Grange**, originally a grange or farm of St Augustine's Abbey, Canterbury. The medieval buildings are now flats; the chapel survives, as does a neat little courtyard in the middle.

The chalk on which Margate is built must be riddled with tunnels and workings. The **Grotto**, at the bottom of Grotto Hill, is a nice underground folly – a network of passages and rooms, covered with an all-over decoration of thousands of sea-shells in an amazing variety of pattern and design. Discovered accidentally by schoolboys in 1837, it has led to all sorts of wild speculations about its origin, of which the theory that it was built in pre-Roman times by Phoenician traders is among the most fanciful. The unromantic eye of the historian, however, sees it as an eighteenth-century shell grotto. Margate also has more conventional caves, at the summit of Northdown Road. Like the Hastings caves, they were discovered by chance about 1800 and subsequently enlarged, though they are on nothing like the same scale. It is more than likely that they were used by smugglers. Murals painted on the chalk in 1798 show redcoats, animals, and the Thanet Hunt galloping across the wall.

The road south from Margate down to Broadstairs passes the **North Foreland** lighthouse, smartly painted in its green and white Trinity House livery and the main landmark on this stretch of coast. There has been a lighthouse of sorts here since 1505, originally just a basket of blazing coals open to the sky. The present tower dates from the seventeenth century, but has been considerably enlarged and adapted down the years. Towards the end of 1998 the North Foreland became Britain's last lighthouse to be switched to computerised remote control, and the proudly self-sufficient race of lighthouse keepers vanished into history.

Broadstairs is a small Stratford-by-the-Sea, with Dickens instead of Shakespeare as its presiding deity. Bleak House, grimly battlemented (though this was done since Dickens's day), dominates one side of the tiny harbour, and every year in June there is a Dickens Festival, culminating in a grand assembly on the front of local people in top hats, frock coats and mutton-chop whiskers, or bonnets, crinolines and twirling parasols.

Dickens had spent a good many holidays in various houses in Broadstairs before he finally rented **Bleak House** (then called Fort

House) as his summer home. When he first took the house, it was far smaller than it is today (a wing was added in the early 1900s), and a cornfield stood between it and the sea. A good deal of it is now open as a museum of Dickensiana. The study where *David Copperfield* was written and *Bleak House* was planned looks out to sea. In a letter to a friend Dickens described his agreeable working life at Broadstairs. 'In a bay window sits, from nine o'clock to one, a gentleman with rather long hair and no neckcloth, who writes and grins as if he thought he were very funny indeed . . . At one he disappears, and presently emerges from a bathing machine, and may be seen – a kind of salmon-coloured porpoise – splashing about in the ocean. After that he may be seen in another bay window on the ground floor, eating a strong lunch; after that walking a dozen miles or so, or lying on his back in the sand reading a book . . . He's as brown as a berry.'

The 'rare good sands' of Viking Bay are still there, as is the weatherboarded harbourmaster's office decorated with painted figureheads, and the Tartar Frigate inn, which a century ago was famous for the strength of its tobacco and rum. If Dickens were to return, he would find surprisingly little changed in the 'old-fashioned watering place' he described for his readers. One of the elegant houses he knew, in Victoria Parade above the beach, is now the **Dickens House Museum**, with rooms furnished in true Dickensian style. In Dickens's time it was the home of Miss Mary Strong, on whom he based the character of Betsey Trotwood in *David Copperfield*. In Albion Street is **St Mary's Chapel**, built in 1601 on the site of the medieval shrine of Our Lady of Bradstow, from which Broadstairs takes its name. The shrine was so venerated that ships used to lower their topsails in deference as they passed.

The medieval church lies well inland. It gives its name to **St Peter's**, which is really a separate village from Broadstairs, with a little T-shaped centre of old houses and open country behind. The church is a splendid building, with a big grey battlemented tower. A local hero lies buried in the churchyard, Richard Joy, known as the Kentish Samson, who died in 1742. He showed off his feats of strength before William III; these included 'pulling against an Extraordinary Strong Horse' and 'the breaking of a Rope wich wil [sic] bear 3500 weight' (thirty-five hundredweight, or one and a half tons). St Peter's tower has the rare privilege of flying the White Ensign, dating from the Napoleonic Wars, when it was used as a naval signalling station.

Ramsgate, the third of the Thanet trinity of holiday resorts, does not thrust itself at you, like Margate, or take refuge in a Dickensian never-never-land, like Broadstairs. It has the nicest harbour in the two counties, with two good piers to walk along, an outer harbour with fishing boats pottering about, and an inner harbour with a marina for small craft and wharves where moderate-sized boats unload their cargoes. The best way to get to know Ramsgate is by looking at it from the eastern pier, past the early nineteenth-century classical Clock House and the obelisk put up in 1822 to mark a voyage by George IV to Hanover; on his return he raised Ramsgate's status by granting the title 'Royal Harbour'. From the pier you can see the unusual symmetry of the original resort town – to the left the tidy seaside Georgian of Nelson Crescent, to the right Wellington Crescent, elegantly colonnaded, both perched on the low cliffs that run down to the harbour and finish off the view in either direction.

The **Clock House** is now a maritime museum, full of navigational instruments, relics of wrecks from the Goodwin sands, lifeboat models and seafaring memorabilia of every description. Until Greenwich Mean Time was established in the 1840s, South Coast captains set their chronometers by 'Ramsgate Mean Time', taken from a north-south meridian line on the Clock House's upper floor.

The old parish church, **St Laurence**, lies well back from the harbour, at the top end of the High Street. Like the other medieval Thanet churches, it was built as a chapel-of-ease to Minster Abbey, probably before the Norman Conquest. It is a dark place, with two rows of Norman arcading round the centrally placed tower, and massive Norman pillars and arches inside. On some of the capitals are strange little devil's heads, which are said to represent the casting of the demon of paganism out of the English church.

The present **Parish Church** was built much lower down the High Street in 1827, nearer the holidaymakers like the young Princess Victoria, who stayed at Albion House (now used in part as council offices). It has a tall pinnacled tower, surmounted by an octagonal lantern. Far more interesting is the **Roman Catholic Church**, in St Augustine's Road. This is the personal testament in stone of Augustus Welby Pugin, the high priest of the Gothic Revival in architecture, whose best-known work is in the Houses of Parliament. A fervent Catholic, converted from Protestantism largely through studying medieval art, Pugin built the church at the end of the 1840s out of the money he earned as an architect. His idea was to build a typical parish church of the Middle Ages: what he actually did was to enshrine an idea in heavy masses of yellow stone, carved woodwork and stained glass. It is of flint banded with stone, with a square tower intended as the base for an enormous spire, which was never built as Pugin ran out of money.

In 1852 he died, aged only forty. He is buried in a chantry on the south side of the church – a delicate-featured effigy in a long robe, with his children kneeling in the medieval fashion round the base of the tomb. He lived at The Grange, over the churchyard wall, and from its battlemented tower used to watch for ships in distress at sea. Pugin was more than a mere visionary. Had his church spire been built, it would have been a landmark for shipping on a treacherous coast. After seeing an injured sailor carried ashore after a shipwreck, Pugin first of all boarded out such sailors at his own expense, and later on bought a house and equipped it as an infirmary – the start of today's Ramsgate hospital. The church and The Grange now form part of a Benedictine abbey and school.

Karl Marx, an idealist of a very different kind, stayed at Ramsgate; and Van Gogh actually lived there. In the 1870s he was a language master at No. 6, Royal Road, before he took up painting as a career.

Westwards along the coast, the low tide retreats for a mile or more across the mudflats and sandbanks of **Pegwell Bay**. At the mouth of the Stour and down towards the Sandwich Bay Estate, the Kent Trust for Nature Conservation runs a breezy seaside nature reserve on the last unspoilt stretch of sand dunes, saltmarsh and tidal mudflats left in Kent. Here sea-holly and wild asparagus flourish, little terns and ringed plovers breed, and summer migrant butterflies like the painted lady and clouded yellow flutter thankfully ashore after their cross-Channel flight.

It was at **Ebbsfleet**, once on the coast but now well inland, that Hengist and Horsa are said to have landed in AD 449. In 1949 an intrepid Danish crew commemorated the 1,500th anniversary of their landing by sailing a replica of a Viking longship across the Channel (in fact, they landed at Broadstairs' Viking Bay). Their ship, the *Hugin*, now makes a brave show in a field by the road, complete with fearsome dragon's head and rows of shields down either side. Hengist and Horsa were followed to Ebbsfleet 150 years later by St Augustine, who landed in 597 and was met by King Ethelbert in the open air, for fear of any magic the Christians might try to practise in an enclosed place. **St Augustine's Cross** (English Heritage), put up in a nearby field in 1884 to commemorate the saint's arrival, stands on a back road near the entrance to the golf club, opposite a lavender farm that scents the air, and a kiosk selling all manner of lavender products. Perhaps the lavender is one reason why Pegwell Bay is a focus for migrating butterflies.

The rush to the coast that has swollen Margate, Broadstairs and Ramsgate into a near-conurbation has passed by **Minster**, once the centre of Thanet. It is still no more than a large village, with a long and very ordinary main street running down to an enormous Norman church. Minster was one of the earliest centres of Christianity in Kent; the nunnery founded there by Domneva in AD 669 reached the height of its fame in the time of her daughter and successor as Abbess, St Mildred. Lambarde describes how Domneva got possession of the land for her nunnery. King Egbert (see Eastry, p. 87) had promised her as much ground 'as a tame deere (that shee nourished) would run over at a breath'. After the earth had opened up and swallowed the king's evil counsellor, Thunor, who advised him against this method of distributing land, 'the hinde was put forth, and it ran the space of fourtie and eight ploughlandes, before it ceased'. The total extent was about ten thousand acres.

By the beginning of the eleventh century the abbey had decayed and was handed over to St Augustine's, Canterbury; nevertheless, the church was rebuilt on the grandest scale in the twelfth and thirteenth centuries. Inside it is huge and bare, with a great Norman arch into the tower at the west end of the nave, wide transepts and a fine Early English chancel. In the choir stalls are misericords with carved heads of all shapes and sizes.

In the 1930s Benedictine nuns returned to the Minster, re-establishing a tradition broken for a thousand years. The **Minster Abbey** where they live is not in fact the original nunnery, which was sacked by the Danes at the end of the tenth century, but a twelfth-century grange of St Augustine's. A certain amount can be visited, including the Norman crypt. The ruined tower on the southern side looks far older, possibly Saxon. The immensely thick walls are pierced with rough, round-headed window openings, and it seems probable that the tower was built early in the eleventh century as a beacon to give warning of further Danish raids.

The coast road south from Pegwell Bay to Sandwich passes the three huge cooling towers of Richborough power station and a miscellaneous clutter of factories and chemical works. **Sandwich,** stranded inland beside the sluggish meanders of the Stour, is in many

79

ways the most fascinating of the ancient harbour towns. Unlike Rye, it has never really had a revival, and still looks back to the days of the Cinque Ports, rather than forward to whatever prosperity the growth of industry may bring.

The **Quay** is the natural place to begin an exploration of the town, with gardens along the town side of the Stour and timber yards on the opposite bank. The **Barbican** gate, built in 1539, still carries much of the traffic out of the town. Until 1978 a toll was charged for crossing the bridge over the river; according to a list displayed under the Barbican, in 1905 you paid 2s 3d (11p) for a 'Chariot, Landau, Berlin Chaise, Chair or Calash drawn by six or more horses or other beasts', but only 2½d (1p) for a drove of calves. The medieval **Fisher Gate,** built in 1384 at the time of the French raids, was the most important entrance to the town for travellers landing at the Quay. Behind it an alley leads up to the old **Customs House,** a medieval timber building with a later brick skin. Here the 'customer' lived and carried out his duties.

St Clement's Church, up Knightrider Street, is now the parish church of Sandwich and the only one of the town's three churches still in good condition. The oldest part is the massive Norman central tower built about 1100, with three rows of arcading round the exterior. The chancel has a curious medieval amplification system consisting of sounding holes cut in the stone below the choir stalls, matched by similar holes high up on the sanctuary walls. The fifteenth-century octagonal font is carved with various heraldic shields, including the arms of the Cinque Ports.

From St Clement's it is only a short step to the high embankment and ditch that still surrounds the old town; there was no town wall proper except on the harbour side. The spine of Sandwich is formed by New Street and the High Street, which bisect it into east and west halves. At the bottom of the High Street is **Strand Street**, which has the finest of Sandwich's timbered houses. The **Sandwich Weavers** has a long beamed front with overhangs; the name derives from the Huguenot refugees who fled from the Low Countries in the 1560s, bringing new prosperity at a time when the effects of the silting of the harbour were beginning to make themselves felt.

Farther down Strand Street, behind a high wall, is the **Old House,** a timbered building where Queen Elizabeth is said to have stayed when she visited Sandwich in 1573. Though the queen ate a banquet of 160 dishes and 'was very merrye', she did nothing at all about a petition to clear the harbour that was presented to her. Nearly opposite the Old House is **St Mary's**, a wreck of a church, damaged by an earthquake in 1578; in 1667 the tower collapsed and brought down much of the rest of the building. What is left, much patched and bedraggled, is a bare damp barn, with tombs huddled at one end and a cluster of pews in the middle.

The **Guildhall** and large market square behind are the hub of Sandwich. Though the outside of the Guildhall looks bogus, the building in fact dates from 1579. On the ground floor is the old courtroom, a sombre chamber of oak panelling, royal arms, and heraldic beasts made originally for Queen Elizabeth's reception in 1573. Above is the council chamber, hung with portraits of local notabilities; on the wall is the moot horn, which was blown before royal proclamations were read out, or as a general summons to the citizens. The Guildhall has a museum of local history, which exhibits among other things a Puritan ordinance of 1646 ordering a day of public humiliation to be inflicted on 'saboth breakers' and other evil-doers, who were held responsible for the unseasonable weather.

The nearby **Congregational Chapel**, one of the prettiest little buildings in Sandwich, was built in 1706. Its roof is supported by two masts from ships in which Protestant refugees reached England after the Revocation of the Edict of Nantes in 1685. (This edict granted French Protestants freedom of worship; its repeal by Louis XIV led to a renewed influx of Huguenots into England.)

The third of Sandwich' s medieval churches, **St Peter's**, is used as a tourist office during the summer. Like St Mary's, its tower fell in the seventeenth century; the ogee cupola on a rebuilt turret is one of the few tall landmarks in Sandwich. Curfew is still rung at 8.00 p.m. from St Peter's by thirty-one men of the town each with his own day of the month; though it is presumably no longer the signal for geese and hogs to be let loose in the streets to scavenge for refuse as it was in the Middle Ages.

If you go to **St Bartholomew's Hospit**al on the saint's day, 24 August, you can get a 'Bartlemas biscuit' stamped with an image of the saint and the date of the foundation in 1190. In fact, the hospital (at the far end of New Street, beyond the railway) is thought to have been founded a good deal earlier in 1217, as a thank-offering for victory over the French. It consists of a peaceful quadrangle of mainly Victorian almshouses around the thirteenth-century chapel.

On each house is the name of the hospitaller who lives there, together with the date when he or she moved in.

In 1998 Sandwich became the first town in the south-east to impose a 20 mph speed limit in its centre.

Sandwich is famous among golfers for its three golf links on the sand dunes towards the sea. The Sandown Road will also bring you (after paying a toll) to **Sandwich Bay**, with its wide beaches and estate of large holiday houses – a Millionaires' Row stuck down here in opulent isolation.

At the western edge of Sandwich a lane leads to **Richborough Castle** (English Heritage), one of the most magnificent Roman ruins in the country. In AD 43 Rutupiae, as the Romans called it, was the landing point for Claudius's invading legionaries. In those days a small and easily defensible island on the south side of the Wantsum channel, it made an ideal jumping-off point for the conquest of Britain. The massive walls, like those of Reculver, date from the last troubled years of Roman occupation, when Richborough served as one of the chain of Forts of the Saxon Shore. On one side the great square of masonry has fallen away; but on the other sides, and especially the north, the wall towers up to twenty-five feet, built of flint and stones set in the iron-hard Roman mortar, with bonding courses of red tiles and a facing of dressed stone.

Inside and outside the walls are the ditches of earlier fortifications, and at the centre is a cruciform foundation where an immense triumphal monument once stood. Built probably about AD 85 to commemorate the Claudian invasion, this was in the form of two arches intersecting at right-angles, faced with marble and topped by bronze statues – the final seal on the Roman conquest and a constant reminder of imperial might. There is an excellent small museum on the site.

Heading back towards Canterbury, **Ash**, just off the main road, has a tall Early English church well worth a look. The needle spire above the mighty battlemented tower is a landmark out to sea, and Trinity House used to contribute to its repair. Inside it has, says Newman, 'the best collection of medieval monumental effigies of any parish church in the county'. Among them is a pretty brass of about 1450 to Jane Kerriell, wearing a strange horned head-dress; and a sixteenth-century acrostic brass on which the name JOHN BROOKE reads downwards to form the first letter of each line of the inscription.

If you had lived at **Wingham** in the Middle Ages, you would have had canons to right of you and canons to left of you. So I was told by

Roman Walls of Richborough Castle, one of the Forts of the Saxon Shore
built at the end of the 3rd century.

the landlord of the Dog Inn, which is one of a row of timbered houses belonging to Wingham College, founded in 1282 by the Archbishop of Canterbury for a provost and six secular canons. The wide main street, lined with chestnuts and pleached limes, has a French look. Wingham's tall green church spire is a landmark for miles around; the church, rebuilt when the College was founded, fell into decay at the Reformation and was propped up by chestnut pillars in the sixteenth century. Wood instead of stone was used, says Newman, because a Canterbury brewer embezzled the money collected for the restoration.

At **Preston**, two miles north of Wingham, the remains of the palace of Juliana de Leybourne, known as the Infanta of Kent, lie under a pond opposite the village church, though no visible trace remains of the home of one of the richest Kent heiresses of the fourteenth century. There is Saxon work in the tower of the homely gabled little church; and inside is a real rarity, a small white cupboard painted with the words 'Dr Bray's Parochia Library for the use of the Vicars of Preston' – a reminder of the days when a poor parson could not afford to buy books. **Elmstone's** pretty little twelfth-century church has a good Norman font of grey Bethersden marble; a medieval priest's stall made from the timbers of a boat wrecked when the priest came by river to conduct a service, as a thank-offering for his safety; and a chamber organ from Hatfield House, said to have been played by Queen Victoria. **West Stourmouth** is a tree-shaded village on a cul-de-sac road, which fades away into a track across the windy watermeadows of the Stour. The small flint church is brick-buttressed and has a weatherboarded tower.

The orchard country between Wingham and Canterbury is packed with villages. **Littlebourne** stretches back from the main road to its church, which has an unusual dedication to St Vincent of Saragossa, Spain's first Christian martyr, tortured to death under Diocletian about AD 303. He was regarded as the patron saint of wine-dressers; possibly the monks of St Augustine's Abbey had vineyards in Littlebourne.

A mile along the Nailbourne stream is **Wickhambreaux** (final syllable pronounced -broo), or Wickham for short, one of East Kent's beauty spots. The fifteenth-century church has a homely wooden entrance porch; inside Victorian angels simper above the arcades, and the nave roof is painted like a starry sky. The village is on a toylike scale, with little houses opening directly onto the road.

Ickham, adjoining Wickham, is a quiet place, with white weatherboarded cottages and a fine Early English church set back behind a narrow green. **Stodmarsh,** reached down zigzag lanes from Wickhambreaux, is a little hamlet whose main interest is in its name, which derives from the marshy ground where the abbots of Canterbury kept their brood mares (*stode* in Saxon, our 'stud'). It stands on the tongue of higher ground that separates the Great from the Little Stour.

6

From Canterbury to the Coast

BETWEEN CANTERBURY AND the populous coastal strip of Deal, Dover and Folkestone is a forgotten land of downs and the remains of great forests. The Romans built their Stone Street and Watling Street undeviatingly across it, and traffic has passed through it without stopping ever since. Until the 1980s much of the region was dominated by the pithead winding gear of the East Kent coalfields, but with the demise of mining this has now vanished.

Patrixbourne, a couple of miles south-east of Canterbury, is a gem of a place, with half-timbered houses clustered along the Nailbourne Valley, and watersplashes to cool you down on hot afternoons. The church, built about 1170, has some first-rate Norman carving; the only place to excel it is Barfreston (see below). Below the centrally-placed tower the main doorway is smothered in a riot of carving – grotesque heads, animals, foliage or pattern-making, surrounding a central tympanum carved with the figure of Christ among angels. Almost as remarkable as the stonework is some of the stained glass, Swiss like the glass at Temple Ewell outside Dover, and dating from the mid sixteenth to the end of the seventeenth century. The scene of Samson slaying the lion is copied from a Dürer woodcut and shows Nuremberg in the background.

A narrow lane and yet another watersplash bring you to Bekesbourne, also with a Norman church. Half a mile away, past the railway, is Howletts Wild Animal Park. A dignified late eighteenth-century house, Howletts is surrounded by a park which dates back to the fifteenth century. It has a large tiger collection and several flourishing gorilla families.

Adisham, two miles east of Bekesbourne, has a long narrow street ending at a triangular open green, with the rugged Early English church and redbrick Adisham Court on a knoll to one side. Outside the west door of the church is a gigantic bronze statue of Thomas Becket, too large to fit in the church, an apocalyptic figure, bearded and grasping a crozier. Even more remote is **Goodnestone**, two miles farther on, a pretty little village of redbrick houses down a cul-de-sac. The name derives from the Saxon Earl Godwin, who also gave his name to the Goodwin Sands. The Early English church was largely rebuilt about 1840. One of the vicars was the Puritan Richard Culmer, notorious for his efforts to smash the stained glass windows of Canterbury Cathedral.

The Rev. William Gostling, Canterbury's eighteenth-century historian, tells the story of how Culmer, standing at the top of a long ladder and 'rattling down proud Becket's glassy bones' with a pike, was asked by a townsman what he was doing. 'The work of the Lord,' replied Culmer. To which the townsman answered 'Then if it please the Lord I will help you,' picked up a stone and threw it at Culmer, 'with so good a will', says Gostling, 'that if the saint had not ducked, he might have laid his own bones among the rubbish he was making; and the place perhaps had been no less distinguished by the fanatics for the martyrdom of St Richard Culmer, than by the Papists for that of St Tho. Becket, though his relics might not have turned to so good an account'.

At the straggling village of **Staple**, two miles to the north-east, the rugged church has a superb octagonal font. On the sides are the symbols of the Evangelists, and on the base bearded wild men armed with clubs, and lions carved with Edward Lear-like fantasy. The name of **Woodnesborough**, three miles east of Staple and almost back in Sandwich, is said to derive, like Wednesday, from the god Woden, worshipped on the hilltop on which the village is built. The church, perched up on the highest point, is basically Norman though much restored, and has a fanciful eighteenth-century wooden balustrade and cupola on top of the tower. Inside there are superb canopied sedilia, with delicately carved tracery.

Eastry (East Rye, as opposed to the better known West, or Sussex, Rye) is a large prosperous-looking village a mile due south of Woodnesborough. The Early English church, down a cul-de-sac of prettily terraced houses, has a monumental west tower, with strange holes gouged in the buttresses. Inside there is a varied collection of monuments. In the chancel is a fine brass to the Elizabethan Thomas Nevynson, who among his military offices was 'scoutmaster of ye Est partes of Kent'. In contrast to the usual individual dedications, a window in the south aisle is a communal one, 'given by the men of this parish in tribute to wives and mothers'.

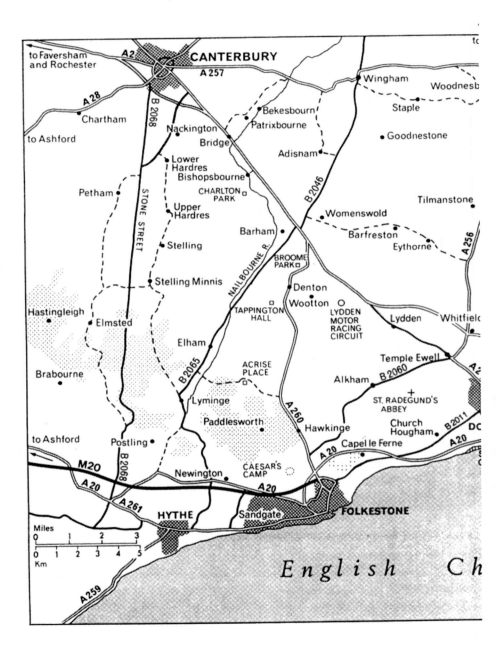

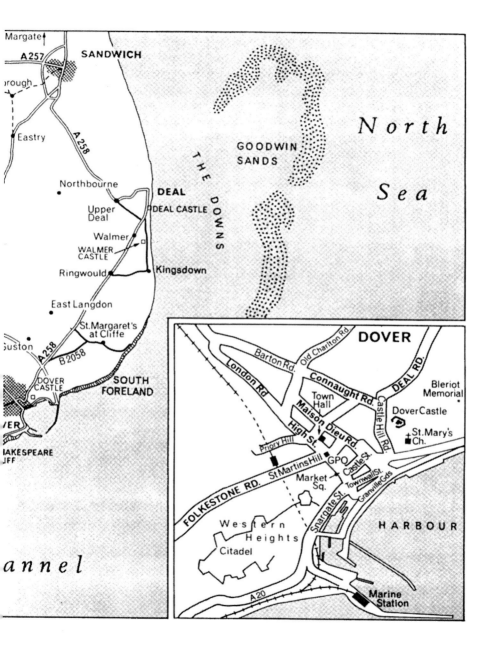

The handsome Georgian Eastry Court, over the churchyard wall, is said to be built on the site of a palace of the Kings of Kent. It was here that the evil nobleman Thunor, wishing to ingratiate himself with King Egbert, murdered the king's two young cousins who might have overthrown him and imprudently buried the bodies under the king's throne. The crime was revealed by a miraculous beam of light which shone down on to the throne, 'replenishing eche corner', says Lambarde, 'with such terrible and fearfull light, that the servaunts shriked at the sight thereof, and by their noise awaked the king'. In expiation of this murder, to which he felt he had half consented, Egbert granted Domneva the land to build Minster Abbey, in Thanet. Becket hid at Eastry before his flight to France in 1164.

Northbourne, down byroads south-east of Eastry and hardly a mile from Deal, has a squat Norman church, which crouches above the village and has a fortress-like look about it. The early priests seem to have lived in the tower in a state of siege, conducting the services through the little window above the nave arch when the Saxons became unduly hostile. In the south transept is a vast ornate tomb to Sir Edwin Sandys and his wife. Sandys, who died in 1629, was Treasurer of the Virginia Company, and drew up the constitution of the new colony, used as a model by later colonies. It laid down among other things that the people should be governed and taxed by their own consent, and should have an assembly modelled on the House of Commons. Beside the tomb is a tablet erected by Americans in 1957, the 350th anniversary of the foundation of Virginia.

The neighbouring hamlet of **Betteshanger** was formerly a centre of coalmining, as were **Tilmanstone**, a tucked-away village of little lanes across the A256, and **Eythorne**. Kent's coal industry had a short and unglamorous history, though the Kentish miners had the reputation of being among the most militant members of their profession. Coal was discovered under Kent in 1891, when test borings for the Channel Tunnel were made. Mining operations started at Tilmanstone shortly before World War I, while Chislet and Betteshanger followed somewhat later. In 1930 an aerial ropeway was built to carry coal the seven miles from Tilmanstone to Dover Harbour, but this fell into disuse.

Though **Barfreston** is only a mile west of Eythorne, it is a world away from anything to do with coalmining. The village is pretty enough in its own right, and provides a perfect setting for the church

The richly carved Norman south doorway of Barfreston Church.

on its hillock above the road. For sheer richness and exuberance of stone-carving there is nothing in the two counties to touch this little Norman church, so small in scale and so richly decorated that it is more like a reliquary than a building. It reached its present form about 1180, and consists of nave and chancel, without even the vestige of tower or turret. You come at once to the masterpiece of the whole church, the south doorway, which gives in a small space a microcosm of the medieval world. On the tympanum above the door is Christ in Glory, surrounded by legendary and symbolic beasts. The outermost semicircle of carving, immediately inside the dripstone, shows scenes from life on the manor house estate – perhaps that of Adam de Port, who held the Barfreston estates at the end of the twelfth century. Whether by design or accident, the topmost figure is the villein on whom the whole system ultimately depended; among the other figures are the minstrel, the cellarer and the estate steward.

The inner semicircle of figures draws on the bestiaries from which the Middle Ages took their garbled ideas of natural history, making comparisons between man and the animals. A hare drinks a toast to a partridge, a monkey rides on a goat, a bear plays the harp. The blocked-up north door is also carved, but far less elaborately. At the east end is a large wheel-shaped window set high in the gable end and decorated with carvings of human and animal heads. The interior cannot help being an anticlimax, though the chancel arch and other carvings would be outstanding anywhere else.

Aylesham, a couple of miles away to the north-west, is back in the twentieth century with a vengeance. It was built in the 1920s for the miners of Snowdon Colliery near by, and consists of acres of orange-roofed semis round a central green. **Womenswold**, a mile away towards the Dover Road, is a complete contrast – a tight little Kentish village, with a church that has a nice Early English chancel and some good eighteenth-century monuments. Its odd name has nothing to do with the sex of its inhabitants, past or present – it derives from Wimlingweald and means 'the wood of the Wimlingas', presumably a local Saxon tribe.

All the villages so far described lie north of the A2. South of the road the first place of any consequence outside Canterbury is **Bishopsbourne**, little more than a cluster of houses by a small green, leading to the long church with its strongly buttressed Perpendicular tower. Two very different writers lived here, the Polish-born novelist Joseph Conrad, and the English theologian Richard Hooker (1554–1600), the champion of the Church of England against both

Catholicism and Puritanism. He spent the last six years of his life as rector here, completing his magnum opus *Of The Laws of Ecclesiastical Polity*. According to Izaak Walton, after arriving at Bishopsbourne in 1594, 'Mr. Hooker had not been twelve months, but his books, and the innocency and sanctity of his life, became so remarkable, that many turned out of the road, and others, scholars especially, went purposely to see the man whose life and learning were so much admired.' There is a bust of Hooker wearing a mortarboard on the south wall, and a statuette of him beside the pulpit. The west window of the church has glass by Burne-Jones (Faith, Hope and Charity), and in the south chapel are panels of sixteenth- and seventeenth-century Flemish glass, including a meticulously detailed Massacre of the Innocents.

At the south end of the village is **Charlton Park**, a long, low, ochre-painted Georgian house, which hides a Tudor manor house behind. The Georgian additions were made about 1790 by John Foote, a close friend of the Prince Regent; the huge ballroom upstairs was built specially for George, who used to relax there with amateur dramatics, after the rigours of reviewing his troops on the windswept **Barham Downs** near by.

Kingston, off the B2065 south of Charlton, is a little village below the downs. Its small church may be Saxon in part. On the south wall is a fine set of funeral armour – helmet, gauntlets and heraldic tabard; and below the tower is a thirteenth-century font, rescued in 1775 by the Rev. Bryan Faussett, from a farm where it was being used for holding pig-food. Faussett was in the true tradition of antiquarian vicars. In 1771 he discovered a magnificent Anglo-Saxon gold brooch up on Barham Downs; it is now in the Liverpool museum.

The redbrick village centre of **Barham** clusters tightly below the church, with its tall green copper spire, the gift, like the similar spire at Wingham, of a nineteenth-century member of the Oxenden family. The late thirteenth-century church is a fine open building, cruciform, and built without any arches at the crossing; a tall arch leads into the Perpendicular west tower. The most notable memorial is not a tomb or a brass, but a flag in the south transept – the White Ensign from HMS *Raglan*, sunk by German cruisers in the Aegean in 1918. The flag was given to the church by Lord Broome, who commanded the ship; luckier than his uncle, Lord Kitchener, he was saved from drowning. In the north transept is a copy of the *Barham Almanack* for 1864 (price twopence, but 'to Barham Labourers Only, One

Penny'), a broadsheet giving such local details as the contributions to the Clothing Club, and the times of the four vans to Canterbury per week. Over the churchyard wall is the large eighteenth-century brick-built Barham Court; an earlier building on the site was the home of Fitzurse, one of the murderers of Becket.

South of Barham the A260 branches off the A2 due south towards Folkestone. If you continue on towards Dover, you pass the **Lydden Motor Racing Circuit** – a little hairpin racetrack, tucked away below the ridge, which must have the prettiest setting of any circuit in the country. **Lydden** village, two miles towards Dover, has a primitive Norman church standing by itself down a side road.

Off the A260, just south of the junction with the A2, is **Broome Park**, now a timeshare development. It is notable for two reasons: it is an outstanding example of a country house built in the 1630s, just before the Civil War made such things impossible for decades to come; and it was owned and adapted by Lord Kitchener, though he never actually lived there. With its E-shaped front and pilasters of cut brick, it has an Elizabethan look about it. Kitchener has left his mark in his motto THOROUGH, carved in giant capitals above the fireplaces.

South and west of the A2 the hills are steeper, the villages more tucked away, and the roads even narrower, often just single track with passing-places, as in the Scottish Highlands – though unlike the Highlands, you cannot see what is coming at you round the next bend. However, there are a couple of main roads before you get to Stone Street.

The first village on the Folkestone road (A260) is **Denton**, a hamlet of tilehung houses, with a little Early English church reached down a grassy track. Outside the village is **Tappington Hall**, the brick and timber Tudor farmhouse which belonged to R. H. Barham's father, and which Barham made the setting for several of his *Ingoldsby Legends*. Their macabre whimsicality and tortuous rhyming schemes tend to put off modern readers; yet in the legends Barham made East Kent peculiarly his own. The jest is compounded inside the house, where old family portraits with Ingoldsby labels hang over the stairs, and a notch on the handrail of the ancient staircase is said to have been hacked when a Roundhead and a Cavalier Ingoldsby met and drew their swords on each other.

Born in 1788, Richard Harris Barham became rector of Snargate on Romney Marsh in 1817; four years later he moved to London as a minor canon of St Paul's, and for the rest of his life combined humorous writing with his unexacting clerical duties. The legends, in which Barham drew on his memories of Tappington and of his time on the Marsh, were mostly written between 1837 and 1844 – those whirling fantasies of ghosts and witches' sabbaths, of Smuggler Bill and Exciseman Gill, of Sir Thomas Ingoldsby who drowned in his own eel-pond and was thrown back into it by his widow because he made such excellent bait, of poor Little Jack, killed by the buccaneer's curse.

Wootton, hidden among trees in the hills behind Denton, has the most secluded of little churches. Few rectors can have had their sermons more charmingly recorded than Edward Timewell Brydges, who died in 1807, and whose enthusiastic though ungrammatical monument reminds posterity that 'he possessed a philanthropy, which glowed with delight at all the refined pleasures of society, a mild eloquence, combined with a melodious voice, gave a charm to his oratory, which could rarely be excelled'.

Four miles to the south is **Hawkinge**, a large village now virtually a suburb of Folkestone, which won glory during the Second World War because of its airfield. From the level plateau high above Folkestone the coast of France is clearly visible on a fine day, and during the crucial summer months of 1940 the young British pilots took off in their Spitfires and Hurricanes to hunt down the bombers of the Luftwaffe. After the war Hawkinge airfield fell derelict; but it has come to life again with the setting-up of the **Kent Battle of Britain Museum**, which has the largest collection of aircraft remains, both British and German, surviving from that epic conflict. The road along the north side of the airfield brings you to **Paddlesworth**, where the church has the unusual dedication to St Oswald of Northumbria, while the pub's name (the Cat and Custard Pot) is a similar rarity.

Acrise is hidden away down lanes a couple of miles north of Paddlesworth. The name has a good many pronunciations, but the one most favoured is 'Ay-cris'. As the name derives from the Anglo-Saxon 'Ac-hris', meaning oak copse, it can only be an approximation. There is no proper village – just a scattering of houses centred on Acrise Place and the church over the garden wall; the church can be visited, but the house is not open to the public. **Acrise Place** is a comfortable, organic kind of a house, which grew over the years from the sixteenth to the eighteenth centuries. It consists of two houses, Tudor and Carolean blocks joined longitudinally, with Georgian portico and decorative trimmings. It

95

was bought by the Papillon family in 1666, and after changing hands several times was bought for a second time and renovated by a branch of the same family after the Second World War. The original Papillon, David, was sent over to England as a boy in 1588 by his French Protestant father; he grew up in this country and had a prosperous career as a civil engineer, being responsible among other things for the fortification of Northampton in 1645. His son, Thomas, was MP for Dover and bought Acrise, doubling the size of the Tudor building by his additions.

The church is a trim little building, surrounded by trees, with a shingled turret and spire perched on top. It is basically Norman, enlarged and altered in the thirteenth century. At the west end is a William III musicians' gallery, and at the east end of the nave the squire's pew, containing some midget Sunday School chairs. Most of the monuments are to members of the Papillon family.

West of Acrise the plateau drops steeply away to the Nailbourne valley – one of the prettiest in the whole of Kent, with **Elham**, as its fitting centrepiece. The name is pronounced 'Eelham', and this has given rise to the suggestion that eels were once caught in the Nailbourne, though this is hardly likely in such an unimpressive little trickle. Another suggestion is that it was originally Yuleham, the home of the yuletide feast. Prosaic modern minds derive it from a Saxon called Ula, since the village appeared as Ulaham in an Anglo-Saxon charter of AD 855.

The **Nailbourne** itself is a so-called intermittent stream; though I have seen it flowing among the thick water plants on the hottest of July days. It has its own legend, going back to the beginnings of Christianity in this country. Soon after St Augustine arrived in Kent at the end of the sixth century there was a drought in the valley. The locals blamed it on the Christians, so to appease them the saint knelt down in prayer, and where he had knelt a stream burst forth and watered the valley. This was too much for Woden, Thor and the rest of the old gods of paganism. They brewed up a tremendous storm, uprooting trees to block the stream and rending open the ground to swallow up its waters. But Valhalla could not be allowed to triumph completely, and so the Nailbourne flows once every seven years, bringing freshness to the parched fields.

Elham has two centres: the wide main street, and the quiet market square, a backwater of timber and tilehanging. The church behind the square is a most impressive place, mainly thirteenth-century, with a massive tower topped by a lead spire. Inside it is sumptuously

96

decorated, surprisingly in Edwardian rather than Victorian times. The sanctuary is panelled in dark oak, with limewood embellishment by the craftsmen who restored Grinling Gibbons's carvings in St Paul's Cathedral. Below the big clerestory windows are seventeenth-century textboards, and elsewhere in the church are rarities like the embossed leather hanging above the side altar, and the English fifteenth-century alabaster panels – the outer pair showing Becket's confrontation with the king and murder, the inner one St Catherine – behind the altar in the south aisle. The Victorian glass in the chancel contains some unexpected faces. In one window David (with the face of Madame Patti, the singer) plays the harp to Saul (Thomas Carlyle); behind the throne stand Gladstone and Disraeli. The vicar himself appears in the next window with his harp, as David grown old.

The most notable building in the main street is the heavily timbered **Abbot's Fireside** restaurant. It was built about 1480 as an inn, and has been dispensing food and drink ever since. Below the eaves the beam ends are carved into grotesque human figures, and inside there is a massive lintel over the fireplace, carved with fearsome dragon-like creatures. Wellington used the inn as his East Kent headquarters in the Napoleonic wars. The Abbot's Fireside is very reminiscent of the Star at Alfriston in Sussex (see p. 279); indeed, Elham and Alfriston are similar in their general atmosphere.

Lyminge (pronounced Limmindge), two miles south along the valley, is a large village; the oldest part, off the main road, faces a central grassy meadow. The church lies at one corner; it is ancient enough, but not nearly as ancient as what it replaces. In AD 633 Queen Ethelburga founded an abbey here. A plaque on the south side of the church marks her burial place, outside the walls of her own abbey church, which can be traced from its apsidal east end by the porch to its excavated west end south-west of the tower. This first church was destroyed by the Danes about 840. The present building has a good deal of later Saxon work, probably tenth-century, in the nave and chancel. The flying buttress at the eastern end was added in the late Middle Ages, and the low sturdy tower was not built until the first decades of the sixteenth century. Most recent of all is the vestry on the north side, ultra-late Perpendicular of the 1960s.

The village of **Postling**, near the southern edge of the downs, has no pub, shop or 30 mph speed limit. But it is set in a wide sweep of magnificent downland, on one of the minor Pilgrims' Ways. Joseph Conrad chose the seclusion of Postling to write some of his greatest novels; between 1899 and 1920 he rented Pent Farm, outside the village, and wrote *Lord Jim*, *Typhoon* and *Nostromo* there. Among his visitors were H. G. Wells, who ate a revolting lunch consisting of dry bread and quinine, and Bernard Shaw, who more predictably stuck to cocoa and a biscuit. Conrad moved to Bishopsbourne (see above) in 1920. If he had followed Kipling in writing downland verse, the gentle green hills round Postling might have become as famous as the Sussex Downs. A fine row of tile-roofed barns run beside the churchyard; the shingle-spired Norman church is dedicated to St Mary and St Radegund, as at one time it belonged to St Radegund's Abbey (see p. 115). There are traces of medieval painting in the nave, and on either side of the chancel are the sawn-off ends of the rood-beam, still painted. On the north wall of the chancel is a small square stone inscribed with the date of dedication, 'the day of St. Eusebius the Confessor' (14 August), but no year to pinpoint the building.

Brabourne, lost in the downs on the other side of Stone Street (B2068), is a compact little village, with an unexpectedly awe-inspiring church, so tall that side-on it looks almost square. The enormously wide, low tower completes the impression. The Norman chancel arch has intricately carved capitals, and the whole north wall of the chancel is Norman work. In this wall is a fine Perpendicular tomb of 'Easter sepulchre' type to Sir John Scott, a fifteenth-century Lord Warden of the Cinque Ports, who was also Comptroller of the Household to Edward IV; the helmet above the tomb was probably that of Sir Thomas Scott, commander of the forces in Kent in Elizabethan times. On the chancel floor are good brasses to the Scott family, among them Sir William Scott, with his feet resting on a greyhound. He died in 1433, and built the Scott chapel on the south side of the church.

By the door opening into the chapel is a small throne-like altar, with a recess at the back for a heart encased in silver or ivory – almost certainly the 'heart-shrine' of John de Baliol, founder of Balliol College, Oxford, who died in 1269. Baliol's son, John Baliol le Scot, King of Scotland, may well have brought the heart south with him after his defeat by Edward I, and entrusted it to his brother, Alexander Baliol, who lived at Chilham (see p. 153). The eastern window on the north side of the chancel still has its original twelfth-century stained glass – a simple piece of pattern-making. Under the tower a rough-hewn medieval ladder leads to the belfry.

Hastingleigh and Elmsted are identical in remoteness, and in having churches that almost form a part of prosperous farms. At

98

Hastingleigh there is an Early English chancel full of lancet windows – there are thirteen of them – and a rustic fifteenth-century rood screen. On the south aisle wall is a faded medieval painting of the Annunciation. From Hastingleigh it is only a short run down to Wye, at the foot of the downs. **Elmsted** church has an odd little shingled belfry on top of the stone tower; inside, the building ranges from Norman (the thick-lipped heads carved below the chancel arch) to Tudor (the almost flat-topped arcading). It is full of monuments to the Honywood family. Best of all is the bust of Sir John Honywood, who died in 1781 – a humorous old man, who looks as though he would have justified the words of the inscription: 'Others may have moved in an higher sphere, But no man ever contributed more To the advantage comfort and happiness of the circle round him.'

    Stelling Minnis, north-east across Stone Street, is a wide-sprawling place, one of several Minnises in the area. Minnis, according to a definition quoted by Walter Jerrold, means 'a wide tract of ground, partly copse and partly moor; a high common; a waste piece of rising ground'. Stelling church is a good mile to the north. Outside it looks like any other unpretentious medieval church in a grassy churchyard; but once inside you are in the eighteenth century, and half expect to see some periwigged Hogarthian cleric thundering from the three-decker pulpit, while the congregation in their Sunday smocks snore behind the tall box pews. Gallery, pews and pulpit are painted white and grey-green – an elegant reminder of what was lost visually when the Victorians seated everyone in austere low-backed pitchpine.

    A little to the north is **Upper Hardres** (pronounced Hards), very much the small farming village; a large barn is even more prominent than the church. This is a fascinatingly bitty building, originally Norman and full of oddments – medieval tiles on the floor, medallions of thirteenth-century glass in the west window, a fine collection of funeral hatchments on the walls. A superb bracket brass shows John Strete, a rector who died in 1405, kneeling in prayer below Sts Peter and Paul balanced on their bracket. **Lower Hardres** is a straggling village with an ugly nineteenth-century church and a good eighteenth-century pub, the Three Horseshoes.

    On the other side of Stone Street is **Petham**, in a broad open valley. The Early English church is a graceful place, with chancel walls that lean outwards at such an angle it is a wonder they remain standing. Above the cool whitewashed interior the beams are painted with naive floral decoration.

At **Nackington** you are almost back in Canterbury again, though you would never guess it in this cul-de-sac hamlet, consisting of a few houses and an odd little church buried among farm buildings. The top half of the tower is nineteenth-century brick, with a lead spirelet poking above the battlements; the lower half is thirteenth-century, as is the chancel, and the nave is Norman. The chancel windows contain some early medieval glass, probably made about 1180; one of them includes a portrait of Becket, done soon after his death and possibly an authentic likeness.

7

The White Cliffs

A S YOU WALK through the quiet back streets of **Deal**, it is hard to believe that this was once the main harbour town of southeast England. Yet in the days when the Downs – the stretch of calm and shallow water between the shore and the Goodwin Sands – was a major anchorage, filled with men-of-war and merchant shipping, Deal was a seething centre of Rowlandson-like marine activity. Sailors, stretching their legs ashore after long and scurvy-ridden voyages at sea, lurched from alehouse to alehouse; pursers stocked up with fresh flour from the mills whose sails whirled near the beach; the press gang roamed the streets, hated and often impeded by Deal's inhabitants; customs and excise men fought the smugglers (and each other); while visiting admirals, and the families of Deal men who had become rich supplying the fleet, picked their way on Sundays to the genteel and reassuring classicism of St George's church in the High Street. But with the coming of steam the usefulness of the Downs dwindled; and Deal itself, with no harbour arm for the steamships to anchor against, slipped into a state of picturesque somnolence.

From the end of the functional concrete pier you can see an up-and-down eighteenth-century roofline that was hardly touched by the Victorian mania for building urban terraces by the sea. Along the steep shingle beach rows of wooden boats – direct descendants of the Deal 'hovellers', which were often built with hollow ribs for smuggling contraband – are drawn up, waiting hopefully for angling parties.

A nearby landmark is the **Time Ball Tower**, used formerly for giving the correct time to shipping in the Downs. The tower was built at the end of the eighteenth century, as the first in a chain of semaphore stations by which messages could be relayed from the Downs to London in two minutes. In 1855 the time ball was added –

A map for this chapter will be found on pp. 88–89

a replica of the one at the Greenwich Royal Observatory and connected electrically to it. At 12.55 each day the black-painted copper ball was raised half way up the shaft, at 12.58 it reached the top, and at 1p.m. it was dropped, and still is, though for the benefit of tourists rather than mariners. The tower rooms have been turned into a 'museum of time and telegraphy', from the days of cliff-top signal fires to the coming of the orbiting satellite.

The story of Deal (or, more correctly, Deal and Walmer, which runs directly into it) begins in 55 BC, when Julius Caesar beached his galleys there after being beaten back from Dover. He would not have landed on the present shingle, which has built up in the past two thousand years, but on a vanished beach somewhere inland. The Belgic tribesmen – not savages, as popularly believed, but the most civilized inhabitants of pre-Roman Britain – were waiting for the Romans with cavalry and chariots, and Caesar later wrote that his men were terrified at disembarking in the face of such opposition. The situation was saved by the standard-bearer of the Tenth Legion. Leaping into the water brandishing the gilded eagle standard, he shamed the rest of the legionaries into following him and engaging, indecisively, with the British.

Deal's name is said to come from the Saxon *dylle*, meaning a low-lying or marshy place. Medieval Deal grew up well inland from the present town centre, at **Upper Deal**, presumably with limited port facilities down on the shore. As the Middle Ages progressed Deal grew in importance to become a 'limb' or associate of the Cinque Port of Sandwich.

The main road from Sandwich passes Upper Deal, a fine collection of Georgian buildings round **St Leonard's Church**. This extraordinary parish church has a redbrick tower, dated 1684, topped by a trim white cupola, and a vastly inflated north aisle, looking from the outside like part of a yellow brick house lit by portholes in the north wall. In fact, the church is basically Norman; the Norman arcades survive, though a pillar on each side was removed to form a pair of wide-spanning arches. The north aisle was enlarged in 1819, and has galleries round three sides; an earlier gallery at the west end announces that it was ' Built by ye Pilots of Deal', and displays a painting of one of the thirteen men-of-war that were wrecked on the Goodwins in 1703, with the loss of 1,200 lives. A model of the ship is on a window-sill nearby.

Deal Castle (English Heritage) is the finest surviving example of the fortresses built by Henry VIII in 1539, at a time when fears of

The Time Ball Tower, Deal, which gave the time to shipping anchored offshore.
The time ball, which dropped at 1.00 p.m., was connected electrically to a
similar one at Greenwich

invasion were as real as they were forty years later, before the Armada. Furious that Henry had defied him over the divorce from Catherine of Aragon, the Pope preached a crusade against him, and urged the French king and the Holy Roman Emperor to invade England. The Downs were among the vulnerable places strengthened, with three fortresses built a mile from one another – Sandown, Deal and Walmer. Sandown, at the northern end of Deal's seafront, is now hardly more than a pile of stones with the remains of vaulting facing the sea, and Walmer has been domesticated; but Deal Castle is still a formidable-looking and efficient place, despite its small scale.

Built for the age of gunpowder, in place of the four-square towers and vertical walls of the Middle Ages these castles have curved bastions for cannonballs to bounce off, and superimposed platforms to give high firepower from a small target. Yet the Middle Ages survive at Deal Castle, in the gateway, with its Tudor brick vaulting pierced with murder-holes, portcullis groove, and massive studded door. In plan it is like a six-petalled Tudor rose, built on three levels around a central staircase shaft. The outer walls are enormously thick – Henry had plenty of stone from dismantled monastic houses at his disposal – but the rooms for the Captain and his men are surprisingly domestic, with exposed beams and wattle and daub between. The upper floors of the keep were reached by an ingenious double staircase; the mortise holes for the second stair can be seen round the central stairpost.

The castle was much fought over in the Civil War, but was not seriously damaged until it had a direct hit from a bomb in the Second World War. Now it is restored as near as possible to the condition it would have been in when Pepys saw it in 1660, as he sailed into the Downs with the fleet, writing in his diary that 'great was the shout of guns from the castle and ships and our answers – nor could we see another on board from the smoke among us'. In the keep is an excellent exhibition showing the evolution of coastal defence from the Romans to the present day.

Behind the castle, in The Strand, is the handsome classical **Barracks** built for the Royal Marines in 1795, until 1996 the home of the RM School of Music. At the time of writing (1999) it is empty and its future is in doubt. The cupola on the barracks is echoed half a mile along the High Street, in **St George's Church**, built as a chapel-of-ease in the early years of the eighteenth century. Work was held up after Admiral Sir Cloudesley Shovell, the man behind the scheme, was drowned off the Scilly Isles in 1707; and the redbrick church was finally completed in 1716. The church has galleries round three sides, and an upper gallery at the back for the boatmen, who could clump up the stairs in their seaboots without disturbing the rest of the congregation.

Nearby, in St George's Road, Deal's **Maritime and Local History Museum** is a boat-fancier's delight. On display are two of the rugged 'beach boats' which in former times ferried passengers between ships anchored in the Downs and the shore, and an example of the four-oared Deal galleys, popular with smugglers as they were faster than the cutters used by the customs service.

On the corner is the brick **Town Hall**, perched up on columns and built for some reason at an angle to the street. In nearby South Street, **Carter House** gets its name from Mrs Elizabeth Carter, a famous eighteenth-century Deal character. She was a great bluestocking, and a friend of Dr Johnson, who found her, says Barbara Collins in *Discovering Deal*, 'as good at making puddings and pies, as translating from Greek, writing poetry, and being proficient in nine foreign languages'. She bought her house with the money she made by translating the works of the Greek philosopher Epictetus. In the eighteenth century the obscurest byways of learning could be profitable. Carter House is at one end of **Middle Street**. This, rather than the High Street, is the true heart of Deal, and though a large section was damaged during the war and is now a car park, Middle Street and the lanes off it are the places to potter about looking for the Dutch gables or humbler weatherboarding of the old town.

The Downs are now empty, except for small cargo boats and pleasure craft, but there is a constant reminder of the menace of the **Goodwin Sands** in the jutting masts of the *North Eastern Victory*, visible from Deal at all states of the tide. She was an American cargo vessel wrecked in 1946 and thus a newcomer to the endless procession of victims that have run aground on the notorious 'swallower of ships'. At low tide you can take a boat from Deal and walk about on the Goodwins, and cricket is even played there from time to time; but as the tide comes in the firm sand softens and becomes a quicksand, with such a power of suction that ships can disappear completely in a few days.

Legends of all sorts have grounded on the Goodwins – tales of the lost lands of the Saxon Earl Godwin, vanished when the sea defences were neglected for more pressing work on Tenterden church tower, or the island of Lomea, buried like Atlantis under the

105

waves after a storm. Sadly, sample borings have shown nothing more romantic than eighty feet of sand resting on chalk. The Goodwins bred a special resourcefulness in the fishermen and smugglers who worked off the Deal coast. In their shallow-draught hovellers they could take refuge over the sands where the deeper revenue cutters could not follow them.

As at Deal, the medieval village of **Walmer** was built well away from the coast; the twelfth-century church and quiet streets round it are north of the Dover Road. Built about 1120 as the chapel to the original Walmer Castle, of which one ruined wall looms at the back of the churchyard, it has a Norman chancel arch with traces of mural painting above. The walls are covered with tablets to naval officers.

While it is still possible to imagine shots being fired in anger from Deal Castle, **Walmer Castle** (English Heritage) has had its fangs well and truly drawn. Since the early eighteenth century it has been the official residence of the Lords Warden of the Cinque Ports; and with its neat Georgian rooms tacked on to Henry's fortifications, picture windows cut in the massive walls, and elegantly landscaped garden it is more of a country house than a bastion of coastal defence.

Of all the Lords Warden who have lived there, Wellington left the greatest mark on Walmer. The room where he died in 1852 has been left virtually unaltered, furnished in great austerity with the camp bed on which he always slept, the wingback chair where he collapsed, and bits and pieces like a counterpoised shaving mirror. In the next room are a pair of the original Wellington boots, the mask taken three days after his death showing a face incredibly gaunt and sunken, and the coat he wore as Lord Warden.

William Pitt the Younger, Lord Warden as well as Prime Minister, spent a good deal of time at Walmer in the 1790s, during the early tense days of confrontation with France. The layout of the gardens was begun in Pitt's time by his niece, Lady Hester Stanhope; earlier engravings of the castle show a very bleak treeless outlook. The most famous twentieth-century Lord Warden, Sir Winston Churchill, never lived there. The present (1999) holder of the office is HM the Queen Mother, who must surely appreciate this enchanting near-folly, facing the wide shingle beach and blue line of the sea. In 1997 English Heritage created a walled garden in her honour, to celebrate her ninety-fifth birthday which had taken place two years earlier. Her great age is echoed in the formal pool which forms the garden's centrepiece: planted with waterlilies and aquatic plants it is exactly 95 feet long.

A couple of miles south of Deal, beyond the faceless resort of **Kingsdown**, the great chalk cliffs begin, sweeping round to Dover and beyond. Kingsdown has a few pretty cottages inland, on the steep hill up from the shore; but the first village of any consequence between Deal and Dover is **Ringwould**, a tight-knit cluster of houses off the main road (A258). The church tower, with its lead-capped corner turret, is a great landmark; it was rebuilt in 1628 after the medieval tower and spire had become unsafe.

St Margaret's at Cliffe could not be better named, as the road down to St Margaret's Bay at the bottom of the hill is precipitously steep. The splendid church is virtually unaltered Norman. Outside there is superb arcading along the nave, at clerestory level; and a really fine west door at the foot of the tower, with a richly carved round arch, surmounted by naive figures possibly representing Christ and the twelve apostles, enclosed in a triangular stone framework. Inside, the solid, round-headed arcading leads to an unusually tall chancel arch; the arch into the tower is pointed, and must therefore be early Transitional, perhaps built about 1180. Since 1696 the church has rung a curfew bell at 8.00 p.m. each night from Michaelmas (29 September) to Lady Day (25 March), to keep lost travellers away from the cliff edge. In that year a shepherd fell over the cliff and was badly injured, but survived long enough to bequeath land to the parish to pay for the curfew to be rung. During the Second World War the church was hit twice by shells fired from across the Channel. A movingly expressive stained-glass window commemorates the *Herald of Free Enterprise* – the Dover-Zeebrugge car ferry which capsized in 1987. Three crew members from St Margaret's died in the disaster; the window shows the ship sailing from the cliffs towards the outstretched arms of Christ.

St Margaret's Bay, the traditional starting and arrival point for grease-covered cross-Channel swimmers, is hardly more than a long seafront carpark, with cliffs rising sheer on either side. It is a marvellous place for watching the Channel shipping go by. A road half way down the steep hill leads to the **Dover Patrol Memorial** on the clifftop – a tall granite obelisk, facing a similar monument on Cap Blanc Nez across the Channel. At the end of Lighthouse Road diametrically opposite is the **South Foreland Lighthouse** (National Trust), built in 1843 to guide sailors past the Goodwin Sands. From the parapet you have a clear view across to France. On Christmas Eve 1898 the Italian inventor Guglielmo Marconi made technological history here, sending the world's first ship-to-shore message (in Morse code) from the lighthouse to the East Goodwin lightship, twelve miles offshore. Less than three months later he sent the first cross-Channel wireless signal from the South Foreland to Wimereux, near Boulogne. His pioneering work is commemorated in a small exhibition in the lighthouse. Nearby a beautifully preserved smock mill stands high above the cliffs. North and east of the bay, towards Kingsdown, the National Trust has safeguarded almost 300 acres of farmland, which includes a magnificent cliff-top walk.

The only right and proper way to approach **Dover** is by sea. This is after all the traditional first sight of England – the distant view of the cliffs which seem at first to form a single wall, and then as you draw nearer separate on the right into the heights of the East Cliff, with the Castle at its summit, and on the left into the white precipice of the Shakespeare Cliff. Between the two is the traveller's goal, Dover's huge harbour; and behind it the town, stretching in a narrow band of buildings up the valley of the Dour. As the gateway to England for over two thousand years, Dover has been a place of passage for kings, armies, embassies, pilgrims, missionaries, artists, writers, and the ever-increasing tide of holiday-makers.

Dover was the first place Julius Caesar made for when he crossed the Channel with his expeditionary force in 55 BC. In those days it was possible to sail right into the estuary of the Dour, which was navigable well inland and did not silt up until Norman times. That ancient haven between the two hills was easily defended, and Caesar had such a hot reception from the Britons on the surrounding heights that he decided against landing there and sailed north to Deal (see above). Dover's subsequent history is based on this constantly evolving harbour, and on the enormously powerful **Castle** (English Heritage) built to defend it. As the castle walls contain much of this history, it is the obvious place to begin an exploration of the town

As you come over the hills from Deal, the stone bulk of its towers and ramparts suddenly fills the whole foreground; indeed, hardly anything else of Dover can be seen. To get to the castle by road, you have to go down the bluff on which it stands and then snake uphill again, passing through successive gatehouses up to the level of the inner bailey. Half way to the sea, surrounded by a high bank from which there is a tremendous view across the harbour, are the most ancient survivals in the castle: the church of **St Mary-in-Castro**, and the stump of a tower at its western end. This is the lower half of the Roman **Pharos** or lighthouse, built soon after the Roman conquest in the first century AD, which blazed on the hilltop as a beacon for the galleys coming over from Gaul, answered by a similar lighthouse, now vanished, on the western heights.

The church is Saxon, rescued from near-dereliction in the nineteenth century and hideously restored. The genuinely Saxon parts of the building, like the round arches made with tiles below the central tower, have to be looked for among the weird mosaic with which Sir Gilbert Scott smothered the interior. At the back of the church a collection of old pictures show the miserable state it was in before restoration. In the eighteenth century it was virtually roofless and was used as a coal store.

Both pharos and church are far older than the present castle, though the site was fortified with earthworks as far back as the Iron Age. The Saxons had a *burh* or fortified township, for which St Mary's church was built; and William the Conqueror strengthened the existing fortifications immediately after the battle of Hastings. But the great keep, the inner bailey and much of the curtain walling – in fact, the basic Dover Castle – were built by Henry II in the 1180s, at the then colossal cost of £3,000. (For comparison, the chief architect was paid a shilling a day.)

The **Keep** is a classic of castle building, combining immense strength with magnificent living accommodation. It has three levels – a basement and two living storeys, each consisting basically of two enormous rooms. Possibly for defensive reasons, the stairs in the keep are completely illogical. There are two separate flights, and the general rule seems to be that in order to go up you have first to go down, or vice versa. The main flight leads past a vaulted antechamber, and then turns up a long stairway which brings you out into the second-storey apartments. A narrow and tortuous passage leads to an exquisite chapel, still used, decorated with fine Norman ornamentation. At the foot of the keep the basement rests on arches of massive strength and thickness. During Marlborough's wars against France at the beginning of the eighteenth century the keep was used for prisoners-of-war, and the walls are covered with the names of Guillaumes and Antoines incarcerated behind these tons of stone.

The latest addition to the keep is an extensive exhibition, partly historical and partly hands-on, entitled 'A Castle Fit for a King'. The apartments have been laid out as if in preparation for a visit of Henry VIII to inspect the Dover defences. Trestle tables are half-prepared, ornate trunks lie in heaps, and a sumptuous bed is ready to receive the monarch's bulky frame.

In 1216 Dover Castle proved its worth when Hubert de Burgh held it for King John against a siege by Prince Louis of France. A tour through the underground works on the north side of the castle is well worth making, as it passes a tunnel thought to have been dug by the sappers of Prince Louis. This was the vulnerable side of the castle; it was defended by the round **St John's Tower** outside the main walls, and by branching tunnels connected to sallyports on the far side of the moat. In the Napoleonic Wars these defences were brought up to date, by a cunning system of spiral staircases, grenade shafts for blowing trapped troops to pieces, and remote-control doors slammed shut by iron bars for taking prisoners without danger.

An exhibition called 'All the Queen's Men' tells the story of the Princess of Wales's Royal Regiment, formed in 1966 from ten separate infantry regiments, in a series of tableaux, together with uniforms, campaign medals, weapons and old photographs. Among the exhibits is a historic football – the last relic of Captain Nevill, who was killed in 1916 while kicking it towards the German lines in a supreme example of the love of sport triumphing over the instinct of self-preservation.

During the Second World War Dover's position in the front line of German air attack earned it the title of **Hellfire Corner**. The name is now linked to an exhibition on the wartime activities carried out in the labyrinth of tunnels that honeycomb the chalk cliffs. They were the headquarters from which Churchill and Admiral Ramsay masterminded the British army's evacuation from Dunkirk in June 1940; later in the war they became an operational command centre complete with hospital, telecommunications network and cipher office for decoding intercepted German messages.

Down a back road behind the castle is the **Blériot Memorial** – the granite outline of Blériot's monoplane set in the turf, on the spot where he flopped thankfully down after making the first cross-Channel flight on 25 July, 1909. It was from a spot near here that two earlier pioneers of flight, the French balloonist Jean Pierre Blanchard and his American sponsor Dr John Jeffries, had taken off for France in January, 1785. Mr Batcheller, who in 1828 wrote his *History of Dover*, gives what must surely be an eyewitness account of their departure. 'The apparatus was prepared for the progress of inflation, and a paper kite kept flying to ascertain the direction of the wind.' By lunchtime they were ready to set off, with a cargo in the basket reminiscent of Edward Lear's Jumblies, or Owl and the Pussycat: 'nine bags of ballast, the French edition of Monsieur

110

Blanchard's aerial voyage with Mr Sheldon, a bladder containing several letters, a compass, a few philosophical instruments, a beautiful English and French silk flag, some refreshments, and two cork waistcoats, to guard against accidents'.

In spite of such precautions, the flight nearly ended in disaster. The balloon began to lose height when only a third of the way across the Channel; and though they threw out their ballast, their food, their pamphlets, and even Blanchard's trousers, they would have landed in the sea but for a sudden air current which lifted them up and dumped them in the Forest of Guines outside Calais.

Another flier, Charles Stewart Rolls has a bronze statue on the Marine Parade overlooking the harbour. In 1910 Rolls capped Blériot's feat by crossing the Channel and returning in a single flight; the statue shows him wearing the flying helmet and gaiters of those incredible early days.

A few hundred yards away the moustachioed bust of Captain Matthew Webb eyes the swimmers in the harbour. In August 1875, using breast-stroke and without wearing goggles, Webb made the first cross-Channel swim, spending nearly twenty-two hours in the water, and keeping out the cold, says the *Dictionary of National Biography*, 'by doses of cod-liver oil, beef-tea, brandy, coffee, and strong old ale'. Though he won his share of fame and money, Webb was a spend-thrift. In a desperate effort to restore his finances, he went to Canada in 1883 to attempt the impossible, by swimming the rapids at the foot of the Niagara Falls. When he reached the central whirlpool his strength failed him, and he was sucked down and drowned in the maelstrom.

With its ultra-modern Eastern Docks, and the huge Gateway wall of flats as its centrepiece, there is little enough left at **Dover Harbour** to suggest its immense history. Indeed, the vast expanse of the harbour dates only from the early years of the twentieth century, when in 1909 an anchorage was opened large enough to take the battleships and cruisers of the Grand Fleet. For centuries ships anchoring off Dover had no artificial protection at all; but steady silting-up at the mouth of the Dour made a harbour arm necessary, and about 1495 the first pier was built, forming a harbour which so delighted the sailors of the time that they called it 'Paradise'. Paradise Harbour now lies somewhere under the Western Dock area, where all the port development took place before the present century. Silting remained a constant problem, and one of the duties of the citizens of Dover was to bring their shovels to clear the harbour bar when a drum was beaten.

From such primitive beginnings grew the Dover Harbour Board, formed as long ago as 1606, with the Lord Warden of the Cinque Ports at its head. The Board's headquarters is near the old part of the harbour, in the elegant white-painted **Waterloo Terrace**, which somehow survived the bombs and the cross-Channel shellfire. Travelling from Dover harbour nowadays has little of the panache of Henry VIII embarking for the Field of the Cloth of Gold, or Henry V landing after Agincourt; yet the international tourist hordes pouring on and off the car ferries, and the constant streams of heavy goods vehicles from all over Europe and beyond, still make Dover the meeting-place of all the world, in spite of competition from the Channel Tunnel.

Dover's **High Street**, with its extensions Biggin Street and Cannon Street, runs inland at right-angles to the harbour, following the line of the Dour. **St Mary's**, in Cannon Street, is the parish church of Dover; its Norman tower, with rows of arcading and leaded spire, is the main landmark in this part of the town. Inside it keeps its Norman arches at the western end, though the rest of it was rebuilt in the nineteenth century. Like the church at St Margaret's at Cliffe, St Mary's has a window commemorating the loss of the *Herald of Free Enterprise* at Zeebrugge. Up the road is the ugly Victorian **Town Hall**, redeemed by the fact that it incorporates the medieval **Maison Dieu** hospital, founded early in the thirteenth century by Hubert de Burgh for pilgrims passing through Dover. The great hall, lit on the south side by a row of traceried windows, is hung with tattered banners and lined with pikes, swords and armour; at the far end, over the door into the council chamber, is a full-length portrait of Churchill as Lord Warden. The town hall incorporates the **Old Town Gaol**, kitted out with a Victorian courtroom, tiny cells and models of murderers, rabbit thieves and other criminals.

Dover's history is told in the **Museum**, a little way towards the sea in Market Square. It emphasises the town's role in defence down the ages and is full of Roman and Anglo-Saxon artefacts, scale models, army uniforms, and anything else from photographs of Blériot landing at Dover to a full-size replica of a German V1 flying bomb. The huge polar bear that used to welcome – or threaten – visitors at the door of the old museum has been banished to an upper floor. The most recent exhibit is a Bronze Age boat, which was discovered during road works in 1992 and has been housed in a special gallery. Europe's oldest sea-going vessel, it was built over 3,000 years ago and consisted of eight enormous oak planks held together with stitches made of twisted yew withies. To stop it leaking, its seams were packed with moss and beeswax. A length of about thirty feet has been recovered, and the same amount may still lie under the road.

Next door is the **White Cliffs Experience**, the museum's ultra-modern younger brother, which uses the latest audio-visual technology, including holograms and hands-on reconstructions for children. It brings history to life in tableaux ranging from Roman legionaries grumbling about life in Britain to the aftermath of aerial bombardment in 1944, when much of Dover was destroyed by bombs and shellfire from across the Channel. Part of the head-quarters of the Classis Britannica – the Roman fleet in Britain – lies under the building, and some of the foundations can be seen as you walk round it.

Nearby, in the 1970s, road-builders uncovered the lower part of a Roman house with the traces of superb illusionist paintings on the walls. Known as the **Roman Painted House**, it was also part of the Classis Britannica headquarters complex, and is thought to have been built around AD 200 as the quarters of a high-ranking naval officer, or as a guesthouse for visiting dignitaries. It was buried around 270, when a later fortress was built on the site, but this protected the coloured plasterwork from weathering or other damage, and it has re-emerged with its brilliance almost intact. Surviving to a height of several feet, the painted dado and *trompe-l'oeil* architectural panels above give a vivid impression of the style in which the wealthy lived in Roman Britain.

The thirteenth-century **St Edmund's Chapel**, near the corner of Priory Road, is only twenty-seven feet long by fourteen wide, and is thought to be the smallest church in regular use in England. It was built for the cemetery attached to the Maison Dieu, and among other transformations became a naval victualling store and a house with forge, before being saved from demolition and restored in the 1960s. The remains of Dover's great medieval priory, founded in 1131 by Archbishop Corbeuil, are incorporated in **Dover College** (entrance in Effingham Crescent). The monks' refectory, still with its Norman arcading round the base of the walls, is now used as an examination hall; the guest house has been adapted for the school chapel; and the gatehouse is a library. In Mr Batcheller's time it was a farm 'occupied by a respectable family of the name of Coleman'.

Corresponding to the magnificent castle on the eastern side are the Napoleonic War fortifications on the **Western Heights** above the town. They are now largely given over to a youth custody centre and cannot be visited; but the brick casements and redoubts are clearly visible rising above the harbour. The barracks at the top were reached from Snargate Street by the **Grand Shaft**, cut through the rock and containing three spiral staircases. According to tradition, notices used to state that one was for officers and their ladies, the second for NCOs and their wives, and the third for soldiers and their women.

In this same direction the dual-carriageway A20 – a controversial road scheme pushed through in the teeth of opposition from conservationists – climbs near the top of the **Shakespeare Cliff**, the whitest and sheerest cliff of them all. It was to this height that Edgar brought the blinded Gloucester in the fourth act of *King Lear*, making him believe that he had fallen over the edge and survived. Shakespeare describes a samphire-gatherer on the cliff, and samphire (an edible green fleshy plant) is still said to grow there, though gorse and brambles are more in evidence.

> *Ten masts at each make not the altitude*
> *Which thou hast perpendicularly fell,*

says Edgar – a good approximation to the estimated height of 350 feet from top to bottom.

At the foot of Shakespeare Cliff the wide chalk platform, formed from the millions of tons of chalk dug from the Channel Tunnel workings, occupies the foreshore between the Folkestone and Dover railway tunnels. It has been landscaped and given the suitable name **Samphire Hoe**. You reach it from the westbound lane of the dual-carriageway A20, down a single-lane tunnel burrowed through the chalk. At the moment it consists of an undulating grassy area crisscrossed by gravel paths; but when the wild flowers that have been sown there have acclimatised themselves, it will be an attractive place to walk, picnic and watch the ships go by. A simple memorial by the car park commemorates the eleven men who lost their lives building the tunnel – sacrifices to the god of speed. The original chalk platform, constructed for the railway in 1843, was an impressive piece of engineering in its day. The base of the cliff was blown away using 185 barrels of gunpowder, and the line was laid on top of the compacted chalk.

The tunnel – Europe's major engineering feat of the twentieth century – was discussed on and off for almost two centuries. Delayed by wars and fears about national security, it was begun tentatively in 1880 and again in the 1970s. It finally received the Royal Assent in 1987 and opened in May 1994, diving underground at Cheriton just north of Dover, and re-emerging at Sangatte outside Calais. One of the giant drills used for the tunnel now stands forlornly on the south side of the M20, opposite the tunnel marshalling yards.

In its spread along the Canterbury road, Dover has swallowed up the village of **Temple Ewell**, which nevertheless has managed to keep its identity. It is a little maze of a place, near the source of the River Dour, which runs through the middle of it past an old watermill. The name derives from the Knights Templar, who had a preceptory there and founded the village church, which still has its original Norman north doorway. In the chancel windows are brilliant little inset panels of Swiss seventeenth-century glass, showing scenes from the life of Joseph in a strange mixture of mock-medieval townscapes, turbans and Roman armour. By contrast, **Whitfield** is a suburb of little character. In the Middle Ages the tenant of Archer's Court, a Whitfield manor house, had the dubious privilege of holding the bowl into which the king was sick on his sea voyages – a royal cupbearer in reverse.

From Whitfield the B2060 brings you to **Alkham**, lying deep in a delectable valley. Alkham is a sheltered little place, clustered below a long low church on the hillside. The Early English church was built early in the thirteenth century by the monks of St Radegund's Abbey near by; its chief glory is the wide and graceful north chapel, arcaded the whole way on slender Bethersden marble shafts, perhaps built by Canterbury Cathedral masons at the end of the century.

St Radegund's is well worth the backhanded journey down minute country lanes from Alkham. Founded by Premonstratensian monks (from Prémontré, in France) about 1191, the abbey was on a fairly large scale. The creeper-covered gatehouse was originally the tower of the church, and the pretty Elizabethan farmhouse behind was made out of the refectory; Henry VIII had most of the stone carted away to build Sandgate Castle.

Radegund was a German princess born about AD 520. When she was ten she was carried off by Clothaire, King of the Franks, and was later forcibly married to him. However, she must have been an uncomfortable lady to live with, as she wore a hair shirt under her royal robes; and Clothaire was no doubt secretly relieved when she left him, took the veil and founded an abbey at Poitiers. Here, according to an eighteenth-century writer, 'the care of lepers and persons afflicted with the most nauseous distempers, constituted her greatest pleasures'. She survived until 587, abstaining from meat, fish, eggs and fruit.

You can get from Dover to Folkestone by two routes – directly along the dual-carriageway A20, which swings well inland, or by the Old Dover Road (formerly the A20 but now downgraded to B-road status) which runs parallel to the coast and passes within a few hundred yards of **Church Hougham** (pronounced Huffem). The most noticeable thing about it is the soaring television transmitter mast near by. The church has a hefty tilehung broach spire, and is much-restored Norman; inside there are blocked Norman arches on the south side of the chancel.

Even more remote is the church of **Capel-le-Ferne**, tucked away behind Capel Church Farm a good mile from the bungalow sprawl of the village, and with sheep grazing in the churchyard. On the clifftop west of the village, the RAF flag flutters above the impressive **Battle of Britain Memorial**, completed in 1993. It consists of a huge aircraft propellor, with blades forty yards long cut into the turf; fittingly, it is used by civil airline pilots to check their instruments. A sculpture on the central boss portrays a Battle of Britain fighter pilot gazing at the sky.

From Capel the road from Capel-le-Ferne coils steeply down Dover Hill into **Folkestone**. This is as good a side as any from which to approach the town, as you arrive almost in the middle of it, and can get a panoramic view by making a short detour to the green slopes by the martello tower, high above the East Cliff sands. From here the resort area of Folkestone is invisible. At your feet is the harbour, with small craft lolling on the low-tide mudflats, while behind rises the steep hill of old Folkestone, crowned by the battlemented tower of the parish church. Below the slopes in the Dover direction is the small wilderness of **The Warren** – a jumble of chalk terraces, grass and undergrowth, bisected by the railway. Bird lovers flock there to watch hordes of migrating birds, and to listen to the songs of nightingales and chiffchaffs.

Folkestone's name in Saxon times was 'Fulchestane', presumably from some prominent lump of rock where the folk assembled. In the Middle Ages it was important enough to be made a 'limb' or associate of the Cinque Port of Dover. Until the growth of its cross-Channel passenger service in the nineteenth century it was hardly more than a few rows of fishermen's cottages down by the harbour, and a scatter of houses up the hill between the harbour and the church. It shared the ferry trade with Dover until the 1990s; but its harbour was too tidal and shallow for today's huge roll-on roll-off ferries, and now only sea-going catamarans ply across to France.

The steep, narrow **High Street** survives from this earlier age, though many of the cottages have been gutted to make restaurants or souvenir shops. It is now closed to ordinary traffic, which has brought it back to the state it was in when R.H. Barham wrote that 'its streets, lanes, and alleys – fanciful distinctions without much real difference – are agreeable enough to persons who do not mind running up and down stairs'. The church on top of the hill stands in the middle of a nice group of Georgian redbrick and weather-boarding.

Seen from close to, the **Church of St Mary and St Eanswythe** is much larger than distant views suggest. It is basically an Early English building, with Perpendicular chapels and central tower added in the fifteenth century. The dedication commemorates Folkestone's patron saint. Eanswythe, the grand-daughter of Ethelbert, the Kentish king converted by St Augustine, founded a nunnery at Folkestone in AD 630; the site is thought to have been on the clifftop east of the present church, but all traces vanished during the great storms and cliff erosions of the Middle Ages. When Eanswythe died in 640, the nunnery was sacked by the Danes, and was probably never restored, though the church was rebuilt by King Athelstan in 927. Lambarde says that her miracles ranged from lengthening a roof beam by three feet when the carpenters had sawn it too short, to forbidding 'certaine ravenous birdes the countrey, which before did much harm thereabouts'. Her relics are kept in a shrine behind an elaborate little door in the north wall of the sanctuary – the bones of a young woman about thirty, who died in the seventh century, discovered in the wall when the Victorian alabaster arcading was being installed.

West of old Folkestone are the unruffled Victorian squares and hotels, which grew up when the railway came to the town in the 1840s. Between the hotels and the sea is that unique Folkestone creation known as **The Leas** – a clifftop expanse of lawns and flower gardens, with a Riviera-like tangle of pine and broom tumbling down to the sea-level promenades. For any South Coast resort to compare itself to the Bay of Naples may seem far-fetched; yet if you look over the treetops on a sunny afternoon to some lonely fisherman in a dinghy far below, the scene is much more

Mediterranean than English Channel. Then you turn round and it is back to waltzes bouncing from the blue curlicued bandstand, the rows of deckchairs, and the terraces behind, disrupted by a lumbering modern office block. A little way along the Leas is a statue of Folkestone's greatest man, William Harvey, discoverer of the circulation of the blood, holding a heart in his hand. Harvey was born in Folkestone in 1578 and died in London in 1657, reputedly by taking poison after he found that he was going blind.

Beyond the Leas Folkestone turns into **Sandgate**, which still has a few weatherboarded cottages left in its High Street. Down on the beach is Sandgate Castle, one of Henry VIII's fortresses, neglected and with its front side washed away by the sea. Presumably in a century or so it will have vanished, like Sandown round the coast.

Farther inland, beyond the M20, are the remains of far earlier fortifications, on the top of the chalk hill known as **Caesar's Camp**. The ditches round the top may be Iron Age or medieval; the one thing that is certain is that they are not Roman. The Camp is a place of painful memory to me, as on a climb up to the top I was bitten by a malevolent horse, furious that I had no sugar to give it; Kent also has its wild animals. A few hundred yards to the east is the smooth cone of **Sugarloaf Hill**, man-made, but no one knows why or when.

Newington, just north of the A20, still has remnants of its rustic past, in spite of its nearness to the huge marshalling yards of the Channel Tunnel terminal at Cheriton. The church has a Norman chancel arch and is packed with monuments; on the south wall is a brass to Dr Christopher Reittinger, a Hungarian who was physician to the Tsar of Russia, and died at Newington in 1612. Four centuries earlier, in 1201, the Lord of Folkestone and the Earl of Guisnes fought for the village in a trial by battle. The Earl won, and Newington was granted to the Abbey of Guisnes, in Flanders.

8

The Borders of Romney Marsh

THE CRESCENT OF land that stretches behind Romney Marsh from Hythe round to Rye marks the ancient southern coastline. At the eastern end, round Hythe, the gentle contours of the greensand ridge cram themselves into a steep escarpment above the levels of the Marsh; and beyond Appledore you are in an estuary area, where old maps show wide tongues of water stretching inland to Tenterden, isolating Oxney as a real island, and splitting Romney Marsh into separate fragments. This coastal strip is clearly defined by the waters of the Royal Military Canal. At the heart of the area is Tenterden, once a harbour town though now ten miles from the nearest sea. There are no trunk roads to speak of, which makes the district ideal for haphazard exploration.

Hythe itself is built on a succession of parallel terraces, rising from the canal to the parish church. The canal gives central Hythe much of its character; shaded by tall trees it runs through the heart of the town, an ideal spot for a stroll or splashing about in a rowing boat. Though now isolated from the sea by the silting up of the estuary and the accumulation of shingle, Hythe was an important harbour in former centuries – the central Cinque Port, geographically speaking, between Sandwich and Dover to the east, and Romney and Hastings to the west. The coast is now a smooth stretch of shingle, and any trace of the harbour has long ago vanished.

The High Street is long and narrow. Half way down is the eighteenth-century town hall, perched on columns and with a clock jutting over the street. From the High Street narrow alleys lead up to the higher levels, where traffic should be deterred (but isn't) by the difficulties of squeezing through. The church, soaring over the town, is a big medieval building; the tower was destroyed by an earth tremor in 1739 and rebuilt in 1750. Inside it is remarkable for its tall chancel, built about 1220 but not finally vaulted until 1886. Below it is a crypt (reached from outside the church) lined like a catacomb

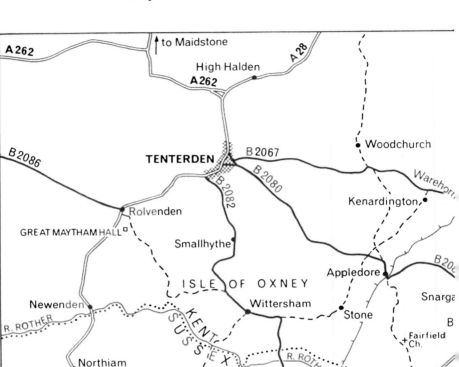

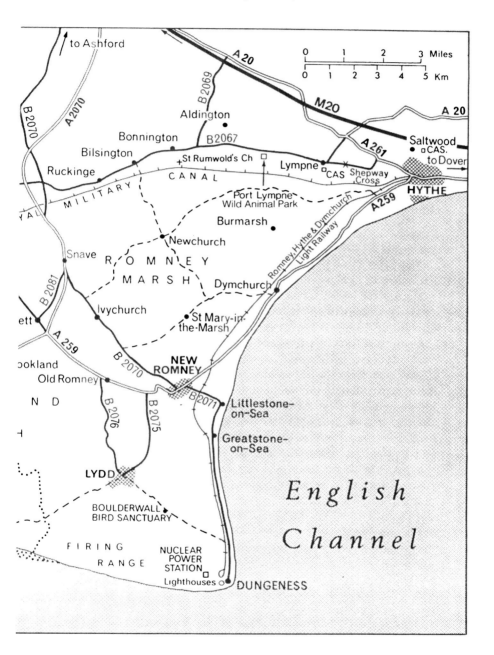

with skulls and thighbones. They were formerly thought to have been placed there after a battle, but were probably dug up in the Middle Ages when fresh burials were made and laid finally to rest in the crypt. There are said to be 2,000 skulls and 8,000 thighbones; presumably these were the parts of the skeleton thought most worthy of preservation, ribs or vertebrae being thrown back into the ground.

When William Cobbett visited Hythe in 1823, he could afford to make light of the Napoleonic threat, and disparage all the military preparations that had been made against it. The martello towers (there are two good examples at the end of the front at Hythe) came in for his special scorn – 'these ridiculous things, which I dare say cost five, perhaps ten, thousand pounds each'. As for the Royal Military Canal, 'those armies who had so often crossed the Rhine and the Danube, were to be kept back by a canal, made by Pitt, thirty feet wide at the most'. What would he have said about the hideous concrete World War II pillboxes that are dotted about the countryside? Perhaps, like the martello towers, they will be tourist attractions in a century or so, though it seems unlikely.

Up behind Hythe is the village of **Saltwood** – a small green, a medieval church lonely in a field, and the high walls of **Saltwood Castle**, the home of Lord Clark, the art historian, followed by his son, the MP and diarist Alan Clark. Saltwood's chief claim to historical fame, or notoriety, came in 1170, when the murderers of Becket met there to plot their crime. As an added irony, the castle previously belonged to Becket, as Archbishop of Canterbury, and had been taken from him; the plotters probably met in the ruined Norman hall on the south side of the courtyard. The towers of the great gatehouse are thought to have been added by Henry Yevele, architect of the nave of Canterbury Cathedral, in the fourteenth century. The enormous room known as the Archbishop's Hall of Audience is now a library. Saltwood is an attractively romantic place to wander about in, as the ancient masonry is still largely creeper-clad, with flowers and even small shrubs growing between the stones of the battlements.

A couple of miles west of Hythe, along the B2067, **Shepway Cross** marks the site of the Court of Shepway, where the authorities of the Cinque Ports met to carry out their official business. The name derives from 'Shipway', since before the channel silted up, boats used to come up to West Hythe, and in Roman times even farther, to Lympne.

Lympne (pronounced Limm) was the Roman Portus Lemanis, one of the Forts of the Saxon Shore built against Saxon sea-raiders at the end of the third century AD. It stood on the now-vanished arm of the Rother that entered the sea at Hythe; indeed, the river itself was called the Limen or Limene, and is so marked on old maps. A Roman road, Stone Street, now the B2068, leads due north from Lympne to Canterbury. If you walk down the steep path beside the present Lympne Castle, you will see the remaining fragments of the Roman fort in a field. The Saxons called it the 'stout wale' or strong fortress, a name down the years transmuted to Stutfall.

Lympne Castle was built overlooking Stutfall about 1360, using stone from the Roman walls below; it was restored early this century. Though of no great interest, apart from a fine hall with kingpost roof, it stands in a superb situation, with wide-ranging views across the rich farmland of Romney Marsh to the hulking blocks of the Dungeness atomic power station in the distance – a lookout point from Roman days down to the Second World War. Next door to the castle is Lympne's medieval church, looking a good deal more fortress-like than the castle.

A mile west of Lympne, three hundred acres of the steep escarpment between the road and the Royal Military Canal are given over to **Port Lympne Wild Animal Park**, the larger of the two Kentish zoos owned and run by John Aspinall (see also Howletts, p. 86). Under the trees and in broad paddocks, buffaloes, cheetahs, cassowaries, tapirs and dozens of other types of animal and bird prowl, browse, preen or sleep in conditions as near-natural as the South of England can provide. The splendid house that dominates the site was begun just before the First World War for Sir Philip Sassoon; designed by Sir Herbert Baker, later one of the architects of New Delhi, its unpretentious redbrick façade conceals such exotic features as a Moorish-style courtyard, and a whimsical room painted as a *trompe-l'oeil* tent by Rex Whistler.

Aldington was the home of one of those victims of delusion thrown up by the uneasy mental climate of the Reformation, Elizabeth Barton, the 'Holy Maid' or 'Nun of Kent'. A maidservant at the Archbishop's manor house during Henry VIII's reign, she seems to have suffered from something like goitre ('a great infirmitie in her bodie', says Lambarde, 'which did ascend at divers times up into her throte and swelled greatly'), leading to fits in which she prophesied and described events that were happening elsewhere. Her fame soon spread beyond Aldington to Canterbury. Archbishop Warham set up a commission to examine her on points of doctrine, which she answered successfully.

If she had confined herself to miracles – 'lighting candels without fire, moistning women's breasts that before were drie and wanted milke, restoring all sorts of sicke to perfect health, reducing the dead to life againe' is Lambarde's comprehensive list – all would have been well. But she tried to intervene in Henry VIII's divorce proceedings against Catherine of Aragon, prophesying that he would lose his throne if he went ahead with the divorce. For this unwise remark she was executed at Tyburn on a charge of high treason.

Aldington's magnificent church stands on a high point above the scattered village. The tall Perpendicular tower is sixteenth-century, but the main building is much earlier, of the twelfth and thirteenth centuries. Inside there is some very fine woodcarving – fourteenth-century choir stalls, with floral carving below the misericords, and a flamboyant pelican on the front of the pulpit. Erasmus, the great Renaissance scholar from Rotterdam, was rector in 1511–12. He is said to have resigned from the living because his English was not up to preaching a sermon; but it is most unlikely he ever came to Aldington.

In complete contrast to this lofty building is **Bonnington**'s church, St Rumwold's, down by the Royal Military Canal. Newman describes it in a pretty simile, 'like a plump little grey hen'. St Rumwold must qualify for the title of England's most improbable saint. Born in Northamptonshire in AD 662, he had the power of speech at birth, preached at Brackley on the second day of his life and died on the third. This was the saint whose image was such a money-spinner at Boxley Abbey (see p. 171). The church is said to be the oldest on the Marsh; it has a curious flat ogee cap on the shingled belfry, and the remains of a precipitously high musicians' gallery at the west end. Fortunately the lane beside it carries little traffic and nothing disturbs the quiet setting of trees and water.

At **Bilsington** a stone obelisk, half chewed away by time, stands on a rise overlooking the Marsh. This was put up in 1835 in memory of Sir William Cosway, MP for the district, who was killed falling from a stagecoach. The small, stumpy church is on the other side of the road, behind a well-preserved moat with farm buildings in the middle. A large bell, presumably too heavy for the flimsy bellcote, stands in a frame at ground level outside. North of the village are the remains of **Bilsington Priory**, of which a fine hall and undercroft survive. The Priory, founded for Augustinian canons in 1253, was used as a lodging by the Archbishop of Canterbury on his periodic visits to Romney Marsh; he was allowed to stay there 'two nights and a day, but nothing more'.

Thomas Aveling, the pioneer of the steam traction engine in the 1860s, came from **Ruckinge**, and the village sign reproduces the smokebox door of an Aveling and Porter steamroller. The church has a Norman tower with a weird lead spire poking through the usual conical roofcap. In the graveyard a plank with an illegible inscription marks the grave of the two Ransley brothers, notorious smugglers who in 1800 were hanged on Penenden Heath outside Maidstone for highway robbery.

Warehorne is a remote hamlet, built round a midget green. The church is large for so small a village; the tower was struck by lightning in 1770 and rebuilt in brick to the old battlemented medieval shape. Inside it has hardly been touched since that date, and with its box pews and mouldering portrait of some forgotten rector would still seem like home to R. H. Barham, who lived in the village when he was rector of Snargate, down on the Marsh.

Lightning must be a hazard along this exposed edge of the Marsh, as **Kenardington** church across the field was struck in the sixteenth century and severely damaged. The nave was pulled down, the fine Decorated tracery of the south aisle blocked up, and the aisle transformed into the nave. With its bare interior it has a desolate air. In the fields below are the remains of earthworks traditionally said to have been built by King Alfred at the end of the ninth century to keep out the Danes. The squarish enclosure can still be traced, and at the lowest level is an entrance that in those days would have opened on to the shore.

Woodchurch, a few miles inland, is a much more consequential place than these quiet hamlets. The big church with its tall broach spire is a landmark for miles around, partnered by a derelict smock mill nearby. It is a straggling village, as big in area as many small towns, built round a large triangular green. The name presumably derives from the first Saxon wooden church on the site. The present building is mainly Early English, of the early thirteenth century, with arcade columns alternately round and octagonal, and three tall lancet windows in the east wall. The tower has enormous buttresses because of subsidence; in spite of them the spire is getting on for two feet out of true. In the south aisle is a thirteenth-century medallion of glass showing the Entombment of the Virgin, a wonderful Rouault-like composition of dark blue and brown. The Bonny Cravat pub opposite the church is said to get its name from a French fishing boat used for smuggling; 'Bonne Crevette' or 'Good Prawn' seems a likely derivation.

From Woodchurch you can continue west for three miles to Tenterden, or head south for **Appledore** on the edge of the Marsh. Appledore was once a busy shipbuilding centre, but it is now a quiet place, with a wide village street, and a church with a squat battlemented tower. It has had its wild past: in the ninth century it was captured by the Danes, who built a fort where the church now stands; and in 1380 it was sacked by the French. The church was rebuilt after this raid with the former north aisle and nave as a single unit, which accounts for the curious appearance of a wide nave leading to a far narrower chancel. The National Trust owns the stretch of the Royal Military Canal between Appledore and Warehorne.

The **Isle of Oxney** still has a cut-off island feel about it, and is still surrounded by water; though round much of the perimeter only ditches and streams remain of the wide waters that once covered the Rother Levels. The name 'Stone Ferry' is a reminder of the days when you had to take to the water to cross from the island village of Stone to the mainland. Outside the Ferry Inn is a list of the tolls that had to be paid until the 1930s to cross the bridge to Oxney, ranging from 1s. 6d. for a charabanc to 1d. for a pig or a Bath chair.

Stone is a small scattered village; the square fortress-like tower of its church is a landmark as you approach Oxney from Appledore. The church was completely rebuilt after a fire in 1464. Inside, below the tower, there are far more ancient survivals – iguanodon bones dug up in a nearby quarry, and a misshapen block of stone that was once a third-century altar to Mithras, the god of the Roman legionaries. This may well have been the garrison altar of Stutfall Castle (see above); the figure of a bull, the emblem of Mithras, can still be traced on the front. **Wittersham**, the 'capital' of Oxney, is a largish village with a long, low church, mainly fourteenth-century. The massive battlemented tower was added at the end of the fifteenth century. In the Middle Ages Wittersham was famous locally for the quality of its miracle plays.

Heading north from Wittersham, you cross the Levels to **Smallhythe**, the ancient harbour of Tenterden. Like Appledore, it was a shipbuilding centre. Henry VIII visited it in 1538, to inspect one of his warships under construction there. But now it is visited for the **Ellen Terry Museum** (National Trust) in Smallhythe Place, down on the Levels. This timber-framed yeoman's house was built about 1480 for the harbourmaster; on the lawn just below is a large rectangular pond, formerly the repair dock and now loud with the croakings of bullfrogs who have begun to colonize the marshes. The leading actress of her age, Ellen Terry lived here for nearly thirty years, from 1899 until her death in 1928; the house is partly a museum and partly rooms preserved as she left them. Her first husband, the artist G. F. Watts, painted her as a young girl with flowing pre-Raphaelite hair, before the breakdown of their short-lived marriage; and subsequent drawings and photographs right through to old age show the same straight nose and determined chin. Her great days as an actress came in the last twenty years of the nineteenth century, when she played opposite Sir Henry Irving at the Lyceum; but of those glittering performances only the brocaded clothes survive, and the superlatives of Bernard Shaw and other writers.

A few yards up the road is another fine half-timbered house, the Priest's House, beside a small church rebuilt in brick after being burnt down in 1514. Apart from the gables, crowstepped in Dutch style, the church is hardly more than a brick barn.

More than any other town **Tenterden** sums up the Weald, both in the beauty of its buildings and in its general air of unruffled relaxation. The great pinnacled tower of its church, which from a distance dwarfs everything else into insignificance, retires into the background once you actually get into Tenterden, as it is set back a little from the High Street. This is the heart of Tenterden – wide and lined with grass and trees at the western end, then narrowing to the main centre of Georgian or half-timbered houses, shops and pubs.

In Saxon times Tenterden belonged to Minster-in-Thanet – the town's name means 'den or forest clearing belonging to the men of Thanet' – which accounts for the rare dedication of the church to St Mildred. This lady, an Anglo-Jutish princess of Kent descended from King Ethelbert and Queen Bertha, was the daughter of Domneva who founded the nunnery at Minster-in-Thanet in AD 669. In the course of time she succeeded Domneva as abbess, and Tenterden was among the lands granted to Minster either before her death or soon after. The church tower is the manifestation of Tenterden's prosperity as a wool town in the fifteenth century. When the sea came right up to Smallhythe Tenterden was a harbour town as well – a 'limb' or associate of Rye and thus a corporate member of the Cinque Ports – and the church was worthy of such a centre of trade. Inside it is an uncomplicated building, with a twelfth-century nave, thirteenth-century south aisle, and fourteenth-century north aisle. In the Lady Chapel is a fine seventeenth-century monument to Robert and Martha Whitfield. Martha was not as meek as she appears, as records show her 'chiding and brawling' in the church with another Tenterden housewife.

It is worth walking a little way along the Ashford Road to the Unitarian meeting house. Built in 1746, it still has the original pulpit and galleries. A painting on the wall shows Benjamin Franklin attending a service in 1774.

Tenterden is well supplied with pubs. At one end of the High Street the William Caxton perpetuates the now suspect theory that the pioneer of printing was born in Tenterden. The White Lion is a coaching inn with courtyard at the back; while the Eight Bells looks the oldest of all, with an enormous stretch of timbered wall along a side lane, and the ostler's bell still hanging in the yard.

Off the High Street, down Station Road, the excellent local museum has displays on every aspect of the town, from the structure of timber-framed houses to the trade in silks and spices that passed through Smallhythe in the Middle Ages.

Tenterden's little station, at the end of Station Road, is the headquarters of a band of enthusiasts who are working to revive a ten-mile stretch of the **Kent and East Sussex Railway** between Tenterden and Bodiam. The waiting room has been turned into a museum of photographs and other historical material relating to the line, and beside the road to Rolvenden, at **Rolvenden Station**, is a wonderful collection of old engines, several of them built in the 1870s and '80s. Opened in the early 1900s, this enchanting country railway ran in a 21-mile loop from Robertsbridge round to Headcorn, and in late summer was packed with hop-pickers down from the East End for their week's annual working holiday. So far, seven miles of track – from Tenterden to Northiam – have been reopened, and from spring to autumn trainloads of steam enthusiasts chug gently along the Rother Valley behind the K & ESR's sturdy little locomotives.

Rolvenden, west of Tenterden along the A28, is like a small-scale version of Tenterden – brick and weatherboarded houses, a wide village street with a grass verge, a tall church tower. The church is mainly fourteenth-century, with columns alternately round and octagonal, as at Woodchurch. Over the south chapel is a large squire's pew, at first-floor level, set out like a comfortable room with carpet, table and chairs. In the sanctuary is a tablet to John Frankish, Rolvenden's martyr vicar, who was burnt at the stake in Canterbury in 1555; and over the door to the north chapel is a memorial by Sir Edwin Lutyens to Lt. Henry Tennant, killed in the First World War.

The Tennants lived at **Great Maytham Hall**, a neo-Georgian mansion designed by Lutyens and built in 1909–10 on the site of an eighteenth-century house that had largely burnt down. Great Maytham is now divided into flats for retired people. In the Middle Ages the estate was owned by a baron who rejoiced in the name of Orable de Maytham; and in Victorian times the Hall was let to Frances Hodgson Burnett, author of *Little Lord Fauntleroy* and *The Secret Garden*, said to be based on the garden at Great Maytham.

The road past Maytham brings you back across the Levels again to Wittersham. South from Wittersham you join the main Rye road (A268) near **Peasmarsh**, an attractive switchback of a place which tends to become a racetrack in summer. The Norman church, shapely and isolated, is down a lane south of the main village. It still has its round Norman chancel arch, carved with splendid heraldic animals; the chancel, enlarged two centuries later, has beautiful Early English lancet windows.

Iden is a quiet little village, dropping down towards the Rother Levels. Its small bright church, tucked away behind the houses, has unusually elegant roof timbers. Alexander Iden, the Sheriff of Kent who killed Jack Cade (see p. 233), is said to have come from here.

At the top of the hill down into Rye is **Playden**. Its church has an exceptionally tall and graceful spire above a centrally placed tower. From the choir a long and ancient ladder leads up into the tower; and in the north aisle is a small sixteenth-century slab to a Flemish brewer, Cornelis Roetmans, carved with barrels and mash forks as emblems of his trade. He was a refugee from the Spanish persecutions in the Low Countries, who settled along with the Huguenots at **Rye Foreign** outside the town. Perhaps a Flemish mason carved the inscription '*bidt voer de siele*' ('pray for his soul').

It is not surprising that tourists flock to **Rye**. First of all, it is indisputably a most beautiful town, full of half-timbered and Georgian buildings that would be exceptional anywhere else, but in Rye hardly get a second glance. Then it is built on a hill, as all good towns should be, so that you can make a satisfying gentle progression from river level up the cobbled streets to the church on the crest of the hill, never in a straight line but always coming to sudden right-angled bends, with some new vista of gable ends and tiled roofs to lure you on. It has a small fishing fleet and a flourishing fishmarket, forming a link with Rye's seafaring and piratical past; and a history rich in raids, disasters, smuggling and general villainy, scarcely credible among the genteel antique shops, tearooms and small potteries that mark the tourist transformation.

Most people approach Rye from London, down the main road, and thus miss the superb distant view of the town across the flats of Walland Marsh to the east. On no two days does this prospect of the town seem the same. When the cold east wind whistles across the marsh the red roofs and low-towered church crouching on the hilltop stand out brilliantly against the backcloth of hills; on hot, still days Rye is almost hidden behind a veil of heat haze; and at dusk on a stormy winter's day it looks unbelievably dramatic, hunched up and twinkling with a few lights under a furious red-streaked sky.

On signs beside the roads into the town the date 1289 is prominently displayed. It was in that year that Rye was raised to the status of a royal borough; it was already an 'ancient town' linked with the Cinque Ports and equal in status, not just a mere 'limb', like so many of the lesser ports around the south coast. In those days Rye really looked like a port. The sea flowed right up to the foot of the cliffs, with the wide inlets of the Tillingham and Rother guarding the town on either side. Rye stood on an easily defended peninsula, entered through the frowning **Landgate**, with other gates now vanished, and a strong town wall of which sections survive.

Though Rye was never affected by the sea to anything like the extent of Winchelsea (see below), a great bite was taken out of the eastern cliff during the terrible storms towards the end of the thirteenth century, and a whole area of the town disappeared below the waves. In the days of its greatness Rye contributed five ships to the Cinque Ports fleet – as many as Romney, Hythe and Sandwich, but only half the number of Winchelsea; and it had the right of supplying fish direct to the king's table, carried up to London by special carriers known as 'rippiers'. It was the French, not the sea, that really finished Rye. In 1377, as the culmination of a long series of attacks, they swept down on the south coast, making Rye one of their chief targets. The town was burnt to the ground, and though it managed a slight recovery during the next two centuries the relentless silting of the estuary prevented it from ever again approaching its former status.

Rye had its share of famous visitors in pre-tourist days. Queen Elizabeth came there on a royal progress in 1573, and, according to tradition, was so pleased with her welcome that she granted the town the right to call itself 'Rye Royal'. A century and a half later George I came to Rye a good deal less willingly. Early in 1726 he was blown ashore on Camber Sands and made his way to Rye, where he stayed four days with the mayor, James Lamb, in Lamb House, and stood godfather to Lamb's child, who was born the night of his arrival. By this time smuggling was in its heyday. It was still flourishing when in 1773 John Wesley preached to the people of Rye, who were quite 'willing to hear the good word', but in spite of all his powers of persuasion 'will not part with the accursed thing smuggling'. Not surprisingly, as smuggling was highly profitable, and Rye might have been built for the purpose, with vaulted cellars below many of the houses for storing contraband, and interconnecting attics so that a smuggler could make his getaway below the eaves while the exciseman was hammering on the door half a street away.

Rye has been an artist's delight since Van Dyck sketched it in the seventeenth century. In the twentieth century Paul Nash and John Piper painted on Romney Marsh, and Edward Burra lived in the town, nicknaming it 'Tinkerbelletown' from its Never-Never-land air of unreality. It produced its own famous literary figure in the dramatist John Fletcher, born in 1579 possibly in the building called Fletcher's House (now tearooms) beside the church. But its greatest literary ghost is an American, the novelist Henry James, who fell in love with Rye at first sight, and from 1897 until two years before his death in 1916 lived at **Lamb House** (National Trust). This superb Georgian house, looking down a quiet cobbled lane, had been built by James Lamb shortly before George I's surprise visit; and its comfortable opulence exactly suited Henry James. The small garden building where he wrote *The Ambassadors* and *The Golden Bowl*, booming out their rolling sentences to his secretary, was destroyed by a direct hit in 1942. A later and far more entertaining novelist who lived in Lamb House was E. F. Benson, Mayor of Rye between the wars, whose Mapp and Lucia stories chronicled the waspish intrigues, backchat and scandal of the town.

James Lamb, the builder of the house, founded a family which ran Rye for well over a century, holding the office of mayor almost nonstop and in strict control of the parliamentary voting in those days of small electorates and rotten boroughs. In 1742 he was involved in Rye's most notorious murder case – the killing of Allen Grebell by John Breeds or Breads, a 'sanguinary butcher'. Breeds had been fined by Lamb, who was mayor at the time, for giving short weight. Burning with resentment, he lay in wait for Lamb late one night in the churchyard, and stabbed a figure he thought was the magistrate with his butcher's carving knife. However, it was not

Lamb at all, but his brother-in-law Allen Grebell, who had borrowed Lamb's cloak for the evening. Breeds was soon arrested, as on the evening of the murder he had been roaming about the streets shouting that 'butchers should kill Lambs', and his bloodstained knife was found lying in the churchyard. He was hanged, and left to rot on a gibbet, which can be seen upstairs in the Town Hall. Only the skull is left; the rest of the skeleton was removed by superstitious old women, who boiled up the bones to make an infusion against rheumatism.

Round the corner from the town hall the huge Perpendicular window of the **Church**'s north transept fills the end of Lion Street. Set back above it is the low tower, dominated by the gilded quarterboys who strike the bells over the clock (it is no use looking hopefully towards the clock on the hour, as they only brandish their hammers on the quarters). Inside, the church is far older than an outside glance would suggest. The transepts are Norman, built about 1120; the nave, slightly later, provides an evolutionary study, from the round arches by the crossing to the full-fledged pointed Transitional at the western end.

The clock dominates the inside as it does the outside; the first thing you see as you go in is the gilded pendulum swinging overhead, and in the north chapel are the two original quarterboys of 1760. The modern replicas on the tower are made of fibreglass, though you would never know it. I was told that someone mathematically minded had worked out that between them the old quarterboys had more than twenty-one million hammer-blows to their credit. The clock mechanism, still going strong after more than four hundred years, can be seen in the belfry, on the way up the tower. Made in 1560 by Lewys Billiard for £31, it is said to be the oldest clock with its original works in any English church. From the tower battlements there are wide-sweeping views across the red roofs of the town to Romney Marsh and the Channel.

Rye is famous for its pubs. There are estimated to be seventeen of them (excluding clubs with bars); and some years ago I was told by the landlord of the Union that the record for the shortest time taken for a drink in each of them stands at twenty-three minutes. They range from the ultra-picturesque and half-timbered, like the Mermaid and the Flushing, to the dignified, white-painted Georgian of the suitably-named George, which has its own assembly room, complete with musicians' gallery.

Rye's thirteenth-century castle, known as the **Ypres Tower**, gets its name from John de Ypres, who bought it in 1430. It stands above a green open space called the Gungarden, where in Elizabethan times 'good ordnance of Her Majesty' threatened the sheep and seagulls on the flats below. Until 1865 it was the town gaol, and its cramped cells can still be visited. It is now owned by the Rye Museum Association; their main **Museum**, in East Street, displays every sort of bygone from mesh 'glasses' for protecting hop-pickers' eyes to Rye's eighteenth-century fire engine.

The Ypres Tower has pottery made in Rye as long ago as the thirteenth century, forerunner of the ware produced in the host of small potteries that have proliferated in recent years. Best known is the Rye Pottery, on the edge of the town, which began operations in 1869 and has now largely abandoned its fine tableware in favour of figures such as Chaucer's Canterbury Pilgrims. Its most typical local products used to be the 'Sussex pigs', which date back to the eighteenth century and were used at weddings. The head was removed, stood snout down and filled with beer, and the guests could thus each manage a hogshead without difficulty. The pig was taken as the stubborn symbol of the county:

And you can pook and you can shove,
But a Sussex pig he won't be druv.

So runs the old verse.

There is no room here to catalogue Rye's fine buildings: Rye's own guidebooks do this very adequately. But it is worth mentioning the ancient black-painted wooden warehouses along the Strand, now restored and converted; and the extensive use of 'mathematical tiles'. These were tiles made to look like bricks, and used as cladding on half-timbered or plastered houses to give them an air of Georgian solidity. The George owes its eighteenth-century appearance to the tiles, though underneath there is a Tudor timber-framed building.

Though quite large boats still moor in the Tillingham beside the Strand Quay, the modern **Rye Harbour** is out towards the sea, reached down a dreary road lined with gravel workings. It has a spiky Victorian church, a martello tower, a few old houses including one with a watchtower on one corner, and a housing estate. A moving monument in the churchyard commemorates the heroism of the seventeen men of the lifeboat *Mary Stanford*, which sank with all hands during a gale in November 1928. Sadly, their self-sacrifice was in vain, as the crew of the ship they set out to save had already been rescued by a passing steamer.

The flatlands towards the sea, cut by drainage ditches where marsh frogs croak in summer, are a nature reserve and a paradise for terns, oystercatchers and waterbirds of all sorts, which can be watched from hides. More than three hundred plant species have been found on the shingle foreshore, including seakale with its blue-green leaves and yellow horned poppy. You can walk across the fields to the low, rounded walls of **Camber Castle** (English Heritage). Like Deal Castle and its fellows round the coast, this was one of a chain of castles built during the invasion threat of the late 1530s. It is stranded far inland today; but when it was built it was placed strategically on a spit of land commanding one side of the Rother estuary.

Winchelsea, hardly more than a mile away across the Brede, is in complete contrast to Rye. Rye seethes with tourist bustle, but at Winchelsea all is quiet, with hardly a shop to be seen among the red brick and white weatherboarding. Rye is so built up that it is bursting at the seams, whereas beyond Winchelsea's few streets of old houses there is nothing but grass, marked with the ghostly traces of the buildings that once stood there. It has hardly altered at all since the mid nineteenth century, when Millais painted his famous *Blind Girl*, now in the Birmingham Art Gallery. Clasping her younger sister's hand, the girl sits by a stream with her eyes closed while a stormy sun shines full on her face; in the backgound a double rainbow arches over Winchelsea's red-tiled roofs and ancient Strand Gate.

Winchelsea is a disaster area from the distant past of English history. The blows that fell on it were the same as those suffered by Rye, though more severe. Both were 'ancient towns' with large fleets; but Winchelsea was more exposed to the sea, standing originally on a shingle spit running north-east from the cliffs near Fairlight. Throughout the thirteenth century the spit was gradually eroded, until a great storm in 1287 finally breached it and washed away much of the town. All the townspeople could do was to abandon it completely and move to higher ground; the old town became the 'Old Winchelsey Drowned' of early cartographers, and was finally forgotten.

Winchelsea was so important a part of the country's defensive system that there were none of the bureaucratic delays usually met with when a complete rebuilding is involved. Public buildings were put up on the new hilltop site; cellars were built for important merchants; and wharves were provided for them on the banks of the Brede. The grid layout of Winchelsea still betrays the hand of the town planner after seven centuries. Though the new town was safe from the sea, it was vulnerable to the French, who attacked and pillaged it seven times in the fourteenth and fifteenth centuries. In one of these raids the magnificent **St Thomas's Church** was largely destroyed. All that remains of this cathedral-like building, the centrepiece of Winchelsea, are the choir and side chapels. To left and right of the present west front, which is roughly where the rood screen would once have stood, are the weathered arches and buttresses of the transept walls, marking the limits of destruction. No one knows when the great west tower and nave were finally thrown down – perhaps not until the final French attack in 1459.

What remains inside is of great beauty. Most notable are the superb tombs in the north and south aisles, with their stone canopies of pinnacled tracery. There are three tombs on the north side: the figures are older than the canopies and are believed to have been brought from Old Winchelsea church. They are of a cross-legged warrior in armour, marvellously preserved, a lady in a head-dress, and a scholarly-looking young man in a long robe.

The two tombs on the south side are even more sumptuous. That on the left is thought to be of Gervase Alard, Admiral of the Western Fleet under Edward I, whose effigy lies in complete armour, the hands clasping a heart. This tomb appears in another Millais painting, *The Last Shot*, which shows a child covered with a soldier's coat uncomfortably asleep on Gervase's effigy. The other tomb, only a little less grand, is probably of Stephen Alard, Captain and Admiral of the Cinque Ports and of the King's Western Fleet under Edward II. For those who might be tempted to add their initials to the already well inscribed Alards, a notice of 1902 warns that those who injure tombs are 'liable to imprisonment for not exceeding six months with or without hard labour and if a male under 16 with or without whipping'.

As striking in their way as the tombs are the stained-glass windows. They form an unusually unified set, as they are all by the same artist, Dr Douglas Strachan, and all date from round about 1930. Their style is half way between the simpering naturalism of most Victorian glass and the chunky abstractions of today; and apart from their decorative function they tell the history of Winchelsea in true medieval manner.

Across the road is the old **Court Hall**, with a museum on the upper floor. The lower floor was once the town gaol. In the museum is a model of the town in its prosperous days, and such strange exhibits as an iguanodon's footprint from the bottom of Fairlight Cliff. Of great local interest are the boards painted with the names of Mayors of Winchelsea since 1295, beginning with Gervase Alard. A new Mayor is elected every Easter Monday, and Winchelsea is the smallest town in the country to have its own mayor and corporation.

Exploring Winchelsea is an unworrying business, as there is no traffic to speak of, except on the main road. On the west side of the churchyard is **Wesley's Tree**, an ash descended from the tree where Wesley preached his last open-air sermon in 1790; a pretty little Wesleyan chapel lies on the westernmost of the Winchelsea roads, opposite the ruins of the medieval Black Friars' house. A short way down this road is the **Pipewell Gate**, at the top of a steep cliff about thirty feet high where Edward I's horse shied and leaped over when the king was at Winchelsea to review the fleet. Amazingly, both horse and rider were uninjured, and the king rode calmly up the hill again and through the gate.

In its great days, before the French destroyed its buildings and its harbour silted up, Winchelsea had about six thousand inhabitants; now it has hardly a tenth of that number. To get an idea of its decline, you can walk across the fields to the black hulk of the post-mill, across bumps and hollows that mark vanished streets and buildings. Best of all is to leave the town by the south exit, continuing down the road that leads past Wesley's Tree. On the left are the ruined chancel arch and choir of the **Grey Friars**, across a field which was once the town's market place. The road turns sharp right to Hastings, but a narrow lane straight ahead leads between fields full of small mounds and depressions down to Winchelsea's loneliest and most evocative ruin, the **New Gate**. It was through this gate that the French are said to have been treacherously admitted in 1380, and one can imagine them systematically pillaging their way northwards through the town, leaving devastation now covered by the grass. Beside the gate is the deep town ditch; but neither gate nor ditch could save the ancient town of Winchelsea.

9

Romney Marsh

EARLY IN HIS career the Rev R. H. Barham (1788–1845) was rector of Snargate, on **Romney Marsh**, and had no doubt of the supreme importance of that unique peninsula. 'The World,' he wrote in one of his *Ingoldsby Legends*, 'according to the best geographers is divided into Europe, Asia, Africa, America, and Romney Marsh. In this last-named, and fifth, quarter of the globe, a Witch may still be discovered in favourable, i.e. stormy seasons, weathering Dungeness Point in an egg-shell, or careering on her broomstick over Dymchurch wall.' Witches are now hard to find, though an occasional warlock can be seen emerging on to the main road from the Dungeness atomic power station. But Romney Marsh is still as fascinating as ever: a fascination made up of the flatness and openness of the place after the little tucked-away valleys of the Weald; of the feeling that Dungeness is the Land's End of the south-east coast – far more so than Beachy Head or the North and South Forelands; and of the impermanence of an area wrested from the sea by dyke and sea-wall, which is yet steadily growing eastwards with the shingle carried along the coast by wind and tide.

Romney Marsh proper is bounded on the south by the road from Appledore to New Romney, which follows the line of the Rhee Wall, the Rivi Vallum of the Romans. South and west of the Rhee Wall is Walland Marsh, almost as large; nevertheless, the whole expanse is generally known as 'Romney Marsh'. Denge Marsh, east of Lydd, gives its name to Dungeness – the 'ness' or point of land of Denge.

Since the Romans, every age has left its mark on Romney Marsh. The Saxons carried on the work of 'inning' or bringing the marshland into cultivation. The Normans and their successors built the superb churches which are astonishingly thick on the ground for

A map for this chapter will be found on pp. 120-121

so small a population. Farmers bred the famous Romney Marsh sheep, which still dot the fields all over the Marsh, though many of the water-meadows are now ploughed up; and if you drive down any of the little byroads the odds are that you will have to pull in for a few minutes while a farmer and his collie work the sheep from one field to another.

Then came the holiday-makers, fringing the coast with bungalows and chalets at Camber on the southern side and along practically the whole eastern side. In the 1960s the Central Electricity Generating Board decided that Dungeness was remote enough for an atomic power station, and built alongside the lighthouses the great grey blocks which loom in the distance across the fields, and which are the focal points for the line of pylons striding westward towards the Kentish hills. Yet in spite of the pylons and gravel workings, the tourists and the holiday camps, Romney Marsh remains a secretive place, its essential character unaltered by this multifarious human activity.

At the heart of the Marsh lies the Romney Marsh group of parishes – not the towns like Lydd and New Romney, which have an almost metropolitan air among so many tiny places, but the hamlets centred on Ivychurch, with a dozen or so parish churches and a couple of ruins thrown in. They lie so close together that they can all be visited in a day, and they form a unity in diversity, with brightly coloured royal arms on the wall, biblical texts gold-painted on oval boards, and clear glass windows letting the Marsh light stream in.

Less than a mile east of Rye, by the A259 just past the Camber turn, the low-crouched brick church of **East Guldeford** is typical of these churches scattered seemingly at random across the Marsh. Built about 1500, it is reached down a grassy path beside a stream. There is no village at East Guldeford, which gets its name from Sir Edward Guldeford, who built Camber Castle soon after 1500. Three miles further on, a lane off the main road brings you to the little church at **Fairfield**, dedicated to St Thomas Becket. He is said to have had lands round here, and the farm where the church key is kept is still called Becket's Barn. The church lies a couple of hundred yards from the road along a grass causeway surrounded by sheep and sheep's droppings: sheep, water, grass, wind and solitude make Fairfield the quintessence of the Marsh. Before the causeway was built parishioners had sometimes to come to church by boat, and a photograph inside the church shows it on a little island surrounded by flood waters in every direction. There was a church here early in the thirteenth century, but the present brick cladding dates from early this century. Inside are tall grey-painted box pews, and a three-decker pulpit. The rector preached from the top level of the pulpit and read the lessons and prayers from the middle level, while his clerk sat in the cramped lowest compartment. Fairfield's font is a numerical curiosity. The basin has seven sides, the base of the column on which it stands has five, and the plinth has ten.

Not far from Fairfield is an exotic importation which has somehow ended up on Romney Marsh as the **Philippine Village Craft Centre**, selling all manner of artefacts from shell decoration to cane furniture. Once a year, on the last Sunday in July, thousands of Filipinos home in on the Centre for a festival of Philippine food and entertainment.

Brookland, on the A259, is the largest of the Marsh villages. It also has the most famous of all the churches, and the most obvious, as it stands right beside the main road. The detached octagonal wooden belfry, looking like three candle-snuffers fitted one inside the other, has attracted various explanations: that it blew down off the church roof twice and after the second occasion was allowed to stay on the ground; that Cardinal Wolsey brought it to Brookland from Lydd; or that it was so astonished when a virgin came to be married at the church that it jumped off the roof of its own accord. In fact it has probably been there as long as the church. The lowest of the massive timbers, stretching tier on tier up into the gloom, are thirteenth-century, as is the church itself.

It contains all sorts of interesting bits and pieces. Most notable is the lead font, Norman in provenance as well as date. It is a cylinder decorated round the outside with the signs of the Zodiac – a complete year from March round to February, and then the first eight months repeated, making twenty panels in all. Below each sign is the work for that month: in June (Cancer) a man mows with a scythe; in September (Libra) corn is threshed with a flail; in December (Capricorn) a man brains a pig with an axe. No one knows how the font got from Normandy to Brookland. One theory is that it may have been seized by English sailors in a raid on the French coast.

On the south wall are fragments of a wall painting of the murder of Becket, with a knight's sword raised over the archbishop's head. At the west end of the south aisle is a wooden enclosure known as a 'tithe pen', where the parson's corn, wine, cloth and other contributions from his parishioners used to be weighed out. The weights and measures for the purpose, beautiful precision objects dated 1795, stand in a glass case against the wall. Brookland church

139

has a reminder of the eighteenth century's care for the comfort of the clergy: a wooden sentry-box known as a 'hudd' or hood, in which the parson protected his wig from wind and rain while conducting the burial service at the graveside.

In the late Middle Ages Brookland was the centre for games and wrestling on the Marsh, and was also renowned for its strolling players, whose Passion plays were much in demand. Like the other Marsh villages, it became a centre of smuggling.

Brenzett church is a much smaller affair, and is the only church in England dedicated exclusively to St Eanswith or Eanswythe (Folkestone church shares the dedication with St Mary.) Its long porch has curious glazed window arcades. Brenzett's chief historical claim to fame is that in 1381 it was the rallying point for Wat Tyler's Romney Marsh supporters, many of them armed only with pitchforks.

Snargate's sonorous name has a prosaic origin in the 'snare-gate', or sluice-gate, which controlled the supply in the waterway leading to Romney Harbour. The big church, built on a mound, dates from the thirteenth century, and has a simple four-square stone tower built about 1400. On the north wall are two lead sheets dated 1700 taken from the roof, one of which shows that church repairers have been known to enjoy themselves. On it appear the names of the churchwarden, the plumber, and 'T. Apps, carpenter, and all his jolly men'. Nearby is a red wall painting of a galleon in full sail. Inevitably Snargate church was used by smugglers. In 1743 revenue men seized a quantity of tobacco in the belfry and a cask of Hollands gin under the vestry table. The north aisle was sealed off from the rest of the church and was a regular smugglers' hide. When Barham was rector here in the 1820s he was often challenged by smugglers on the lanes to his home at Warehorne a couple of miles away.

The largest and most prosperous of these buildings is at **Ivychurch**; the name has nothing to do with creeper, but means 'the church on the island in the waters'. It is a Decorated church of complete uniformity, as it was all built in the decade 1360–70. The stone entrance porch is battlemented like a castle gatehouse; above is a parvise or upper room, where a chantry priest may have lodged, and which was put to use as a secret food store during the Second World War. The Marsh has always been a possible landing-point for an invader, and during earlier centuries the beacon turret on the corner of the lofty tower was a watchman's lookout post. Inside the church there is a feeling of great spaciousness, as the nave is

140

completely bare, with seats in the choir alone. Along part of the south wall run stone seats, reserved for the aged and infirm before the days of church pews – one explanation of the expression 'Let the weakest go to the wall'. In the nave is a hudd, as at Brookland.

The north aisle is now partitioned off along its whole length. Cromwell's soldiers are said to have stabled their horses on its rough brick flooring, and in later centuries smugglers used a vault below to conceal brandy, gin, tea and tobacco, hiding the contraband in coffins emptied for the purpose. One Sunday the rector was even turned away from the door by his own sexton with the words 'Bain't be no service, parson. Pulpit be full o' baccy, and vestry be full o' brandy'. Tea in those days was so expensive that the locals had to make their own out of marsh herbs, and a jug of Hollands gin was cheaper than a pot of China tea.

Snave church, north along the road towards Ashford, is a forlorn place, and recalls the dilapidation of all of them remarked on by travellers a generation ago. You can only reach it on foot, down a grass track between tall trees. The south porch seems to be crumbling away; the whitewashed interior is of puritanical austerity.

The church at **Newchurch**, three miles to the north-east, has a similarly forlorn, neglected look. It stands in an overgrown grave-yard, with bushes forcing their way between the bars of family tomb enclosures. The battlemented tower leans away from the body of the church at an angle of at least five degrees. Inside there are unusually wide aisles, with the north aisle the same width as the nave.

Most easterly of the group is **Burmarsh**, only a mile outside Dymchurch. This is one of the earliest of the Romney Marsh settlements, the name deriving from the Saxon Bur-wara-mersce, the 'men of the burgh of the marsh'. The little church, reached by a foot-bridge across a stream, is largely Norman, with a good rustic Norman south doorway. The tower was rebuilt in the fourteenth century.

Dymchurch, on the coast a mile to the south, crouches behind the massive sea-barrier of Dymchurch Wall, first built by the Romans. John Davidson, one of the largely forgotten 'Georgian poets' writing in the years round 1900, vividly evokes the Marsh scene here a century or so ago:

As I went down to Dymchurch Wall
I heard the South sing o'er the land;
I saw the yellow sunlight fall
On knolls where Norman churches stand.

Dymchurch strikes a balance between being a seaside resort and an unspoilt little town. In spite of an amusement arcade, the centre of Dymchurch, with its curving main street, and church down a side road, has very much the Kentish village feel. The church is an enlargement of 1821, and much of the old Norman work remains hidden inside; the original Norman west door now forms the inner arch under the tower.

Opposite the church is the eighteenth-century **New Hall**, now the headquarters of the boards which control the complex land-drainage system of the Marsh. Upstairs is the old Court Room, which can be seen on request; it still has high box seating and the royal arms of George II, together with a small museum of Romney Marsh exhibits. Especially interesting are the old maps of the area, showing Dungeness much blunter than it is today, and the Marsh subdivided into sections called 'waterings'. Down by the wall **Martello Tower No. 24** (English Heritage) is full of exhibits showing the preparations against invasion during the Napoleonic wars; it also has a cannon mounted in a suitably anti-Bonaparte position on the roof. The tower was built where it is to protect the sluice controlling the water level of Romney Marsh – of paramount importance, as the whole of the Marsh is below mean high tide level, and Dymchurch itself is more than seven feet below.

The legendary exploits of smugglers, excisemen and redcoats in and around Dymchurch were celebrated, and glamorised, in Russell Thorndike's series of novels about Dr Syn, a fictional vicar of Dymchurch at the end of the eighteenth century. Dr Syn himself has the best of both worlds by leading a Jekyll and Hyde or Scarlet Pimpernel life as both parson and smuggler; the sordid and brutal realities of the constant war of attrition between lawbreakers and revenue men have been transmuted into a gentlemanly contest by the novelist (brother of the great actress Sybil Thorndike). Every other year in the summer Dymchurch is turned over for a day to a Dr Syn carnival, when cargo is landed on the beach, battles are staged, and one of the locals leads the proceedings disguised as Dr Syn and his alter ego, the smuggling Scarecrow.

At **St Mary-in-the-Marsh**, a couple of miles inland to the west, you are back among the churches of the central Marsh. The building is simple and remote. Inside the door on the west wall is what seems to be a medieval altarpiece, with three scenes separated by carved wooden saints, and by the door is a tablet to E. Nesbit (1858–1924), author of *Five Children and It* and *The Railway Children*, who is buried in the churchyard.

Old Romney church, the last of the central group, lies down a little side road, and is separated from the main road by a field full of sheep. There may well have been a church here since Saxon times, as the Saxons reclaimed or 'inned' a large area where Old Romney now stands. Originally there was a single port of Romney – the ancient Cinque Port, called by the Saxons Rumenea, sometimes interpreted as 'island of the Romans' – but as the sea retreated the seaward part grew in importance, and Old and New Romney were being differentiated by the early thirteenth century. This church is the most delightful of all the Marsh group. It stands in a beautiful setting, with a giant yew in the churchyard, and has a sturdy tower with a squat spire on top, and a higgledy-piggledy roofline which reflects its gradual growth from the thirteenth century on. Inside there is an air of homely tidiness. The box pews are trimly painted pink, as is the splendid gallery at the west end, which still has the church band's pews in place, as in the days of Thomas Hardy. The roof beams are rough-hewn, and the stonework is equally massive.

The altar in the north chapel is a smooth black stone slab, marked with five consecration crosses – the original medieval *mensa*, discovered during restoration work in use as a step. It is an extremely rare survival, as both Edward VI and Elizabeth ordered all stone altars to be destroyed as undesirable links with pre-Reformation days. In the chancel floor a stone slab commemorates John Deffray, rector for nearly half a century. He was a French Huguenot who fled from France after the Revocation of the Edict of Nantes in 1685 abolished Protestant worship, and ended up as rector of Old Romney in 1690. Ten years after his arrival he wrote how he had found the church and services neglected, but instituted a choir and set up a 'religious society'. The outcome of his labours was that 'to the joy of all pious souls, our shepherds, ploughmen and other labourers, at their work perfume the air with the melodious singing of psalms'.

New Romney is the capital of the Marsh. It has a long, straight country-town High Street, with a grey-painted town hall on the south side. Farther up on the north side the imposing redbrick front of Priory House keeps its Dickensian shop windows on either side. New Romney church, built about 1100, is one of the glories of the Marsh. Before the great storms at the end of the thirteenth century altered its course, the River Rother ran into the sea in a large bay with New Romney at its apex; and ships could moor beyond the churchyard walls. The land still drops away below the walls, but it needs the eye of faith to see a harbour in the haphazard collection of bungalows and yards that now stand there; though there is still a narrow, sluggish watercourse under a bridge.

As you come down the street towards the church, the massive tower looms over you, bewildering in its variety of stonework and window pattern, like some textbook of late Norman masonry. Steps lead down into the church; presumably with the years the roadways to north and west have been gradually built up. Inside, the church has the Marsh pattern of nave and aisles of equal length, and no transepts. The tower was a little later than the original church. If you walk through the high arch beneath the tower and look upwards, you can see the patterned arcading which decorated the original west front, and was cut through or blocked up when the tower was added.

In earlier times the church was a centre for local government, with the sessions of the Jurats, the yearly Cinque Port meetings and the election of the Mayor all taking place there. It is worth looking downwards as well as upwards, as the floor is a grand mix-up of tiles of all periods, surrounding black memorial slabs whose beautifully incised inscriptions are a copybook of seventeenth- and eighteenth-century lettering. Above one of the sedilia is a carved stone head of a tonsured priest, individual enough to be a portrait.

A mile from New Romney, where once the sea flowed in between two spits of land, are the resorts of **Littlestone** to the north and **Greatstone** to the south. Littlestone has an air of faded Victorian gentility, with a large pink granite Diamond Jubilee fountain on the sward in front of the hotels. Greatstone forms part of the largely bungalow sea frontage which stretches south as far as Dungeness. At low tide a sunk section of the Second World War Mulberry harbour which never got towed across the Channel to France can be seen offshore.

If Romney Marsh is a world on its own, then **Dungeness** is a world within that world. It is a place where incongruities meet on a few square miles of windswept pebbles – a pair of lighthouses, the bird sanctuary at Boulderwall, sea anglers shoulder to shoulder, the vast masses of the atomic power station, gravel pits, the Pilot Inn with a cluster of houses round it, a shanty town of old railway carriages. A good first impression can be got from the top of the old lighthouse, which is open on most summer afternoons. The view takes in the whole coastline from Fairlight round to Folkestone.

Immediately at the foot of the lighthouse, and beyond it to the shore, the grasses have colonized the shingle in successive waves, with bare patches between, so that waves of green seem to be reflecting the grey of the sea. Immediately to the north the road is lined with small cottages and shacks. A black-painted bungalow belonged to the film-maker Derek Jarman (1942–94), who created an imaginative and haunting garden round it, full of sea-loving plants and totem-like structures made from objects washed up on the beach. The power station itself is only a few hundred yards away on foot, yet a good three miles by car, as you have to go half way back to Lydd and then double back on your tracks to get there by road.

A light of sorts has stood on Dungeness Point since early in the seventeenth century, when an open coal fire was kept alight there, financed by dues levied on passing shipping. By the mid eighteenth century the sea had receded considerably, and there was obviously need for a large and permanent structure. This need was met by Samuel Wyatt, who in 1792 built a tower over a hundred feet high, lit by eighteen sperm oil lamps instead of a coal fire. An electric light was installed as early as 1862, and the lighthouse continued in use until the beginning of this century, when it too had been stranded inland by the build-up of shingle. The black tower which superseded it, and which visitors now climb, operated from 1904 until 1961, when the atomic power station obscured its light, and it had in turn to make way for the elegant black and white minaret of the new automatic lighthouse, worked from complex control panels in its base. The new tower is floodlit, which makes it more visible to shipping, and also reduces deaths among migrating birds which might otherwise collide with it. The ground floor can be visited in the afternoon, but 'only if the fog signal is not sounding'.

The shingle movement that makes lighthouses obsolete could leave the **Nuclear Power Station** on an island, and means that for much of the year lorries are kept busy carting shingle westward from the point to the far side of the station, in a perpetual motion of stone. Visitors can learn about the mysteries of the atom at the large information centre, or experience them at first hand on a guided tour. Going round Dungeness is like a conducted tour of the temple of an esoteric religion, with clicking geiger counters to measure the strength of the invisible power. The fact that it is like any other power station, except that it uses atomic fuel instead of coal, tends to be overlooked. The tour takes in one of the reactors; through a window you look down into an enormous hall, where white-clad

145

figures pad silently below a gigantic gantry, which rolls gently forward laden with fresh fuel elements for the living heart of the reactor. In the central control rooms banked dials monitor every activity of the uranium core, of the gas that is heated by the energy produced in the reactor, and of the steam that drives the turbines; while computer printouts snake into racks. A concrete-sided whirlpool outside marks the return to the sea of the huge quantities of water used for cooling purposes – one reason that led to the choice of Dungeness as a site. The rows of sea anglers on the steep shingle seem singularly unworried by the much publicized radiation risks of atomic power stations; and you can buy superb fresh-caught fish at many of the roadside shanties.

Before the present network of little roads the locals had to walk everywhere on the shingle, and for this evolved their own footwear – 'backstays' or 'backsters', wooden overshoes rather like snowshoes.

Dungeness has lost much of its ancient windswept solitude; yet if you stand on its eastern shore, with nothing between you and the sea except a few fishing boats and black-painted huts standing out against the shingle, you can recapture that sense of remoteness, until the damp mist blows in from the sea and the world shrinks to the pebbles round your feet.

Anyone with children will certainly want to see Romney Marsh from the **Romney, Hythe and Dymchurch Railway**, which has one of its termini – if that is not too pretentious a word – at Dungeness. On its thirteen-mile journey it passes over roads, dykes and ditches, and gives a complete picture of the Marsh terrain, from the naked shingle of Dungeness to the meadows round Hythe. For enthusiasts, there is a 'model land' at New Romney. The main section of the railway, covering the eight miles between Hythe and New Romney, was opened as long ago as 1927, to link up the Southern Railway terminals at each of those towns. The five-mile extension out to Dungeness was opened two years later. Though its gauge is only fifteen inches, the railway can carry an amazing amount of traffic; motorists are liable to be held up while the *Green Goddess* or *Samson* chugs slowly by (maximum speed of trains at level crossings, 5 mph), bursting with an axle-bending load of holidaymakers. The RH and D was considered of such strategic importance that it was requisitioned by the army in the Second World War, and carried much of the material for Pluto – the pipeline under the ocean from Littlestone to France which supplied our forces in Europe after D-Day in 1944.

On either side of the Dungeness–Lydd road huge water-filled gravel pits have been gouged out of the shingle. Here, at **Boulderwall**, the Royal Society for the Protection of Birds maintains a major reserve covering more than a thousand acres, where ornithologists can spy on the nests of ringed plovers and little terns, or listen in spring to the songs of willow warblers and whitethroats.

With its nearness to Dungeness power station, **Lydd** now rivals New Romney in importance. Yet it is still hardly more than a village, overshadowed by its enormous church which has been called the 'cathedral of the Marsh'. Thomas Wolsey, the future cardinal, was vicar here early in the sixteenth century. The noble pinnacled tower, 132 feet high, was built in the 1440s and looks as though it should belong to an Oxbridge college rather than a parish church. At the foot of the tower are twin pairs of doors set in the base of a single arch. Originally a Saxon basilica stood on the site and there is still some Saxon stonework in the north aisle. A plan inside the church shows its conjectural Norman predecessor engulfed by the present long, low bulk of nave and aisles.

Much of the fabric, including the chancel, is new, as the church suffered a direct hit in the Second World War, which destroyed the chancel, and damaged the chapels and roofs. A painting under the tower inside the west doorway shows the extent of the damage. The new chancel ceiling is white, with coloured oak leaves and Tudor roses; and the new east window has three narrow lancets, full of glowing purple and red glass. As at New Romney, the church at Lydd was used for local affairs. The Jurats and commons of Lydd used to meet around the Stuppeny tomb, in the North Chapel, to elect their Bailiff – a custom that carried on until 1885.

Behind the church there is a pretty little triangular green surrounded by small shops and houses, and near it on the main road some big eighteenth-century houses. Down towards the coastal firing ranges Lydd peters out in a waste of derelict army hutments. Lydd gave its name to the explosive called Lyddite, which was first tested here towards the end of the nineteenth century.

Along the southern side of the Marsh the steep shingle beach of Dungeness merges into the huge level expanse of **Camber Sands**. Camber is a holiday village built among or on the sand dunes, and when the wind blows hard from the south you may find yourself in a whipping hail of sand which is the nearest approach to a Sahara sandstorm the South Coast has to offer. The vast dunes, topped with

147

marram grass and gorse scrub, are a favourite with film-makers. Outside Camber the dunes provide natural bunkers for the Rye golf course, one of the finest championship links in the country.

10

Ashford and the North Downs

SOUTH-WEST OF CANTERBURY the valley of the Great Stour cuts through the North Downs, and gives easy access to Ashford and the farmlands of central Kent. The main road (A28) takes the line of least resistance and follows the same course through a landscape of hill and woodland, seldom more than a few hundred yards from the waters of the river.

Chartham, the first separate village beyond the outskirts of Canterbury, reconciles the medieval and the modern in an unusually successful way. From the main road your eye is caught by the enormous church, with its row of Decorated windows down the side; but it is not until you have crossed the railway into the village that you realize there is also a large paper mill on the other side of the Stour. Chartham has two village greens – a large open space directly in front of the church, and behind it a smaller triangular green forming the heart of the village.

The church belonged to the monks of Christ Church, Canterbury, which accounts for its great size; it dates mainly from the 1290s, with a Perpendicular tower added about two hundred years later. The magnificent chancel windows are of the type known as 'Kent tracery', in which the stonework in the upper part seems to burst apart into starlike shapes. The roof is equally splendid – a forest of close-set beams, linked at the crossing by a carved boss. In the north transept is a very fine early brass to Sir Robert de Septvans, who died in 1306. On his shield and surcoat are the seven winnowing fans (*sept vans*) which form a rebus on his name.

From Chartham you can continue along the main road to Chilham, or turn off through the delightfully named **Old Wives Lees** for the villages on the northern slopes of the downs. None of them is of particular importance individually, but jointly they make a composite picture of quiet remoteness. **Selling** straggles up and down the hills; its cruciform church, with commanding brown rendered central

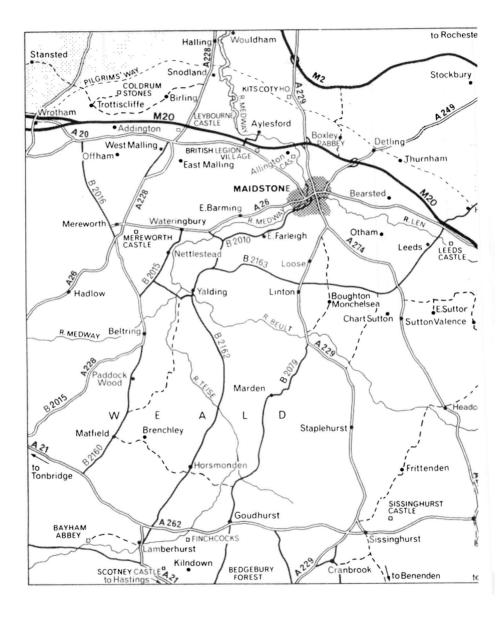

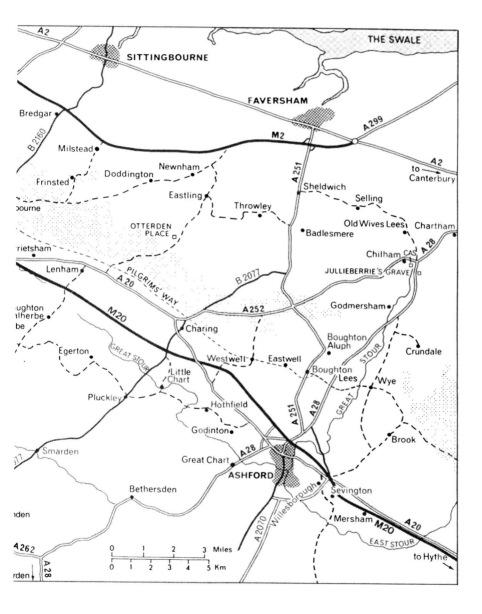

tower, has a fine Early English chancel and chapels. The church at **Sheldwich** has a unique fourteenth-century window, high above the chancel arch, a wild triangular affair with blob-like excrescences on the whirling tracery. The tiny Early English church at **Badlesmere** (down a road signposted Fisher Street) has hardly been touched since the eighteenth century. It still has box pews, three-decker pulpit and textboards painted in cream on brown; the pew-ends nearest the altar were carved about 1415.

Throwley is right up on the high downs. Its stark Perpendicular church tower is visible miles away across the fields; in the north chapel is a statue to George, first Lord Harris, a tough campaigner who captured Seringapatam in 1799, during the victorious campaign against Tippoo Sahib in India led by General Wellesley (later the Duke of Wellington).

Eastling is an open little village, with a good pub called the Carpenters Arms. Two miles to the south is **Otterden Place** (not open), which still keeps the look of a Tudor brick mansion, though it was largely rebuilt in the early nineteenth century. There are a large number of portraits of the Wheler family, who bought Otterden early in the eighteenth century and still own it. Most interesting of them was the Rev. Granville Wheler, Prebendary of Southwell, whose sharp-featured clerical face gazes down from the library wall. In 1729 he carried out electrical experiments in the long gallery upstairs, charging a glass rod by rubbing it with a silk handkerchief, and holding it near one of the Otterden pageboys to make his hair stand on end. His son, another Granville, gambled away much of the Wheler fortune. At his death in 1786 Otterden was ruinous, and could only be salvaged by pulling down much of the Tudor courtyard house and remodelling what was left. The house has a very rare survival: in a back courtyard is a horse wheel used to draw water from the well.

Newnham has an unspoilt village street, with one outstanding half-timbered house decorated on its plaster panels with red swirls of foliage. The church at **Doddington** is worth a short detour up a tree-lined lane. It has an exceptional dedication to the Beheading (Decollatio) of John the Baptist. Externally its oddest feature is the pretty west tower, white weatherboarded up to the battlements. It is largely Norman, with the original east window arrangements of three small openings and another above. In the side chapel a monument to George Swift, a young law student, records an early road fatality. He died in 1732, 'By an Unfortunate Fall from a Chariot'.

Milstead has a good village centre; the church faces across the road to the superb half-timbered manor house. **Bredgar** is larger, with a good deal of modern building going on, and a neat village pond in the middle. The name derives from the 'broad gore' or wide forest clearing of a Saxon settlement, and there was probably a church here in Saxon times. The present church is mainly fourteenth-century, though the Norman west door survives from an older building. On the other side of the Sittingbourne road (A249) is **Stockbury.** From a distance the church tower, solitary on a bluff overlooking the valley, looks like the keep of a fortress; and in fact it stands near the site of a vanished castle. Below the church the orchards tumble into the valley, and behind it the road slopes down to Stockbury village, built round a tiny green.

Chilham, back again in the Stour valley, is one of Kent's most self-conscious beauty spots. Isolated from through traffic, its enchanting square of half-timbered houses is now a large car park; if it was in France, the cars would be made to park outside. The village stands, in proper feudal manner, between the churchyard and the gates of the castle. The church has a fine Perpendicular tower, built in a flint and Caen stone chequering; the nave is fifteenth-century, while the transepts are a hundred years older. For a few years after St Augustine's Abbey in Canterbury was dissolved, the gilded shrine that contained Augustine's body was kept in the church, but in 1541 it was removed and disappeared. It is a simple and stately building, with several remarkable tombs to members of the Digges family.

Largest of all is the tall black marble column in the south chapel, commemorating Lady Mary Digges, who died in 1631 and was the wife of Sir Dudley Digges, builder of the present Chilham Castle. The column, eleven feet high, is surrounded by figures of the cardinal virtues – Justice, Prudence, Temperance and Fortitude. In the north aisle is a more typically seventeenth-century monument to Sir Dudley's sister, Lady Margaret Palmer, who died in 1619 and was, according to the inscription, 'fayrer then most women wiser then most men'. Here the polished Bethersden marble has been cut away in an intricate pattern to give a luxuriously inlaid effect. Such tombs are a whole world away from the Victorian pathos of the memorial in the chancel to the two little Hardy boys, sons of the owner of the castle. With their arms round each other, they are reading the *Babes in the Wood*, while their battledore and shuttlecock lie on the ground beside them.

153

The **Castle** (not open to visitors) is set in a park of over 300 acres. Below the Norman keep of the original castle Saxon construction has been discovered, and there may well have been some kind of fortress on the site even in pre-Roman times. Sir Dudley Digges completed his brick Jacobean mansion in 1616; he was a highly successful diplomat and lawyer, who in 1618 went on an embassy to Moscow for James I, and when he died in 1639 held the office of Master of the Rolls. His house, whose design has been attributed to Inigo Jones, is a typical assemblage of gables, tall chimneys and stone-mullioned windows. What is not typical is the ground plan, which forms five sides of a hexagon, with an open side at the back, enclosing a central courtyard. This shape accounts for the strange angles the sides of the house make with one another.

Below the castle the gardens fall away in a series of terraced lawns towards the Stour valley, with a lake on the valley floor, and a heronry at the western end of the park. They were landscaped by two of England's greatest gardeners – John Tradescant in the seventeenth century, and 'Capability' Brown in the eighteenth.

Though the downs hereabout are poor in prehistoric remains, there is one impressive example, the long barrow known as **Jullieberrie's Grave**, across the Stour from Chilham. The track below the Jullieberrie Downs runs fairly close to it, but the barrow takes a bit of finding. To get to it you have to skirt a field and come down almost to the banks of the Stour; the barrow is there right enough, but is heavily overgrown. A copse of tall trees grows along one side of it. The strange name Jullieberrie is said to be a corruption of the name Julius Laberius, one of Julius Caesar's tribunes killed in a battle near Chilham in Caesar's second expedition to Britain in 54 BC.

At **Godmersham**, set in the rich parkland of the valley floor, there is no village to speak of. A semicircle of road crosses the Stour, which meanders through watermeadows studded with enormous oak trees, and brings you to **Godmersham Park**, a wide Georgian brick mansion. In the 1790s it was inherited by Jane Austen's brother Edward; she often stayed here, and may well have drawn on her memories of this idyllic place when she wrote *Mansfield Park* (though the story is set in Northamptonshire). In order to inherit Godmersham and other properties, Edward had to change his name from Austen to Knight, which seems a small enough price to pay for so many pastoral acres. The church, outside the brick wall of the park, has a Norman tower built on the north side; the tower has its own eastern apse, showing that it was used as a separate chapel. In the chancel a naive medieval relief carving shows a mitred bishop, possibly Becket, seated below his own cathedral.

On the other side of the main road is **Crundale**, up terrifyingly narrow lanes in the heart of the downs. Its isolated church, backing on to a wide downland valley, has a good deal of Norman work remaining, including the arcade cut through the nave wall into the north aisle. Inside the door is a huge fifteenth-century stone graveslab, incised with the figure of a priest in full canonicals. A stretch of the downs between Crundale and Wye is now a nature reserve, famous for orchids and rare butterflies and moths.

Wye is chiefly known as the home of one of this country's main agricultural colleges, but it is in addition a smart little country town, between the placid waters of the Great Stour and the steep scarp of the downs. Its most prominent landmark is up on the hillside – a large crown, carved in the chalk by students of the college to commemorate Edward VII's coronation in 1902. The churchyard and the college fill the centre of the town, looking across to the Green with its timbered houses, and to the Georgian dignity of Church Street. Wye's church is an odd-looking building, reflecting the disasters of its history. It was originally a large cruciform building of about 1300; the nave and aisles survive from this period. In 1572 the steeple was struck by lightning and set on fire, and in 1686 the tower collapsed, bringing down the whole east end. This was never rebuilt; instead, in the eighteenth century, the present little apsidal chancel was built where the old tower once stood, and the massively buttressed and pinnacled tower was built in the south-east corner.

Wye was the birthplace, in 1640, of Mrs Aphra Behn, the Mata Hari of Restoration England, who spied for Charles II on the Continent, and had a second career as the first woman to earn a living as a playwright and novelist. Her best-known novel was *Oroonoko, or the History of the Royal Slave*, published in 1688, the year before she died. Virginia Woolf praised her for her 'plebeian virtues of humour, vitality and courage'.

Wye College has now expanded far beyond its medieval beginnings at the corner of the churchyard. It was founded in 1447 by Cardinal John Kempe, who was in his time Lord Chancellor to Henry VI, Bishop of Rochester, Chichester and London, and Archbishop of York and Canterbury. At the Reformation the college for secular priests was disbanded, but Kempe's grammar school survived until 1893, when the buildings were turned into an agricultural college for the south-east, and later into the agricultural branch of London University, including a 720-acre farm.

The college has a museum at the village of **Brook**, three miles outside Wye. A vast medieval barn houses a collection of every sort of farming bygone, from carts and ploughs to a land-measuring wheel that turns three hundred times per mile. An oasthouse at the back has smaller exhibits like sickles and bird scarers. Brook, in a fine open situation below the downs, gets its name from the stream that runs along the edge of the road. The Norman church, next door to the museum, has an enormously wide, square west tower; apart from the windows, the whole building has remained unaltered since early Norman times. Above the tower arch two windows, from a chapel or priest's room in the tower, look down into the nave. There are remains of medieval painting right along the south wall, and in the chancel are scenes from the life of Christ, set in painted roundels to separate them from one another.

Ashford stands at the hub of all the communications of central Kent. From it roads radiate in six different directions and railways in five; and it is now connected firmly to Europe as the site of the Ashford International Station – the half-way stop for Eurostar trains running between Waterloo and France. It is expanding fast, and swallowing up outlying places in a sea of industry and housing estates; yet it still has a recognizably Georgian town centre, isolated by a ring road in a sea of swirling traffic and dwarfed to some extent by hulking new office buildings. This centre stands on a spur of high ground above the Great Stour, and is separated from most of the later suburbs by the river and its tributary streams.

The **High Street**, at the heart of old Ashford, is very much the main street of a country town, with some good Georgian buildings left, like the three-storey redbrick County Hotel. Half way down is the little rabbit warren of gabled shops called Middle Row, all overhangs and unexpected corners. At one end of the High Street is Castle Street, worth the short stroll to have a look at the green-painted First World War tank preserved there as a memorial; and at the other end East Hill, dropping steeply down to the river, has some of the best Georgian houses in the town. These are incorporated into Ashford girls' public school, whose main buildings take up much of the north side of the hill.

Away from the High Street, on the south side behind Middle Row, is the calm of the churchyard, surrounded on all sides by good brick or white-painted houses. On the west side is the single tall brick gable of the old grammar school, dated 1635. The **Church**'s soaring tower, with a gilt-vaned pinnacle at each corner, is a landmark for miles around; it formed part of a major rebuilding scheme for the church begun and financed by Sir John Fogge about 1470. Fogge was a leading Kentish landowner, who served in Parliament and became Treasurer of the Royal Household to Edward IV. After weathering the storms of Richard III's reign he held office under Henry VII, and died in 1490. His huge stone table tomb is in the chancel, north of the altar. Fogge's additions were the final stages of an overall reconstruction that had been going on for well over a century. Nave and aisles are wide, with galleries round all three sides. The elaborate nave ceiling, panelled and embossed, is dated 1638. Even finer is the ceiling below the tower at the crossing, part of the original Fogge decorative scheme of the 1470s, painted in grey and black, with gold rosettes.

In the south transept are the three enormous effigied tombs of Sir Thomas Smythe and two of his sons. Smythe, who died in 1591, is carved reading a book. Known as 'Customer' Smythe because he was in charge of the Port of London customs, he was a man of great wealth; under the tax-farming system of the day he paid the Queen an annual rent of £30,000 for the customs and no doubt made a handsome profit. The Latin inscription commends him for his 'singular liberality towards those of the higher rank and love for the trading interests'. In short, a Customer who was always right. Also in the transept is a superb Charles II royal arms, put up in 1660.

After centuries of somnolence as an agricultural centre, Ashford was dragged into the industrial world with the coming of the railways in the 1840s. The locomotive works down Newtown Road were opened in 1847 and remained one of British Rail's chief construction and maintenance centres until they closed down in 1981.

The Templer Barracks, on the north-western edge of the town, is the home of the **Intelligence Corps Museum** (visits by appointment only). The displays cover four centuries of British military intelligence, from the wily Sir Francis Walsingham, head of Queen Elizabeth I's intelligence-gathering network, to 1960s operations in Aden and the Far East.

East of the town a string of villages leads you into the open country. **Willesborough**, now embedded in Ashford, has a church with a 'candle-snuffer' spire like the one at Upchurch; **Sevington** is hardly more than a hamlet, with an isolated medieval church; while

Mersham (pronounced Merzam) is a good deal larger. Its church, down a cul-de-sac, has a spectacular west window, with a row of thirteen lights along the bottom, presumably for glass depicting the apostles with Christ in the larger central panel. It is full of Knatchbull tablets and memorials. The epitaph on the tomb of Lady Bridget Knatchbull (died 1625) in the chancel begins with an unforgettable couplet:

The dust closed up within this Marble Shrine
Was (when it breath'd) a Blossome feminine.

A mile west of the town, off the A20, is **Godinton House**, set comfortably in a hollow, with topiary yew hedges between the house and the noble trees of the park. The greatest of these, on the side opposite the entrance front, was the Domesday Oak, which split asunder and collapsed on September 3, 1939, while Neville Chamberlain was making his broadcast announcing war with Germany. The outer appearance of Godinton, with its rounded Dutch-style gables, and stone mullions setting off the mellow brickwork, is due to Captain Nicholas Toke, who remodelled the old house in 1628 – at least, that is the date on the rainwater heads. The fifteenth-century Great Hall, spanned by an enormous chestnut tiebeam, is still medieval in character, despite the plaster ceiling put in by the Captain, and the flamboyant chimneypiece surmounted by a Lely portrait of James, Duke of York, later James II, as Lord High Admiral. The hall's rich panelling is a foretaste of the incredible wood-carving found elsewhere in Godinton. The most sumptuous is on the staircase, which is lit partly by fretted arcades opening from the Great Hall.

Upstairs the Captain left a permanent record of his military leanings in the carving and panelling of the Great Chamber, the showpiece of Godinton. Below the ceiling a carved wooden frieze depicts in a series of panels the complexities of musket and pike drill, carried out by little soldiers in the padded trunk-hose of Queen Elizabeth's reign. Hasted called these militiamen 'a very droll exhibition', as indeed they are; but they are of historical interest as well, and the pikemen's drill is still performed by the Honourable Artillery Company today. Above the fireplace the frieze shows the Captain's non-military interests – hunting, pig-sticking and bear-baiting. Captain Nicholas lived on until 1680; he survived five wives and died at the age of ninety-three while on his way to London to look for a sixth. He is buried in the church at Great Chart (see below).

Downstairs, the Priest's Room, opening off the hall, may have been the chapel of the medieval house. Fittingly, it has a carved confessional box, turned into a cupboard. This room was used by the Victorian artist R. B. Martineau as the background for his painting *The Last Day in the Old Home*, now in the Tate Gallery.

Godinton has fine formal gardens laid out in the eighteenth century, contrasting with a woodland garden which in spring is a mass of daffodils and other flowers.

West of Godinton you can make your way from village to village by the back roads. **Hothfield** has a long, low thirteenth-century church, down a cul-de-sac and beside a vast kitchen-garden wall that is about all that is left of Hothfield Place, apart from a fine park. The church was struck by lightning and largely burned to the ground in 1598, and five years later it was rebuilt by Sir John Tufton – hence the very late Perpendicular windows which flood it with light. The Tufton tomb, between the chancel and the north chapel, is a magnificently pompous object, made of different kinds of marble. Sir John, who died in 1624, 'lived peacefully in this country and was allwayes ready and well furnished to defend ye same'. So the inscription runs.

On the other side of the Great Stour from Hothfield a high ridge gives the villages built along it magnificent views across the plain of the Beult to the south. **Pluckley** owes much of the consistency of its appearance to the whim of a nineteenth-century squire, Sir Edward Cholmeley Dering, who had every window in the village altered, giving them rounded lights under an overall exterior arch, in the curious belief that this shape would bring luck. Outer arches and window frames are all white-painted, which makes Pluckley's houses look as though they have their eyebrows permanently raised in surprise. You can see similar windows at Little Chart. Pluckley is a ghost-hunter's paradise: its apparitions include a lady of the Dering family who flits about the churchyard looking for her unbaptized child; a gypsy woman who burnt to death when a spark from her pipe set fire to her gin-sodden shawl; and a labourer at the local brickworks who fell into the knives of a mixing-trough for clay. In the early 1990s the village appeared on millions of television screens as the setting for the series *The Darling Buds of May*, based on H.E. Bates's novels.

Egerton is an unassuming village, dwarfed by the tall Perpendicular west tower of the church. Inside, a lofty arch runs the full width of the tower. The most noticeable fitting is the enormous multi-branched eighteenth-century chandelier, hanging from a cherub's head. The fifteenth-century octagonal font is carved with symbols of the evangelists; and an armorial wooden memorial panel to Henry Hussey (died 1694) makes a fine splash of colour by the door. The modern altar rail is supported by figures of Becket, Augustine and other saints.

There is no village at all at **Boughton Malherbe** – only an austere stone church superbly placed above the valley, and backed by dour farm buildings. The chancel is raised high, five steps above the nave; on the walls and floor are brasses to the Wotton family, and in a recess three domesticated-looking marble lions, which once formed part of a monument. The farmhouse is all that is left of the Elizabethan mansion of the Wotton family, the birthplace in 1568 of Sir Henry Wotton, a diplomat who described an ambassador as 'an honest man sent to lie abroad for the good of his country', and a poet best known for the lines:

> *How happy is he born and taught*
> *That serveth not another's will,*
> *Whose armour is his honest thought,*
> *And simple truth his utmost skill.*

Harrietsham, two miles to the north, is a good tilehung and weatherboarded village cut in two by the A20. There are fine Georgian houses in the southern part; but best of all are the low brick almshouses, built originally for Mark Quested, of the Fishmongers' Company, in 1642 and rebuilt in 1770. A stream fed from a reed-lined lake flows through the northern half of the village. The grey-brown stone church, battlemented all round, is a little north of the village, near the Pilgrims' Way; it has a tall Perpendicular west tower and an Early English chancel. It is worth going round the back of the church to see the massive square tower, possibly Saxon, on the north side. The sundial above the porch, put up in 1853, is accurate to within five minutes.

Lenham is bypassed by the A20 and can enjoy being a beauty spot – though it is only half a mile from the M20, and dozens of massive container lorries park nearby at an enormous freight depot. The square is a fine mixture of building styles from medieval to Georgian. At one corner is the Saxon Pharmacy, named after a Saxon grave discovered outside in the course of restoration work.

The Pharmacy is part of a typical Wealden timber-framed house, with a tall medieval window, and a kingpost roof rising above the glowing glass bottles and blue drug jars of an old-style chemist's shop. It was restored from dereliction in the 1940s by Robert H. Goodsall, an erudite delver into the byroads of Kent history, who had previously bought and restored Stede Hill, above Harrietsham. The long white Dog and Bear inn has a brilliant royal arms over the door, to commemorate Queen Anne's stay there. Another small square forms a kind of antechamber to the churchyard; on one side is a long tiled barn, with a pond in front and a farmhouse dated 1672 in the background.

The original church was maliciously burnt down in 1297, and though the incendiarists were excommunicated by the Archbishop they were never discovered. The present building consists of nave and north aisle, with a good Perpendicular west tower. It still has its medieval stone altar slab, which was let into the floor and thus survived the destruction of the Reformation. North of the altar is the tombstone to the prolific Mary Honywood, who died in 1620 aged ninety-two, leaving behind her a village-sized population of 367 descendants – sixteen children, 114 grandchildren, 228 great-grandchildren and nine great-great-grandchildren.

The magnificent Perpendicular church tower of **Charing** is a great local landmark. Fortunately for this delightful little town, the main roads to Ashford and Canterbury split to the west of it and the traffic passes by on either side, leaving the High Street to wander gently uphill in peace. Charing's prosperity had two causes: it lies by the Pilgrims' Way, and so its guesthouses were always put to good use; and it had belonged to Canterbury since Saxon times. The Archbishop's Palace (in fact the manor house), where Henry VIII was entertained by Archbishop Warham in 1520 on his way to the Field of the Cloth of Gold, is beside the road down to the church. The ivy-covered remains of the gatehouse are still standing, and across the courtyard a Tudor brick farmhouse dated 1586 has been built among the ruins of the palace's medieval stonework. The huge barn was once the banqueting hall.

The church itself is a good deal older than the tower; it has no aisles but consists of a nave and transepts, with windows ranging from Early English lancets to the latest of square Perpendicular shapes. The arch from tower to nave is enormously high and graceful. The elaborately carved and painted roofbeams were put in after a fire that destroyed all the woodwork in 1590, caused, says a contemporary account, 'by means of a birding-piece discharged by one Mr Dios, which fired in the shingles, the day being extreme hot and the same shingles very dry'. The church guide suggests that the Spanish nature of the roofbeams may be due to Mr Dios making amends for the damage he had caused. Like Ashurst, Sussex (see p. 332), Charing church has an eighteenth-century vamping horn, in its original case (kept in the vestry). It still makes a most efficient megaphone.

Behind the church is the medieval vicarage. A plaque attached to the ancient yew tree nearby has given two centuries of vicars something to think about on their journeys past the church. Dated 1772, it reads: 'O Vicar, who ever thou art, reflect and profit by the reflexion how small the distance and perhaps quick the transition from yon house thou inhabitest to the caverns of the Dead.'

The High Street provides a good amble of ten minutes or so – unpretentious brick or black-and-white timbering, broken here and there by grander places like the gabled Peirce House set back a little from the road, or the fine Georgian Wakeley and Ludwell Houses.

From Charing a lane full of right-angled kinks brings you to **Westwell**, a pretty little village miles from anywhere. The church is a curious muddle from outside, cement-rendered, with brick buttresses and a broach spire awkwardly perched on the narrow tower. But inside it is a wonderful forest of stone columns, alternately round and octagonal in the arcades, leading to a stone-vaulted Early English chancel, with an additional pair of columns in the chancel arch to take the weight of the vaulting. In the chancel are fine sedilia, and a memorial to the infant son of R. H. Barham, author of the *Ingoldsby Legends*, who was curate here from 1814 to 1817. **Eastwell** is even more remote – a ruined church right by the Pilgrims' Way, with nothing left except the tower at the edge of a romantic lily-covered lake. **Eastwell Park**'s monstrous flint and stone gatehouse, built in the 1840s, is an unforgettable sight as you leave Ashford on the A251. The huge grey stone Victorian house is now a hotel.

The broad green of **Boughton Lees** is a good mile from the fortress-like church of **Boughton Aluph**. The Saxon village was known as Boctun, and in the thirteenth century the manor belonged to the sonorously named Alulphus of Boctune – hence the present name. He is thought to have replaced the Saxon church by a building of his own; this was in turn greatly enlarged and adapted in the fourteenth century by Sir Thomas de Aldon, King's Yeoman to

Edward III. The armorial glass of the Black Prince and other members of Edward III's family dates from his time. The church has undergone heavy restoration after incendiary bomb damage in 1940 and later weather deterioration. Its bare interior is acoustically perfect for music; when I went there on one occasion an early-music group was recording Renaissance polyphony, and the strands of sound formed an aural reflection of the intricacies of the stonework. At the back of the church is a little brick porch with a Tudor fire-place, traditionally said to have been adapted for travellers along the Pilgrims' Way, who would rest there before the final stage of the journey to Canterbury. It makes a nice fancy to imagine the weary pilgrims warming their hands in front of a blazing fire before pressing on through the robber-infested woods above Godmersham; though as both porch and fireplace look Elizabethan if not later, it may be only a fancy.

South-west of Ashford, the Tenterden road (A28) brings you first to **Great Chart**, a good solid Kentish village. Its grey stone church, a little way out of the village, stands out strikingly on the skyline. In Saxon times Great Chart was far larger than it is today, but it was burnt to the ground by the war-party of Danes who established themselves at Appledore in 893; the destruction of Great Chart led to the early growth of Ashford. At the entrance to the churchyard is a small white-painted timber-framed building, with widely overhanging eaves – the fifteenth-century predecessor of countless modern bungalows. It may have been built for a chantry priest, or as an office for church business.

The church itself dates mainly from the fourteenth century, when a small Norman church was rebuilt; finally, after a fire in the mid fifteenth century, there was a major restoration in which the Perpendicular aisle windows and clerestory were added. The man responsible for the building's ultimate grandeur was James Goldwell, who was rector at the time. He is portrayed in the stained window at the east end of the south chapel; much of it is the original fifteenth-century glass. In 1472 he became Bishop of Norwich, where he built the cathedral's magnificent spire. In the north chapel is a large altar tomb to his parents, William and Avice Goldwell, who died within a month of each other in 1485. In the same chapel are brasses to members of the Toke family, who lived at Godinton nearby (see above): two sixteenth-century brasses to John Toke and his son, also called John; and a very late brass to the much-married Captain Nicholas Toke, who died in 1680 and is shown in a full suit of armour – the latest brass on which such armour appears.

Bethersden, four miles towards Tenterden, was famous in the Middle Ages for its marble – 'thin limestone', S.W.Wooldridge tells us in his book *The Weald*, 'made of the shells of the fresh-water snail-like *Paludrina*'. It was used as embellishment in Canterbury and Rochester Cathedrals, as well as numerous smaller churches. Bethersden is a typical Wealden village, with plenty of good weatherboarded houses, built tidily around an oval arrangement of roads. The church is a big Perpendicular building, with tall battlemented west tower and an uncomplicated interior. A modern stained-glass window in the south chapel shows Bethersden's farming concerns of cabbages, chickens and oasthouses.

11

Maidstone and District

FOR A COUNTY town, **Maidstone** is a haphazard, incoherent place. This is due partly to its plan, as it is bisected by the Medway, and thus has not grown in a unified way; and partly to its history as a small market town. The old town lies east of the river, on either side of the High Street which runs uphill from the twin bridges. Maidstone's eighteenth-century Town Hall stands on an island site at the top of the High Street, right in the centre of everything; while the bulky County Hall from which Kent's affairs are run is out of the main swim, along the road to Chatham. The river that severs Maidstone is the most attractive feature of the town, especially upstream from the two bridges, where you can stroll along the riverside walk below the stone walls of the medieval Archbishop's Palace, looking across the water to the hulking County Courts building and the sprawling Lockmeadow market building next to it. The whole riverside is eventually due to be improved by Millennium funding.

Maidstone pushes its prehistory back a hundred million years or so, when iguanodons plodded about the shores of the great Wealden lake; an unlikely-sounding 'iguanodon proper collared gules' appears on the town's coat-of-arms. The Medway valley was a natural site for Stone Age settlement. Stone implements are constantly being found there, and the area was an important one for Neolithic burials. In spite of Maidstone's commanding position at the upper end of the Medway gap in the North Downs, the Romans do not seem to have built any kind of township there, though a major highway ran through it, giving access to the Weald. Even in Norman times it was little more than a manor and associated farming community.

Its prosperity began in the late Middle Ages, when it became the focus for Wealden agriculture and an industrial centre. Ragstone

A map for this chapter will be found on pp.150-151

quarried nearby was shipped down the Medway for such buildings as Hampton Court and Eton College, and was also shaped into cannon balls; fuller's earth was both exported and used for Maidstone's own cloth industry; and local sand was used by glassmaking pioneers. The seventeenth century saw the start of Maidstone's main industries of papermaking and brewing. Maidstone was the scene of a major Parliamentary victory in 1648, when Fairfax defeated the Royalist forces under Lord Norwich in a battle which was fought right up through the streets of the town and ended at midnight after five hours of conflict.

The oldest buildings in Maidstone are in the cluster by the Medway south of the High Street. Most prominent is the **Archbishop's Palace**, which consists of a stone Elizabethan E-shaped front on a massively beamed medieval building; the bulk of it was moved here from Wrotham (see below). It is now owned by the Corporation. The ground floor contains the registry office, while one of the upper rooms – the medieval solar – is now a restaurant with a fine view across the Medway. The palace gatehouse has been turned into Maidstone's tourist information centre, and the Master's House next door is the headquarters of the Kent Music School, which has been running the county's music teaching for the past fifty years. Near the palace a wide flight of stairs leads down from the gardens to the River Len, a tributary of the Medway, with a medieval bridge cowering in the darkness below the concrete span of Mill Street.

Across Mill Street is a long low stone building, with external staircase, once thought to have been a tithe barn, but now called with more probability the Archbishop's Stables. It houses the **Tyrwhitt-Drake Museum of Carriages**, crammed with painted and polished triumphs of the carriage-maker's art, from an Italian gig of about 1670 which perched its driver among a riot of carved wooden dragons and centaurs, to the sober blue and black landau still used by the Mayor in Maidstone's annual carnival. A comfortable-looking travelling coach has a sad story attached. It was built at great expense for the Earl of Moray's honeymoon, in about 1840, but the girl called off the wedding, and the disappointed earl shut the coach away in his coach house for good, and shot the six white horses that were to have hauled it.

The **Parish Church** (usually closed) is just upstream from the palace. It was built by Archbishop Courtenay at the end of the fourteenth century, and is an enormously wide Perpendicular building, with spacious aisles and narrow chapels on either side of the chancel, and sumptuously ornate roof beams. There was originally a spire, which rose nearly a hundred feet above the tower; it was destroyed by lightning in the eighteenth century. The north aisle is the regimental chapel of the Royal West Kents, and is hung with tattered banners. Near the tower door is a tablet to Laurence Washington, related to an ancestor of George Washington, chiefly interesting for the Stars and Stripes appearing on the family arms. William Shipley, founder of the Royal Society of Arts, lived in the tall three-storeyed Knightrider House in nearby Knightrider Street.

Maidstone is not a comfortable town to wander about in, as much of it has been turned into a one-way nightmare of swirling traffic. Fortunately a group of small central streets has been pedestrianised, including Gabriel's Hill, which has some half-timbered or weatherboarded houses, and Bank Street, which has one notable house, decorated with flamboyant pargetting (painted plasterwork) dated 1611. In the High Street is the dignified eighteenth-century town hall, and below it a cannon captured at Sebastopol points down the hill towards the Medway. North of the High Street is Earl Street, with the medieval Brotherhood Hall, which belonged first to the Corpus Christi Fraternity, then to the grammar school, and at present appears to be in limbo. Higher up is the large white house of Andrew Broughton, Mayor of Maidstone during the Civil War, a Roundhead who read out the death sentence on Charles I. Though a regicide, he survived the return of Charles II, and lived on until 1688.

Maidstone Museum is in St Faith's Street, opposite some handsome almshouses of 1700. The actual museum building, Chillington Manor, is worth more than a passing look; it is an E-shaped redbrick Elizabethan manor house, with long gallery and bewildering staircases, and gives the museum authorities all sorts of interesting rooms and passageways to play around with. The collections naturally concentrate on Kent, with displays beginning in the Palaeolithic age, including stone implements collected by Benjamin Harrison, the archaeologist-shopkeeper from Ightham. The museum has portraits of Kent writers and their families, like the early nineteenth-century essayist William Hazlitt (Maidstone's theatre is named after him), and Edward Hasted, the eighteenth-century historian of Kent; and the museum of the Royal West Kents, full of uniforms, pistols, medals and trophies. Its international collections include Japanese and Islamic art, and there are also natural history displays from Kent and further afield. A fascinating curiosity is the row of medieval 'acoustic jars', which came from

Leeds church (see below). Made of clay, they were placed at the side of the church to increase the resonance of the chanting during services.

Seven major roads converge at Maidstone, and the town is spreading rapidly out along all of them. At the south end of Sandling Road (which becomes the Chatham Road) are the County Hall buildings, with a grandiose pedimented front facing the roundabout and a white crescent stretching behind. Most of the square island on which the County Hall stands is taken up by Maidstone Prison, of which nothing can be seen but a blind white stone wall. Off the Sittingbourne Road is Penenden Heath, now a public open space, where in Saxon and later times the shire court was held, chosen for its central position in Kent; it was also used for public executions.

Maidstone's finest open space is **Mote Park**, south of the Ashford Road. The white eighteenth-century Mote House stands on a rise overlooking a large artificial lake, used for boating, formed by widening the River Len. Behind a wall in Mote Park is the Turkey Mill, converted from fulling to papermaking by James Whatman in 1739, and the origin of 'Whatman' and 'Turkey Mill' first-class papers. The main entrance is under redbrick railway arches on the Ashford Road.

Maidstone has no castle of its own, except for **Allington Castle** (not open), built on a bend in the Medway half way between Maidstone and Aylesford. It is a comfortable place, in spite of its thick stone walls, battlements and arrow slits, and stands in a peaceful setting of lawns and trees. In 1492 it was bought by Sir Henry Wyatt, who restored it, built a Tudor range with a long gallery right across the medieval courtyard, and settled down to a life of prosperous entertainment. In the time of Richard III he was imprisoned in the Tower and is said to have been racked in the presence of the king. The brown pigeons that flutter about the castle may be descended from birds brought back from the Near East by Sir Thomas Wyatt, Sir Henry's son. According to legend, during his imprisonment Sir Henry was kept alive by a cat which brought a pigeon to his cell every morning, and Sir Thomas introduced the brown birds as a living reminder of his father's sufferings.

Sir Thomas Wyatt (often called the Elder, to distinguish him from his son, also Sir Thomas) was born at Allington in 1503. He was the archetype of the Tudor courtier – diplomat, musician, linguist, jouster and poet, who introduced the Italian sonnet into England. He died in 1542, from a fever caught while on his way to the West

Country to meet the ambassadors of the Emperor Charles V. Sir Thomas Wyatt the Younger's life was a brief chronicle of disaster. Born in 1521, he succeeded to his father's Kent properties; but on the accession of Queen Mary in 1553 feared for the estates acquired at the Dissolution and led the men of Kent in revolt, with the object of replacing Mary by the Protestant Lady Jane Grey. He had some success at first, including the bombardment of Cooling Castle, but his defeat was inevitable, and he was captured and executed in 1554.

With the downfall of the Wyatts Allington fell into neglect. When Lord Conway bought it in 1905 it was virtually a ruin; he spent a quarter of a century and £70,000 on its restoration, and his signature is the statue of St Martin on horseback, set in a niche above the courtyard.

You can get a perfect view of Allington Castle – spoilt to some extent by rows of houses on the slopes behind – from the **Museum of Kent Life** on the other side of the Medway. Hemmed in between the quiet river and the headlong traffic of the M20, this imaginative open-air museum is a salvage operation for traditional Kentish farming methods, animals, arable and fruit crops. Hops are grown here by the sixteenth-century method of planting them on low mounds and letting them grow up clusters of three hop-poles per mound; and by the later and still current technique of an overhead framework of wire, with the hops growing up radiating networks of string. Kent's hop-gardens are under threat both from the Common Market's distaste for English-grown hops, said to be too bitter for our cross-Channel neighbours, and from imports coming from as far afield as Japan. But as you drive around Kent you will still see plenty of hopfields about – the perfect Kent calendar, from the first green climbing shoots in May, to the heavy clusters up the strings and over the wires at the summer's end.

Aylesford is the home of a vast paper works (successor to a mill founded in the seventeenth century), and of all the small towns in Kent must be the one least adapted by its layout to heavy modern traffic. For years the graceful five-arched medieval bridge over the Medway was shaken by heavy lorries; but fortunately this has now been syphoned off by a new bridge a little way to the east.

The **Church** stands commandingly above the bridge; it has a square tower with a Norman base, and a pair of naves of equal size, built in the early fifteenth century. High on the chancel walls are swords, helmets and gauntlets, the funeral armour of the Colepeppers and other local magnates. The sober tomb of Sir Thomas Colepepper (died in 1604) is overshadowed by the pompous arrogance of the memorial to Sir John Banks, who died in 1699. He stands in full-bottomed wig on one side of an urn, with his wife on the other; at the foot lies their son Caleb Banks.

Sir John lived at **The Friars**, beside the river, and Pepys has left a lively description of a visit to Aylesford in March 1669 to see him on Admiralty business, though Banks was away. 'A mighty cold and windy but clear day, and had the pleasure of seeing the Medway running, winding up and down mightily, and a very fine country.' Pepys found The Friars 'mighty finely placed by the river; and he keeps the grounds about it, and the walls and the house, very handsome'. Very handsome it still is, back in the hands of its original occupants, the Carmelite friars, who built themselves a priory in 1242, were expelled by Thomas Cromwell in 1538, and returned four centuries later in 1949.

Sir John Banks did a great deal to it in the seventeenth century; but most of its present appearance is due to restoration work on the old buildings and the building of new shrine chapels by the Carmelites. The centre of the complex is now an arcaded shrine, with seating in the open air for a large congregation of pilgrims. Off the main shrine, which is on the site of the medieval monastic church, are a number of smaller shrines, remarkable for ceramics by Adam Kossowski, a Polish artist who throughout the 1950s and '60s worked steadily at Aylesford like some medieval illuminator, taking concentration camp heroes as well as biblical themes as materials for his inspiration. He died in 1986, and is buried at The Friars. Seen from the other side of the Medway, The Friars appears as a harmonious range of gables, tiled roofs and stone walls, and would not seem alien to the medieval traveller, arriving footsore in the evening from the Pilgrims' Way.

From Aylesford you can get to Rochester along the still-countrified eastern bank of the Medway; though the villages – Eccles, Burham and Wouldham – have little to offer, apart from **Wouldham** church. This has a rough-hewn effect, with the chancel walls leaning alarmingly outwards. Below the west window of the south aisle are two cannon balls said to be from the *Victory*, and just outside the church is the grave of Walter Burke, purser on the *Victory*, who stayed with Nelson after he was mortally wounded, and held him in his arms as he died. Burke himself died ten years later, aged seventy; which means that he must have been sixty at Trafalgar, well past the normal age of active service.

North-east of Aylesford, just off the A229 to Chatham, is **Kits Coty**, a Neolithic tomb of three large upright stones and a single huge horizontal, standing on an open slope of the downs and reached by a steep track with hedges joining to shut out the light overhead. At the foot of the hill is **Little Kits Coty**, or the Countless Stones, a much less impressive affair. The story goes that a local baker vowed to count the stones of Lower Kits Coty by placing a loaf on the top of each one, but every time he started, the devil knocked off the loaves and foiled the attempt.

At the foot of the downs a string of villages marks the line of the Pilgrims' Way. **Boxley** consists of little more than a church, a pub and a group of old houses. The church lies well back from the road, at the end of a long narrow green; a stone path points straight as an arrow from the church entrance to the pub door. In the Middle Ages Boxley was famous for its Cistercian **Abbey**, founded in 1146 by William of Ypres. What remains can best be seen from the minor road that runs parallel to the M20 half a mile south of Boxley village – broken, creeper-covered stone walls, with a redbrick house built inside them, and an enormous and magnificent tithe barn thought to be thirteenth-century.

Boxley Abbey owed its prominence to two miracle-working images. First and foremost was the Rood of Grace, a figure of Christ on the Cross, which Lambarde described as follows (spelling modernized). 'Compacted of wood, wire, paste and paper' it was 'able to bow down and lift up itself, to shake and stir the hands and feet, to nod the head, to roll the eyes, to wag the chaps, to bend the brows, and finally to represent to the eye both the proper motion of each member of the body.' In a darkened church, in an atmosphere of chanting and incense, this rood must surely have given the pilgrims their money's worth.

The other image was simpler – a statue of St Rumwold, the child saint (see Bonnington, p. 124), which could only be lifted from the ground by those of pure life. According to Lambarde, if a pilgrim had not offered them enough money the monks kept the statue on the ground by means of a pin running into a post, while if they were satisfied they lifted the statue themselves by a crank mechanism. As a result, 'chaste virgins and honest married matrons oftentimes went away with blushing faces, leaving (without cause) in the minds of the lookers-on great suspicion of unclean life and wanton behaviour; for fear of which note and villainy women stretched their purse strings'. Boxley was dissolved in 1538, and the rood was publicly burned in

St Paul's churchyard the following year. Perhaps St Rumwold is still somewhere among the abbey ruins, waiting for a lady archaeologist of blameless life to lift him up.

From Boxley eastwards the Pilgrims' Way can be driven along for several miles, though it is extremely narrow, needing the passing places provided at intervals. **Detling** has an unobtrusive church on its outskirts, with a sumptuous medieval lectern, thought to have been carved about 1340 and to have come from Boxley Abbey. The intricate design is made up of foliage, flowers, abstract patterning and animals, including an elephant with a howdah on its back. Beside the main road, on the downs high above Detling, is the Kent County agricultural showground.

In the quiet churchyard at **Thurnham** is the grave of Alfred Mynn, one of the fathers of Kent cricket, who died in 1861. The inscription says that 'four hundred persons have united to erect this tombstone, and to found in honour of a name so celebrated the Mynn Memorial Benevolent Institute for Kentish Cricketers'. With Victorian thoroughness the amount raised is specified – £121 10s. invested in India 5 per cent stock.

Hollingbourne is a long village rambling uphill from a stream, with some fine half-timbered houses by the flint and ragstone church. The road through Hollingbourne is used by heavy traffic on the way to Sittingbourne, and the village suffers accordingly.

Leeds Castle, across the M20 south of Hollingbourne, is unrivalled in Kent – some would say in the whole of Britain – for the grandeur of its buildings and the beauty of its setting. Built on two islands in a natural moat formed by the River Len, it was the favourite country retreat of the medieval queens of England. A Norman castle was built here at the beginning of the twelfth century by Robert de Crevecoeur. Under Edward I at the end of the next century it became a royal castle, and from his time date the walls and turrets whose bases rise sheer from the waters of the lake. The older building on the small island is called the Gloriette, the French for arbour or summerhouse, joined to the main island by a two-storey stone bridge, the Pons Gloriettae. The main building on the large island, though rebuilt as recently as 1822, fits in remarkably well with the spirit of the whole place, with its unadorned stone walls and battlements. Edward I's gatehouse still stands at the inner end of the bridge, and on the landward end are the ruined walls of a fortified mill and the barbican which guarded the approach in medieval times. The park, laid out in the eighteenth century, is a marvellous place to

Leeds Castle, which seems to float in the middle of its lake.

The ruined cloisters of the thirteenth-century Bayham Abbey

stroll in, with its giant horse chestnuts, oaks and beeches, and its fine turf shorn for the golf course. The reed-fringed lake is full of ornamental ducks, geese and gliding black swans.

In 1976 Leeds Castle was given in perpetuity to the nation by Olive, Lady Baillie, its last private owner. You can wander through Henry VIII's gargantuan banqueting hall, or revisit the Middle Ages in a suite of rooms laid out in the style of 1400, made ready for Henry V and his beloved Queen Kate. The castle is also used as an international conference centre, while in summer the park becomes the setting for classical music concerts, firework displays, and all kinds of cheerful events. If you want to know what the well-dressed dog was wearing in Queen Anne's time, it is worth taking a look at the unique dog-collar collection in the castle gatehouse. Leeds has one of the most challenging mazes in the country, planted in 1987. At its centre is an ingenious matching of Renaissance-inspired fantasy with modern technology – a shell-lined grotto, dominated by the huge water-gushing face of a god, with a rock-lined tunnel to lead you once more up into the light of day. Nearby is an aviary crammed with exotic birds.

The village of **Leeds** lies west of the park, straggling uphill from the church. This has one of the oddest towers in Kent: a squat thirteenth-century stronghold, which looks as though a giant fist has come down on a tower of normal proportions and flattened it out. Inside there is a finely traceried fifteenth-century rood screen right across the church; and on the outside of the north wall is a blocked-up window said to have belonged to an anchorite's cell – a tame hermit like an Indian holy man, who was kept at public expense because of the benefits arising from his spirituality.

In spite of its small size, **Otham**, on a back road west of Leeds, has more than its share of good half-timbered buildings. **Stoneacre** (National Trust) is a fine yeoman's house of about 1480; the great hall is lit by two-tiered windows and has an oak screen across one end, and the ceiling has a rare kingpost made of a cluster of four engaged shafts.

Bearsted, across the main road from Otham, is a growing Maidstone suburb, but still manages to keep an attractive unity of its own. Round the enormous village green are some really good half-timbered and Georgian houses, with a glimpse of tall oasts behind. The church stands on a hill at the end of a dogleg road and is not at all obvious from the village; it is remarkable for the stone beasts, including a lion with a paw raised and an eagle, that peer over the parapet of the Perpendicular tower like sinister watchmen.

West of the British Legion Village, the A20 takes you past the two Mallings, both a little way south of the road. The road to **East Malling**'s neat village centre runs past the trees of a leading fruit-growing research station. **West Malling** is far larger, and qualifies as a small town; it is a fine place to stroll about in, with a High Street that is unusually wide for this part of Kent, lined on either side by mainly Georgian houses. South of the town is **St Leonard's Tower** (English Heritage), a square eleventh-century building with arcaded windows, like a keep without a castle to go with it. It is ascribed to Gundulf of Rochester, the leading tower-builder of the region. The church, at the south end of the High Street, has a tall spindly spire on a sturdy medieval tower; apart from the chancel, the rest of it dates from a rebuilding in 1901.

At the bottom end of the High Street, Swan Street leads down to **St Mary's Abbey**, an enclosed community of Church of England Benedictine nuns. The medieval gatehouse (now a private dwelling) leads to a large open space, with a free-standing tower on the far side. This tower, with pyramidal pinnacles and Norman blind arcading, bears a strong resemblance to the west front of Rochester Cathedral, and must be a survival of Gundulf's Benedictine nunnery founded here in the 1080s. Behind the tower is the modern abbey.

West Malling airfield, along the road to Mereworth (see below), was one of the centres of fighter resistance in the Battle of Britain. It is now the site of housing estates, a business park and the offices of the Tonbridge and Malling Borough Council.

Offham's open triangular village green has a quintain in the middle, consisting of a white-painted upright with a centrally pivoted horizontal piece of wood on top. The quintain was originally used by knights practising for tournaments, but simple contraptions like this one were used at village merry-makings. The quintain in action had a target board attached at one end and a sack of sand suspended at the other. The competitor rode or ran at it, trying to hit the target with his lance; he might hit it squarely, miss it altogether, or not get out of the way in time and be struck on the back of the neck by the rotating sack.

North of West Malling, the main road along the west bank of the Medway (A228) to Rochester runs through an industrialized landscape of cement works and their belching chimneys. Near the M20 interchange are the ruins of **Leybourne Castle** – the bases of rounded towers, and an entrance gateway – with a 1930s house tacked on the front. Leybourne was the castle of Sir William de

175

Leybourne, friend of Edward II who visited him in 1286 and awarded him the title of '*Admiral de la Mer du Roy d'Angleterre*' – the first time an Englishman had been given the title of Admiral. A Victorian squire of Leybourne, Sir Joseph Hawley, won the Derby four times with horses trained there; he engaged Sir Arthur Blomfield to restore the church in 1874. The window-like opening in the chancel wall is the 'heart shrine' of Sir Roger de Leybourne; the left-hand of the two little stone caskets contains the embalmed heart of this famous crusader, who died about 1271.

Towards Rochester the terraces of **Snodland** and **Halling** (pronounced 'Hauling') are strung out like Yorkshire industrial villages. Until the 1980s they were made intolerable by cement lorries thundering by; but bypasses have now relieved them of most of their traffic. In Snodland's case, this has meant severing the old High Street and putting the new road in a deep cutting half way along it – a cure that is not much better than the disease. Snodland's stocky medieval church is built on a mound directly above the Medway, next door to a large paper-mill, and its classical station building might have come straight from France. In the sixteenth century William Lambarde, the great Kentish antiquarian, lived in Halling in the long-vanished Bishop's Palace beside the church-yard. Inside the patchwork-looking church, a naive monument commemorates his wife, Silvester or Sylvestre, who died in 1587, a fortnight after giving birth to twin sons, shown in a cradle beside her.

On this side of the Medway there are several villages below the downs, near the Pilgrims' Way though not actually on it. **Birling,** a mile north of Leybourne, consists largely of stone Victorian cottages with pinched-up gables. **Addington** is a rapidly expanding place, with a small green, and a remote church, built on a mound and hidden among tall trees. Two fifteenth-century chapels give the building an unusual T-shape. In the south chapel are some fine brasses, notably one on the wall to William Snayth (died 1409) and his wife.

Near **Trottiscliffe** (pronounced Troslif or Trosley, but never as spelt) is one of the finest Neolithic remains on the North Downs, the **Coldrum Stones** burial chamber. It consists of a chalk mound surmounted by a group of large stones, mainly fallen, a stone circle and a ditch round the outside. Looking eastward from the main group you can see for miles across the valley to the next spur of the downs in the distance – as nobly sited a burial place as a king could wish for. It is now a permanent memorial to Benjamin Harrison of Ightham.

Trottiscliffe church forms the centrepiece of a group of farm buildings and a big rectory, outside the residential sprawl of the village. It is worth looking at the outside of the west wall of the church, which was rebuilt in 1885 from flints meticulously cut square by a local craftsman. Inside is a case containing human and animal bones from Coldrum. Study of the bones has revealed a good deal about the physique of these ancestral Kentish Men. They were, says Ronald Jessup in his *South East England*, 'long-headed and short in stature, good-looking and of moderate muscular strength with wide feet free in movement; they had healthy teeth with an edge-to-edge bite; the aged suffered from rheumatism which was not helped by the constant squatting posture'.

High up on the other side of the Gravesend road is **Stansted**, the perfect downland hamlet, built on a switchback of hills, with a large village green in the valley, and an impeccable flint church, complete with giant yew tree outside the door. At the edge of the churchyard an art nouveau black granite memorial, surmounted by scroll-carrying angels, commemorates Sir Sydney Hedley Waterlow, one of the founders of the great Waterlow printing firm, who lived at Trosley Towers nearby. Born in 1822, he began printing in 1844 in partnership with his brothers, starting with £120 from their father. They made their fortunes from cornering the market in railway printing and stationery. Waterlow was a philanthropist as well as a businessman. As Lord Mayor of London in 1872, he was responsible for opening the Guildhall Library to the public.

Wrotham (pronounced Rootam) has a narrow High Street which widens out into a little square, with the church looming over the north side, the Tudor brick gables of Wrotham Place appearing above the wall opposite, and a cluster of pubs and back streets of cottages, some opening straight on to the pavement. The church is magnificent; its big fifteenth-century tower has an outside passage right under it, perhaps made for processions around the church, with a stone which may once have held a sanctuary ring granting safety to criminals who grasped it. Inside it is spacious, with wide aisles and some finely traceried windows; the east window was brought from St Alban's, Wood Street, in the City, and is thought to have been designed by Wren.

On the corner of White Hill, the old main road, is an inscription to Lt-Col. Shadwell, 'shot to the heart by a deserter' in 1799; there is a memorial to him in Maidstone church. Beyond is the Bull Hotel, an old coaching inn, and next door on the edge of the town (easily seen from the road) is what is left of the Old Palace, after most of it was carried off to Maidstone to make the Archbishop's Palace there.

The grandest house hereabouts, **Mereworth Castle** (pronounced Merryworth), five miles south-east of Wrotham, is not open to visitors. However, you can get a brief view of it through the main gates on the A26; and occasional glimpses as you approach it from the north. Mereworth, with its grey dome, orange walls and Ionic columned porticoes, is a complete Italian villa stuck down in the Kentish countryside. It was built in the 1720s for John Fane by Colen Campbell, one of the leaders of the Palladian revival, and is a direct copy of Palladio's Villa Rotonda at Vicenza. The two lodges are now on the opposite side of the road to the castle, as the road was shifted after they were built.

Unlike the castle, **Mereworth Church** can be seen. In its way it is as unusual as the castle: a hybrid of London churches, the main body with its huge overhanging eaves copied from St Paul's Covent Garden, and the west end crowned with a replica of the steeple of St Martin-in-the-Fields. There is also a semi-circular columned porch to the main entrance below the tower. John Fane (by this time Earl of Westmorland) built in here in the 1740s, after he had pulled down the medieval church near the castle. No one has ever dealt so high-handedly with their architectural neighbours as these Georgian grandees. The best thing about the church is a semi-circular lunette at the east end, glowing with golden sixteenth-century armorial glass.

Wateringbury, back towards Maidstone, is half way between a village and a small town. The main street has some good Georgian houses, and arcaded shops with slim cast-iron pillars. The church is reconstructed, slate-roofed and ugly; what it was once like can be seen from a drawing inside, dated 1852. Over the door is a unique object called a 'dumb borsholder' – a staff of office dating back to Saxon times, carried to the Court Moot and in use until about 1740. It has a spike at one end for breaking down the doors of suspected wrongdoers.

Wateringbury's most interesting character was Edward Greensted, parish clerk and schoolmaster at the end of the eighteenth century, and author of a local history. He has left a vivid description of the great storm of 19 August, 1763, when hailstones up to ten inches in diameter hurtled down on the houses, orchards and livestock of Kent. 'The storm over, how shocking was the prospect! Our houses flowing with water, scarcely a pane of glass to be seen, the roofs and walls of our houses shatter'd, the waters roaring in torrents down the streets, the surface of the earth covered with the prodigious hailstones and water, the corn, fruit and hops destroy'd, scarcely any saved.' Not surprisingly, it took the farmers years to recover.

Another place that suffered severely in the storm was **Nettlestead** church near by. This extraordinary church is nearly all window – a nave with enormous Perpendicular windows, tacked on to a simple thirteenth-century tower. The nave was built by Reginald de Pympe in the first half of the fifteenth century; he campaigned at Agincourt with Henry V, and it is thought that he saw in France what could be done with stained glass. There are six windows in the nave, and three in the chancel added about 1465 by John de Pympe. Several of the saints survive in softly coloured blue or red robes on an architectural background. The 1763 storm wrecked all the windows on the south side, but much of the shattered glass has since been cleverly replaced or restored. The painted and gilded memorials on either side of the chancel arch commemorate the two wives of Sir John Scott, an Elizabethan soldier. The Scotts took over Nettlestead Place from the de Pympes in the sixteenth century; the grey stone house, a product of successive rebuildings from the Middle Ages on, can be seen over the churchyard wall.

Yalding, where the Beult joins the Medway, is a place of boats, locks, islets and medieval bridges. The waters here are deceptively inviting on a hot day; but there are weirs and a lock, with 'danger of drowning' signs everywhere. The village runs uphill from the seven-arched Town Bridge – at 450ft Kent's longest medieval bridge – across the Beult. Big oasthouses stand right in the village, and the main street has the usual nice Kentish mixture of redbrick and weatherboarded houses. The church has a square tower, which looks strange, as it is without battlements, and even stranger because of an onion dome on its turret, like something strayed from Austria, made of lead and dated 1734. In one of the chancel windows is a small engraved panel by Laurence Whistler to the poet Edmund Blunden (1896–1974), who lived at Yalding; a verse from his poem *Forefathers* epitomises a vanished rural past, and could stand for any village of the Weald:

> *From this church they led their brides,*
> *From this church themselves were led*
> *Shoulder-high; on these waysides*
> *Sat to take their beer and bread.*
> *Names are gone – what men they were*
> *These their cottages declare.*

Downstream from Yalding, a superb medieval bridge, with no houses anywhere near, crosses the Medway between West Farleigh and Teston (pronounced 'Teeston').

East Barming's isolated church lies down a lane; the tower with its spindly spire is a landmark from the main road. There has been a lot of restoration, but the east end still keeps its three little arched Norman windows. The carved bench ends are thought by Newman to be German about 1300; he calls them 'very wild', and certainly Samson rending the lion and St George spearing the dragon (or St Michael the devil) are explosively energetic. The modern altar is well carved in traditional linenfold style.

The medieval bridge at **East Farleigh** was where General Fairfax crossed the Medway before taking Maidstone in 1648 (see above). Above the river, with its boats, locks and weirs, the shingled spire of the church stands out on the skyline.

A couple of miles away is **Loose**, on the southern outskirts of Maidstone – a secretive little place, tucked away in a valley off the A229. It is perched on a hillside and is full of the sound of running water, with a causewayed path running between two streams. The **Wool House** (National Trust) has long, low beamed rooms inside, and close vertical timbering on the walls outside. The stream that splashes down beside it still looks sparkling even in this age of pollution.

12

The Sevenoaks Ridge

STANDING HIGH ON the greensand ridge above the Darent valley, **Sevenoaks** is a breezy town, consisting mainly of successive generations of commuters' houses spreading north from the old town centre, and expanding into the area between the London road and the splendidly landscaped bypass. On the south it ends abruptly south of Sevenoaks School, where the grass and trees of Knole take over from the houses.

It seems likely that the town's name means exactly what it says – that in Saxon times a clump of seven oak trees made a good meeting-place in this heavily wooded area, and the name stuck. At any rate, belief in this origin was perpetuated in the 1950s, when seven young oaks were planted on the southern edge of the town. The trees (in a row, not a clump) are on the west side of the Tonbridge road, south of the White Hart; they are now about forty feet tall. The town was put on the map by Sir William Sevenoke or Sennocke, a foundling who rose to be Lord Mayor of London. Said to have been found in a hollow tree, or, less romantically, lying in the street, some time in the 1370s, he became an apprentice in the City, joined the Grocers' Company, and made a fortune. He endowed Sevenoaks School by his will in 1432, though it had been founded some years earlier; today's sober ragstone building, with almshouses on either side, was designed by Lord Burlington about 1724.

The tall Perpendicular church tower opposite is a great landmark; part of the building goes back to the thirteenth century, but it is much restored. Inside there are monuments to Sevenoaks' varied collection of notabilities: Lord Amherst, who captured Montreal and accepted the surrender of the French in 1760, at the end of the campaign in which Wolfe was killed; William Lambarde, author of the *Perambulation of Kent*; Dr Thomas Fuller, an eighteenth-century investigator of flea bites and eruptive fever. A tablet to John Donne records that the great love poet and Dean of St Paul's was rector here

from 1616 to 1631. The Sackvilles of Knole are not buried here but in the family mausoleum at Withyham.

Going north into the town from the church and school you pass any number of fine old buildings, among them The Chantry, a brick house with two projecting wings, built about 1700, and the Red House, the home of Dr Thomas Fuller and later of Francis Austen, the uncle of Jane. The old trading area of the town was built at the junction of the High Street and the London Road. The Old Market House is an 1840s building decorated with swags made of red tiling. Local JPs used to meet in its upper room to sentence malefactors, and it is now used as offices. Beyond is a little alley leading through a tunnel to The Shambles. Much of this warren of cobbled lanes and cottages has been knocked down and cleared right through to the High Street, but enough still remains to give an idea of the cramped conditions under which the ordinary townspeople lived and worked.

Farther down the High Street is Bligh's Hotel, built as a farm-house about 1600. In the eighteenth century it became known as Bedlam Farm, as it was used as a country home for mental patients from Bedlam Hospital in Moorfields. Nearby is the **Vine Cricket Ground**, the original home of Kent cricket. The earliest recorded match was played on the ground in 1734, when the home side of Kent defeated Sussex. The ground was given to the town by the cricket-loving third Duke of Dorset in 1773; in those days it was right in the country, with one or two houses to the north. It is a smallish and rather sloping pitch, with a tremendous view away to the North Downs. The cricket pavilion, built in 1850, is an elegant single-storey white wooden building, looking far more Regency than Victorian, with pediment and sash windows. During the great storm of 16 October, 1987, the Vine lost six of the seven splendid oak trees planted beside the ground in 1902 to commemorate the coronation of Edward VII.

On the town's northern outskirts, a chain of gravel pits near the A25 has been turned into the **Sevenoaks Wildfowl Reserve** – the perfect place to watch waterbirds from hides and footpaths, and to learn about their lives from the excellent visitor centre.

Though modern Sevenoaks is expanding northwards along the roads towards London and Dartford, its centre of gravity is still very much **Knole** (National Trust), on its southern side. If a house can be said to have a character, then Knole has more character than any other house in the two counties. It is often coupled with Penshurst nearby; but by comparison with Knole, Penshurst is a straight-forward, open house, with none of the twists and turns, the dark corners, the sense of mystery that give Knole its endless fascination. You can see Knole in the distance from the Tonbridge road; but when you approach it through the park it is hidden behind the tree-covered hills or knolls (on one of which the house stands, hence its name), until you round the last bend and the jumble of stone walls and turrets lies close before you.

Before going into the house, it is worth getting an idea of its scale and complexity by walking a short way on to the golf course, on the left-hand side as you stand facing the house. Over the high stone garden wall rise gables and oriel windows, and a bewildering series of stone towers and long tiled roofs; while through the gates set here and there at odd angles you catch glimpses of workshop yards and storage sheds.

Knole is intimately bound up with the history of the Sackville family, as the title of Victoria Sackville-West's lovingly detailed

Companion Guide to Kent and Sussex

chronicle, *Knole and the Sackvilles*, implies. Yet though the Sackvilles transformed the interior, adding the rich decoration, furnishings and pictures down the centuries, the external appearance is due to an earlier owner, Thomas Bourchier, Archbishop of Canterbury. Bourchier bought it in 1456 from Lord Saye and Sele, and turned it from a medieval muddle into the Oxford college-like appearance it has today. In Archbishop Cranmer's time Henry VIII coveted the palaces at Knole and Otford nearby, remarking to Cranmer that Otford was damp and would do for his retainers, but 'as for Knole, it standeth on a sound, perfect and wholesome ground; and if I should make abode here, as I surely mind to do now and then, I will live at Knole'. Naturally Cranmer complied (though this did not save him from being burnt at the stake by Henry's daughter Mary I); and Knole remained almost continually in royal hands from 1536, until in 1566 Queen Elizabeth gave it (subject to lease) to her cousin, Thomas Sackville. In 1603 Sackville bought the freehold, and from then on it was firmly in the Sackville family.

Whether by accident or medieval astrological design, Knole is linked to the passing of time; it is said to have seven courtyards corresponding to the days of the week, fifty-two staircases for the weeks of the year, and 365 rooms for the days of the year, no doubt involving some cheating with anterooms and lobbies. You go under the outer gateway into the Green Court, an austere stone quadrangle. Facing you is yet another gatehouse, which brings you into the Stone Court, at the heart of Knole. All the great staterooms lie behind or beside this court. Below the flagstones are huge reservoirs of water. The court carries reminders of the Knole Sackvilles: the initials T.D. (Thomas Dorset) and the date 1605 on the beautifully shaped lead water pipes; and the name Shelley's Tower for the square gate tower on the left looking back towards the entrance. ('Shelley' was the nearest the Knole retainers could get to the name of the third Duke's mistress Giannetta Baccelli, an Italian dancer he met while ambassador in Paris just before the French Revolution and kept in style at Knole.)

You go into the medieval Great Hall under a Jacobean colonnade surmounted by a Georgian balcony – a mingling of the centuries typical of Knole. The bulbously carved oak screen was put in by Thomas Sackville, who sat down to dinner on the low dais at the opposite end, surveying a small army ranging in importance from the chaplain to the scullery-maid. Sackville was created first Earl of Dorset in 1604; his portrait, painted about 1600, hangs in the hall.

184

He was a sober politician, Lord Treasurer under Elizabeth and James I, and died in harness at the Privy Council table in Whitehall in 1608. Knole was his passion: after getting full possession in 1603, he spent thousands of pounds on beautifying it, importing craftsmen from Italy to work on the magnificent carving and plasterwork. Behind the hall the Great Staircase – a Jacobean *tour de force* of heraldic carving and grisaille wall painting – leads to the galleries and state bedrooms. At the foot of the stairs is a life-size plaster nude of the seductive Giannetta Baccelli, which was banished to the attics when the third Duke brought a wife home to Knole. John Frederick Sackville preferred cricket to politics or diplomacy, though this did not prevent him from being sent as ambassador to France, a suitably frivolous envoy during the final frivolous days of the old regime. After his return from Paris in 1789 he sobered up, married, had a family, lost his good nature, and died only ten years later at the age of fifty-four.

At the top of the staircase is the Brown Gallery, the most typical gallery of Knole. The sombre room stretches into the distance, lined with a double row of portraits in identical frames; in the dusk of a late autumn day these rows of gloomy historical personages gaze down with hypnotic effect. Below the paintings stand rows of seventeenth-century chairs; even their brocade has been preserved in the uncorrupting timelessness of Knole.

In complete contrast are the small rooms opening off the end of the gallery, where Lady Betty Germain, an eighteenth-century friend of the Dorsets, lived for forty years, engaged in needlework, letter-writing, and making pot-pourri to sweeten the air of Knole (you can still find bowls of it here and there, made to her recipe). On the other side of the gallery is the Spangle Bedroom, whose giant four-poster once sparkled with sequins, now turned black with age; this great bed is challenged by the huge green-velvet-hung four-poster in the Venetian Ambassador's Bedroom, across the Leicester Gallery. The focus of interest in a small room is the original drop-end Knole sofa, the Jacobean original of countless modern settees.

All these rooms are on the east side of the house. Another vast suite opens off the top of the staircase, leading along the south or garden front towards the west front of the house. The huge ballroom was decorated by Thomas Sackville with a sumptuous frieze of gryphons, mermaids and monsters; below are portraits of the Sackvilles, ending, as did the direct line, with the young fourth Duke of Dorset, killed in a hunting accident in 1815, soon after his twenty-first birthday.

The Reynolds Room takes its name from the portraits by Sir Joshua that line the walls. Among them is a delightful painting of the third Duke's Chinese pageboy, Wang-y-Tong, who was taught at Sevenoaks School across the park, and was called Warnoton, as the locals could not pronounce his name. The last and most formal of the galleries is the Cartoon Gallery, so called because one long wall is covered with dull copies of the huge paintings by Raphael done for a series of tapestries on the lives of Saints Peter and Paul. And finally comes the grandest of all the bedrooms, the King's Bedroom, reputedly prepared for James I, with a tall four-poster crowned with ostrich plumes. This room houses the extraordinary silver furniture – everyday objects like mirrors and tables, transmuted to a degree beyond vulgarity by a heavy silver overlay, and teased by the silversmith's art into a riot of swirling ornamentation.

Though part of Knole is still occupied by the Sackville family and life goes on there, the vast house gives off a feeling of time transfixed that is almost palpable. A return to the broad daylight of the park breaks the spell; yet behind those grey walls the ghosts of Knole linger on, staring down from the walls on to the sombre opulence that they created, and we can wonder at.

The park that surrounds the house suffered terribly in the great storm of October 1987. Knole's herd of deer pick their way among the huge trunks and broken branches that still lie on the ground where they fell, and though 200,000 new trees have been planted and are beginning to take the place of the shattered giants, it will need decades of growth before the park is restored to anything like its former glory.

Seal is the first largish village on the main road east from Sevenoaks, notable for Old Seal House, a handsome half-timbered building, now shops and offices, which stands at the central crossroads. Seal church, begun in the thirteenth century, has a fine Perpendicular tower. A little statue of St Peter, complete with keys, stands in a niche over the entrance door. Inside is the bewigged stone head of Lord Camden, Attorney-General and Lord High Chancellor in the reign of George III, who lost his job for opposing the American War of Independence.

Oldbury Hill (National Trust) is the most impressive earthwork of the Sevenoaks ridge. It is on the north side of the A25, above Ightham, and is so heavily wooded that you have to use the eye of faith to convince yourself that it is an ancient site at all. The main entrance is from a small lay-by, where the road widens briefly into a dual carriageway. You walk up a steep track, and after a minute or two stone steps to left and right lead to the dip that marks the Oldbury ramparts. These were constructed about 100 BC by Iron Age tribes, and may have been defended against the Romans during Claudius's conquest of Britain in AD 43.

Below Oldbury is **Ightham**, a delectable village, which rambles up and down, and has a superb cluster of half-timbered houses at its centre. For many years the village shop was kept by Benjamin Harrison, who became internationally known in Victorian times as an archaeologist; the Coldrum Stones burial chamber is now a permanent monument to him. He died in 1921 aged eighty- four and is commemorated by a tablet in the church. This is notable for its brickwork: the north aisle was constructed entirely of brick in 1639. These seventeenth-century bricks are longer than later varieties (ten inches as opposed to nine).

Harrison's modest tablet is overshadowed by the monuments of the Cawnes and Selbys, who owned Ightham Mote nearby. In the chancel, life-size in full armour, lies the stone effigy of Sir Thomas Cawne, who died about 1374; the window above, with strange cork-shaped carving in the tracery, forms part of the tomb. More eye-catching are the seventeenth-century Selby monuments. One is a double memorial to an uncle and nephew, both called Sir William. Before they came south to the soft airs of Kent in the 1590s, the Selbys were Lords of the Marches on the Scottish Border. Their talent for rough justice is commemorated on the monument, which mentions that the younger Sir William executed or exiled '1,500 wicked and desperate thieves' in that wild region. Smaller but far more interesting is the wall monument to his wife, Dame Dorothy Selby (died 1641). In her day she was a famous needlewoman, and two of her pictures, *The Gunpowder Plot* and *The Golden Age* (Adam and Eve), are depicted on the monument.

Ightham Mote lies hidden away down side roads a couple of miles south of the village. Through the hamlet of Ivy Hatch, you suddenly plunge down a steep-sided lane with hardly room for two cars to pass, and ahead of you is the stone manor, with a small lake beyond. The house may get its name from its moat, or 'Mote' may mean the place where the moot or Saxon council met. There can be few places in this country more peaceful or unspoiled after six centuries. It was this tranquillity that struck a young American, Henry Robinson, who first saw it as he was cycling through Kent in the early 1900s. In 1953, after he had made a fortune as a paper-maker, he saw his dream house advertised for sale in a magazine. He bought it, did it up, stocked it with old furniture, and lived there until his death aged 93 in 1985, when it passed by bequest to the National Trust.

Even though Ightham Mote is in the heart of the countryside, it has been under attack from atmospheric pollution and general decay ever since it was built. So since 1989 the Trust has been carrying out an incredibly thorough restoration. The country was scoured for the finest craftsmen in brick, stone, wood, metal and glass, and every phase of the operation was carried out using the techniques of the period when the house was built. For example, when the walls were replastered the laths were not sawn but made from split chestnut, while the plaster that was smoothed on them was a witches' brew of putty, sand and goat's hair mixed with cowdung. Today's craftsmen met the same kind of problem as their medieval forebears – they found that the dung, and hence the plaster, was a different colour depending on whether the cows had been eating beetroot in winter or grass in summer.

Though it now appears as a single harmonious building, in the form of a hollow square with a moat around it and an imposing stone gatehouse leading to it, in fact the construction spans about three hundred years, from the Cawnes in the fourteenth century to the Selbys in the seventeenth. Across the courtyard is the old core of the house – the Great Hall, built about 1340. As well as the huge oak beams, the ceiling is supported by a stone arch resting on comic little human corbels. Two portraits of the needlewoman Dame Dorothy Selby preside over the room.

In spite of its comparatively small size, Ightham Mote makes room for two chapels: a medieval one above the hall, connected with the solar or ladies' retiring room by a squint through which services could be watched; and the Tudor chapel built about 1520, complete with linenfold panelling, pews and pulpit, and with a sanctuary ring at which criminals could take refuge. Like many things about Ightham, this 'new' chapel lends itself to conjecture. Tree-ring dating (dendrochronology) on its timbers gives a date of about 1470 for the actual building; but the elaborate Tudor painting on the curved ceiling panels has led the Henry VIII historian David Starkey to suggest that the chapel was done up by Sir Richard Clement, the owner of the day, as a guest chamber for a visit by Henry and Catherine of Aragon in 1525. The boards are painted with royal emblems, including Henry's Tudor rose and Catherine's pomegranate, which makes such a connnection possible at least.

Plantagenet stonework and Tudor timbering form such an integrated whole that it is strange to find a Palladian window in the drawing-room, especially noticeable from outside the house. Apart from odd bits of carving like the Saracen head on the staircase, the drawing-room is the only light-hearted thing about Ightham, which tends to the rich and melancholy. A flamboyant Jacobean oak frieze, carved with Saracen heads, vultures, fruit and flowers, runs round the room below the ceiling; and there is a huge, almost obese overmantel. Frieze and overmantel were put in by the younger Sir William Selby, husband of Dame Dorothy.

Below the Palladian window on the north side of the house is a little water-gate opening on to the moat. Legend links this with the Cromwellian suit of armour in the Great Hall. A soldier of the time, the story goes, fell in love with one of the Selby ladies, but while trying to get into the house through the water-gate he slipped into the moat and drowned. But peaceful rather than tragic memories rule over this beautiful house, in its calm setting of hill, water, grass and huge dark trees.

Two of the prettiest villages in the Sevenoaks area lie on the Pilgrims' Way, north of the A25 and M26 – Kemsing, right off the main road, and Otford, where the old travellers crossed the Darent. **Kemsing**'s chief claim to fame is St Edith's Well, at the junction of the road from Seal into the village. It stands in a little lawn by the war memorial, and feeds a small stream. St Edith, daughter of King Edgar the Peaceful and Lady Wulfrith, was born in Kemsing in AD 961; she lived most of her life at the Wilton Abbey, in Wiltshire. After her death at the age of twenty-four a cult grew up round her, a shrine with a miracle-working statue was built in the churchyard, and the church prospered from the offerings of pilgrims. Lambarde tells how for a consideration the priest at Kemsing would bless corn and other grain in the name of St Edith to protect it from mildew and blight. The church, with its wood-shingled spire and belfry, and white doves cooing on the buttresses, is as pretty as the village.

Otford has been much more in the mainstream of history. It is strategically placed at the crossing of the Darent; Roman remains have been found here; and it was the site of battles in 774 and 1016. In medieval and Tudor times the Archbishops of Canterbury had a palace here. The remains of the Tudor palace lie back from the main road. They consist of a single-storey building used as a storehouse, a gallery, now turned into cottages, and a three-storey brick tower. This, the last of the Otford palaces, was built by Archbishop

Warham early in the sixteenth century in preference to Knole. Becket is reputed to have started the palace's water supply by striking his staff into the ground at St Thomas's Well, now in a private garden. Lambarde says he 'was much hindered in devotion, by the sweete note and melodie of a Nightingale'; and at once put a miraculous ban on birdsong in the palace park.

Otford church has a magnificently sturdy twelfth-century tower, covered in an ugly layer of cement. There was originally a Saxon church here, and much of the masonry in the nave dates from about the time of the Norman Conquest. On the west wall of the nave are eight sombrely painted funeral hatchments in memory of members of the Polhill family (after whom the steep hill up the downs north of Sevenoaks is named). In the middle of Otford is a tidied-up village pond, with weeping willows on either side, and ornamental waterfowl swimming about on it.

Chevening, off the B2211 north-west of Sevenoaks, is little more than the great mansion, a few small houses built against the high outer wall, and an ancient church. The house is now a country retreat for the Foreign Secretary of the day and cannot be visited, but the north front, facing up the slope of the downs, can he seen by walking a short way up the footpath to Knockholt. The nucleus of the present house was built between 1616 and 1630; the architect is said to have been Inigo Jones. It was bought in 1717 by General James Stanhope, George I's Foreign Secretary and Head of Government. In 1718 he was made Earl Stanhope, but died only three years later, leaving the vast alterations he planned to be carried out by his widow.

Its appearance is largely due to Charles, the third Earl, who was a vintage example of the wealthy English eccentric. He was a keen republican, and his sympathies with the French Revolution gained him the nickname 'Citizen Stanhope'. He was also a scientist, who experimented with steam-driven ships, and invented the first iron printing press and a machine to do multiplication and division, now on view in the London Science Museum. Eccentricity continued in the next generation with Charles's daughter, Lady Hester Stanhope, who kept house for her uncle, the Prime Minister William Pitt the Younger, until his death in 1806. Thereupon she travelled to the Near East and built herself a castle on the slopes of Mount Lebanon, where she bossed the Arabs, surrounded herself with vast numbers of cats and other animals, and lived like an Oriental princess for nearly thirty years.

Chevening church is a pretty little thirteenth-century building, thought to have been built here because at this point the east-west Pilgrims' Way crossed the north-south main road; but both sections where they ran through the park were closed by the eccentric third Earl, who built the present road from Sundridge at his own expense. Inside the church is the Stanhope Chantry, kept locked since visitors started removing armour and other mobile trophies from the walls. The most notable memorial is the white marble figure of Lady Frederica Stanhope, who died in childbirth in 1823, aged twenty-three. Carved by Sir Francis Chantrey, she lies quietly asleep, cradling the child who killed her.

West of Sevenoaks, Sundridge and Brasted now form an almost continuous village along the A25. **Sundridge**'s tall-towered church is on the hillside south of the main road; the finest house in the village is Sundridge Old Hall, a Kentish yeoman's timber-framed house built about 1458. The great hall is lit by a superb oak twelve-light window.

Combe Bank, the big house of Sundridge, is a large white Georgian building, now a girls' convent school. In Victorian times it belonged to Dr William Spottiswoode, a mathematician and physicist who combined the job of Queen's Printer with that of President of the Royal Society. The great scientists of the period – Darwin, Huxley, Herbert Spencer – used to meet here. Not only was Combe Bank the first house in the neighbourhood to be wired for electricity, but the work was carried out under the supervision of Michael Faraday himself. A later scientific owner of Combe Bank was Robert Mond, one of the founding fathers of ICI.

Brasted's old name, Bradestede, may derive from Bredsted in Jutland, where the original Jutish settlers came from; or it may simply be the 'broad steading', or sprawling village, which it still is. Half way along the straight High Street is a pretty green, backed by some fine old buildings, including a row of Tudor cottages. A side road leads down to the church, on the other side of the Darent. The medieval tower is still standing, but the rest of the church was pulled down and rebuilt in the 1860s, in a discreet and non-Gothic-Revival way. In 1944 it was badly damaged by a flying bomb, which blew out all the glass and cracked the chancel walls. The original church's great age is recalled by a Saxon tombstone below the tower, discovered during demolition in 1865. About 1840 Napoleon III lived for some time at **Brasted Place** (now a Church of England training college), before returning to France as emperor.

For a practical demonstration of the steepness of the sandstone ridge, you can take the **Toys Hill** road in the middle of Brasted, which shoots up to 770 feet. There is marvellous National Trust woodland up here for walking and picnicking. The **Ide Hill** road, running parallel to the east, will also take you up and over the ridge. Ide Hill village is not much more than a green and a few houses, with a spiky little Victorian church; but the view across the Weald from the car-park below it must be one of the most spectacular anywhere in England. The superb National Trust garden at **Emmetts**, 700 feet up on the summit of Ide Hill, gives magnificent views across the Weald as far as Ashdown Forest. Its shrubs and specimen trees were devastated in the 1987 storm – though miraculously a giant wellingtonia, whose summit is the highest treetop in Kent, survived the onslaught. A thoroughgoing scheme of clearing and replanting has now restored the garden to much of its former glory.

Two or three miles to the south the landscape is dominated by the **Bough Beech Reservoir**. This caused an outcry when it was created in the 1960s, as it inevitably drowned houses and good farmland; but on the credit side it enhances the landscape as only water can do, and is used for fishing in summer and boating in winter. The Kent Trust for Nature Conservation runs a nature reserve and information centre at **Winkhurst Green**, on the north side of the reservoir.

As its name implies, **Westerham** is the westernmost town in Kent. On the green at the top of the hill are statues of Westerham's most famous men, General James Wolfe, who spent his childhood at Quebec House, and Sir Winston Churchill, who lived at Chartwell a couple of miles to the south. Wolfe's statue, put up in 1911, shows him leading his men to victory with drawn sword, while Churchill, in a bronze by Oscar Nemon, slumps back in a chair, with his chin thrust aggressively forward.

Behind the green is an attractive group of old houses, mainly antique shops, pubs and tearooms. The church still keeps its Early English tower and chancel, though most of it was reconstructed at the end of the fifteenth century. Inside there is a splendid fourteenth-century timber spiral staircase running up into the tower. Only one other like it is known, in Hemel Hempstead church, Hertfordshire. Hexagonal in shape, it still looks as sound as ever, and seems to have undergone very little repair. Wolfe is commemorated in the church of his youth. by a memorial window – a glowing Pre-Raphaelite Annunciation scene designed by Burne-Jones and made in the William Morris workshops.

Wolfe was born in January, 1727, at Westerham Vicarage, not at Quebec House; his mother stayed at the vicarage for her confinement, while her husband was away with his regiment. The Wolfes had moved to **Quebec House** (National Trust) the year before, and lived there until 1738. The downstairs rooms are full of Wolfe relics – portraits, caricatures, his massive field canteen, the dressing gown in which his body was brought back to England. Though he died in a blaze of glory, Wolfe's military success only came at the very end of his life. After a swift rise to the rank of lieutenant-colonel by the age of twenty-three, he spent seven years stagnating in Britain; but in 1757 this period ended when Pitt the Elder came to power, and Wolfe was sent out to Canada. Throughout the campaign he was ill with the gravel and rheumatism, and was already broken in health when in 1759 he defeated the French spectacularly on the Heights of Abraham, falling mortally wounded at the moment of victory and dying with a smile on his face. He is buried at Greenwich.

You can follow Wolfe's trail along the dogleg of Westerham High Street to **Squerryes Court**, on the west side of the town. Wolfe is said to have received his first commission, at the age of fourteen, in the garden of Squerryes; the spot is now marked by a small classical urn at the top of the garden terraces. Squerryes is the ideal middling-sized country mansion, redbrick and welcoming, with a small lake in front and a garden and park behind. It dates from the 1680s; in 1731 it was bought by John Warde, and has remained the Warde family home ever since. As a boy Wolfe became friendly with the Warde children, who all appear in a conversation piece in the drawing-room, painted by Wootton in 1735. The Wolfe Room contains documents and pictures, including the only portrait for which Wolfe is known to have sat, probably painted about the time he received his commission at Squerryes. His mother's recipe book is on view; among other things, it tells you how to make 'a good water for a consumption' from ground snail shells, sliced earthworms and herbs, simmered in milk and served two spoonfuls at a time.

Squerryes is full of good pictures, from simple family portraits to the huge equestrian figure of Philip II of Spain, partly by Rubens, which dominates the Picture Gallery. Prominent among the Warde portraits is the glum, red-robed figure of Sir Patience Warde, Lord Mayor of London in 1680; he was given his strange name because his father was fed up with having a string of sons and only one daughter. Far more cheerful is the Falstaffian portrait of a later John

Warde, painted in 1829 sitting ponderously on the back of his favourite horse Blue Ruin, so called because he bought him from a gin merchant. Warde has been called the father of foxhunting, and was a master of foxhounds for fifty-seven years. The first John Warde was a racing enthusiast; the gazebo he built about 1740 to watch his racehorses at their training gallops still stands on a hill overlooking the lake, on the other side of the road.

South of Westerham the roads run up on to **The Chart**, a wide expanse of mixed heath and woodland that stretches over the county border into Surrey, and is a splendid place for walks, with its alternation of trees and open ground. The Chart gives its name to Chartwell, which you can find easily enough on summer weekends by following the nose-to-tail queue of cars and coaches through the back roads. **Chartwell** (National Trust) is built on the side of one of the combes which cut into the southern side of the ridge and give magnificent views across the fields and woodlands of the Weald. It was certainly the views rather than the house that appealed to Churchill; when he bought it in 1922 it was a gloomy, creeper-covered Victorian barn of a place.

As it now stands, Chartwell is nothing special in the way of English country houses; but for its association with one of the giants of the twentieth century its plain façade would hardly deserve more than a glance through the open front gates. Though Chartwell has the elements of a shrine, it is far too much of a home to let the reverential aspects get the upper hand. In the entrance hall you are immediately confronted by an umbrella stand full of walking-sticks; and in the drawing-room – the first large room you come to – a pair of splendid George II mirrors and a glowing pink and yellow Monet painting of London Bridge look down on a small card table set for bezique. Upstairs, several bedrooms have been converted into display rooms, full of medals, photographs of the generals of both World Wars, and the gifts Churchill accumulated, many of them hideous, like the two silver and crystal bowls from Stalin. Of far greater interest is the famous Boer War poster offering £25 for Churchill's capture '*levend of dood*', dead or alive.

Churchill's literary side is centred on the study, a magnificent room where the architect Philip Tilden removed the Victorian ceiling to show the great beams and rafters of an older Chartwell. Here Churchill wrote much of his life of Marlborough, his chronicle of the Second World War, and his *History of the English-speaking Peoples*. A vast painting of Blenheim hangs above the fireplace, and on the left is a small portrait of his father, Lord Randolph Churchill, who died a disappointed man in 1895, and whose life formed the subject of an early book by Churchill, written in 1906.

Much of the character of Chartwell is concentrated in the garden: in the lawns and terraces where Churchill strolled with his dog – or on occasion a pet sheep – at his heels; in the pond where he fed the golden orfe; in the orchard whose trees he planted; in the Golden Rose Garden planted to mark the Churchills' golden wedding in 1958. Round this part of the garden runs the wall with which Churchill busied himself during his years in the political wilderness, a relaxing contrast to the frustrations of the 1930s. Far from being some little piece of do-it-yourself bricklaying, it is enormous, about eight feet high, built stepwise down the hill round all four sides of the kitchen garden. Typically, Churchill sparked off a union uproar when in 1928 he took out a card as an adult apprentice in the Amalgamated Union of Building Trade Workers; just as typically, he finished the wall.

At the far end of a little group of cottages near the wall is Churchill's studio, lined with paintings and with an unfinished canvas still on the easel. He describes how he was inspired to start painting by watching the wife of Sir John Lavery. 'Splash into the turpentine, wallop into the blue and white, frantic flourish on the palette – clean no longer – and then several large fierce strokes and slashes of blue on the absolutely cowering canvas. Anyone could see that it would not hit back.' Churchill seized a brush, did likewise, and so began his career as the patron saint of amateur artists.

Crockham Hill, the nearest village to Chartwell, is another place of spectacular views; Samuel Palmer is thought to have drawn the landscape here, though his viewpoints cannot be identified exactly. Suitably enough for a village so embedded in beautiful countryside, the church contains the tomb of Octavia Hill, one of the founders of the National Trust. 'Noble in aim, wise in method' as the inscription calls her, her recumbent effigy lies in the sanctuary, a smiling female crusader in a stone-carved shawl.

13

The Eden and Upper Medway

THE THREE COUNTIES of Kent, Sussex and Surrey meet at a point somewhere among the fields and woods four miles south of Edenbridge. Though their boundaries may seem to have little logic behind them, in fact they follow for a good way the streams that once separated the kingdom of Kent from its neighbours – Kent Brook from Surrey, and Kent Water from Sussex.

Edenbridge is strung out along the Roman road which led south across the Weald to Lewes and north to London. At its northern end fields have given way to factories and housing estates; but its centre still keeps something of the feeling of an old market town. The central square is little more than a widening of the High Street. The church is north of the river, set back from the square and built on the site of a Saxon predecessor. Some Norman work survives, but it is mainly Early English, with a heavily buttressed tower that seems to grow from the soil, topped by a well-proportioned shingled spire. Inside, the wide south aisle has almost the effect of a double nave. The monuments are not particularly noteworthy; though there is one curiosity, a memorial window in the south wall commemorating a bewhiskered Victorian station master, who gazes down from the glass disguised as a prophet.

The Roman road was used to bring iron down from the hills to the south, and round **Cowden** (accent on the -den), one of the local beauty spots, there are visible reminders of the time when the skies were red with the glow from primitive blast furnaces. West of Cowden down a small lane is Furnace Pond, now a quiet thirty-acre stretch of water surrounded by trees and lined with bulrushes. This supplied the water power for the furnace of Richard Tichborne, who built **Crippenden Manor**, north of Cowden, in 1607. In the garden of Crippenden is the 'Cowden gun', made at Furnace Mill and the only local gun known to survive. The Tichbornes were strong Parliamentarians, and the gun, a small type known as a falconet, may have been made for Cromwell but never supplied because it was faulty.

Cowden village – a short street of white-painted and half-timbered houses – is tucked away from the outside world. The church has an unusually tall spire (127 feet), and both spire and tower are shingled. The building is mostly fourteenth-century, with a nineteenth-century north aisle added. Inside it is remarkable for the timbers below the tower, and for the fine kingpost roof. Before the Reformation it housed an image of St Uncumber, the popular name for St Wylgeforte, to whom wives wishing to get rid of their husbands – 'uncumber theym of theyr Housbondys', wrote Sir Thomas More – used to make offerings. As a girl she was beautiful, but so pestered with suitors that she prayed to be rid of them, grew a flourishing beard, and passed the rest of her life in hirsute sanctity.

At **Holtye**, a little east of the White Horse Inn, a sign by the road marks a stretch of the Roman road where it continued south from Edenbridge. At the bottom of the hill, down a footpath, the Sussex Archaeological Society has uncovered and protected a few yards of the original surface, made of rammed iron cinders. Unfortunately much of the exposed section is now green with moss, and grass is starting to re-invade it.

East of Edenbridge the Eden meanders through a broadening plain, full of villages but preserved from major expansion by lack of anything that can be called a main road. Immediately downstream is **Hever** (pronounced Heever). The much-filmed **Hever Castle** dates back to 1270, but much of what we see today – the 'Tudor' village, 35-acre lake and Italian garden – was created by an American millionaire early this century. It all makes a perfect film set, complemented by the trim village church outside the gates and the old pub opposite. There is no village to speak of; Hever exists by virtue of its castle, with the pale ghosts of Anne Boleyn and her grasping father flitting somewhere in the background.

The castle started life in the thirteenth century, as a fortified manor house inside a moat. From the de Hever family it passed to the Cobhams, and in the mid fifteenth century was bought by Sir Geoffrey Bullen, a former Lord Mayor of London. In 1505 his ambitious grandson, Thomas, inherited Hever, when Anne was five years old. When she was thirteen she was sent to the glittering French court and spent eight years in that cosmopolitan atmosphere before returning to Hever. Henry VIII's regular visits to Hever to woo Anne began in 1525 – an infatuation encouraged by Thomas

Bullen, who was created Earl of Wiltshire and Ormond as a reward. (His wife Elizabeth and elder daughter Mary had already been among Henry's many mistresses).

Anne – who adopted what she thought was the more elegant spelling of 'Boleyn' – became Queen in 1533, but instead of producing the male heir Henry wanted, she gave birth to the future Queen Elizabeth, followed by three stillbirths. Only three years later, after the 'thousand days' of her reign, she was beheaded on Tower Green, with a single sweep of the sword, by an executioner brought specially from Calais, as death by the axe was thought unsuitable for the Queen of England. The pretext was adultery with five men, including her brother George Bullen. With her last words she forgave her bloated ogre of a husband – 'one of the best princes on the face of the earth, who has always treated me so well that better could not be'.

The best portrait of Anne (by an unknown artist) is in the room known as the Anne Boleyn Book of Hours Room, which she occupied as a child. With her parchment skin and hair drawn severely back, she hardly looks the *femme fatale* of legend. The Venetian ambassador said of her: 'Madame Anne is not one of the handsomest women in the world. She is of middling stature, swarthy complexion, long neck, wide mouth, bosom not much raised, and in fact has nothing but the king's great appetite, and her eyes, which are black and beautiful.' The Book of Hours Room gets its name from the prayer book (book of hours) she carried with her to the scaffold. Inside she inscribed it with the tragic couplet:

Remember me when you do pray
That hope doth lead from day to day.

Only a few months after her marriage Henry was being unfaithful to her, and warned her to 'shut her eyes as her betters had done'. The Long Gallery on the second floor, running the full width of the castle, is set out with lifelike tableaux of figures in Tudor costume, showing scenes from Anne's life, and Henry and his six wives.

In 1538 Thomas Bullen died at Hever, broken and neglected by his friends. Henry took possession of Hever and in 1540 gave it to Anne of Cleves, his recently divorced fourth wife On her death it passed into three and a half centuries of obscurity.

In 1903 it was bought by the American tycoon William Waldorf Astor, an Anglophile who maintained that America was 'no longer a fit place for a gentleman to live'. In the 1880s he was American Minister in Paris, and in 1899 became a naturalised British subject, confirming his new allegiance by buying the *Observer* newspaper in 1910. With his architect F. L. Pearson, he transformed Hever. He filled the interior with replica Tudor plasterwork and wood-carving, sent agents to scour Europe for fine furniture and works of art, built a village of mock-Tudor cottages beyond the moat for guests and servants, planted a yew maze, and created a splendid garden bordered by a man-made lake where the Eden flows through the grounds.

He was followed at Hever by his second son, John Jacob, proprietor of *The Times*. The Astor connection is documented at Hever in a suite of upstairs rooms. In 1983, after 80 years of improvement and embellishment, the Astors sold Hever to a property company, who have turned the Tudor village into a residential conference centre and made all sorts of improvements, like planting a herb garden and creating a 'water maze' which soaks you with jets of water if you take a wrong turning.

Though Hever has a moat (now filled with waterlilies), a drawbridge and a neat stone gatehouse, it is hard to imagine them ever being used for defence; fortunately, they were never put to the test. The inner courtyard, with its timbering, gabled windows and giant climbing plants, is small; inside, the house is chiefly remarkable for its portraits, as magnificent a gallery of sixteenth-century royalty and notables as you could find anywhere. Among them are the three great Tudor sovereigns: a canny Henry VII, a majestic Henry VIII painted by Holbein, and a hawk-eyed and forbidding Elizabeth.

Hever gardens are brilliant at all times of the year, from spring when the orchard is carpeted with daffodils, to autumn when the leaves of the vast horse chestnut trees are beginning to turn. The herb garden has been planted with the medicinal plants and flowers that Anne would have known – borage, hollyhock, saffron, basil and dozens more. The formal Italian gardens, with a lavishly planted pergola walk along their southern side, are like an open-air museum, crammed with busts of emperors, giant jars, urns and fragments of pillars, all collected in Rome by William Waldorf Astor. Beyond the formality the lake, lined with reeds and trees, stretches away into the distance.

Hever church, like the castle, is of sandstone, with a tall shingled spire visible a couple of miles away across the meadows. The earliest parts of the building are Norman. The most important memorial is the tomb of Anne Boleyn's father, Sir Thomas Bullen, north of the altar; the brass on top shows him in the robes and insignia of a Knight of the Garter. Across the road is the Henry VIII Inn; the story goes that it was originally called the Bull, but after the execution of Sir Thomas Bullen's son and daughter it became known as the Bull and Butcher (or 'Bullen Butcher'). But Henry, as always, had the last word.

A mile and a half to the east, down winding byroads, is **Chiddingstone**. When you walk down the short village street you feel like a time traveller visiting the Tudor world; it is now preserved from everything except traffic by the National Trust. Like Hever Castle, Chiddingstone village is a favourite with film-makers, who find it a perfect period backdrop. Some of the houses, with their overhanging first storeys and heavy beams, are known to have been there since the fifteenth century. Built and owned mainly by small farmers and tradesmen, they epitomize the rural affluent society.

The church is a serene sandstone building, with a Perpendicular pinnacled tower. It was largely rebuilt by Sir Bartholomew Burghersh, a famous soldier of his day, about the middle of the fourteenth century, with further reconstruction after 1624, when it was struck by lightning and severely damaged. The interior is spacious, with nave and aisles of the same length. The south aisle is almost a private memorial chapel to the Streatfeilds, the neighbourhood's leading family for over four hundred years. Sophia Streatfeild, who has a small tablet on the wall, was a friend of Dr Johnson, a bluestocking, and well known among her friends for her ability to weep to order – a useful attribute in the age of sensibility. She died in 1835 aged eighty-one.

At the end of a pathway that leads round behind the houses opposite the church is the 'Chiding Stone', a bulbous lump of sandstone to which scolds were brought to learn the error of their ways, and which is supposed to have given the village its name. More prosaic etymology derives it from 'Ciddingas', the people of a Saxon called Cidd.

Chiddingstone Castle, formerly the Streatfeild family home, lies on the other side of the tall gates at the end of the village street. The first Streatfeild settled here in the early sixteenth century, in a Tudor house where the castle now stands. About 1680 a descendant built a new brick house, in the latest Carolean fashion, called High Street House, which lasted until Henry Streatfeild inherited the estate at the beginning of the nineteenth century. He employed a rising young architect, William Atkinson, to remodel High Street House in the popular 'castle style', with battlements, towers and turrets, and a great hall – a process completed by Henry Streatfeild's son about 1835. The High Street, which had run directly in front of the earlier house, was diverted to run north of the property; the stone used in the reconstruction was probably quarried from the site of the present three-acre lake.

When the last Streatfeild occupant died in 1938 the castle was sold, and during the war it was occupied by troops – Field Marshal Montgomery once held a review there – and then by a school. In 1955 it was bought by the antiquarian Denys Eyre Bower, who left the castle and its contents to the nation on his death in 1977. His superb collections of Jacobite relics and Oriental *objets d'art*, including fine Japanese swords and lacquer, can be enjoyed by the public as he wished, in a secluded country-house setting.

The lake in the grounds is very popular with local anglers; in 1945 it produced the largest bream ever caught in the British Isles. Across the lake are tunnels cut in the sandstone, which are said to have been used by brandy smugglers in the great days of contraband.

Leigh (pronounced Lye) consists mainly of bogus Victorian half-timbering, but is full of character nevertheless, and has an excellent village green perfect for summer cricket. North of the road the grounds of Hall Place run the whole length of the village. The park and lake can be seen here and there over the wall, and there is an assortment of turreted and gabled entrance lodges. The church is on a rise looking across the green; it is basically medieval, but much of it, including the tower, is Victorian. Inside on the north wall there is an odd Tudor brass showing a woman rising from the tomb at an angel's trumpet call, leaving her shroud behind her.

Penshurst clusters round a T-junction, at the gates of Penshurst Place. At either end are bridges, one over the Eden and one over the Medway, and in between are houses of Kentish brick and weatherboarding, the former smithy with a horseshoe-shaped door, the big village hall, and the creeper-covered Leicester Arms Hotel. Opposite the hotel is the prettiest corner of Penshurst – a group of half-timbered cottages shaped like a hollow E, and forming a large inhabited lychgate at the entrance to the churchyard.

The eye-catching feature of the church is the Perpendicular tower, with disproportionately vast pinnacles on the corners; the rest of the building is twelfth- and thirteenth-century, much altered by the

Victorians. The interior has been brightly painted in places, especially the roof of the Sidney chapel, which was reconstructed about 1820, and the medieval font. The main memorials in the Sidney chapel include the mutilated thirteenth-century effigy of Sir Stephen de Penchester, and the altar tomb of Sir William Sidney, the first of the Penshurst Sidneys. (The most famous Sidney of all, Sir Philip, was buried not here but in St Paul's, where he was given a state funeral in 1587, the year after his death. A new monument was placed there in 1986 to mark the four-hundredth anniversary.) In the west wall is a window, full of Becket references, installed in 1970 to mark the eight-hundredth anniversary of his murder. It is by Lawrence Lee, who designed the nave windows for Coventry Cathedral.

At first glance **Penshurst Place**, with its vast stone west front rising from a broad expanse of grass, may seem on the dull side. But a longer look shows that the uniformity of a first impression is in fact an illusion: the walls themselves separate into a number of distinct parts, and above them gabled roofs lead the eye back into the hinterland of the great house. Sir Philip Sidney wrote that it was 'built of fair and strong stone, not affecting so much any extraordinary kind of fineness as an honourable representing of a firm stateliness; handsome without curiosity and homely without loathsomeness'. When Sidney described Penshurst towards the end of the sixteenth century it was already old. The centrepiece then, as it still is today, was the magnificent medieval hall, built by Sir John de Pulteney in 1329–49.

Visitors reach the house from the east side, through a gate in the sixteenth-century garden wall – an approach that gives the impression of a small village. To the south are ten acres of formal gardens, little changed since Tudor times. Seen from this side the Pulteneys' hall and its associated rooms are on the right; to the left of them is the fifteenth-century addition known as the Buckingham Building with the Elizabethan galleries built on at right-angles to form the western side of the forecourt. There is no particularly striking feature, yet it all fits comfortably together.

Sir John de Pulteney, who bought Penshurst from the Penchester family in 1338, was a medieval magnate on the grand scale, four times Lord Mayor of London, and buried in the church of St Lawrence Pountney, which was named after him. His Great Hall is the first place you enter, after passing through the Garden Tower and across the forecourt. Over sixty feet long and nearly forty wide, and lit by tall traceried windows, its massive beams are of chestnut instead of the more usual oak, and are supported by grotesque human figures carved in wood – the peasants on whom the whole social structure ultimately rested. A staircase leads down from the hall to a vaulted crypt, which contains an exhibition devoted to the history of the Sidney family.

Elizabethan and medieval Penshurst meet in the State Dining Room, up a flight of stairs from the hall. This was the solar of Pulteney's house; it still keeps the squint or small window where the ladies could keep an eye on the goings-on in the hall below. The walls are hung with Sidney portraits, starched and ruffed, in the stylized postures of the Elizabethan studio. Penshurst came into the Sidney family in 1552, when Edward VI granted it to Sir William Sidney, Chamberlain and Steward of the Household, who years before had fought at Flodden, and gone with Henry VIII to the Field of the Cloth of Gold. Sir William died soon after taking over Penshurst, and it was his son Sir Henry who really established the Sidneys there.

Henry Sidney was brought up with Edward VI; 'as the prince grew in years and discretion, so grew I in favour and liking of him', he later wrote. Among his strangely assorted court offices were those of Chief Cupbearer, Otter Hunter and Chief Cypherer; and as early as 1550 he was sent as ambassador to France. He remained in favour in Mary's reign, and was Elizabeth's Lord Deputy in Ireland. His campaigns there wore him out physically and financially, and he met the usual lack of appreciation from the Queen. To add to his worries his wife caught smallpox after attending Elizabeth when she had the disease. Little wonder that his portrait at Penshurst (in the Panelled Room next door to the Nether Gallery) shows a thoroughly despondent face beneath the luxuriant beard. When he was fifty-four he described himself as 'toothless and trembling'; and he died shortly after, in 1586. Nevertheless, he found time from his burdensome public life to build the north and west fronts to the house, and the fine gatehouse on the northern side.

Ironically enough, in 1554, when his eldest son was born, he named him Philip after the Spanish king, who was the boy's godfather. Perhaps Elizabeth's harsh treatment of Sir Henry was partly due to this. Sir Philip Sidney's life was a contrast to his father's in every way, brilliantly successful, and cut off in its prime before court envy and intrigue could exact their toll. As a poet he was famous for his *Arcadia*, inspired by the country round Penshurst and written in conjunction with his sister Mary, and above all for the sonnets he wrote to Penelope Devereux, calling himself Astrophel and her Stella.

His death from a wound received before the walls of Zutphen in the Low Countries has been told and retold, but still remains a classic parable of heroism and waste. After his thigh had been shattered by a bullet he rode from the field; then, as his friend Fulke Greville put it, 'being thirsty with excess of bleeding, he called for drink, which was presently brought to him; but as he was putting the bottle to his mouth he saw a poor soldier carried along, who had eaten his last at the same feast, ghastly casting his eyes at the bottle, which Sir Philip perceiving, took it from his mouth before he drank and delivered it to the poor man with these words, "Thy necessity is greater than mine".' After undergoing the crude surgery of those days he lingered on for a few weeks at Arnhem until gangrene set in, and then quietly died. His portrait is in a corner of the Long Gallery, sandy-haired, thin-faced and pensive.

On Sir Philip's death in 1586 his younger brother Robert (subsequently made Earl of Leicester) took over Penshurst, adding the Long Gallery, and the Nether Gallery on the floor below, in a southern extension to the house. The Nether Gallery contains a collection of armour, including one of Penshurst's most fascinating relics, the helmet carried at Sir Philip Sidney's funeral in 1587, surmounted by a porcupine, the Sidney family crest. Lord Leicester had a remarkable quartet of grandchildren. The only girl, Dorothy, inspired the Roundhead poet Edmund Waller, who addressed her in his verses as 'Sacharissa' in the stilted manner of the seventeenth century. A portrait of her in the Queen Elizabeth Room shows, a plump middle-aged lady, good-natured but no longer inspirational.

Two of her brothers, Philip and Algernon, fought for the Parliamentarians. In later life Algernon became friendly with William Penn and helped to draft the Pennsylvania constitution. As a prominent Whig he was accused of joining in the 'Rye House Plot' of 1683, which aimed to assassinate Charles II, was tried and condemned before Judge Jeffreys, and died stoically on the block. The youngest brother, Henry, was instrumental in the accession of William III; but perhaps his greatest claim to fame lies in the fact that, as Master of the Ordnance, he adopted the broad arrow or 'pheon' of the Sidneys as the mark of government property. A combined portrait of Philip, Algernon and a fourth brother, Robert, painted in boyhood, is in the Long Gallery.

In the eighteenth century the male line of the Sidneys died out, and Penshurst decayed. Fortunately, as has so often happened, new owners revitalized and restored it. These were the Shelleys (related to the poet), who inherited the house at the end of the eighteenth century. Sir John Shelley Sidney, who took the old name (his grandmother's maiden name was Sidney), his son the first Lord De L'Isle and Dudley, and their successors restored and rebuilt, in a style as near the 'firm stateliness' of the ancient building as the nineteenth century could provide. They also planted the yew hedges that are one of today's outstanding features. In 1945 Viscount De L'Isle – who was both a VC and a KG – inherited Penshurst and carried on the work of his predecessors until his death in 1991. He restored the Nether Gallery and the gardens, and kept the house going by opening it to visitors only two years after taking it over.

The fifteenth-century Buckingham Building, a much altered fragment of medieval Penshurst, links Pulteney's hall with Leicester's galleries. The state rooms on the upper floor – the Queen Elizabeth and Tapestry Rooms – contain the finest furniture at Penshurst, together with the hangings from which the Tapestry Room takes its name. A toy museum, in a converted stable at the back of the house, is a delightful assemblage of dolls, dolls' houses, rocking-horses, and toys enjoyed down the years by generations of Penshurst children.

Penshurst, like Knole, is set deep in parkland. It was devastated during the 1987 storm, but the present Viscount has embarked on an ambitious long-term plan to restore it. Over the fence the wide expanse of grass beyond the north front is the local cricket pitch. On the south side of the great house is a formal Italian garden, with neat borders, edged by trimmed box, laid out symmetrically round a fountain; while the orchard mixes apple trees and roses behind a massive yew hedge, like a garden in a medieval illumination.

Bidborough, across the Medway two miles east of Penshurst, consists mainly of prosperous-looking houses running along the ridge, with wide views northwards across the valley from it. The old village and the partly Saxon church are down a side road. The church still has its tiny children's pews, installed about 1790 at the beginning of the Sunday School movement.

Two miles to the south is **Speldhurst**, a neat village on top of a hill. The half-timbered George and Dragon claims to date from '*c.* 1212' and might even do so. The original church was struck by lightning in 1791 and burnt down; the present Victorian building does not look

Companion Guide to Kent and Sussex

much at first sight, but has windows – a number of them designed by Burne-Jones – which are among the masterpieces of the William Morris factory. With the sun behind them, the saints in the south aisle windows stand out almost three-dimensionally against their dark backgrounds.

Ashurst, on the East Grinstead–Tunbridge Wells road, consists of little more than a steep hill, a stretch of river and weir popular with fishermen, a station and a pub. But it has a dainty little church perched up above the road, with a white weatherboarded bellcote on top. There has been a church of sorts here since the tenth century; no one seems to know the date of the present building, though the porch is dated 1621. Near the porch is a pillar sundial made in 1634 by Elias Allen, the most famous instrument-maker of his time.

Groombridge, a couple of miles to the south, is half in Sussex and half in Kent. The Sussex part, which grew up when the railway came, is nothing special, but the Kent part, across a tributary of the Medway, is an attractive spot – a triangular green with weather-boarded and tilehung houses along two sides; the redbrick symmetry of Groombridge Place, a superb Charles II manor house, across a moat; and a chapel-of-ease in similar brick at its gates. The name is said to derive from a Saxon, Gromen (the name means simply 'the man', as in 'bridegroom'), who built a moated castle where the Place now stands.

A Norman castle was later built on the site; in the fifteenth century it passed to the Wallers, one of whose descendants was Edmund Waller, the seventeenth-century poet (see Penshurst, above); and in 1618 it was bought by Charles Packer, who built the present Jacobean house. As Clerk to the Privy Seal, Packer accompanied Charles I to Spain in 1623, on his unsuccessful mission to seek the hand of the Infanta in marriage. Packer built the chapel as a staunch Protestant's thank-offering for the expedition's failure. It is Late Perpendicular in style, with big traceried windows, one of which has magnificent armorial glass designed in part by Packer himself.

The house is privately owned and cannot be visited, though the state rooms can be hired for weddings and other functions. However, the gardens and park are open, and include a vineyard, fields of brilliant sunflowers, a circular woodland walk and a raptor centre where birds of prey are put through their paces. A small garden chalet is given over to relics of Conan Doyle, who lived at Crowborough and featured Groombridge Place in his novel *The*

206

Valley of Fear. Its formal topiary garden was the setting for Peter Greenaway's film *The Draughtsman's Contract.*

Between Eridge Green, south-east of Groombridge, and Frant is the expanse of **Eridge Park,** which takes the form of a rough circle about three miles in diameter. Eridge Castle is the home of the Nevills, Lords Abergavenny, who were originally tycoons of the Tudor iron industry (spelling their name Bergavenny). Around the whole circumference of the estate are small cottages and lodges in every variety of Gothic, all emblazoned with the letter A, used by the nineteenth-century Abergavennys to sign their properties. In the park's south-west corner is the Iron Age **Saxonbury Camp,** with an easily traceable defensive ditch round the summit. At the top, within a tangle of pines, oaks and rhododendrons, is a vintage folly – a round tower, complete with arrow slits, machicolations and conical roof. Over the door is a coroneted 'H. A.' and the date 1828. A perfect place for the Sleeping Beauty to lie imprisoned.

Frant is built round a vast irregularly-shaped green, with plenty of large Victorian and neo-Georgian houses for commuters. The village nucleus is at the northern end. A short street leads from the green to the dark stone pseudo-Perpendicular church dated 1821, with tall pinnacles on the tower and a slate roof. The little village school, built in 1816 and rebuilt in 1852, is inscribed with a quotation from the Book of Proverbs, as a reminder of the days when educationalists knew what they wanted, if not necessarily how to get it: 'Train up a child in the way he should go; and when he is old he will not depart from it.' Frant station, over a mile away, is a Victorian railway gem.

For years **Tunbridge Wells** was a byword for quiet gentility; indeed, 'Disgusted of Tunbridge Wells' is still shorthand for the kind of blimpish ex-colonel popularly supposed to live there. Even the revivalist names of the main streets – Mounts Sion, Ephraim and Pleasant – conjure up a vision of the sort of place where you would not be surprised to meet John Wesley on the street corner. But nowadays it is something of a boom town, with office blocks in the centre, a modern shopping mall, and many of its large nineteenth-century houses converted into flats.

Its beginnings were far from respectable. It owes its existence to a jaded young courtier in the time of James I, Lord North, who in 1606 was riding back to London from Eridge Castle after convalescing with his friend Lord Bergavenny. North rode past a spring of iron-flavoured water, tasted it, took a sample up to London to have it tested, received glowing reports of its health-giving properties, and returned the following year after another round of dissipation. By 1620 the wells four miles south of Tunbridge, as Tonbridge was then spelt, had become a popular summer resort for the courtiers. In 1630 Queen Henrietta Maria came there to recuperate after the birth of the future Charles II, camping in tents on the common, and Tunbridge Wells was made. (The 'Royal' was added to the town's name much later, by Edward VII in 1909.)

As early as 1632 a Dr Lodwick Rowzee brought out the first book praising the qualities of 'Tunbridge Water', recommending those in search of health to drink up to fifteen pints a day. It could cure 'tedious agues, the black and yellow jaundice, scirrhus of the spleen, scurvey, green-sickness, flour albus, and in the menses, deficient or redundant; . . . all inward ulcers, especially for those of the liver, the kidnies and the bladder; . . . vomiting, the hiccup, and in worms; likewise in the gonorrhea simplex et venerea; . . . in behalf of the women, there is nothing better against barrenness, and to make them fruitful.' Fifty years later another medical man, Dr Madan, was more specific. Tunbridge Water, he wrote, 'naturally incites men and women to amorous emotions and titillations, being previous dispositions enabling them to procreation.' Lured by such promises, no wonder the hypochondriacs flocked to Tunbridge Wells!

Though the town's centre of gravity has shifted north up the hill to the administrative centre and the large stores, the Pantiles, where the chalybeate water still trickles, remains the chief attraction of Tunbridge Wells. This is a town-planner's dream which has grown up by chance, a pedestrian precinct, surrounded by harmonious buildings, some of which go back to the seventeenth century. The original spring is in a recess below ground level, beside a chemist's shop; in summer you can buy a glass of the iron-laden water from ladies still known as 'dippers'. The precinct gets its name from the large roofing tiles that once paved it. They were laid after a complaint by Queen Anne in 1698 that the walks were unpaved; the work had still not been done when she returned the following year, and she never came back again.

The Pantiles reached their heyday in the mid eighteenth century. In 1735 Beau Nash arrived at Tunbridge Wells, established himself as Master of Ceremonies, and remained in charge for a quarter of a century. His innovations were a recognized and rigidly enforced code of behaviour, and the introduction of organized gambling. Nash was accompanied from Bath, his previous kingdom, by a forbiddingly effective lady called Sarah Porter. Known as the 'Queen of the Touters', she pursued visitors around the Pantiles until she had worn down their resistance to entering the gambling rooms. But with the increasing popularity of the seaside in the second half of the century Tunbridge Wells lost its appeal as a summer resort for the jaded, raffishness gave way to respectability, and the town was colonised by retired Empire-builders. Visitors can recapture something of the town's eighteenth-century atmosphere at an audio-visual exhibition on the Pantiles called 'A Day at the Wells'.

Across the road on the north side of the Pantiles is the **Church of King Charles the Martyr**, whose plain brick walls, gabled roof and white-painted clock tower hide a sumptuous interior. It dates from 1678; most of those who took the waters and subscribed to the church were royalists, which accounts for its dedication to the king. It is square in plan, with dark-stained galleries on either side, and a plaster ceiling of great panache, decorated with cherubs' heads, flowers, fruit and leaves. Before Tunbridge Wells was a properly defined unit, the altar was in Tonbridge, the pulpit in Speldhurst and the vestry in Frant.

From the Pantiles, Tunbridge Wells grew northwards. Off the High Street, cobbled and brick-paved alleyways of small eighteenth-century houses lead uphill to the tree-planted playground of The Grove. Past the station, at the top of Mount Pleasant, is what is left of one of the most ambitious development schemes of the early nineteenth century – the Calverley Estate, designed by Decimus Burton, a brilliant young architect of the day who was also responsible for the screen at Hyde Park Corner and the Athenaeum Club in Pall Mall. Half way down Crescent Road a large stone archway complete with a lodge and Doric columns leads into **Calverley Park**, a curve of big widely spaced houses, separated from the public park by mighty shrubberies. Far more attractive is the sweeping curve of Calverley Park Crescent, with its colonnade of white-painted iron pillars. Burton's largest building is the former **Holy Trinity Church**; its pinnacled tower is a local landmark. It is now the headquarters of a flourishing arts centre.

The neo-Georgian town hall – built in the 1930s on the site of a fine Decimus Burton terrace – is worth going into for a look at the portrait of Beau Nash at the head of the stairs. In wig, flowered waistcoat and brown velvet coat, with his cocked hat under his arm, he looks every inch the man who drove into Tunbridge Wells 'seated in a magnificent post chaise drawn by six greys, with outriders and postillions blowing French horns, and every appendage of parade'. The same building complex includes the town museum, which has a large collection of Tunbridge Ware – a local craft which consisted of decorating boxes or trinkets with mosaics built up of minute squares of different types of wood.

West of the town is the common, crisscrossed by roads and footpaths, and studded with some of the strange rock outcrops that jut from the earth for a mile or two around. Most impressive of all are the **High Rocks**, which cover several acres. Though hardly fifty feet high, they include such a variety of chimneys, overhangs, crevices and other formations that they are used for practice by local mountaineers. Those less strenuously inclined can amble among oaks, pines and rhododendrons, crossing the gorges by walkways.

Eastwards, Tunbridge Wells runs virtually without interruption to **Pembury**, a swollen village whose nucleus is a small triangular green on the north side of the road surrounded by big Victorian houses. Opposite is a large stone church with a tall spire, quite medieval-looking but in fact built in the 1840s. The medieval church, well over a mile from the village, is a lonely and impressive stone building, with a good kingpost roof and a vast and hideous marble reredos.

Capel, a mile and a half away down winding lanes, is a church virtually without a village, as the houses are said to have been deliberately burnt after the Black Death to prevent further infection. Inside, the north wall is covered with medieval paintings. The Last Supper can still be made out fairly easily. **Tudeley**, a mile towards Tonbridge, is another tiny hamlet with a church worth looking at. Reached past farm buildings, it is mainly eighteenth-century red brick with a squat tower; its uniqueness lies in its stained glass by Marc Chagall. The east window, in memory of Sarah d'Avigdor Goldsmid, who was drowned in a sailing accident in 1963, shows Christ on the cross looming above the waves, where the girl lies as if asleep – a gentle lullaby rather than a harsh lament.

Though **Tonbridge** is far more ancient than Tunbridge Wells, it is a good deal less interesting. The Saxons had a fortress on the castle mound, guarding an important crossing on the Medway, and to the Normans it was a strategic point for controlling the tribes of the Weald, so important that the lands around it had the special title of 'lowy', meaning the league of ground in every direction which formed its domain. The castle is now a peaceful enough place, overlooking the river. The great thirteenth-century gatehouse, on the landward side, survives up to three storeys; it now houses audio-visual and other displays. In the early Middle Ages the castle was owned by the de Clares, rebellious barons who often came into conflict with the king. The fortifications were slighted (made undefendable) by the Parliamentarians in the Civil War, and the castle was finally tamed at the end of the eighteenth century by a Mr Hooker, who built beside the gatehouse a smart Gothic mansion, now local government offices.

The rest of old Tonbridge also lies north of the river. On the west side the High Street widens slightly by two fine gabled Tudor black-and-white buildings, one of them a clothing shop with rows of suits hanging among some superb internal timbering. The parish church, down an alley across the street, is built on the site of a Saxon church, and is mainly fourteenth-century, enlarged in the nineteenth. The east window is an ambitious composition of modern glass by Leonard Walker, dating from 1954: Christ together with saints and prophets, thrown confusingly together in big pieces of brilliantly coloured glass.

The main buildings of **Tonbridge School** are in the form of an open E facing directly on to the High Street. It was founded by Sir Andrew Judd, ex-Lord Mayor of London and Master of the Skinners Company, in 1553. Old prints show a long range of buildings fronting the street; the present strenuously worthy Gothic block, set back behind a courtyard, is mid-Victorian and later. The school chapel, built in 1902 was gutted by fire in 1988; but in the 1990s the shell was restored and the interior rebuilt in a dignified semi-modern style. Judd School, the boys' grammar school founded in 1888 at the southern end of the town, perpetuates Sir Andrew's name.

Tonbridge has an unusual hour-glass plan, as it has grown on the higher ground north and south of the Medway, with the flood plain between. Before a flood barrier was built a couple of miles upstream, the High Street that links the two halves of the town was liable to severe winter flooding; and even with today's industrial expansion downstream the fields still come almost into the heart of the town.

Shipbourne (pronounced Shibburn), due north of Tonbridge on the A227 and half way to Ightham, is sandwiched between acres of Forestry Commission conifers and the park of Fairlawne, formerly the home of the Cazalet racing stables. The village centre of Shipbourne – a Victorian feudal creation of church, pub and cottages – was built about 1880 by Edward Cazalet. The hefty stone church, on the site of a former chapel of the Knights Hospitallers, has vast

211

gargoyles protruding from the tower. The few houses that make up Shipbourne are along the sides of an enormous undulating common that forms the village green.

The road to **Plaxtol** runs along the north side of Fairlawne Park. Plaxtol is very much a beauty-spot, with a crossroads church and a village street running down to a small tributary of the Medway. The church is said to be the only complete seventeenth-century church in Kent, and has no dedication. It was commissioned by Archbishop Laud, and is dated 1649 above the inner door in the porch. The interior is simple – apart from the roof, which is a forest of hammerbeams – with light flooding in through the clear window glass. A Victorian stone reredos makes an incongruous background for medieval oak carvings of the crucifixion and other scenes.

Isolated in the undulating orchards a mile east of Plaxtol is **Old Soar Manor** (National Trust, in the guardianship of English Heritage), a thirteenth-century stone solar block, with a redbrick Georgian farmhouse attached. The house is on the site of the medieval hall; and what is left is the first-floor solar, with garderobe (lavatory) at one corner and chapel at the other. Below are vaulted undercrofts, and a garderobe pit that could be cleaned out when need arose. For all its two-light windows and king-post roof, Old Soar must have been uncomfortably primitive to live in.

The main landmark of the flat Medway plain below Tonbridge is **Hadlow**'s fantastic folly tower. Hadlow, three miles south-east of Plaxtol, is an attractive village, with a core of good eighteenth-century brick and weatherboard, a medieval church down a back street, and an agricultural college on the outskirts. But the tower, soaring up to 170 feet, is the one thing you cannot get away from, in Hadlow itself or in the countryside for miles around. Apart from a Gothic coach house and other outbuildings converted into private houses, it is all that remains of Hadlow Castle, a vast house pulled down in 1951. It was begun by Walter May about 1790; and the tower was built half a century later by his son, Walter Barton May, inspired by the tower of William Beckford's palace at Fonthill, in Wiltshire. It was a good deal better constructed, as Fonthill fell down in 1825.

According to local legend, May built the tower to keep an eye on his wife's comings and goings after she left him, or alternatively so that he could see the sea – though the lie of the land would make this impossible. It was used by the Royal Observer Corps as a watch tower in the Second World War. In recent years the pinnacles that once crowned it have had to be removed for safety reasons, and at the time of writing (1999) the future of the whole structure is in doubt.

14

The Heart of the Weald

EAST OF TUNBRIDGE Wells lies the '-den' country, where names like Marden, Biddenden and Horsmonden perpetuate the clearings in the thick Wealden forest where the Saxons fattened their pigs in summer. Now in place of the forest it has some of the best of the Kent orchards, white and pink with blossom in the spring; yet in spite of its prosperity and accessibility, hardly any of the dozens of tilehung villages have grown even as far as the small-town stage. At the entrance of the orchard country the River Teise wanders gently along through woodland, before swinging north to join the Medway near Yalding.

The monks, as always, picked the most beautiful place on the river to build **Bayham Abbey** (English Heritage), whose ruins lie four miles east of Tunbridge Wells, north of the road from Frant station to Lamberhurst (B2169). The abbey dates from the earliest years of the thirteenth century. Much of the gatehouse survives, facing north over the river; as does the roofless east end of the great church: the transepts, still with unworn faces on the corbels; and the grass-lined chancel, its stones clutched by the roots of a vast beech tree. As the Teise forms the boundary between the two counties, the ruins are in Sussex, while the 'new' Bayham Abbey – a gabled stone Victorian house on the slope north of the river – is in Kent, which must lead to problems with the local authorities. The arms of the Camden family, an elephant's head, can be seen on many of the Victorian cottages round about.

At **Lamberhurst** the Hastings-bound traffic thunders down the A21 to a bridge over the Teise (though a bypass has been promised). However, much of this good old Kentish village is spared, as it is off the main road. The church is down a lane north of the village, on a bluff surveying the Teise; it is fourteenth- and fifteenth-century, much restored. The Scotney chapel is full of tablets to the Hussey family; and by the main entrance a stained-glass window by John

Piper, showing the angel announcing Christ's birth to two shepherds, is a marvellous modern parody of the medieval style, with the shepherds' hands shown grotesquely large, and their dog begging up at the dark blue sky. In the churchyard a tombstone to a couple who died aged ninety-six and a hundred and one bears the inapposite inscription 'Surely I come quickly'.

Lamberhurst was an ironworking centre, with a foundry on the Teise near Bayham. In 1782 Edward Hasted wrote that the iron railings round St Paul's – 'the most magnificent balustrade perhaps in the universe' – were cast there; but Ernest Straker, author of the classic book *Wealden Iron*, thought they were probably made in conjunction with other furnaces. A short section of the balustrade can be seen outside the village hall. Straker devotes a good deal of space to Lamberhurst or Gloucester Furnace, which was powered by water supplied by a 1,300-yard-long cut across a bend in the Teise. As early as 1548, he tells us, a complaint was made about its impact on the local economy: 'Alexander Collyn hath begun to make a hammer for iron making . . . and hath cut down the most part of all the oaks standing in the same wood and ground and beginneth to cut down the beeches standing and being in the same; by mean whereof in short time the same woods if that hammer do there continue wll be utterly wasted and destroyed, to the utter undoing of a great number of the inhabitants and tenants in that part.' Such complaints went unheeded, and the furnace was still going strong at the end of the eighteenth century.

Just south of the village are the neatly trimmed vines of the Lamberhurst Vineyards, one of the pioneer wine making ventures of the Weald.

There are two **Scotney Castle**s: the austere stone house built for Edward Hussey in the 1830s; and the romantic ruin at the foot of the hill, with its single round fourteenth-century tower reflected in the still waters of the moat. Apart from the tower and medieval stone approach, old Scotney is mainly seventeenth-century. Edward Hussey deliberately knocked it about to make it still more picturesque; then all around, and especially in the quarry from which the stone for the new house was excavated, he planted the forest trees and the brilliant rhododendrons and azaleas which are the glory of Scotney in early summer. Old Scotney and the gardens were left to the National Trust by Edward Hussey's descendant Christopher Hussey (1899–1970). For more than forty years he was a pervasive influence on the growing appreciation and love of English architecture and the landscape in which it was set; and Scotney is his finest memorial. It is now one of the National Trust's regional headquarters.

Another Lamberhurst garden worth a visit is that of **Owl House**, off a minor road north-west of the village. With its water garden, wide lawns and woodland ride it makes a spacious setting for the modest tilehung house.

Anglers, windsurfers and birdwatchers can enjoy themselves to their heart's content on and around **Bewl Water**, a couple of miles south of Lamberhurst and invisible from the main road. This reservoir – the largest area of inland water in south-east England – was formed by damming the little River Bewl or Beult (a tributary of the Teise) and flooding three small valleys; the thirteen-mile walk round its perimeter makes an enjoyable though strenuous day out. A short way below the dam the Bewl forms the moat of Scotney Castle.

A mile or two down the A21, a backhanded turn along the B2079 brings you to the **Bedgebury Pinetum**, which forms part of the 2,000-plus acres of **Bedgebury Forest**, run by the Forestry Commission since 1924 as an open-air laboratory of tree-growing. The pinetum was begun as an offshoot of Kew Gardens after increasing London pollution started to kill off Kew's conifers. It is planted on a hilly site, with broad avenues leading through the cypresses, spruces and pines, and narrow paths among the rhododendron undergrowth. The trees sprawl, or tower, or droop, with an infinite variety of greens and silvers in their foliage; the few specimen oaks that stand here and there are modern interlopers, botanically speaking, into this ancient coniferous world. At the end of an avenue is a lake, with rhododendrons crowding to the edge, and a stand of swamp cypresses, pale green in spring and glowing brilliantly russet on an afternoon of pale autumn sunshine.

Kilndown, on a back road a mile or so from Bedgebury, is an unremarkable small village, except for its grey stone church, austere on the outside but startlingly decorated within. This Gothic Revivalist's ideal was consecrated in 1841, and during the next few years was painted, gilded and enriched to the specifications of Alexander Beresford Hope, who lived at Bedgebury Park and was one of the leaders of the Revival movement. Gold, red and blue are the dominant colours, on the chancel screen, on the font cover, on the pulpit.

Goudhurst stands at the summit of a steep spur of land rising from the Teise, with magnificent views, especially to the west over the river valley, and south to the Hawkhurst ridge. The traffic-choked village street proper begins at the pond; the houses, half-timbered, tilehung and weatherboarded, climb stepwise to the church at the summit. At the top the road seems to end abruptly, with the churchyard on one side and a tilehung house with vast overhanging eaves on the other; the illusion is caused by a bend so sharp that the traffic disappears from view. Near the top the street widens a little, with the Manor House facing straight up the hill, and two pubs opposite, almost next door to each other; one of them, the Star and Eagle, adjoins the churchyard and is thought to have had monastic connections.

There was a church here as early as 1117; the present building is thirteenth-century, enlarged in the fourteenth when the population grew with the influx of weavers from Flanders – the medieval influx, as opposed to the sixteenth-century flight that followed the Spanish domination of the Low Countries. The medieval tower was destroyed in a storm in 1637 and replaced the following year by the present stocky structure, with its square-cut window and classical doorway. The top of the tower is over five hundred feet above sea level, and was used as a lookout point in both World Wars. The stained glass was blown out by landmines in 1940. Goudhurst church is a treasury of splendid monuments. Best of all is the table tomb in the south aisle to Sir Alexander Culpeper and his wife, dating from the 1530s. On top the two figures lie side by side; unusually, they are carved in wood, he in armour, with head bare, wearing a red and gold surcoat, she in a red cloak over a black dress, with a Holbein-style head-dress fastened under her chin.

Goudhurst church saw the last act of the fight against the Hawkhurst Gang of smugglers. Their leader, George Kingsmill, was a Goudhurst man; and another local, William Sturt, formed a militia to deal with him. After capturing a member of the militia and torturing him to get information, Kingsmill sent him back with the message that he was coming to attack Goudhurst. Sturt evacuated the women and children and posted his militia in the church tower. Swearing that he would 'boil four of the militiamen's hearts and eat them for his supper', Kingsmill led 150 of his gang to the attack; but the militia beat them off and routed them. The church register laconically records the burial of Kingsmill, 'leader of the scoundrels killed by the discharge of a lead bullet'.

Finchcocks, a couple of miles west of Goudhurst, is a large and striking redbrick Georgian house among the meadows by the Teise;

Newman calls it 'the most notable Baroque house in the county'. It consists of a central block, with symmetrical wings, three storeys high, and was built for Edward Bathurst in 1725. A battered statue of Queen Anne, rescued from the old Royal Exchange, stands uncomfortably in a niche over the front door. An enormous hall, bigger than any of the other rooms, runs from front to back. Finchcocks belongs to the pianist Richard Burnett, who has filled its spacious rooms with his unique collection of harpsichords, fortepianos and every variety of early keyboard instrument. In summer he gives conducted 'musical tours' round the collection, playing Scarlatti, Mozart or Schumann on the type of instrument for which they wrote.

As you come into **Cranbrook**, four miles east of Goudhurst, you pass a painted sign punning on the town's name, showing a crane standing in a brook. Neither bird life nor water is particularly obvious today, yet it was to its water as much as anything else that Cranbrook owed its vanished prosperity. Cranbrook is a town built by industry. It was the centre of cloth-making in Kent; the industry began in the fourteenth century, when Edward III lured cloth-makers from Flanders to break the Flemish monopoly and make England self-sufficient in cloth manufacture, and lingered on into the eighteenth. Cranbrook was the ideal centre for the trade, as there were plenty of streams which could be dammed to provide power for the fulling mills, oak trees from which the mills could be built, and fuller's earth to clean the cloth. When Queen Elizabeth visited Cranbrook, she is said to have walked to the manor of Coursehorn, half a mile away, on a path made entirely of Cranbrook-woven broadcloth.

The most lasting reminder of this trade is the magnificent **Parish Church**, a gloriously wide and airy place, which dates almost entirely from the fifteenth and sixteenth centuries, with elegant Late Perpendicular columns and clerestory windows. Above the tower clock is a figure of Father Time, who, according to legend, jumps down from his perch at midnight and scythes the churchyard grass; the legend is said to have been started by a former rector, who could not afford to pay for the grass to be cut and did the job himself under cover of darkness. Another rector left a unique and useless addition to the fittings of the church – the tall stone 'tub' for total immersion, standing against the south wall and reached by a flight of steps. This was installed in 1710 in an attempt to lure Baptists back to the church on the grounds that 'anything you can do we can do better'; but it was only used once. It is certainly an uninviting bathing-place.

Leading from the churchyard are the varied buildings of **Cranbrook School**, founded early in the sixteenth century and granted a royal charter by Queen Elizabeth in 1574. The school owns an outstanding collection of Kent and Sussex birds, assembled around the turn of the century by the African explorer Boyd Alexander, who seems to have shot anything that flew in the two counties, including an osprey killed on Bedgebury lake. Expertly stuffed by a local bootmaker of the time, the birds are now in Cranbrook's excellent little **Museum**.

The rest of Cranbrook is typical Kent weatherboard and tilehanging, with the narrow Stone Street turning a corner into the gentle slope of the wider High Street. On the corner is the long low George Hotel, where Queen Elizabeth stayed on her visit to Cranbrook in 1573; the town's many pubs are relics of the thirsty days of the clothiers. Up the hill at the eastern end of Stone Street is the stately **Union Windmill**, a tall smock mill on a high brick base, built in 1814 for Henry Dobell. It got its name because for a period it was run by a union of local tradesmen. Now fully restored, it once again grinds and sells its own flour. You can climb up the inside by ladders worn smooth by grain dust, to the topmost level where the driving shaft enters and meshes with the cogs high up in the roof.

Benenden, three miles south-east of Cranbrook, is mainly known for its girls' public school, founded in 1923. Its premises are a large redbrick mock-Tudor building, quite handsome with its stone-mullioned windows, built in 1859 for Lord Cranbrook and bought and modernized by Lord Rothermere in 1912. The house was originally called Hemsted, and superseded an Elizabethan house of the same name. Benenden village is a single straight street, with a long tongue-shaped green leading up to the church. Outside there is still plenty of the medieval church remaining, but inside it is an object-lesson in nasty restoration, with sharp-sawn Victorian pillars between nave and aisles. In fact, these replaced classical rather than medieval columns, as the church was largely destroyed by a storm in 1672 and rebuilt in the next few years.

Sissinghurst Castle (National Trust), off the Goudhurst–Biddenden road (A262) is a marvellous fragment set in a beautiful garden. It is a memorial to the creativity of Harold Nicolson and his wife Victoria Sackville-West, who found the place a wreck when they took it over in 1930. Over the next decade they restored the Tudor buildings and made a garden which expressed their personalities by means of planning and planting, a place of controlled romanticism where one open-air 'room' leads inevitably into another. Harold Nicolson's diaries give a running commentary on the progress of this rescue operation, which provided an idyllic refuge from the threatening international scene of the 1930s. A photograph of Sissinghurst taken in 1932 shows a scene of virtual dereliction, with the long entrance block in decay and the tower standing gauntly behind; a few walls form the skeleton of the garden still waiting to be born.

The existing buildings – low entrance block, tower and two cottages –are all that remain of a great Tudor manor house built in the sixteenth century by the Baker family of Cranbrook, whose most famous member, Sir John Baker, was a successful politician and acquirer of property in the reigns of Henry VIII, Edward VI and Mary. Beyond the tower was a vast courtyard building stretching well back into the present orchard; the south cottage stands at the bottom corner of the courtyard. Sir John became known posthumously as 'Bloody Baker', because of his persecution of Protestants, and all sorts of horrors, including rape and murder, were attributed to him. However, he seems now to have been the typical grasping and self-seeking man of his age, who used the offices of Attorney-General, Chancellor of the Exchequer and Speaker to his advantage. It was probably his son, Sir Richard, who built the gate tower and mansion early in Elizabeth's reign.

In the following century the Baker fortunes declined and Sissinghurst began to slide downhill with them. The final degradation came in the 1750s, when it was used as a prison for French sailors captured in the Seven Years War. An unlikely officer on guard duty there was the historian Edward Gibbon, who wrote that 'the duty was hard, the dirt most oppressive'. The prisoners were jammed together; they murdered their guards and were murdered in reprisal, and tore out all the woodwork to burn as fuel. Sissinghurst was left a wreck, and the main mansion was finally pulled down about 1800.

Though it now leads nowhere except to the garden, the tower with the Sackville-West flag flying above it makes a fine sight. The first floor was Victoria Sackville-West's study, and is still furnished as she left it, with writing table, books and souvenirs. An exhibition in an oasthouse in the grounds has the clumsy hand printing-press of the Hogarth Press, used for the first edition of T. S. Eliot's *Waste Land* and works by Virginia Woolf, Robert Graves, E. M. Forster and other *avant-garde* writers of the 1920s; with splendid impracticality this was the first piece of furniture to be brought to Sissinghurst in 1930. There are also photographs showing the transformation of the house and garden. The book-lined library in the entrance block can also be seen; with its Sackville portraits and silver mirror it is like a small offshoot of Knole.

It is the garden of Sissinghurst that most people come to see: the White Garden planted entirely with white or grey plants; the walk of pleached limes; the herb garden with a medieval profusion of herbs, such as caraway, fennel, tansy, borage and woad; the roses in formal beds or clambering over the warm brickwork of the gateway.

The French prisoners at Sissinghurst are said to have given its name to the Three Chimneys, a pub on a bend in the road half way between Sissinghurst and Biddenden. The inn sign shows a soldier looking at a signpost, and wondering which of the *'trois chemins'* (three roads) he should take. However, as the name Three Chimneys was current two centuries earlier, the bewildered Frenchman is just another local myth.

Frittenden, in the hinterland north of the Sissinghurst–Biddenden road, is a quiet village on a hillside, with a tall-spired church and a pub called for some reason the Bell and Jorrocks. It is full of ponds and streams which flow down to join the Beult in the valley below.

Biddenden's most famous residents were the two 'Maids of Biddenden', Eliza and Mary Chulkhurst, Siamese twins joined at hip and shoulder. Though they are supposed to have been born about 1100, the sign on the village green shows them dressed in blue Elizabethan costume. They died aged thirty-four, within a few hours of each other. The Maids are perpetuated in an Easter charity which provided cheese and two four-pound loaves to be distributed to each poor parishioner of Biddenden, paid for from twenty acres of ground called the 'Bread and Cheese Lands'. Nowadays on Easter Monday visitors can eat biscuits embossed with images of the Maids.

It is not surprising that Biddenden is touristy, full of antique shops, pubs and restaurants in the fine half-timbered buildings of the main street. The pavements on either side are made of irregular ankle-twisting slabs of Bethersden marble. A little way north of the green is the magnificent six-gabled Old Cloth Hall, the centre of the local cloth trade in prosperous medieval and Tudor times. The house contained workshops for the weavers, and was probably the collecting point for cloth to be taken to Cranbrook for final inspection and sealing. This is one of the grandest of the Biddenden houses; and you cannot go down a side road without seeing some splendid example of a half-timbered house built by the proceeds of the cloth trade.

Biddenden church separates the old village from the lapping tide of modern housing. It is mainly thirteenth- and fourteenth-century, with a later tower, begun about 1400. The tower, like the village pavements, is made of Bethersden marble – a misnomer for anyone expecting gleaming white walls, as it looks much like any other building stone. Inside there are some fine brasses, mainly quite late; to see them you have to roll back the carpet below the chancel step. Several of these sober clothiers in their ruffs and long robes are portrayed with two or more wives; 'cocks with their hens', as Newman aptly puts it. Like Lamberhurst, Biddenden has a flourishing vineyard, a little way south of the village.

Smarden, three miles north-east of Biddenden, is high on the list of villages that should be banned to heavy traffic. A small village, built on a dogleg, it is loud with the noise of lorries negotiating its angles; and the walker who tries to cross the street to get to the churchyard is in danger of his life. Apart from that, it is a most beautiful spot. Coming from the west you suddenly see a compact cluster of tiled roofs and weatherboarded walls; then round the corner the main street widens out, with a few hundred yards of old houses juxtaposed in casual perfection. The village name derives from the Saxon 'Smeredaenne', meaning 'butter valley and pasture'.

You enter the churchyard below the first storey of an overhanging building called the Pent-house. The church looks ordinary enough from the outside – early fourteenth-century, with a Perpendicular tower of about 1475 – but inside it is structurally very unusual. The single aisleless nave, thirty-six feet wide, is spanned by a timber roof of great ingenuity, known as a scissors-beam roof, because the timbers intersect. The church has been called the 'Barn of Kent' for this reason. On the south wall is a copy of the charter granted by Queen Elizabeth in 1576, allowing Smarden to hold a weekly market and annual fair; this confirmed an earlier charter granted by Edward III in 1332.

Though **Headcorn** is quite a commuting centre, it still keeps the feel of a small town based on agriculture. It is at the heart of the rich watermeadows along the river Beult; Queen Elizabeth is said to have been so impressed by the crops grown locally that when she visited the town she said it should be called 'not Hedecron' – the old name – 'but Hedecorn', and the anagram has stuck. The High Street has several half-timbered houses; the most prominent is Shakespeare

House (no connection with the poet except for the period), with an excessively tall and startled-looking gable. At the corner of the churchyard is the old Cloth Hall, and behind the church is Headcorn Manor (in fact built in 1516 for the parson) with a noble two-storey oriel window lighting the central hall.

The church is set right back from the end of the High Street behind a large and well-filled graveyard; on the north side a nice row of cottages leads to the Manor. By the south porch is a vast hollow oak tree, nearly fifty feet in circumference, and venerable enough to lend credit to the story that King John held a bull-baiting below it. From the north side the Perpendicular church, with its massive battlemented tower and severe roof line, looks like a fortress. Inside, the wide nave and south aisle are darkened by the Victorian stained glass. There is a battered wall tomb decorated with the Culpeper arms; and inside the door are two curious paintings on wood, more like icons than anything else, one showing a turbanned priest swinging a censer, and one wearing a robe fringed with bells. They are said to depict Moses and Aaron, as described in *Exodus* – Moses with his face shining when he came down from Mount Sinai (Chapter 34), and Aaron wearing the robe fringed with bells and pomegranates prescribed in Chapter 28, so that 'his sound shall be heard when he goeth in unto the holy place before the Lord, and when he cometh out, that he die not'.

Outside the town, on the road to Frittenden, is the narrow medieval Stephen's Bridge, possibly built by and named after Stephen Langton, Archbishop of Canterbury at the beginning of the thirteenth century.

Ulcombe, along byroads three miles north of Headcorn, has a fine church, isolated high above the village at the foot of the hill. This is one of a whole row of churches, beginning at Boughton Malherbe, that run at about the same level along the slope of the greensand ridge; it is thought that an old road to Canterbury, now vanished, may have linked them. The churchyard has two vast yews; the church interior has been stripped of choir stalls and provides an austerely modern setting for the medieval painting on the walls: red, black and yellow chevrons under a north aisle arch; a corresponding pair of outline crucifixions in the south aisle; and two fragmentary scenes, one of Dives and Lazarus, and one of St Michael fighting a fiercely horned and winged devil. In the north chapel is a splendid brass to Ralph Sentleger (died 1470) and his wife. He wears fanciful and most unmilitary armour, while she is wasp-waisted, and elegantly coiffed and mittened. The church's setting is spoilt by a vast corrugated-iron barn directly behind.

A mile to the west as the crow flies, though at least three times the distance as the lanes wander, is **East Sutton**. Its little gem of a church is virtually the private chapel of East Sutton Park, whose redbrick gables can be seen over the churchyard wall. The Park (now a prison) was the home of the Filmer family, Royalists who were besieged there by General Fairfax in the Civil War, though the house hardly looks martial enough to stand up to a siege. Sir Robert Filmer, friend of Charles I and author of a book on the divine right of kings, was captured by Fairfax and imprisoned in Leeds Castle. The north chapel, added to the thirteenth-century church about 1345, has two delicate windows which show perfectly the change from the Decorated to the Perpendicular style. Inside there are numerous Filmer memorials, including a very large brass, about seven feet long, on the floor of the north chapel, and a stained-glass portrait of Sir Robert, the last baronet, in the east window of the south chapel; he was killed in the First World War, and is shown in his red full-dress uniform.

Below **Sutton Valence** the main road falls steeply away down a one-in-eight slope to the plain of the Beult. Most of the little town lies east of the road, terraced on different levels to give wide-ranging views across the plain. The centre is dominated by the grey stone walls of the boys' public school, founded in 1576 by William Lambe, the town's most famous citizen. Lambe, born in Sutton Valence in 1495, was a wealthy cloth-maker, whose school was an extension of the almshouses he had founded some years previously; Victorian successors to the original almshouses stand at the far end of the elliptical green. His portrait hangs in the main school building, entered from the main road a short way up the hill: a benevolent face with an iron-grey beard, topped by a flat Tudor black hat. He is commemorated in London by Lamb's Conduit Street, north of Theobald's Road, marking the place where he brought fresh water to the people of Holborn in 1577.

Sutton Valence is an attractive place to wander about in, with its different changes of levels; it is free of traffic, as the side roads on which it is built lead nowhere in particular. The church is on the other side of the main road, a stone Victorian building with a well-scrubbed look, on the site of an older church.

The line of hillside churches continues westwards with **Chart Sutton**; and **Boughton**, crouching against the slope and surveying immense views southward, a harsh Victorian reconstruction redeemed by a medieval lychgate. Beside Boughton church is the stableyard entrance to **Boughton Monchelsea Place** (not open to the public); the main driveway runs through immensely tall beech trees – decimated by the 1987 hurricane – from the road at Boughton Green. The name Boughton (pronounced Borton) in fact derives from the Anglo-Saxon for beech tree, 'boc-tun' being a clearing among the beeches. The rest of the name comes from the Montchensies, a Norman family who were granted the manor by William the Conqueror. The present house is basically a stone Elizabethan mansion, completed in 1575 by Robert Rudston, who had joined Wyatt's Kentish rebellion in 1554, soon after buying Boughton, and was imprisoned in the Tower. He was pardoned in 1555, perhaps on the grounds of his obscurity, and allowed to repurchase the house, buying it back for half what he had first paid for it.

Later owners added to the house. A fine broad oak staircase was put in about 1685, and a century later battlements and dormer gables were added, and the hall was given fashionably Gothic pillars and vaulting. During nearly two centuries, from 1728 to 1903, there were children about the house for only twenty years. For ninety-eight years it belonged to two bachelors; but it is once again a family home. The herd of fallow deer in the park was first mentioned in 1660.

Linton is the westernmost of these hill villages. The church has a chapel full of tombs, and on the other side of the road is a nice group of old buildings, including the Bull Inn, dated 1574. North of Linton it is only a mile up the road to the outskirts of Maidstone. To the south the road divides just over the Beult. The A229 brings you to **Staplehurst**, built on either side of a switchback rise in the dead-straight Roman road. The gaunt church, built right at the summit, has a tremendously high opening to the rood loft, and some simple modern windows in the north wall, plain glass, with shields at the centre. In 1865 Staplehurst was the scene of one of the worst railway disasters of Victorian times, when the Dover-London boat train was derailed there. Charles Dickens was on board but unhurt; though severely shocked, he went to the help of the injured.

Marden, three miles west of Staplehurst, is as ancient a Kentish village as any, going back to Saxon times; though Edwardian and later houses are now more prominent than timber or tiling. The church stands right at the centre of the straggle, a big building, with a tower capped by a white weatherboarded belfry, and a pyramidal slate roof. It is mainly thirteenth- and fourteenth-century, much

225

enlarged about 1400 with the influx of Flemish weavers. Inside, the most immediately striking thing is the glass in the chancel, both the east window and the two side windows – harsh gashes of reds and blacks and greens that make the rest of the glass seem placidly insipid by contrast. Dating from 1962, they are by Patrick Reyntiens, who worked with John Piper and was greatly influenced by Graham Sutherland; the theme is St John's vision in *Revelation*. The font has a massive seventeenth-century cover which does not lift off but has opening panels. Beside the porch stand the old village stocks, moved here from outside the wooden lockup in the village square.

Horsmonden, across the Teise south of Marden, was a centre of iron-working. (The final syllable of the name is still stressed, Horsmon*den*, as are most of the -den names.) Nearby is one of the finest of all the iron-masters' artificial lakes, a great sheet of water over a quarter of a mile long. The beauty of this Furnace Pond is that the footpath takes you right over the spillway, with the water cascading down from step to step, and a circular basin at the bottom where the giant wheel (now vanished) once turned. The overgrown mounds on either side would surely give the industrial archaeologist something to get his spade into. Horsmonden village is large and not particularly memorable, except for the square green at the centre, which gives it the feel of a small French town.

If you follow the footpath sign pointing to the church, you will have a walk of a good two miles, as it is so far from the village that it seems to have nothing to do with it. But it is well worth driving along the narrow lanes to get there. The tall embattled tower, rising from a cluster of barns and oasthouses, looks across orchards, hopfields and water meadows to the Teise. Inside the church is very plain, apart from a magnificent chandelier, the gift of the rector in 1703. Behind the church you can look across to Goudhurst, perched compactly on top of its hill.

A couple of miles west of Horsmonden two vintage villages, Brenchley and Matfield, almost run into each other. **Brenchley** is self-consciously perfect. The centre is full of weatherboarding and pubs, built round a small triangular open space where the village pound once stood. The Old Palace, across the road from the church, is the most prominent of the secular buildings; there certainly was a Tudor house there, but most of its heavily timbered appearance is due to the modern restoration which turned it into cottages.

The church has a curious concave-sided pyramid cap on its corner turret. Most of the exterior is hidden as you approach it by a double row of tall yews clipped into cylindrical shape. The original foundation is said to have been in 1233; the tower is probably fourteenth-century; and the Victorians did a great deal of restoration. The first immediate impression is of width and light, as there is hardly any stained glass in the main windows or clerestory. Round the chancel arch and easternmost aisle arches texts are painted, picking up the far older texts and decoration on the beams and kingposts; above is an area of roof boarded in and painted blue – the 'celure' decorated to honour the rood which once stood below it. The linenfold panelling along the organ loft at the back of the church may have come from the rood screen. Though Brenchley hardly looks an industrial area, in the last century it was famous for its beaver hats.

Matfield is completely different, wide open rather than cosy, built round an enormous village green. At its northern end is a pond full of ducks and swans, and behind it Matfield House, the height of Georgian elegance, with a large stable block set back on one side. The clock tower on the coach house says 'Mind the time' in large letters. The rest of the green is surrounded by smaller Georgian houses; and it is no wonder that on a fine day the photographers are as thick on the ground as the admirers of the ducks. As Matfield was part of Brenchley parish until the 1870s, it has to be content with a little Victorian church, attractively set in trees at its southern end.

North of Matfield, dreams of the idyllic country life are shattered by the housing estates of **Paddock Wood**. Beside the railway is the huge square yellow box of the English Hops building, and behind it taller though less bulky grain silos. At least Paddock Wood's industries are rooted in the area; the hop theme is taken up by the pub sign of the Hop Pocket (a pocket is an outsize sack) next door.

Through Paddock Wood, on the low-lying fields near the Medway at Beltring, is a monumental cluster of oasthouses – the ranks of pyramid roofs and white-painted cowls of the **Hop Farm** (until recently the Whitbread Hop Farm). The oasts are no longer used for drying hops, but have been turned into a museum devoted to the arts of hop-growing, beer-making, coopering and agriculture in general. Each summer, the famous Whitbread shire horses are let loose into the Beltring paddocks for their annual holiday and lumber friskily about, free from the drudgery of hauling drayloads of barrels round the London streets.

15

The Rother Valley

BOTH EAST SUSSEX and West Sussex have a River Rother, and neither will agree as to which the Rother is. I am naturally prejudiced, as I lived for nearly ten years near Bodiam, where the eastern Rother emerges from hill-surrounded seclusion and ambles through an ever-widening spread of water-meadows to Rye and the open sea. In addition, the western Rother is a mere tributary of the Arun, and even rises over the border in Hampshire. Finally the eastern Rother is the most typical river of the Weald, cutting a deep channel which is still only crossed in its upper reaches by twisting steep lanes, and with its tributary the Dudwell producing a landscape of dramatic ridges which is amazingly spacious despite its small size on the map.

Rotherfield, seven miles south of Tunbridge Wells, is a suitable place to begin, as the Rother is said to rise in the cellar of one of its houses, and several of its small tributaries rise nearby. It looks westward across a narrow valley to Ashdown Forest and the creeping expansion of Crowborough, and is built round an irregular crossroads, with plenty of good tilehung houses and a church whose tall spire crashed to the ground in the hurricane of 16 October, 1987; it has since been rebuilt. In recent years the village has begun to expand beyond its ancient nucleus.

The church is a big friendly building, with a complete array of old box pews inside. The dedication to St Denys pushes the foundation of a church here back to the eighth century, when Bertwald, Duke of the South Saxons, was cured by the monks of St Denys near Paris and built a church as a thank-offering. A small monastery was also established, and it is thought that the remains lie under fields south of the church. A track called 'Chant Lane' is by tradition named after the chanting monks of St Denys.

The present building dates from the twelfth century on. Apart from the pews, there is some fine woodcarving, especially a

Perpendicular screen between chancel and side chapel, a Jacobean pulpit complete with sounding board, and a sixteenth-century font cover. The Burne-Jones east window, symbolizing the 'Te Deum' and showing musicians surrounded by tendrils of foliage, was made by William Morris in 1879. Sussex iron can be seen in the grave slab bearing a double cross by the north door; this may be fourteenth-century, about the same date as the medieval frescoes which survive, especially over the chancel arch. Old Rotherfield can just be deciphered from a painting on the wall of the north aisle, which shows the village, with a good deal of artist's licence, as it was in about 1710.

As this is a land of hills, it used to be a land of windmills as well. More survive here than anywhere else in the two counties. There is a well preserved post mill half way between Rotherfield and Mayfield, on a high point with the improbably Greek name of **Argos Hill**. From it you can see Mayfield with its church tower a little to the south-east, and due south across the Rother valley to the Heathfield ridge.

Round Rotherfield and Mayfield you continually come across the broken-down bridges and derelict cuttings of the branch line that once ran from near Eridge to Heathfield. Though **Mayfield** is now railwayless, it is still the most prosperous-looking place in the neighbourhood. Its most prominent feature is the cluster of buildings that form the Roman Catholic convent (St Leonards-Mayfield School), at the eastern end of the High Street. The school is built around the remains of **Mayfield Palace**, one of the great residences of the medieval Archbishops of Canterbury and an important administrative centre for church affairs. The first in the succession of archbishops to live at Mayfield was St Dunstan, who in the tenth century built a small wooden church there. It was at Mayfield that his famous encounter with the devil took place. As a good blacksmith the saint was forging a horseshoe when the devil visited him. He seized the devil's nose with his red-hot tongs, whereupon the Prince of Darkness leapt in a single bound to Tunbridge Wells and plunged his nose in the water to cool it. Hence the sulphurous (and health-giving) qualities of the water. Visitors to the convent are still shown the saint's supposed tongs and anvil, and the well reputed to have flowed when he struck his staff on the ground.

The finest part of the palace still survives – the fourteenth-century great hall, now used as a chapel. It is built on an enormous scale (seventy feet long and forty wide), with three giant stone arches

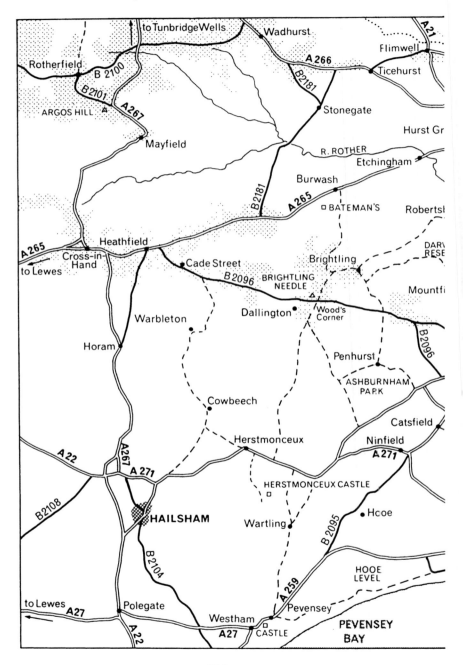

230

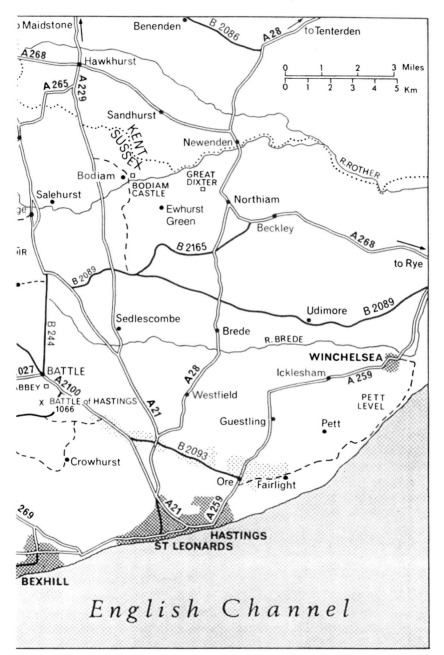

supporting the roof and resting on grotesque corbels which are themselves of unusual size. In a recess off the hall is the tomb of Cornelia Augusta Connelly, who died in 1879 and was the American foundress of the Society of the Holy Child Jesus. After the Reformation, the palace eventually passed to Sir Thomas Gresham, the Elizabethan financier and founder of the Royal Exchange; his grasshopper crest is carved on one of the fireplaces shown to visitors. After changing hands a good many times the palace fell on hard times. In the mid eighteenth century the roof was stripped off the great hall, and for the next hundred years the palace mouldered away as a picturesque and much visited ruin.

In 1862, on an outing from her school in St Leonards, Mother Connelly saw the palace; later the Duchess of Leeds, an American friend, bought the property and gave it to her. Edward Welby Pugin was commissioned to design the restoration, and only two years later the hall was re-roofed and in use as a chapel. The stone tower west of the hall is medieval; the gatehouse to the main street is Tudor, probably built by Archbishop Warham. (The palace is open to visitors at most reasonable times, though notice is appreciated.)

Apart from the palace, Mayfield was prosperous in its own right as a centre of Wealden iron-working. The main street is dignified, with wide brick pavements and some good timbered buildings, notably Middle House, built by Sir Thomas Gresham for his retainers and now a hotel, which has the date 1575 carved on the bargeboards. The figure of a girl on top of the tall village sign refers to the origin of the town's name from Maghfeld or Maid's Field.

The **Church**, naturally dedicated to St Dunstan, is set back a little from the street, with open country behind. Most of it was built after a fire in 1389, in which much of the village was destroyed. It has an odd-looking interior, with some late Perpendicular arcading cut short where it meets the chancel. There are two very fine eighteenth-century candelabra, a rustic octagonal font with the date 1666 carved on it, and two cast-iron grave slabs in the nave, one by an obviously inexperienced founder, as several of the figures and letters have come out the wrong way round.

South of Mayfield a pretty road leads direct across the Rother valley to Heathfield. The main road makes a wide loop via **Cross in Hand**, an important road junction, with a post mill on its central triangle, not as good as the one on Argos Hill but worth a glance.

Modern **Heathfield** is undistinguished, with little character either of Sussex or anywhere else. East of the town is the wide expanse of

Heathfield Park, behind a seemingly endless wall. Over the wall down a side turn you can see the round castellated folly known as Gibraltar Tower, built in honour of General Sir George Augustus Elliot, Governor of Gibraltar, who successfully defended the Rock against combined French and Spanish attacks from 1779 to 1783. Old Heathfield, at the south-east corner of the park, is a pretty group consisting of a church, a pub and a few cottages. At **Cade Street** nearby, an inscribed monument north of the road to Battle marks the spot where Jack Cade, leader of the Kentish rebellion of 1450, was killed by Alexander Iden, Sheriff of Kent. The inscription ends with the moral: 'This is the Success of all Rebels, and this Fortune chanceth ever to Traitors.'

The most memorable thing about **Horam**, a couple of miles south of Heathfield, is a large cider press beside the main road, which belongs to the makers of Merrydown cider and fruit wine.

To the east is a jumble of inconsequential lanes and small villages, reminiscent of the North Downs. **Warbleton** is hardly even a village – just a large and noble church, set in magnificent country, with a farm next door and a long low house opposite. The interior is dominated by a galleried manorial pew, dated 1722, with two compartments at first-floor level, ideal for sleeping during sermons or keeping a check on church attendance among the tenantry. Hanging on the wall is a Victorian engraving which shows Richard Woodman, an ironmaster of Warbleton, being burnt at the stake with nine others at Lewes in 1557. When the rector handed him over to the authorities, Woodman rebuked him for 'turning head to tail' to satisfy the Catholics. An iron-bound door in the church may come from the strongroom where Woodman kept his workmen's wages.

Another village well off the beaten track is **Dallington**, which has some old half-timbered buildings and a church with a spire covered in stone slabs instead of the usual shingle. The nave is a Victorian rebuilding, with turned beams like enormous chair legs stretching right across.

At **Wood's Corner**, half a mile east of Dallington on the road to Battle, is a folly built by 'Mad Jack' Fuller, the squire of Brightling, who died in 1834 aged seventy-seven. It stands near the Ordnance Survey triangulation point (558 feet), and takes the form of a cement-rendered sugar-loaf, put up after Fuller had bet a friend that the spire of Dallington church was visible from the Grecian temple in the grounds of Brightling Park (then known as Rose Hill). When Fuller found he was wrong, he had the sugar-loaf built on the skyline. Inside it is reminiscent of a Mycenean beehive tomb; it was inhabited until 1880 and could still make a bizarre weekend cottage.

From Wood's Corner a side road leads up to **Brightling Needle**, an obelisk built on the highest point for miles around (646 feet), and the most prominent of Mad Jack's constructions. Brightling Park's broken-down stone wall runs from near the beacon to **Brightling** village; the dignified two-storey house can be seen over the churchyard wall. Fuller lies buried underneath the massive pyramid in the churchyard. According to legend, he sits inside wearing a top hat and holding a bottle of claret; but the church guide punctures this story by stating that 'he died a natural death and is buried in the ordinary recumbent position beneath the floor of the pyramid'. Inside the church is a tablet to Fuller on the south wall of the nave; the bust shows the fleshy face of a man who enjoyed the good things of life. He was interested in music, and in science, as is shown by the observatory he built on a hill near Brightling Needle, still used for amateur astronomy. Fuller bought Bodiam Castle when it was about to be demolished, and commissioned a number of paintings of Sussex from Turner. He sat as MP for Sussex from 1801 to 1812, after an election that cost him and his supporters a total of £50,000. On one occasion he was ejected from the House for calling the Speaker an 'insignificant little fellow in a wig'. A window in the north wall of the church contains the coat-of-arms of the Fullers, with the motto 'Carbone et Forcipibus' ('by charcoal and tongs'), referring to their trade as ironfounders.

William of Wykeham – the future Chancellor of England and founder of Winchester College and New College, Oxford – was rector here in 1362. His coat-of-arms can be seen outside the church on two shields above the small door in the south wall of the chancel.

East of Brightling the road passes over the aerial ropeway of British Gypsum, with endless chains of containers gliding silently by. Apart from occasional glimpses of this nature, the biggest industrial concern in the area is virtually invisible.

From Brightling a lane runs north of Darwell Reservoir, a brilliant sheet of water seen here and there through the trees or across a field, and then swings down to **Mountfield**, the quintessence of a forgotten Sussex village: a big house set in a park full of old oaks; a few cottages; and a small church with squat tower, simple nave with Norman chancel arch, and organ gallery at the back. Beyond Mountfield a dead straight road leads south to Battle, a couple of miles away.

Robertsbridge, north of Mountfield, on the main Hastings road, used to be called Rotherbridge; the road runs uphill from the Rother between a jumble of old houses, many of them half-timbered. At the top of the hill there is a small green with a varied group beside it, and the red tilehung bulk of the George, an old coaching inn, facing down the street. Robertsbridge was once the junction for the Kent and East Sussex Railway, used in the summer by hop-pickers making for the hopfields round Bodiam.

Robertsbridge grew as an appendage to a Cistercian abbey, founded towards the end of the twelfth century. The ruins are now part of a private house in a lane by the Rother about a mile east of the town. The house has an inordinately high-pitched roof, protecting what remains of the abbot's house, including the tall west window; and in the garden are the ruins of the refectory.

Across the river from the abbey is **Salehurst**, whose large gaunt church is used by Robertsbridge, which has no church of its own. The name comes from the Anglo-Saxon 'sealh' (willow) and 'hurst' (wood), and the area is still famous for its cricket bat willows. In medieval times Salehurst was on the main road to London, and until the Reformation was more important than Robertsbridge. The present church was begun in the thirteenth century, and greatly enlarged by the abbots of Robertsbridge in the fourteenth. Inside is a remarkable font, carved with salamanders running round the foot; by tradition it was given to the church by Richard Coeur de Lion in gratitude for being released from imprisonment in Bavaria by Abbot William of Robertsbridge.

From Heathfield to the Hastings road at Hurst Green, the A265 runs along the crest of the high ridge that separates the Rother and the Dudwell. **Burwash**, five miles east of Heathfield, consists of a single main street, with the church at the eastern end and an exceptionally harmonious collection of houses, which can all be seen by five minutes' walk along the brick pavement. Most imposing of all is the high-roofed Carolean house near the church, which according to Pevsner is timber-framed under the elegant brickwork.

Charming though Burwash is, it is not so much the village that people come to see as **Bateman's** (National Trust), the house below the ridge where Kipling spent the last three decades of his life. Bateman's is a handsome stone house built in 1634 possibly by a wealthy ironmaster; aptly enough, the stone from which it was built has rusted in places where ore runs through it. Kipling came here in 1902 from Rottingdean, and tells of his first visit with his usual

235

whimsy. 'We had seen an advertisement of her, and we reached her down an enlarged rabbit-hole of a lane. At very first sight the Committee of Ways and Means said: "That's her! The Only She! Make an honest woman of her quick!" We entered and felt her Spirit – her Feng Shui – to be good.'

Kipling was thirty-seven at the time and at the height of his fame. At Bateman's he wrote *Puck of Pook's Hill*, *Rewards and Fairies* and the Sussex poems; and he lived there until his death in 1936. Among the relics in the drawing-room is a small watercolour of Lake Rudyard in Staffordshire, where Kipling's parents met and which no doubt they remembered nostalgically when they christened their first-born out in Bombay. Kipling's father, Lockwood Kipling, was by profession an architectural sculptor and went to Bombay as the principal of an art school there; he was later curator of the Lahore Museum. He carved the terracotta plaques which were used as illustrations for *Kim* and other books, and which hang on the walls at Bateman's.

The best of the portraits of Kipling, painted in 1891, shows him in a white Indian-style jacket. His study is very much as he left it: the long table still with ink-well and pipe cleaners; the chair raised on blocks for his short stature; the novels, histories and books of travel and poetry lining the walls; the personal oddments picked up in the course of a wandering life. From the bedroom across the corridor can be seen the small dome-shaped rise which was the original of Pook's Hill. A large room with powder closet leading off it is used as an exhibition room, with early magazine editions of the short stories, more plaques by John Lockwood Kipling, and a remarkable seventeenth-century Sussex fireback showing an ironmaster, Richard Lenard of Brede, holding a hammer and surrounded by his wares.

The garden was largely planned by Kipling and was paid for by funds from his 1907 Nobel Prize for Literature. It leads down to the banks of the Dudwell, with a watermill that Kipling harnessed for electricity when he first came to Bateman's. In one of his poems he personified it:

See you our little mill that clacks
So busy by the brook?
She has ground her corn and paid her tax
Ever since Doomsday book.

The mill has been restored and produces stone-ground flour sold in the National Trust shop.

Kipling's only son John was killed at Loos in 1915, aged eighteen. There is a tablet to him on the south aisle of the church. Until the end of his life Kipling felt responsible for John's death – he was not fit enough to join the army, but Kipling pulled the necessary strings to arrange this. The church has a fourteenth-century iron grave slab, said to be the oldest in existence. The tower was built about 1090, and in spite of much Victorian rebuilding the graceful chancel arch was left untouched.

Like Heathfield, which used to be pronounced 'Heffle', Burwash was 'Berrish' to the locals. A Victorian rector of the village, John Coker Egerton, left a marvellous picture of Burwash life a century ago in *Sussex Folk and Sussex Ways*. In his day the roads were so bad that six horses had to be used to pull a two-wheel cart; and a farm labourer's life was no rustic idyll, but was summed up in the rhyme:

> *Pork and cabbage all the year,*
> *Mouldy bread and sour beer,*
> *Rusty bacon, stinking cheese,*
> *A chaff bed full of fleas –*
> *Who do you think would live here?*

Etchingham is a scattered village, with a commuter station and a massive fourteenth-century church. In the Middle Ages the fortified manor of the de Echyngham family stood roughly where the station is now, guarding the crossing point of the Rother, which was navigable as far as here for the ships of the time. The manor has disappeared, but Sir William de Echyngham's baronial church still stands, with its centrally placed tower held together by metal cramps, its flowing tracery which suggests a French architect, and its brasses. In front of the altar lies Sir William (headless now) in chainmail, over an inscription 'Of earth was made and formed, and to earth returned, William de Echyngham was his name. God on my soul have pity.' The copper vane on the tower is the original fourteenth-century one.

The road to **Bodiam** branches off the A21 a mile south of Hurst Green; or you can get there from Salehurst by twisting back lanes. Though **Bodiam Castle** (National Trust) seems remote and pointless today, it was built to guard an important crossing of the Rother, which in the Middle Ages was a navigable river and a possible invasion route for the French right into the heart of Kent and Sussex.

The castle is a classic of medieval fortification, austere in the symmetry of its walls, round corner towers and square-cut gatehouses. In the summer it dozes peacefully above its reflection in the moat; but a better time to see it is on a lonely winter afternoon, with a cold rain whipping the water and battering the walls – a reminder of the chill grimness of the Middle Ages that lay behind the pageantry.

It was built by Sir Edward Dalyngrygge in 1385, at a time when the French fleet had virtual command of the sea, and is thought to be unique as a combination of private dwelling and part of the national defence system. Fortunately, it was never attacked, though it was held by an opponent of Richard III during the Wars of the Roses, and was probably slighted (made undefendable) by Cromwell in the Civil War. By the mid eighteenth century its teeth had been so thoroughly drawn that it was used to grow vegetables. It belonged to various owners, including Mad Jack Fuller (see above), before its final restoration by Lord Curzon, formerly Viceroy of India, who bought it in 1917 and left it to the National Trust when he died nine years later.

The main entrance to the castle is on the north side, through the gatehouse which still has its portcullis, now rusted into place. Inside there is a single large courtyard, with buildings round all four walls: great hall, chamber, ladies' bower and chapel for Sir Edward; servants' hall and massive kitchen; household offices. By the standards of the time it must have been comfortable, though damp; looking up the south-east tower, for example, you can see three storeys of bedrooms each with its own shapely fireplace. The south-west tower is also worth a close look, as it houses the castle's well, and cut in the stone round the upper levels are rows of nesting boxes for pigeons. A small museum next to the ticket office has a model of how the castle looked in its prime – like a college quadrangle of the same date, crouching behind a shield of stone.

A rectangular depression between the southern side of the moat and the Rother marks the site of the harbour, and a flat area towards the village is said to have been a tilting yard (though more prosaically it is now thought to have been the village mill-pond).

From Bodiam the most prominent landmark is the spire of **Ewhurst** church on the ridge to the south. Ewhurst (now called Ewhurst Green, to distinguish it from Ewhurst in Surrey) used to be a rustic backwater, but has undergone an arty transformation right in its centre.

The centre of **Northiam** is full of character, though the outskirts down towards the Rother are unprepossessing. Not all that long ago the name was pronounced 'Norgam', as Bodiam was 'Bodgem', and a local rhyme testifies to patriotism if not to any great poetic talent:

O rare Norgam, thou dost far exceed
Beckley, Peasmarsh, Udimore and Brede.

Northiam's showpiece is the ancient battered oak on the village green, now virtually branchless and held together by chains and clamps, under which Queen Elizabeth I dined in August 1573, on her progress through Kent and Sussex. She took off her green shoes there and let the people of Northiam keep them; they are now at Brickwall, the home of the Frewen family, and are put on show when the house is open to the public. All round the green are fine examples of weatherboarded eighteenth-century houses. The church, with its tall stone spire, lies hidden away behind; the base of the tower is Norman, and the rest of the building was built at various times in the Middle Ages. In early Victorian times it was considerably altered, and the Frewen mausoleum was added on the north side.

Northiam's two main houses are at opposite ends of the village. **Brickwall**, now a boys' school, takes its name from the high walls that surround the gardens. The front has a close-set pattern of elaborate timbering, with the date 1633 on the bargeboards of the central gable. The walls of the drawing-room are lined with Frewen family portraits, which must be among the most comprehensive collection of any prosperous squirearchal family in the country. The first Frewen came to Northiam as rector in 1573; the portraits begin in the seventeenth century, and include paintings of Stephen Frewen, Alderman of the City of London, and his brother, who had the Puritan name of Accepted Frewen and became Archbishop of York. (Northiam went in for original names. When vaccination became compulsory in the nineteenth century one furious inhabitant saddled his daughter with the name Annie Antivaccinator.) Also in the drawing-room is the sedan chair belonging to Martha Frewen, who burnt to death in her bedroom in 1752, while passengers in the Rye coach listened helplessly to her screams.

Great Dixter, at the end of a lane off the main street, is a timber-framed late fifteenth-century manor house of more architectural but less personal interest. In 1910 it was bought in a state of semi-dereliction by the architectural historian Nathaniel Lloyd, who employed Lutyens to restore and add to the building, and to design the gardens. The great hall is a magnificent room, with an enormous central tie-beam supporting a kingpost, and hammerbeams on either side; the hammers are ornamented with armorial bearings of local families connected with the early days of Dixter. The tilehung extension on the front of the building was designed by Lutyens, and at the back is a small hall house of about 1500, brought timber by timber from Benenden and re-erected at Dixter.

The sunk garden was designed by Lloyd after the First World War, but the rest is by Lutyens, who also preserved and incorporated the fine old farm buildings near the house. The gardens have an incredible amount of topiary yew, including eighteen peacocks, pyramids and battlemented walls, and spectacular herbaceous borders full of contrasting colour. Since 1950 they have been presided over by Nathaniel's son, the writer and garden expert Christopher Lloyd, who among many alterations and improvements has converted the Lutyens-designed rose garden into a garden for exotic-looking plants.

Towards the end of the Second World War Northiam had a brief taste of world-shattering affairs, when on 12 May, 1944, four Allied prime ministers met on the playing fields before D-Day, and held an inspection of the troops of Southern Command. Their names are recorded on a plaque on one of the gates: Churchill of Great Britain, Mackenzie King of Canada, Smuts of South Africa and Huggins of Southern Rhodesia.

Beckley, on the road to Rye, is a pretty, strung-out village, with a grouping of medieval church and Georgian houses at the Northiam end. Alfred the Great, who died in AD 900, referred in his will to lands at 'Beccanleah' (Beckley), and there was certainly a Saxon church on the present site. With its homely dormer windows breaking the roofline, squat Norman tower and top-heavy spire, it is a church full of character. Inside, there are two 'jack-in-the-green' corbels (grotesque stone heads with leaves growing from their mouths) and a dug-out oak chest that may be eight centuries old. On still nights the quiet of Beckley is said to be broken by the hoofbeats of Sir Reginald Fitzurse, one of the four murderers of Becket, riding unavailingly to the church for sanctuary after the crime.

Newenden, over the Rother from Northiam across a narrow humpbacked bridge, is a trim little village. The church, right on the road, is a fragment of a much larger medieval building; it has a fine

Norman font, carved with a design of dragons and other fabulous beasts. According to Lambarde, in 1241 the first Carmelites to arrive in England 'made their nest at Newendene, which was before a wooddie and solitarie place'.

Two miles to the west is **Sandhurst**, not much to look at except for its church, which is a mile away from the village down the back road to Bodiam. The original village is said to have been near the church, but after the Black Death of 1349 the surviving inhabitants moved to healthier ground up on the ridge. Part of the churchyard is still reputed to be a plague pit where victims were buried. The church has a massive stone tower, built in the fourteenth century and perhaps used as a watch tower for Bodiam Castle below. Half a century ago Sandhurst had a mill claimed to be the only five-sailer in Kent.

Hawkhurst has grown considerably in recent years, and is now at the uneasy half way stage between village and town. It reached the height of its fame, or rather notoriety, in the first half of the eighteenth century, when the 'Hawkhurst Gang' of smugglers held a reign of terror over much of Kent and Sussex. They regularly murdered or tortured opponents, and were so self-assured that after a successful smuggling run to Rye they would celebrate at the Mermaid there with their loaded pistols lying on the table in front of them, without any interference from the magistrates.

The old part of Hawkhurst, known as The Moor, lies half a mile south of the main crossroads, round a large triangular green. The long, low ragstone church has magnificent Perpendicular window tracery in the aisles, which were added about 1450. Finer still is the Decorated east window dating from the previous century, a five-light masterpiece rising to a star at the apex. The glass was blown out, and the church put out of action for thirteen years, by a flying bomb which landed in the churchyard in 1944. One of the new windows on the south side commemorates Sir John Herschel, the nineteenth-century astronomer, who lived at Hawkhurst for the last thirty years of his life; the fitting subject is the Wise Men and the Star. Church and green are surrounded by prosperous brick and weatherboarded houses.

Up the hill, in the more recent part of Hawkhurst, is what looks from a distance like a large Wealden church, with a spire dominating the ridge; a closer look shows it to be Victorian Gothic (built by Sir George Gilbert Scott in 1861). It is now disused. Opposite is a civilized country-town row of shops, with weatherboarding above and an arcade of cast-iron pillars below.

At **Flimwell**, where the A268 crosses the Hastings road, you pass an extraordinary collection of steep-gabled Victorian farm cottages, set well back from the road behind gardens crammed with vegetables. They are just as much a part of the history of the countryside as any half-timbered Tudor cottage. On the brow of the hill behind, at the southern edge of Bedgebury Forest, the lattice tower and saucer aerials of a television relay station intrude on the landscape.

Ticehurst, a couple of miles beyond the crossroads, is a good tilehung village. Down the road to the church is an unusual little row of shops with an arcade of spindly iron pillars. The church is thirteenth- and fourteenth-century, and still keeps some of its medieval glass, originally in the east window but now in the north wall of the chancel. One of the lights is a 'doom window', showing souls being trundled off to hell in a tumbril by grinning devils.

Wadhurst, a good deal larger than Ticehurst, was a centre of the iron industry. The big Queen Anne vicarage which dominates the High Street was built by John Legas, chief ironmaster of the town; and if the church is not actually built of iron it is largely floored with it. The tall slender spire, nearly 130 feet high, which shoots up behind the main street, has been struck by lightning six times down the years; the tower is Norman, and the rest of the church Early English or later.

On the floor of the chancel, nave and aisles are thirty iron grave slabs, mainly of the seventeenth century. The earliest ones have a simple repetitive design of shields; but as the century progressed the founders grew more assured, and by the end of the century were producing complex and ornate designs, like the embossed slab of William Barham in the chancel, dated 1701. Recent examples of ironwork are the cast-iron cross and candlesticks on the altar, and the wrought-iron and glass screen protecting the bell-ringers, decorated with lambs, hops and flowers. In the porch are memorials to the Luck family, one of which is decorated with terracotta plaques made by Jonathan Harmer of Heathfield, an early nineteenth-century potter whose work can be found on monuments here and there in East Sussex.

At the Tunbridge Wells end of Wadhurst is a group of Victorian workshops with walls largely of glass – an early example of a factory estate, looking like a set from a Keystone Cops or Charlie Chaplin movie.

The last important prize fight in England was held at Wadhurst in December 1863. To get there, enthusiasts caught a special train from London Bridge at six in the morning.

The Rother Valley

During the 1950s the late Sir Michael Tippett lived at **Tidebrook Manor**, on a back road half way between Wadhurst and Mayfield, completing his opera *The Midsummer Marriage* and composing several major orchestral works.

16

The Norman Shore

THOUGH WILLIAM THE Conqueror landed his army along the coast in Pevensey Bay, and defeated Harold and the Saxons six miles inland, at Battle, **Hastings** has appropriated for itself the name of the most crucial conflict in English history. Hastings was an important port in Saxon times; the name Haestingas is a Saxon tribal name, and in Edward the Confessor's reign the town was renowned for its sailors and ships. It was the first place William made for on his landing. The Bayeux Tapestry has a scene of Normans throwing up a motte or earth mound, and constructing one of William's prefabricated castles – wooden structures, brought over in sections from Normandy – on top of it. It was from this strongpoint, where the ruins of Hastings Castle now stand, that the Normans marched along the high ridge to Battle on the morning of 14 October, 1066.

Nine centuries later it needs an effort to visualize that early Hastings. The topography is now quite different, as the sea has carried away much of West Hill, and over half the stone Norman castle which was built almost immediately after the Conquest. It is thought that the Saxon harbour was in the centre of the modern town, with a creek leading out to sea along the line of Harold Place; West Hill would both have protected the harbour from the wind, and dominated it as a site for fortification. Old Hastings is across to the east of the castle, in the sheltered valley between West and East Hills. The inland harbour gradually fell into disuse as the creek became blocked by shingle, and was finally abandoned after the colossal storms of 1287. From being one of the most powerful of the Cinque Ports, Hastings fell into decay.

The combined outcrop of West Hill and Castle Hill, a rolling stretch of mown grass, is the natural place to begin an exploration of Hastings, as it gives a bird's-eye view of the layout of the place, from the fishing boats drawn up on the shingle below, to the looming bulk of the St Leonards Marine Court building two miles to the west.

The **Castle** itself is fragmentary. All that remains is part of the curtain wall. the lower sections of the western gatehouse, and a few arches and part of the tower of the collegiate church, begun about 1070 by the Norman governor, Robert d'Eu. William entrusted the whole of Sussex to six of these great barons, dividing the county into six administrative areas, or 'rapes', each with a port defended by a castle, and extending inland from south to north. Hastings was the easternmost of the rapes, the others being Pevensey, Lewes, Bramber, Arundel and Chichester.

The original motte survives in the angle of the curtain wall, but there is no trace of a keep. Presumably it was built in the southern part of the castle, and collapsed and fell as the cliff was eroded. Outside the curtain wall is a honeycomb of passages in the sandstone, shown to visitors as dungeons, but thought by experts to have been used as storehouses. However, they have the extraordinary property of making even the smallest whisper audible along all their twists and turns, and would have made excellent oubliettes for political prisoners. An audio-visual show, housed in a replica of a medieval siege tent, illustrates the confrontation between Normans and Saxons.

West Hill also contains some far more extensive underground passages, the **St Clement's Caves**, a naturally formed network of tunnels with a good deal of man-made embellishment. In the nineteenth century they were leased by a Mr Joseph Golding, who spent years underground, hewing galleries, arcades and statues from the sandstone, and producing one of the commercial wonders of Hastings. During the war the caves were used as air raid shelters, protected by eighty feet of rock. They now form a suitably eerie background for lurid smuggling tableaux.

From West Hill steep alleys lead down to **Old Hastings**. This consisted originally of two main streets, All Saints Street and High Street, running roughly parallel down to the shore; but about forty years ago a third street, The Bourne, was brutally gashed through the old buildings to take the increase of traffic – 'the Rape of Hastings indeed', as Pevsner savagely puts it. Fortunately it is easy enough to forget this miserable assemblage of neo-Georgian housing while exploring the streets around it. Near the southern end of the High Street is **St Clement's Church**, one of the two medieval churches surviving from Hastings's original total of seven. This is the borough church of Hastings, containing the mayoral pew, marked by a gilded rail; it was begun about 1270, suffered severely in an attack by the French in the 1370s and was largely rebuilt soon afterwards. The west end is cut off at an angle, to fit in with the hilly site. It is the only church in Sussex dedicated to St Clement, the patron saint of black-smiths and sailors. (Old Romney in Kent has the same dedication.)

The other medieval church, **All Saints**, is at the north end of All Saints Street, at the entrance to old Hastings. It stands on a bluff overlooking the town, and was rebuilt like St Clement's after the French raids, probably a few decades later. Though it is not a particularly large building, it has a feeling of great spaciousness, with lofty vaulting under the tower. Over the chancel arch is an extensive piece of medieval wall painting, much better preserved than most – a 'Doom' painting, showing Christ in judgment, seated on a rainbow. A brightly painted rhyme under the tower, dated 1756, tells of the joys of bellringing, with a warning to the would-be ringer:

> *But if you ring in spur or hat*
> *Sixpence you pay be sure of that.*

All Saints faces directly across the road to the Catholic church of **St Mary Star of the Sea**, a timelessly Gothic nineteenth-century building with walls of rounded pebbles. It was founded by the poet Coventry Patmore, famous in his day for *The Angel in the House*, a lengthy hymn to Victorian domesticity. From 1876 to 1891 he lived in the splendid Georgian Old Hastings House, whose redbrick stables are now a theatre.

An alley beside All Saints churchyard leads up to the **Tackleway**, one of the prettiest streets in any of the South Coast resorts – a row of small weatherboarded houses, painted white, blue, orange or green, facing on to the gorse-covered slopes of East Hill. The name has nothing to do with fishing tackle, but comes from an old French word *tegill*, meaning tile. From the Tackleway a number of steep alleys lead down to All Saints Street, the best preserved street in the old town, full of half-timbered houses, with occasional unexpected patches of wilderness. Shovells, a fifteenth-century house with jutting upper storey, was the home of the mother of Sir Cloudesley Shovell, the seventeenth-century admiral who drowned off the Scillies in 1707. The **High Street** has a dignified Georgian look; many of the houses have been turned into antique shops, and the old town hall is now a museum of local history. A final reminder of antiquity is a fragment of the medieval town wall, marked by a plaque, in Winding Street.

In George Street you are out of the antique-selling area and into that of shops that stock oilskins and waders, and cafés specializing in

Hastings Castle, built by William I immediately after the Norman Conquest.

mussels and jellied eels. Hastings is still very much a fishing town, centred on the tall black 'net shops' of the Stade. These unique wooden structures, used for storing nets and tackle, are thought to date back in general design to Elizabethan times. Built of tarred wood, they are about eight feet square and three storeys high, with the upper floors reached by internal ladders. The nets drying in the sun outside them are nowadays mainly of orange nylon; but the sailors mending their nets or busying themselves about the boats still have a piratical look – like their ancestors who, says Augustus Hare, were known as 'Chopbacks' from their habit of chopping an axe down the backs of their enemies.

Next to the net shops is the **Fishermen's Museum,** built in 1854 as a chapel. Its central exhibit is the *Enterprise,* the last of the Hastings sailing luggers, built in 1909. The walls are hung with faded photographs of ancient mariners with white fringe beards; and as a fitting companion there is an enormous stuffed albatross. The nearby **Shipwreck Heritage Centre,** as its name indicates, is largely given over to recording disasters at sea, with displays of treasures salvaged from wrecks down the centuries, and films of shattered hulks on the seabed. Visitors can see for themselves how modern technology anticipates such disasters by studying the traces of offshore shipping on the Centre's radar screen.

Like Brighton, Hastings owed its beginnings as a resort to an eighteenth-century medical man, a Dr Baillie; and by 1800 it was already becoming popular. The two miles of seafront, from East Parade down to the far end of St Leonards, now form a single unit; but in fact the twin resorts of Hastings and St Leonards grew gradually outwards, until they coalesced in the 1870s. One of the earliest developments was Pelham Crescent, built in 1824 by Joseph Kaye – a grey row of buildings directly below the castle, with a grey classical church in the middle. The best part of early nineteenth-century Hastings is Wellington Square, built on a steep site west of Castle Hill. In the Town Hall the **Hastings Embroidery** is displayed in a special room; this latter-day Bayeux Tapestry, nearly 250 feet long, was made in 1966 to mark the 900th anniversary of the battle, and is a needlework strip cartoon of more than eighty historic or dramatic events in British history, ranging from the murder of Becket to the conquest of Everest.

Hastings pier is nothing much in the way of piers, though it has all the necessary adjuncts. Opposite is one of the town's showpieces, the **White Rock Theatre,** built in the 1920s and faintly Oriental-

248

looking, with cream walls, and tiled pyramidal rooflets, surmounted by green spikes, at either end. In a hall under the auditorium, Norman England has been resuscitated in the **Domesday Exhibition**, which portrays life nine centuries ago in a series of tableaux of monks, princes and peasants, along with a 'talking head' of the Conqueror himself. The original White Rock was a prominent landmark which blocked the promenade near where the pier now stands. As it was very much in the way and, according to Mr W. H. Dyer's guidebook, 'gave the young Princess Victoria a hazardous passage when she came to the town', it was broken up and carted away in the 1830s. Across the White Rock Gardens is the town's main museum and art gallery; among the paintings of old Hastings is an especially evocative one by C. Powell, showing the shore as it was in 1790: a sea like a mirror, fishermen wading in the shallows, and grass stretching from the foot of Castle Hill to the shingle of the beach.

The only layout of any character west of the White Rock is Warrior Square, spaciously green and a welcome break in the terraced monotony.

St Leonards was the first, and remains the best, of the host of exclusive seaside residential developments where speculation and amenity make uneasy bedfellows. In 1828 the builder and architect James Burton, together with his more famous son Decimus, began to lay out a new resort at what was then a respectable distance from Hastings. The centrepiece of the scheme, the white stuccoed Royal Victoria Hotel, is still there; but the symmetry has been spoiled by the vast 1930s bulk of Marine Court, fourteen storeys high and designed to look like the sun decks of an ocean-going liner. Behind the Royal Victoria is the classical block of the Assembly Rooms (now a Masonic headquarters). A little entrance lodge leads to the landscaped valley of St Leonards Gardens, still with a good many Burton houses surviving on either side. Over a fence, in the gardens of Gloucester Lodge, a memorial portrait plaque of James Burton benevolently surveys his garden city by the sea. Visitors coming to St Leonards from the north used to have to pay a toll before being allowed under the arch of North Lodge, at the upper end of this highly desirable piece of marine exclusivity.

St Leonards church was destroyed by a flying bomb in 1944 and rebuilt in safe modern style in 1961. Inside it is impressive, with lofty paraboloid arches round the windows, and dark blue glass of saints and prophets by Patrick Reyntiens.

To get to **Battle** by the route William took, you should not go by the London Road from St Leonards, but take the Old London Road, and turn east in Ore, along The Ridge. If the Normans did not keep exactly to this line they must have stayed very near it, as in 1066 it was the only practicable route to Telham Hill, where William drew up his troops that October morning. It was not until late in the afternoon that Harold the Saxon died from an arrow in the eye – or from blows to the head and body, as some recent historians have suggested. The battle can be easily visualized from the terrace in the grounds of **Battle Abbey** (English Heritage), and followed on foot from a waymarked walk round the circuit of the battlefield – tiny by the standards of later conflicts, but still large enough to alter the course of a country's history.

The Saxons were drawn up on Caldbec Hill, barring William's advance to the north. They must have been exhausted after their long forced march down from the north of England, where they had defeated the Norwegian army under Harold Hardrada at Stamford Bridge, near York, less than three weeks before. Nevertheless they were so sure of victory that they spent the previous night drinking, unlike the dour Normans, who had passed the time in prayer. According to one account, the battle started when the Norman minstrel Taillefer made a suicide charge against the Saxon ranks; and with shouts of '*Dieu nous aide!*' from the Normans and 'Out! Out!' from the Saxons the slaughter began.

Harold should have won the battle by wearing the enemy down, as the Norman strength lay in their heavily armoured mounted knights, who could not penetrate the strong Saxon shield line. But late in the day the Normans on the right flank (seen from the Saxon side) made a feint retreat. The Saxons on that flank charged into the valley in pursuit, defying Harold's orders to stay put, and were slaughtered by the Norman cavalry. The Normans now had a way open up the hill and came in behind the Saxon army; and the battle was over. True to their practice, the Normans butchered anyone they caught, leaving the Saxon bodies to rot. It is not known what happened to Harold's body. According to one story, Harold's mistress, Edith Swan-neck, buried it at Waltham Abbey in Essex; while another account says that William wrapped it in purple linen and buried it on the cliff at Hastings. There is also the belief that some of his remains were buried at Bosham, near Chichester.

Before the battle William had vowed to build an abbey in the event of his victory, and it was in fulfilment of this vow that the

Abbey of St Martin was founded, with the high altar on the spot where Harold fell. The original abbey, consisting of church and monastic buildings, was completed by the end of the eleventh century; but the magnificent remains we see today are what is left of later rebuildings. Most splendid of all is the great gatehouse, built about 1338, which looms over the market square of Battle and closes the vista when you look down the High Street. During the Middle Ages the abbot was a man of tremendous consequence, with absolute power within his 'lowy' or area of sway, and able to pardon any criminal throughout the whole of England.

At the height of its glory the abbey had a long church with numerous side chapels, together with a cloister and the usual monastic buildings; but at the Dissolution in 1538 it was granted to Sir Anthony Browne, 'Master of the Kings Majestes Horcys' as his tomb in Battle church describes him, and was largely demolished by him. However, a good deal still remains, notably the monks' dorter or sleeping quarters over a series of beautifully vaulted common rooms, and a row of cellars built into the side of the hill up which the Normans advanced. Browne converted the abbot's house to his own use; altered and added to down the centuries, it is now a co-educational boarding school.

A melodramatic curse was laid on Sir Anthony as he feasted in the abbey: one of the dispossessed monks marched up to him with the prophecy that his line would end 'by fire and by water'. In 1793 the curse was finally fulfilled. Cowdray House, the home of the Montagues (Sir Anthony's son was the first Viscount Montague), was burnt to the ground, and the last Lord Montague was drowned in the Rhine (see Cowdray, p. 399).

In the Abbey precincts is a monument put up in 1903 by the French in honour of '*le brave Harold*'; it stands on the spot where the Saxon king stood to command his army.

The town of Battle is an attractive place. A mainly Georgian High Street slopes up from the abbey, leading to Mount Street (the original road to London), with a white-painted windmill at its summit. Outside the abbey gates, set back from the market square, is the timbered Pilgrims' Rest, fifteenth-century and possibly built for the abbey's cellarer. As a reminder of Battle's brutal past, a brass plate in the square marks the spots where bulls were tethered for baiting.

The **Parish Church** is very much in the shadow of the abbey walls. It was begun soon after the abbey, at the beginning of the twelfth century; the tower was added in the fifteenth century, and the whole thing was restored by Butterfield in Victorian t mes. In the sanctuary is the ornate tomb of Sir Anthony Browne and his wife, with a frieze of winged cherubs' heads round the side and alabaster effigies on top. On the north wall is a copy of the *Roll of Battle Abbey*, a document of dubious authenticity on which the sonorous Norman names of William's knights are listed – Columber, Grendoun, Malebraunch, Wardebois. **Battle Museum** (in Langton House) has a reproduction of part of the Bayeux Tapestry.

Sedlescombe is a pretty village, with its share of tearooms and antique shops, and a long narrow green running up its gently sloping hill. The church is north of the village, end on to the road, and was greatly enlarged and restored in 1868. The hierarchy of rural society three centuries and more ago is well illustrated by a church seating plan of 1632 that hangs inside. Sir Thomas Sackville, family and retainers sat in the front; behind were pews of villagers like the Widows Van, Stint and Sloman, and right at the back 'Youths and Strangers'.

At the south end of Sedlescombe is the **Pestalozzi Children's Village**. Johann Heinrich Pestalozzi (1746–1827) was a Swiss educationalist who took charge of orphans during the Napoleonic wars. After the Second World War another Swiss, Walter Robert Corti, founded the first Pestalozzi village at Trogen in Switzerland, and Sedlescombe was its English offshoot. The Village was opened in 1959 as an international home for children from displaced persons' camps in Europe. Since the mid 1960s it has cared for children from developing countries, including Zambia, Zimbabwe, Thailand, Nepal and the Tibetan refugee communities in India; thirty-five young people aged between sixteen and twenty now live there. In 1997 it began a new programme in conjunction with the Hastings College of Arts and Technology. The presence of young people from so many developing countries means that British schoolchildren meet their contemporaries from a wide range of cultures, which can do nothing but good.

When Battle Abbey was built, stone for its construction is said to have been brought by boat as far as Sedlescombe along the River Brede, then much wider and navigable far inland. **Brede** village, three miles east of Sedlescombe, perches on a spur of land north of the river; its large church has a fortress-like appearance as you come up the hill towards it. Brede is a compact little place, with a typical mixture of brick and weatherboarding at its centre.

The church is a vast enlarging of a small Norman building of about 1140; the tower is mid fifteenth-century, and a chapel with fine tracery in the east window was added as late as the 1530s. In this chapel is the tomb of Sir Goddard Oxenbridge, who died in 1537. In effigy he looks harmless enough, but like Col. Lunsford of East Hoathly, it was rumoured that he ate children for his supper. The children of Sussex finally got their own back by making him drunk with beer and then sawing him in half with a huge wooden saw, the children of East Sussex sitting on one end and those of West Sussex on the other.

Near Sir Goddard's tomb is a tall and gentle Madonna, carved in oak by Clare Sheridan, the sculptress cousin of Winston Churchill. A woman of extraordinary persistence, she travelled to Russia soon after the Revolution and carved portrait busts of Lenin and Trotsky, staying for two months in the Kremlin and provoking Lenin to get the expression she wanted. She learnt to carve oak during a six months' stay on a Red Indian reservation; this Madonna was in memory of her son, drowned while sailing before the mast in a windjammer. Like the Oxenbridges, she lived at Brede Place, a small brick and stone manor on a terrace overlooking the river valley. She died in 1970 aged eighty-four.

Westfield is largely a redbrick eyesore in a fine high position. Its church has a solid tower, Saxon in origin, with vast buttresses, and a perfect Norman chancel arch with squints on either side. It suffered greatly at the hands of the Victorians, notably in its hideous columns between the nave and new north aisle. Hastings is creeping out so rapidly towards Westfield that the village will soon be swallowed up.

The eastward expansion of Hastings along the coast is blocked by the sandstone cliffs that begin at East Hill and stretch right round to Fairlight Cove. Between Hastings and Fairlight, more than 500 acres of clifftop are given over to the **Hastings Country Park**. Unlike the grass-covered chalk cliffs beyond Eastbourne, which fall sheer to the sea, the Hastings cliffs are split by sloping glens, full of gorse and bracken, and overhung by trees. Most beautiful of all is **Fairlight Glen**, where a stream, runs between huge boulders below the tangled woodland. A memorial plaque in the country park commemorates 'Grey Owl', the Hastings-born author (real name Archie Belaney), who between the wars lived the life of a Red Indian in Canada. His books and lectures did much to draw attention to the downtrodden plight of the Indians, and to the threats to the wildlife on which the survival of their culture depended.

Fairlight is little more than a collection of old coastguard cottages, and a ponderous grey stone church in a breathtaking position. The church is a complete nineteenth-century rebuilding, but it has a grandeur that suits the place. Its tower is a landmark for miles out to sea. The churchyard has a luxuriant collection of tombstones, including one, sadly neglected, to Richard D'Oyly Carte, founder of the opera company. From Fairlight the road drops steeply down to **Pett Level**, a flat expanse of watercourses and meadows, dotted with small lakes that are sanctuaries for wildfowl. The beach hereabouts is held in place by a barricade of groynes and cross timbers. Pett village lies well inland on top of a hill; its spiky Victorian church has a curious octagonal tower and spire, and a complement of large and sinister gargoyles.

Icklesham, two miles north of Pett along winding lanes, is the only substantial village in the area, and marks the eastern end of the Hastings peninsula, which William made the bridgehead for his invasion. It has a fascinatingly irregular Norman church, with a centrally placed tower rising in three successive steps. The Norman capitals on the nave columns are all different; the finely carved roof corbels above, in the forms of flowers and fruit, are Victorian work. Icklesham was first mentioned in 772, in a royal charter granting land to the Bishop of Selsey (see Bexhill, below). From Icklesham it is little more than a mile to Winchelsea.

Guestling, three miles back towards Hastings, has no village centre. The isolated church, Saxon in origin with a squat tower built about 1100, is down a side road beside a farm. It was largely rebuilt after a fire in 1890, but still has a good Norman arch, with chevron moulding, in the north aisle. Guestling was probably the meeting place of the governing body of the Cinque Ports, known as 'Court Guestling'; off the beaten track and on neutral territory, it would certainly have been a suitable spot.

The main road from St Leonards to Bexhill (A259) is now so built up that you can get little idea of the local topography as you drive along it. In medieval times an area of undrained and over-grown marshland stretched inland as far as Crowhurst (see below), protecting the Hastings peninsula on its western side; hence the strategic importance of Battle, half way between the Crowhurst gap and the Brede levels. The pub called the Bo-Peep, at the west end of St Leonards, is said to be named after the games of hide-and-seek the smugglers played with the revenue men. According to a notice inside, the famous nursery rhyme was written by 'Old Humphrey', a

Hastings character, after watching the landlord's little daughter playing in the fields.

At **Bulverhythe** the wreck of the Dutch East Indiaman *Amsterdam* is visible occasionally at extremely low tides. In January 1749 she set out on her maiden voyage from Holland to Java laden with chests of silver bullion, thousands of bottles of wine and bolts of cloth. She ran into a gale, and her rudder was torn off in Pevensey Bay. The captain wanted to repair it and sail on, but the crew mutinied, broke into the wine store and ran her aground at Bulverhythe, where she was soon swallowed up by the soft clay of the shoreline. The Dutch East India Company recovered the silver, but little else. By the 1990s the timbers were so decayed that the ship was in danger of disappearing, so their positions were plotted and fed into a computer to give a complete record of the ship's construction.

Bexhill is a latecomer to the status of a seaside resort, and has never summoned up the self-assurance to build itself a pier. Development began only in 1885, when Lord De La Warr gave the first impetus by building on a large tract of his land between old Bexhill and the sea. Bexhill is a featureless place. Its pride and joy is the De La Warr Pavilion, built in the 1930s by Erich Mendelsohn and Serge Chermayeff, both refugees from the Nazis and apostles of the then-revolutionary functional style of architecture. With its great bows of glass and spacious stairway, it is still way ahead, architecturally speaking, of most if not all the major buildings on the South Coast. Chermayeff, who died in 1996 aged 95, was described in his *Guardian* obituary as 'the most flamboyant of the modernists, a lover of theatre, jazz, adventuring, sunbathing and sea'. In other words, the right man in the right place at the right time. Next door to the pavilion are two groups of buildings in delightful contrast to it, Marina Arcade and Marina Court Avenue, built at the beginning of the century. With their green onion domes and glimpses of inner courtyards, they are like small great-nephews of Brighton's Royal Pavilion.

The old village is inland, north of the railway at the top of Upper Sea Road – a small oasis of weatherboarding round the ancient parish church. Though the church was vastly expanded in the nineteenth century, it still has traces of Saxon work, a powerful tower of about 1070, and Norman arches at the west end. Bexhill is first mentioned, along with Icklesham, in a charter of 772, recording the grant of land at 'Bexlei' by Offa, King of Mercia, to Bishop

Oswald of Selsey. In its homely attention to detail, this charter takes us back beyond the harsh efficiency of the Normans to the 'good time of the smaller things' whose passing G. K. Chesterton lamented in his *Ballad of the White Horse.* 'These are the bounds of the 8 hides of inland of the people of Bexhill. Firstly at the servants' tree, from the servants' tree south to the treacherous place, so along the shore over against Cooden cliff, eastward and so up on to the old boundary dyke, so north to Kewhurst, and so to the Benetings' stream, and so north through Shortwood to the boundary beacon, from the beacon to the bold men's ford, from the ford along the marsh to the road bridge, from the bridge along the ditch to Beda's spring, from the spring south along the boundary thus to the servants' tree.'

The church's chief treasure is an eighth-century Saxon stone, probably carved at much the same time as the charter was written. It is decorated with crisply carved interlaced cable ornament, and may have been the lid of a reliquary placed there when the church was consecrated. About 1750 the medieval glass depicting saints in one of the north windows came by devious means into the possession of Horace Walpole, who incorporated it into his jackdaw's nest of antiquities at Strawberry Hill, Twickenham; it was finally restored to Bexhill in 1921.

Bexhill straggles westwards along the A259 as far as the prison; and then you are away from buildings and in the flat expanse of **Pevensey Levels**. Half a mile north of the road is the small village of **Hooe**, with a medieval church at the end of a farm track, dozing in an unenclosed and peaceful churchyard. Inside is a rough-hewn muniment chest, supposedly Saxon. An alternative route from Bexhill to Pevensey is along the coast road, through the smart resort of Cooden, and skirting the not-so-smart shanty town of Norman's Bay.

When William landed in 1066 this area of dyke and meadowland was a swampy inlet of the sea; the ancient names – Manxey, Rickney, Chilley and Pevensey – all have the Saxon '-ey' suffix meaning 'island'. The Bayeux Tapestry shows the Normans landing at Pevensey on 28 September, 1066; some of the ships are already unloaded, while elsewhere sailors are lowering the masts or leading the horses through the shallows. Apart from being a convenient landing-point, **Pevensey** had the great advantage from William's point of view of having a ready-made **Castle** (English Heritage) – the Roman fortress of Anderida, probably built about AD 280 as one of the 'Forts of the Saxon Shore'. The Roman walls are not built to the usual rectangular plan, but in a rough oval, corresponding to the raised ground of the 'island' of Pevensey. They are still remarkably well preserved round three of the sides, especially the massive west gateway, with its rounded stone buttresses, striped every few feet with courses of thin Roman brick. When the Romans left Britain in 410, the Romanized Britons occupied the castle; but in 477 the Saxons under Aella attacked Anderida and slaughtered every man, woman and child within the walls. The Saxons took over its name and applied it to the dense forest that spread north into Sussex and Kent – the Andredsweald, or Forest of Andred, shortened in course of time to the Weald.

The Normans built their own castle in the south-eastern corner of the walls. Much of the inner bailey survives, including the base of the gatehouse, the foundations of the chapel, and the lower levels of the keep, strengthened by gigantic semi-circular bastions. The keep was built about 1100, the gatehouse about 1220. Unlike so many medieval castles, Pevensey seems to have been really defensible, withstanding sieges by William Rufus in 1088 and Simon de Montfort the Younger after the Battle of Lewes in 1264. It was even incorporated in the South Coast defences in 1940: a camouflaged gun emplacement is marked by a notice as prominently as the Roman postern and medieval oubliette.

Like all self-respecting castles, Pevensey has a ghost, reputedly of Andrew Borde, a Pevensey character who lived in the fifteenth-century **Mint House** (now an antique shop) outside the castle gates. Borde was court physician to Henry VIII and Edward VI, and was Henry's unofficial jester, reputedly the original 'Merry Andrew'. Born in 1490, he took holy orders, studied medicine on the Continent and acted as secret agent for Thomas Cromwell. His sense of humour is typified by the punning Latin name he made up for himself – 'Andreas Perforatus', Andrew 'Bored full of holes'. Like Till Eulenspiegel, his irresponsibility led to his downfall. In 1549 he was imprisoned on a trumped-up charge of debt by an enemy he had satirized, and died in the Fleet prison the same year. The house gets its name from the mint established by the Normans immediately after the Conquest; a 'minting chamber' with beams of enormous antiquity is at the back.

The Mint House has its own ghost, an Elizabethan woman who was horribly done to death there. She was the mistress of Thomas Dight, a London merchant, who lived at Pevensey in the 1580s.

Dight came home unexpectedly and found his mistress in bed with a lover. He ordered his servants to cut out her tongue, and made her watch while her lover was roasted to death over a fire in the minting chamber – a scene as macabre as anything in a Jacobean tragedy. Dight's men threw the body into the harbour, and took his mistress to an unlit upper room, where she was starved to death.

Old Pevensey's justice was administered from the Court House, a small white building with a museum of local relics, up the road from the castle. If a condemned criminal was a freeman of Pevensey, he had the right to be drowned rather than hanged. Tied hand and foot, he was thrown from the parapet of the bridge into the harbour; if he took his time drowning, there was a pile of stones ready at hand for his fellow-townsmen to finish him off.

The **Parish Church**, a completely uniform thirteenth-century building, with the tower centrally placed on the north side, is dedicated to St Nicolas (spelt thus in the French way), the patron saint of sailors. The old town seal shows the saint stilling the waves. In the seventeenth century the chancel arch was walled across, and the chancel was used as a cattle byre and storehouse for smuggled brandy. Andrew Borde's brother, Richard, was vicar here in the early days of the Reformation. After announcing to his parishioners that he 'would rather be torn to pieces by wild horses than acknowledge King Harry as head in spiritual matters of the Church of England', he prudently fled overseas without waiting for the repercussions.

On the other side of the castle from Pevensey is **Westham**, with a pretty village street and its own parish church, which has one of the most ruggedly beautiful church towers in Sussex, built in the fourteenth century and patched, braced and mended down the years. In the south chapel is the original Norman altar stone, with five consecration crosses, restored to its original purpose. Half a mile beyond Westham you are in the spreading suburbs of Eastbourne.

Pevensey is now cut off from the sea by the bungalow development of **Pevensey Bay**; but inland from the castle the Levels are still an empty expanse. The main landmark, due north, is the silver dome that formerly marked the Royal Greenwich Observatory at **Herstmonceux Castle**. The observatory moved to Sussex from Greenwich in 1957 because of atmospheric pollution and the glare of artificial light; but by the late 1970s the atmosphere of Southern England as a whole was no longer sufficiently clear, and in 1979 the giant 100-inch Isaac Newton telescope, housed in the great silver dome, was dismantled and refurbished, and five years later was installed on top of an extinct volcano in the Canary Islands. The astronomical buildings have been turned into the Herstmonceux Science Centre, which still has a magnificent 26-inch telescope *in situ* – used by the astronomer Patrick Moore in 1994, the Centre's guide tells us, 'to observe the collision of Comet Shoemaker-Levy 9 with the planet Jupiter'. The Centre has all sorts of hands-on science exhibits, which introduce children to magnetism, light and other scientific phenomena in a clear and simple way.

The castle itself has taken on a new lease of life as an international study centre for Queen's University of Kingston, Ontario. It has been so meticulously restored that it looks almost bogus; yet its battlements and turrets, following in brick the stone fortifications of the time, in fact date from the 1440s. It was built by Sir Roger de Fiennes, a veteran of Agincourt, to defend the Levels against possible French invasion. Large-scale building in brick was copied from Flanders, and Herstmonceux was one of the first extensive brick buildings in this country since Roman times. After it had passed down the centuries from one family to another, the interior was largely dismantled in the 1770s to build Herstmonceux Place (up the road towards the village). In the last century guidebooks referred to its 'desolation and decay', but successive owners since 1911 revived its mellow glory. In pre-scientific days a ghostly drummer nine feet tall was said to stride through the castle beating a spectral tattoo, but this has been explained away as a device used by smugglers to frighten off inquisitive locals.

Outside the castle gates is All Saints Church, an attractively varied little building, with a fifteenth-century chapel at the west end, built of brick, like the castle. On the floor of the chancel (under a carpet) is a splendid brass showing Sir William Fiennes, father of Sir Roger, in full armour. Herstmonceux village was the birthplace of the Sussex trug or garden basket over a hundred years ago; and the craft is still going strong.

Ninfield, five miles east of Herstmonceux, is a jumble of a village spreadeagled on a ridge. The little church is worth a glance inside for the magnificent blue-framed clock mechanism working away below the tower.

A couple of miles to the north is **Ashburnham Park**, where Capability Brown formed a chain of lakes to fill the low ground in front of **Ashburnham Place**. Brown's glorious park, with its plantation of great trees dropping steeply down to the water, still survives on the grand eighteenth-century scale. The redbrick house is only a fragment of its former vastness. It now consists of a central two-storey section with single-storey wings, whereas before 1959 it was three storeys high throughout. A new block was added in 1967, and the house is now used as a conference centre for Christians of all denominations.

Between the main house and the stable block is Ashburnham church, medieval-looking but largely rebuilt by John Ashburnham in the seventeenth century. The Ashburnhams – a family of wealthy ironmasters – have their monuments in the chapel on the north side of the chancel. John himself lies against the north wall, carved in anachronistic armour. A devoted Cavalier, he accompanied Charles I on his last journey to the scaffold, and was imprisoned by Cromwell in the Tower during the Protectorate. After the execution he got possession of the shirt, underclothes and watch that the king was wearing at the time; and the sheet that was thrown over the body later came into the possession of the family. They used to be kept in the church as relics for those who wanted to touch them against scrofula, a glandular disease known as the 'king's evil'; as recently as 1859 a child suffering from the disease was wrapped in the sheet.

The road that runs round the back of Ashburnham Park brings you to **Ashburnham Forge**, once powered by the Ashbourne stream which runs on through the park. The forge, together with Ashburnham Furnace nearby, continued working until the first decades of the nineteenth century, the last survivor of the Sussex iron industry. Beside the cottage you can still see the race that fed the undershot wheel, and the base of the supports that held it. The cottage garden has lumps of iron slag to edge the paths. It seems incredible that this little hollow, miles from anywhere, was once a centre of industry; but so it was. **Penhurst**, at the top of the hill, is a perfect little spot, like a Morland painting of gabled manor farmhouse, tiled church and great barn behind. The church still has its fifteenth-century oak screen.

Catsfield, south of the Battle road, is dominated by the tall spire of the Methodist church, which looks as though it has strayed across the Channel from North France. The parish church is tucked away down the road to Crowhurst, beside the manor house. Inside is an extraordinary encaustic tile memorial to Annie, Lady Brassey, showing a yacht against the setting sun. Lady Brassey died in the Indian Ocean aboard her schooner *Sunbeam* in 1887, and her body was 'committed to the deep at sunset'. The trophies she collected on her voyages round the South Sea Islands are now in the Hastings Museum.

Crowhurst, a couple of miles towards Hastings, is a hamlet on a steep hillside. The church is a Victorian rebuilding, apart from its fifteenth-century tower. The giant yew tree in the churchyard is said to date back to the days when Harold held the manor.

17

Eastbourne and the Downs

EASTBOURNE, TEN MILES from Bexhill on the other side of Pevensey Bay, has avoided the twin traps that lie in wait for the seaside resort: brashness at one extreme, and timid gentility at the other. Admittedly it does not allow a single shop along the whole three miles of its landscaped seafront; but it has a fine pier, with all the Victorian greenhouse effects that a good pier should have, and gardens along its sweep of elegant Parades.

Like Bexhill, Eastbourne was laid out as a speculation by a wealthy landowner; but it was laid out earlier, on a grander scale, and caught the high tide of nineteenth-century holidaymaking. The man responsible was William Cavendish, later the seventh Duke of Devonshire, who developed it from about 1850 onwards. His statue, robed, bewhiskered and slumped in an ornate throne, stands at the seaward end of Devonshire Place. Indeed, in the seafront area, you still feel as though you were visiting the Devonshires' private seaside estate: in the gardens west of the Wish Tower stands Spencer Compton, the eighth Duke, with his back to the sea; Devonshire Park is inland from the front; and the Devonshire Park Theatre, with its pair of handsome campaniles, looks across Compton Street to the Devonshire swimming baths.

Eastbourne is hemmed in to the west by the rampart of the Downs, with Beachy Head (the 'Beau Chef' or 'beautiful headland' of the Normans) as their culmination. But there is nothing to hinder its sprawl in other directions. To the north it has swallowed up Willingdon and Polegate (worth a detour for its restored early nineteenth-century windmill), and to the east housing estates are proliferating towards Pevensey, and creeping eastwards over the shingle of the Crumbles, within recent memory a wild stretch as lonely as Dungeness.

The original East Bourne is a mile or so inland, along the main Brighton road, and consists of a few streets of old houses, much

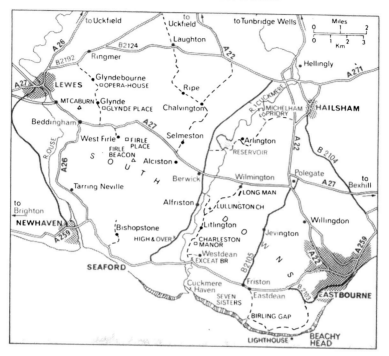

bitten into by haphazard modern development, round the **Parish Church**. This is a big building, mainly of about 1200, on the site of a Saxon church. The flattened chancel arch is ornamented with a double row of late Norman dogtooth moulding; the wooden screens have survived since the fourteenth century; and in the chancel are fine sedilia and an Easter sepulchre of about the same period. Behind the church is the stone-built Old Parsonage, a sixteenth-century hall house, and across a lane is the Lambe Hotel, said to date back to the thirteenth century.

On the other side of the road from the church is the **Towner Art Gallery and Local History Museum**, formerly the Manor House, a good sensible Georgian house built by Dr Henry Lushington, vicar of Eastbourne. At the beginning of the nineteenth century it was owned by Davies Gilbert, President of the Royal Society, friend of Thomas Telford, and a leading civil engineer. In the 1920s it was turned into the municipal art gallery, with emphasis on pictures of local interest. Most fascinating are the watercolours of Eastbourne as it was about 1850, painted by a local girl, Louisa C. Paris. She draws

263

cliff and beach, Sea Houses (the first resort, popular since 1780 when George III's children came there on holiday), and the new Eastbourne rising from the countryside, like Cornfield Terrace, a row of town houses waiting for neighbours literally in the middle of a cornfield.

Eastbourne makes full use of the Napoleonic relics at either end of the seafront. At the western end, opposite the hideous brown bulk of the Amalgamated Engineering Union building, is the **Wish Tower**, a martello tower (No. 73 in the South Coast chain of forts) made into a small museum illustrating the history of coastal defence. The odd name comes from the Saxon word *wisc*, meaning a marshy place. On the roof is a twenty-four pounder gun, still pointing out to sea as a deterrent to Bonaparte. Near the Wish Tower, the **Lifeboat Museum** has a collection of mementoes of the boats and their crews, with scale models beginning at the first lifeboat of them all, built on the Tyne in 1789.

At the eastern end of the front, past the elegant blue-domed bandstand and pier, is the far larger **Redoubt**, a squat circular redbrick fortress which still looks as substantial as any modern gun emplacement. It is now the home of the Sussex Combined Services Museum, and also houses an aquarium, where you can stare back at the goggling tropical fish when you have had your fill of warlike paraphernalia. A short stroll along Royal Parade brings you to the tropical illusion of the **Butterfly Centre**, where you can walk among hibiscus, jacaranda and bougainvillaea and watch exotic butterflies and moths fluttering in total freedom. At the eastern extremity of Eastbourne, on the shingle of Langney Point, is an unexpected and praiseworthy example of an environmentally friendly building, designed by the Council Architect's Department for Southern Water – a redbrick construction built to hide Eastbourne's new sewage-treatment works, which looks vaguely like a martello tower. The area round it has been landscaped and planted with thousands of trees, and no doubt by 2020 the whole thing will look convincingly Napoleonic. Beyond a genuine martello tower is the new Sovereign Harbour marina, hemmed in by modern housing.

As the hotels went up along the front between the Wish Tower and the Redoubt, the visitors flocked to Eastbourne, arriving at the station at the top of Terminus Road – very much a part of the Eastbourne scene, with its iron-framed clerestory on top. An improbable visitor, in 1905, was the French composer Claude Debussy, in search of peace and quiet after the break-up of his first marriage. He wrote to a friend: 'It's a little English seaside place, silly as these places sometimes are. I shall have to go because there are too many draughts and too much music.' The sea off Eastbourne is woven into his own greatest orchestral work, the glittering sparkle and surge of *La Mer.*

In **Beachy Head** Eastbourne has the most spectacular chalk precipice in England, not excluding Dover's White Cliffs. At the highest point the sheer drop is over five hundred feet – a scale brought into focus by the lighthouse a few yards out from the base of the cliffs, a large enough structure anywhere else, but here dwarfed to the size of a toy. Why the public is kept well away from the edge was shown in January 1999, when hundreds of thousands of tons of chalk were dislodged by rain followed by frost and crashed down from the cliff, creating a new causeway almost out to the lighthouse. Beachy Head is notorious for the number of its suicides, known locally as 'jumpers'; and as you watch the choughs and gulls that launch themselves dizzyingly above the foreshore and the sea, you may well feel like soaring after them. Adjoining the Beachy Head Hotel is a countryside centre where you can find out about the local geology and wildlife, peer into a Bronze Age hut, and even talk to a downland shepherd via an audio-visual presentation.

A mile away along the road to Birling Gap is the old **Belle Tout** lighthouse, now a private house. It was built in the 1830s by Mad Jack Fuller, of Brightling (see p. 234), and shows that his addiction to follies could give way to something far more practical. The stone is said to have been dragged by oxen from as far away as Maidstone in Kent. By the beginning of 1999 it was only a few feet away from the crumbling edge of the cliff; so in a unique experiment in house-moving the 850-ton granite structure was first jacked up onto rails and then inched by hydraulic rams to a safe new site fifty feet inland.

Crumbling chalk is also menacing the old coastguard cottages and sprawling pub at **Birling Gap,** the first break in the cliffs past Beachy Head and a favourite landing-place for smugglers in the eighteenth and nineteenth centuries. According to Augustus Hare, it was once guarded by a gate and portcullis. From Birling Gap you can follow the South Downs Way over the top of the Seven Sisters cliffs to Cuckmere Haven.

Eastdean, a mile to the north, is a vintage downland village of flint-walled houses neatly built round an oblong green. The church, in a hollow at the bottom, is a small aisleless building, with eleventh-century nave and thirteenth-century chancel, joined on askew. A new west end was added in 1962, with the organ high on an arch cleverly linking the old and the new. The low tower, said to be tenth-century, is hidden away on the north side and is invisible from the front of the church.

At the top of the steep hill beyond Eastdean is **Friston**, with a squat little church crouched beside the road. In part it may be pre-Conquest; it has magnificent roof timbering of about 1450, which gives it the effect of a large yeoman's hall. The south door is in memory of Frank Bridge, the teacher of Benjamin Britten and one of the pioneers of twentieth-century English music, who was born in Brighton, lived in Friston, and died in Eastbourne in 1941.

The byroad north across the downs from Friston brings you to **Jevington**, an old smugglers' village. The church, up a tree-shaded lane off the main street, has a Saxon tower probably built in the tenth century. Inside, on the north wall of the nave, is a wild and primitive Saxon sculpture – a small stone tablet carved with a stylised Christ, wearing a loincloth to symbolise the Resurrection and thrusting a tall cross into the throat of a beast squirming at his feet. Apart from the tower, the church is mainly Early English. **Filching Manor**, half a mile towards Polegate, is a fifteenth-century hall house, with a collection of vintage racing cars and speedboats, including Sir Malcolm Campbell's *Bluebird* hydroplane, in which he set the world's water-speed record in 1937.

From Friston the main road skirts the gloomy coniferous acres of Friston Forest and plunges down to **Exceat Bridge** across the Cuckmere, with a bird's-eye view of the wide meanders of the river on its final mile to the sea. Like Birling Gap, **Cuckmere Haven** at the mouth of the river was much used by the smugglers (see Alfriston, below). Why no port ever grew here is a mystery, as it would seem a perfect place – a shelving bay, protected by the cliffs of Seaford Head on one side and the Seven Sisters on the other. It is reached down a track, and is still lonely and remote, except during the height of the season.

On the east side of the river, seven hundred acres of downland and watermeadow have been set aside as the **Seven Sisters Country Park.** You can walk along a three-mile trail over every kind of terrain from shingle to grassy clifftop, past badger setts, traces of ancient cultivation, and the foundations of a long-vanished Napoleonic barracks. Beside the main road, a cluster of sweeping-roofed, flint-walled Sussex barns contains **The Living World**, an interpretation centre for this stretch of unspoilt and undeveloped

South coast relaxation: Eastbourne seafront.

The garden at Nymans, planned as a series of outdoor 'rooms'.

coastline – the only such stretch (apart from half a mile or so at Ferring) from Eastbourne right round to beyond Littlehampton.

The gap in the downs made by the Cuckmere has a road on either side. The eastern road is much the prettier, though it lacks the spectacular viewpoint of High and Over (see below). Past Exceat a lane by a stream brings you to **Westdean**, seemingly miles from anywhere, buried among trees deep in a downland combe. King Alfred is said to have had a palace there, and certainly he could hardly have chosen a more idyllic spot. It is a village of high flint walls and giant barns; the church (Norman but much altered) has a curious shingled cap to the tower. Inside there are two modern memorial bronzes: a bust by Epstein, to Sir John Anderson the politician (1882–1958), who took the title Viscount Waverley of Westdean; and a head by Clare Sheridan above a plaque to Sir Oswald Birley, the artist (1880–1952).

Charleston Manor, where Birley lived, lies in a narrow valley north of Westdean. The garden, planted on the rich soil of the valley floor, is a remarkable one, long and narrow, and far more Continental than English with its parterres and terraces divided by low yew hedges. The house is a fascinating centrepiece. The oldest section, at the back, is Norman, traditionally said to have been built about 1080 for William the Conqueror's cupbearer; behind this there once stood a Norman chapel, built for the cupbearer's mother and pulled down after her death to avoid the possibility of sacrilege. On to this Norman building later generations added a Tudor block and finally a Georgian front, so that within this one small house there are three distinct sections.

As far as Charleston the road runs by watermeadows and reed-beds. At **Litlington** the valley narrows, hemmed in by spurs of the downs on either side, which gives the narrow village a rather cramped feeling. However, it is all very unspoiled, with a pretty little church, white weatherboarded below the spire.

You get to Wilmington past **Lullington** church, a tiny building in a sacred grove on the hillside. The church, which only holds about twenty people, is in fact the chancel of a much larger building, stumps of which appear here and there above ground. **Wilmington** is best known for its **Long Man** – a giant outline cut in the chalk, with a staff about 250 feet long in either hand. No one knows his date; he has traditionally been thought to be Bronze Age. He faces north, and can be seen from miles away across the flat plain of the upper Cuckmere.

Apart from the Long Man, Wilmington has a trim village street, and the remains of a medieval **Priory**, founded by King William's half-brother, Robert de Mortain, soon after the Conquest. The priory had decayed well before the Dissolution and become a farmhouse, so that early Tudor and medieval are inextricably jumbled together. Upstairs is an agricultural museum, crammed with every sort of bygone from a metal bottle for feeding lambs to a tripod for holding down recalcitrant oxen. Both the Long Man and the priory belong to the Sussex Archaeological Society.

The parish church next door was begun about the same time as the priory for the two or three monks who lived there, and the villagers; the monks would have used the chancel and the parishioners the nave. There is a fine Jacobean pulpit complete with sounding-board; and a small window worth hunting for behind the organ, depicting butterflies, moths and a bee. The church is overshadowed by an immense and ancient yew, its limbs held together by chains and supported by timber uprights, which may be as old as the priory itself.

The road along the west side of the Cuckmere crosses the A27 a mile west of Wilmington. Just south of the crossroads is **Drusilla's**, which has been a child's delight for the best part of half a century. When I first knew it in the 1960s it was little more than a tearoom, with a miniature railway in the field behind and a few wallabies bouncing round the garden; it is now a full-blown 'entertainment centre' complete with zoo, butterfly house, traditional-style pub and Japanese garden. Next door is the **English Wine Centre**, which has its own vineyard and wine museum, and each September runs the English Wine Festival.

Alfriston, a mile to the south, is the most substantial of the downland villages, with timbered medieval inns and low brick and weatherboarded cottages, many of them now turned into tearooms and antique shops. It can be a bedlam of traffic; even the stone market cross, one of the last two in Sussex (the other is at Chichester), was smashed by a lorry some years ago and now has a new shaft. Alfriston's chief beauty is not its old street, fine though it is, but the broad green behind the houses, stretching to the majestic fourteenth-century parish church, symmetrically cruciform, with nave and chancel the same length and low central tower. Beside it is the thatched and timbered **Clergy House**, a bare hall of about 1350, with a kingpost roof, where the vicar lived in medieval times. It was the first building acquired by the National Trust, who bought it in

269

1896 -- for £10! Its floor has been recently relaid in the traditional Sussex way, with lumps of chalk rammed down and sealed with sour milk, said to last far longer than the plain earth floors found in other counties.

The Star Inn was built early in the fifteenth century, probably as a resthouse for pilgrims going to and from the shrine of St Richard at Chichester. On the front timbers are carvings of weird and wonderful medieval beasts, heraldically painted, including two snakes, and a basilisk being slain by St Michael. In the square is the Market Cross Inn, otherwise known as the Smugglers. At the beginning of the nineteenth century it was the home of Stanton Collins, leader of the Alfriston Gang, a highly successful group who knew every inch of the Downs and used Cuckmere Haven as their landing-point. They were a savage lot, like the Hawkhurst Gang over in Kent. One unfortunate revenue man, following a clifftop path marked out by lumps of chalk, fell over the edge, as the smugglers had deliberately moved some of the blocks to mislead him. He managed to cling to the top of the cliff and begged the smugglers to rescue him, but they stamped on his fingers and sent him hurtling to his death. Stanton Collins was finally arrested and transported, not for smuggling but for sheep stealing.

From the green at Alfriston you can walk across the Cuckmere by a footbridge and up a hillside path to the tiny **Lullington Church,** only sixteen feet square. The walk back is the ideal way to appreciate Alfriston's harmony of church, village and watermeadow.

South of Alfriston is a stretch of road called the **White Way,** the haunt of a well-vouched-for ghost which used to appear every seven years. Towards the end of the eighteenth century a young local man was taking his dog for an evening walk along the White Way. He was set on by robbers, who knocked him down, killed him and buried him in a field near the road. The dog ran off, but came back and started whining by the grave, so the robbers killed it and buried it in the bank by the road. Seven years later to the day a couple walking along the road were accompanied by a mysterious white dog, which suddenly vanished into thin air – or rather, into chalk bank; and every seven years thereafter it made an appearance. Then, during a road-widening scheme, the skeleton of a young man was found by the road where the dog was seen to vanish. The bones were buried in Alfriston churchyard, and the hauntings ceased.

The road rises steeply to the aptly-named **High and Over,** hardly more than a gear-change or two to the driver, but a necessary place for a breather in the days of horsemen and stagecoaches. From High and Over, with its huge expanse of the downs all around and the glint of sea ahead, you drop down to the dull prosperity of **Seaford**, all golf courses, private schools and well-mannered housing estates, the quintessence of seaside gentility.

Before the great storm of 1579 which changed the course of the Ouse, Seaford was at the mouth of the river and the port for Lewes, but after the storm the 'New Haven' superseded it. There are still traces of the old town in the streets round the church; this is basically medieval, much rebuilt in the last century, with a stepped tower that shows astonishing contrasts of stonework in its various layers. The modern esplanade has a high concrete sea wall: an obvious necessity, if you have ever tried to drive or walk along the front at Seaford during a high wind, with tons of water hurtling at you from the Channel. At the end of the front a martello tower has been turned into a small local history museum, and beyond it the cliffs rise sharply to **Seaford Head**. Round towards Cuckmere Haven a clifftop nature reserve is a favourite stopover for migrant birds, and also provides the classic view of the white undulations of the **Seven Sisters** cliffs.

When the Saxons built **Bishopstone**, they sensibly placed it a good mile from the sea. It is still quite separate from Seaford, consisting of a large white-painted manor, a few houses and a noble church. This must be one of the few churches where the modern work is in fact Norman, as much of it, including the porch, was built before the Conquest, perhaps as early as the ninth century. The porch has a Saxon sundial over the door, inscribed with the name of the donor, Eadric. Inside there is some exceptionally fine arcading; and under the tower is a coffin lid decorated with crisp twelfth-century carving, including two doves drinking from a pitcher of water.

A half-mile walk along the seawall from Seaford towards Newhaven brings you to the ruins of the Victorian **Bishopstone Tide-mill**. This jumble of massive brick walls and ancient sluice-gates once harnessed tidal power to grind grain, and in its time was the largest watermill in Sussex. With today's emphasis on pollution-free renewable energy, it is surely time that such structures were repaired and brought back into use, or new ones built.

From Seaford you can either cross the Ouse to Newhaven, or follow the downs along the east bank of the Ouse. The Ouse is a more workaday river than the Cuckmere, but for that very reason its occasional surprises are all the more striking. The surprise on this road is **Tarring Neville**, a small square-towered church, with a sweep of mellow tiled roof, behind a group of large flintwalled barns basking in the sun. Across the river you can see the round tower of Piddinghoe church, and on the left the cranes of Newhaven docks.

Round a corner of the downs you are brought back to earth by a cement works, whose belching chimney covers all the ground and plants on the leeward side with white dust. **Beddingham** is a church without a village, but an impressive one, with a sturdy battlemented Perpendicular tower built in a pattern of flint and dressed stone.

Rising above Beddingham – and the most prominent landmark for miles around – is the grass dome of **Mount Caburn**, on the outlying bulge of downland that rises east of Lewes. About the third century BC, Celtic tribes built one of their strongholds there, surrounding it by the massive dyke and rampart that still form a great trough in the grassland. Caburn was hardly a town by modern standards – it is thought to have housed about seventy families – but it would have been the rallying point for defence for the villages round about, and the centre of organized crafts like cloth- and iron-making.

West Firle, a mile east of Beddingham, at the end of a cul-de-sac below the downs, is still very much the feudal English village. **Firle Place** was built by the Gages in Tudor times, possibly incorporating an older house on the site, and after four and a half centuries they are still there. The main front of the house, symmetrically classical, faces away from the village across an enormous park; the downland turf leads uninterrupted to the side of the building. Behind the eighteenth-century skin lies a Tudor courtyard house, with its great hall; a Tudor gable survives on the south front.

This house was probably built by Sir John Gage, a tough soldier and uncompromising Catholic. Born in 1479, he fought in France and was appointed Comptroller of Calais; in 1542 he commanded the army that defeated James V of Scotland at Solway Moss. Henry VIII made him captain of the royal guard and Constable of the Tower of London. He still held this post in the reign of Mary, and presided at the execution of the seventeen-year-old Lady Jane Grey in 1554. He died in 1556. His portrait in a long silver cloak dominates the white-painted staircase hall, a grand approach to the upper floor, which is part of the eighteenth-century rebuilding. Below the stairs a door leads into the great hall, still with its hammerbeam roof hidden by the eighteenth-century plasterwork. On the walls are a huge Vandyck portrait of the Count of Nassau and his family, a pair of fine tapestries, and a portrait of General Gage, who was defeated by the Americans at Bunker Hill.

If the eighteenth century sits uneasily in the great hall, the downstairs drawing-room is a perfect period piece. Gilt Ionic columns, portraits and furniture form a harmonious unity. The man responsible for Firle's reshaping was the first Viscount Gage, who set himself in a broken-pedimented frame at the end of the room; his wife, Benedicta Hall, looks down from the centre of the prettily ornate mirror over the fireplace. Upstairs the main feature is the long gallery, built by the first Viscount and stretching the length of the east front. It has a good sound collection of pictures, many of them from the collection made by the third Earl Cowper in the eighteenth century, and some elaborate pieces of furniture.

Firle church, with its massively buttressed thirteenth-century tower, is surprisingly wide and spacious for so small a village. It reached its final form only in the sixteenth century, when the Gage chapel was added on the north side of the chancel. By the door from the north aisle into the chapel are some very fine brasses; the chapel itself is dominated by the tomb of Sir John Gage and his wife Philippa, with every detail, from belt buckles to crowsfeet round the eyes, meticulously carved in alabaster. A stained-glass window by John Piper, symbolizing the Tree of Life, commemorates the sixth Viscount Gage.

Above Firle is **Firle Beacon**, at 713 feet the highest point on this stretch of the downs. To reach it is a good half-hour's walk from the end of the road, but it is a walk well worth doing for its views southward of ridge beyond ridge of hills, with the glint of sea and the line of Newhaven breakwater in the distance. The width of the downs is hardly more than three miles as the crow flies, yet on a misty day they take on an illusion of immensity quite out of proportion to their actual size. The trackway runs past clusters of burial mounds – sunken in the middle and presumably plundered of their contents – to the Beacon, one of the South Coast warning beacons at the time of the Armada. From there it is another three miles' walk along the tops and down to Alfriston.

On the eastern side of Mount Caburn a narrow switchback road runs through Glynde, a quiet little village on a hill, generally ignored by those making for Glyndebourne a mile up the road. **Glynde Place** is a magnificent flint-built Elizabethan house, built in the 1560s on the site of a now-vanished medieval house. You get to it literally through the stables, passing under a white cupola and then between massive gate piers surmounted by a pair of fearsome wyverns. These date from the mid eighteenth century, when Glynde belonged to Richard Trevor, Bishop of Durham, who inherited it in 1743, after his cousin committed suicide.

The Bishop sensibly left the outside of the house unaltered, but thoroughly reconstructed the interior along classical eighteenth-century lines. His main innovation was to turn the whole place back to front, making the east side, facing across a sleepy expanse of parkland, into the main approach. The outcome is a kind of time-travelling, straight through an Elizabethan façade into a Georgian hall, with columns at either end, made of wood painted to look like marble. On either side of the front door are a pair of Allan Ramsay's coronation portraits of George III and Queen Charlotte. Ramsay churned out these portraits; there is another pair at Firle a couple of miles away.

Upstairs, in the splendid Long Gallery, is a portrait of Bishop Trevor, a sleek prelate with a well-scrubbed countenance, who cut such a majestic figure in his canonicals that George II called him 'the Beauty of Holiness'. In the middle of the gallery is an enormous silver centrepiece, with a statue of Victoria on top and plaques of politicians all around, given to Henry Brand (Lord Hampden), who was Speaker of the House of Commons in the 1870s. Throughout the house are Italian old master paintings brought back by Thomas Brand in the 1750s.

At the gates of Glynde Place is the parish church, built in 1763–5 on the site of the medieval church by Bishop Trevor. It is like a miniature version of St Paul's Covent Garden, in flint, with an open bellcote above the pediment. The architect was Sir Thomas Robinson, a follower of Wren and an enthusiast for Italian architecture. The interior is heavy with wooden columns and Victorian stained glass; unusually, the walls are covered in hessian with a faded arabesque design, which appears contemporary with the church.

Glyndebourne is now so much an international opera centre that it is hard to see it any longer as a prosperous country house with opera house attached. After more than sixty years, evening dress in mid afternoon and champagne and cold chicken by the lake have lost their novelty; but Glyndebourne still remains unique. The perfection of the setting has a lot to do with it – the clipped yews, the croquet lawn, the distant view of the downs beyond the lake, the cattle grazing on the other side of the ha-ha.

The whole place is stamped with the personality of its founder, John Christie, schoolmaster, music-lover, and inheritor of the Glyndebourne estate. His marriage to an opera singer, Audrey Mildmay, confirmed him in his ambitions to bring opera to the English countryside, and on 28 May, 1934, Glyndebourne was launched on its way by the cheerful intrigues of Mozart's *Marriage of Figaro*. Christie's local interests in and around the estate included hotels, building works and forestry, and it was this eminently commercial base that enabled him to survive without over-reaching himself. He set out the principles on which Glyndebourne should be run: 'One, we should aim at the sky, but have our feet on the ground. Two, our work (being opera) depends on having the necessary funds. It is our fault if we cannot get the funds.' Spike Hughes, in his history of Glyndebourne, pointed out that the building of the opera house in the lean years of the early 1930s saved many local labourers and craftsmen from penury. Glyndebourne is now masterminded by John and Audrey Christie's son George.

During the 1990s the old and much-loved opera house was pulled down and replaced by a far grander and more spacious structure. Many of those who knew Glyndebourne in the past mourned its passing, cramped and inconvenient though it was – but the doubters were silenced by the elegance of the new auditorium, and the Glyndebourne aim of producing opera to as high a standard as possible remains.

Ringmer, the gateway to Glyndebourne for motorists, is a spacious village, with an enormous green, and a good deal of modern building going on. The patron saint of Ringmer (if a reptile can be a patron saint) is the tortoise who appears in the centre of the elaborate village sign (on a triangle of land by the road up to the church). This was Timothy, who belonged to Mrs Rebecca Snooke, the aunt of Gilbert White, the clergyman-diarist of Selborne, in Hampshire.

On his visits to Ringmer, White became fascinated by Timothy's activities, and on his aunt's death in 1780 took the tortoise back to Selborne with him. In *The Natural History of Selborne* White observes the lethargic movements of Timothy with his usual sharp-eyed amusement. 'It scrapes out the ground with its forefeet, and throws it up over its back with its hind; but the motion of its legs is ridiculously slow, little exceeding the hour-hand of a clock; and suitable to the composure of an animal said to be a whole month in performing one feat of copulation.' Like all sensible tortoises,

Timothy disliked rain: 'though it has a shell that would secure it against the wheel of a cart, yet does it discover as much solicitude about rain as a lady dressed in all her best attire, shuffling away on the first sprinklings, and running its head up in a corner.' Timothy's rain-proof carapace is now in the Natural History Museum.

Ringmer church is basically fourteenth-century, with wide side chapels of about 1500 which give a feeling of great spaciousness and light. The chancel is slightly skewed on its axis from the nave. The south chapel, known as the Springett chapel, has a superb painted wall monument to Sir Harbert Springett, who died in 1620. After heavy rain he used to be driven to church over the atrocious local roads in a cart drawn by oxen. Ringmer must surely have been the 'country village, not far from Lewes', where Daniel Defoe on his tour round Britain in the 1720s, 'saw an ancient lady, and a lady of very good quality. I assure you, drawn to church in her coach with six oxen; nor was it done in frolic or humour, but mere necessity, the way being so stiff and deep, that no horses could go to it'. Defoe's 'ancient lady' was no doubt a Springett still using the family ox-cart. The derivation of Ringmer from Ryngmere, 'a place ringed by swamps and marshes', was more than justified by the notorious mud of the area before the days of field drainage and asphalt roads.

East of Ringmer the B2124 runs along the northern edge of a flat plain, full of rich farms and crisscrossed by watercourses. Its angular grid of roads, reminiscent of Romney Marsh or the Fens, is said to have been laid out as a land-settlement scheme for Roman army veterans. **Laughton** is a scattered village; its church, half a mile south of the main road, has a long chancel built of flints, and a lofty kingpost roof. It is dominated inside by a stone war memorial featuring a soldier and a sailor, with rifles carved down to the minutest details of bolt action and sights.

Beyond Laughton church the road zigzags down through **Ripe**, **Chalvington** and **Selmeston**, a trio of peacefully unmemorable villages. In the last century, when Selmeston was misleadingly pronounced Simson, its vicar was the Rev. W. D. Parish, who published his *Dictionary of the Sussex Dialect* in 1875. Apart from his dialect studies, he compiled collections of poetry for elementary classes, wrote an instruction book on the electric telegraph, and edited the Sussex Domesday Book. The *Dictionary* was a salvage operation. Even a century ago local dialects were dying out; so the vicar wandered among his parishioners, jotting down words, phrases and sentences. What could be more descriptive than 'Fluttergrub' for 'a man who takes a delight in working about in the dirt', 'Sussel' for 'disturbance; impertinent meddling', or 'Guess-sheep' for 'young ewes that have been with the ram and had no lambs'?

Alciston, across the A27 from Selmeston, once belonged to Battle Abbey, and is full of reminders of its monastic past – fishponds, a ruined dovecote, and a giant flint-built tithe barn which looms in front of the church, with its ancient roof timbers patched and repatched down the centuries, and sweeping red-tiled roof.

A mile along the A27, heading back towards Firle, the country outpost of the 'Bloomsbury Group' lies well hidden in the fields south of the road. **Charleston** (not to be confused with Charleston Manor, see above) is an unpretentious sixteenth-century house, modernised around 1800, where two generations of artists and writers lived and congregated. From 1916 on it was the home of a talented *ménage à trois* – Vanessa Bell, the artist sister of Virginia Woolf (who lived at nearby Rodmell, see p. 340), her husband the art critic Clive Bell, and her lover and fellow-artist Duncan Grant. Apart from entertaining T. S. Eliot, E. M. Forster, Maynard Keynes and other leading between-the-wars intellectuals, Vanessa Bell and Duncan Grant painted the walls, cupboards, bedheads, tables and chairs with abstract patterns and naturalistic designs, which make Charleston a unique monument to a vanished artistic world. The house with Duncan Grant's cluttered studio, its contents and its high-walled garden are now lovingly preserved by the Charleston Trust.

The interior of Charleston has an endearing and muddled amateurishness about it. Vanessa Bell died in 1961, while Duncan Grant lived on at Charleston until his death in 1978, at the age of 93. In her autobiography *Deceived with Kindness*, their daughter, Angelica Garnett, describes a typical unappetising meal dispensed by Vanessa. 'In the Charleston dining-room she presided over the table painted by herself; it was round, but where she sat was the indubitable head of it . . . In front of her stood the joint of cold beef from which day after day she cut a few grey slices, while at the bottom of the salad bowl there lurked some leaves of lettuce.'

A mile east of Alciston is **Berwick**, an isolated farming hamlet, down a dead end like the neighbouring villages. From the outside its church is a simple twelfth-century building with broach spire; but inside it is a remarkable experiment in bringing the art of mural painting up to date. Commissioned by the go-ahead Bishop Bell of Chichester, Duncan Grant, Vanessa Bell and Quentin Bell (Vanessa's son by her husband Clive) decorated the upper surfaces of the walls with paintings including the Annunciation and Nativity (side walls), and Christ in Glory (chancel arch). The paintings, carried out in 1941–3, are not strictly murals, as they were painted on plasterboard and then fixed to the walls. Like Stanley Spencer's Cookham scenes, the Biblical stories are set in the countryside round about; thus for the Nativity Mount Caburn appears in the background, and two local shepherds were used as models. Bishop Bell and the rector of Berwick both appear on the Christ in Glory, beside the chancel arch. Nowadays the paintings look old-fashioned, yet as an overall scheme of decoration they make Berwick church well worth a visit.

The featureless landscape round the upper Cuckmere is greatly enhanced by the **Arlington Reservoir**, best seen from the road north of Berwick station. Apart from supplying water to Eastbourne, it adds something of positive worth to the countryside, whether you look nearby to **Arlington**, now a lakeside village, or in the distance to the downs, with an unexpected foreground of water. Arlington's church is Saxon and later, with an obviously Saxon window in the south wall and a few remains of medieval paintings on the walls.

A couple of miles north of Arlington the Cuckmere was turned to good account by the Austin (Augustinian) canons of **Michelham Priory** (owned by the Sussex Archaeological Society), who came here in the thirteenth century, taking over the site of a moated Norman manor house. At first sight, apart from the fourteenth-century gatehouse, Michelham is not obviously medieval, as the later stonework of a Tudor farmhouse masks what survives of the priory buildings. The present building corresponds roughly to the south side of the priory; to the north (marked out by stones set in the paths and lawns of the immaculate garden) were the cloister, the chapter house, and the long narrow church, of which nothing remains.

You go into the priory through the best of the medieval survivals – a vaulted room which may have been the visitors' parlour, now dominated by a lifesize figure of an Austin canon, in black habit and wearing a broad leather belt. The Tudor rooms are furnished with an impeccably presented collection of Dutch paintings, Flemish tapestries and old English furniture. Over the staircase is the upper half of the tracery of the refectory's great west window; and at the top of the stairs, above the vaulted parlour, is the Prior's Chamber, presided over by the figure of a fork-bearded prior sitting at his desk. In the gatehouse is a good group of brass rubbings, and a reconstruction of a Sussex forge.

At the back of the priory is a neat little 'Physic Garden', laid out with the herbs grown by the monks in the Middle Ages to cure all the ills that flesh is heir to. Among them you will find mugwort (good for gout and rheumatism), creeping jenny (relieves children's coughs when boiled in wine), yarrow (stops nose-bleeds) and calamint (an antidote to poison). Across the moat from the priory, the monks' watermill, which dates back at least to the fifteenth century, has been restored and is once again turning out stone-ground flour.

Hellingly, three miles upstream from Michelham, is a pretty, loose-knit village, built between the Cuckmere and a small tributary stream. The churchyard may well date back to the eighth century, as it is in the form of a circular mound or 'ciric' typical of the early days of Saxon Christianity. Later builders followed the circumference of this circle, so that even the tilehung houses on the north side of the churchyard are built round a curve. The church itself was built far later, about 1190, and has a good Early English chancel and north transept. The battlemented tower is a Victorian addition. Inside, the church is dominated by a splendidly gilded organ on the western gallery.

A couple of hundred yards down the road is the magnificently timbered **Horselunges Manor**, built about 1475 on a much older moated site. The timbers are a mellow grey, as opposed to the usual startling contrast between black wood and white infilling. The extraordinary name is probably a corruption of the names of two fourteenth-century owners of the house, Herst and Lyngyver. It was near Horselunges that in 1541 Lord Dacre of Herstmonceux murdered a gamekeeper while out on a poaching expedition; he was taken to the Tower and hanged at Tyburn after Henry VIII had turned down his plea for mercy.

Hailsham is a cheerful go-ahead place, with a shopping precinct which is in scale and keeping with the Georgian buildings of the High Street. The fifteenth-century church has a sturdy pinnacled Perpendicular tower, built in chequers of flint and squared stone; the only trace of an older medieval building is an Early English capital set in a niche in the south chapel. In the last century, according to Augustus Hare, Hailsham's rope factory had 'the privilege of supplying the cords used in prisons for executions'. Its cattle market is one of the largest and most important in Sussex; in the nineteenth century it attracted drovers from as far afield as Wales.

18

Around Ashdown Forest

ASHDOWN FOREST, LIKE Dungeness, is a world on its own.
But whereas Dungeness is constantly altered and renewed by
fresh additions of shingle washed round the coast, Ashdown Forest
is immeasurably old – a tract of sandy heathland, where bracken,
heather and scrub form an oasis of wildness amid the rich farmland
that lies all around. A glance at a geological cross-section diagram
through the Weald will show the reason for the Forest's uniqueness.
It lies equidistant between the North and South Downs, and is made
up of the lowest strata that lie beneath the great chalk dome which
once covered Kent and Sussex. Millions of years of earth
movements, erosion and weathering have worn away the crest of this
dome, scouring the clays and greensands so that as you go inwards
from the Downs the soils get progressively older, with the sour sands
of the Forest as the ancient core.

In shape it is a rough equilateral triangle, with the apex pointing
downwards and the corners marked by Forest Row, Crowborough
and Maresfield. It stretches for 14,000 acres, on nearly half of which
the public is allowed to wander. On summer weekends it is full of
picnickers, walkers and riders, who come here for the exhilaration of
its tremendous views and wide expanse of sky. But you can get a
better sense of the true solitude of the Forest on a sparkling winter's
day, with the pine trees cut out against a blue background; while on a
day of cold mist and sleet, when the views are hidden and all you can
see are shrouded bushes by the road and the occasional startled
sheep, it can seem hostile to your intrusion.

Indeed, it is only modern town-dwelling man who has enjoyed the
Forest as a place to relax in. Previous generations thought of it much
as William Cobbett did when he rode across it in 1822. He called it
'a heath, with here and there a few birch scrubs upon it, verily the
most villainously ugly spot I ever saw in England. This lasts you for
five miles, getting, if possible, uglier and uglier all the way, till, at

last, as if barren soil, nasty spewy gravel, heath and even that stunted, were not enough, you see some rising spots, which instead of trees, present you with black, ragged, hideous rocks.' Cobbett crossed it in January, so he may have been unfairly critical.

Like other high places, Ashdown Forest was used for trackways by prehistoric man. The Romans drove the road from London to the South Downs straight across it, using slag from the local iron bloomeries for the surface; stretches survive here and there. By Norman times the rights of the commoners living on the fringes of the Forest had become well established: the right among other things to graze cattle and pigs; to collect wood for fuel and bracken for roofing; to cut peat. Much of the story of the Forest is concerned with the struggles of these stubborn Sussex men to maintain their rights. Their enemies might be kings or barons hunting deer in the Middle Ages, or landlords who wished to enclose and 'improve' the Forest in the eighteenth century. The commoners retaliated by poaching or illegally taking small bits of land for their own use; they were also great smugglers, even smuggling cannon to the enemies of England in the sixteenth century, as well as the usual brandy and lace in later years.

These feuds and squabbles were not laid to rest until 1885, when the Board of Conservators of Ashdown Forest was set up by Act of Parliament, to resolve the conflicting claims and administer the Forest. In 1988 its owners, the De La Warr family, sold it to the East Sussex County Council. The Conservators run the forest's affairs from the **Ashdown Forest Centre**, on a by-road a couple of miles south of Forest Row. It consists of three oak-framed barns, removed from elsewhere and reassembled, and originally roofed with thick heather thatch cut on the forest, replaced with tiles when the thatch began to let in water. Two of the barns are used by the Conservators, while the third is a visitor and information centre, explaining the forest's history and wildlife.

Nowadays the Conservators have all the usual environmental problems that arise where a large car-borne public is involved: first of all, what to do with the cars themselves; and secondly, how to make sure that the occupants do not set fire to the tinder-like gorse and scrub, obliterate the rare mosses and heathers, or scare off the badgers, fallow deer, and all the other creatures that survive in this delicately balanced wilderness. The Conservators make themselves plain enough by frequent small green notices telling you what is not allowed; however, gorse and withered bracken can be set alight by a

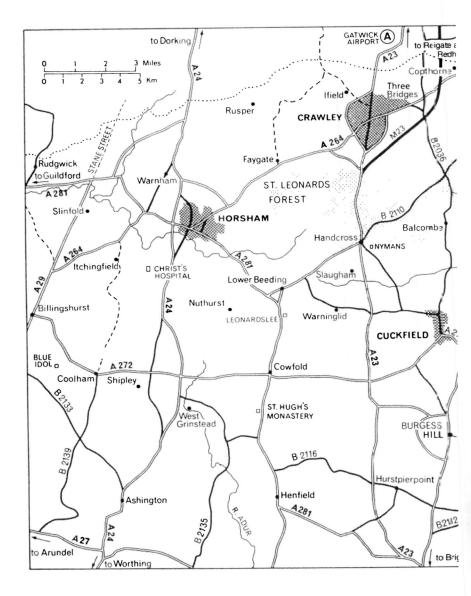

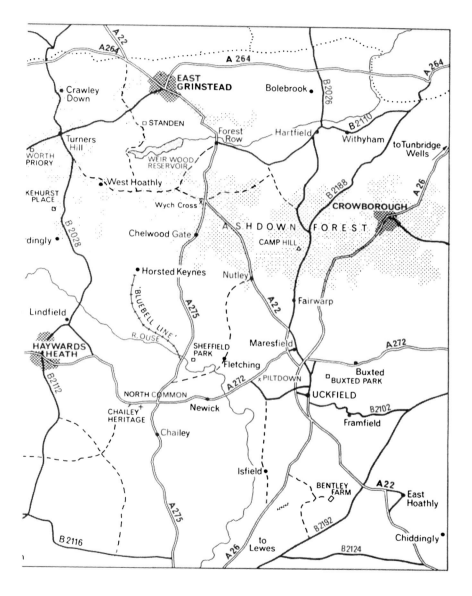

cigarette end, and in a dry spring or summer brush fires are a recurrent menace.

Since the great trees were cut down for fuel to heat the ironmasters' forges, Ashdown has been a forest in name only. But there are still large woods here and there, like Five Hundred Acre Wood; while names like Hindleap Warren and King's Standing – the hunting post from which Edward II shot his game – perpetuate the chases of the past. The Forest's most famous sporting owner was John of Gaunt, Duke of Lancaster, who was granted it in 1372. For the next three hundred years it was known as Lancaster Great Park; and as recently as the nineteenth century the locals spoke about 'King John' as a living memory. But the sixteenth century saw the end of most of the large trees. The clumps of Scotch pines which are now prominent landmarks on every high point were planted in the last century, to give some relief from the monotony of which Cobbett complained.

Though the main coast road (the A22) cuts across the western side of the Forest, the best quick impression of its wild spaciousness can be got from the B2026 between Maresfield and Hartfield (incidentally following the Roman road for much of the way). The road climbs past the isolated Victorian church of **Fairwarp**, nothing much architecturally, but a curiously attractive place, with the hill rising steeply behind, and a backcloth of pine trees. The nearby hamlet of **Duddleswell** was formerly a haunt of smugglers and poachers. The summit plateau of the Forest begins at **Camp Hill** (650 feet), by the chain-link perimeter fence of the former Diplomatic Wireless Service Station – until a few years ago a forest of lattice aerials – where messages to and from embassies all over the world were transmitted and received. Code-named 'Aspidistra', the station was opened in 1942 to broadcast anti-Nazi propaganda, and remained in use until 1985. Three years later, a local newspaper carried the story that a large bunker was being constructed behind the fence as a seat of local government in the event of a nuclear attack – after which, presumably, the officials both civil and military would emerge to gaze upon a devastated world. Across the road a short section of Roman road has been exposed beside a small car park.

Since the 1920s Ashdown Forest has infiltrated the minds of children through A. A. Milne's *Winnie-the-Pooh* books, and especially through E. H. Shepard's illustrations to them. Milne lived on the edge of the Forest near Hartfield; and all Pooh's adventures

284

by sandy banks and streams, by gorse, thistles and snow, and above all by trees, have a firmly realistic setting, meticulously observed. From the car-park at Gills Lap, a ten-minute downhill walk will bring you to the 'Enchanted Place' – a viewpoint with tremendous views to the north across the Weald. A memorial to Milne and Shepard carries the inscription 'and by and by they came to an enchanted place on the very top of the Forest called Galleons Leap'.

A couple of miles to the north you leave the Forest again by **Chuck Hatch**, one of the many Gate and Hatch names that mark the perimeter. They date from the years when the Forest was a royal hunting park, and the gates/hatches gave access through its 'pale' or boundary. This was a ditch and earth bank, topped by a wooden fence; a short section has been constructed at the visitor centre.

Hartfield, past Chuck Hatch, has no trace of the wilderness about it, but is thoroughly smart, to the extent of a painted-up Sussex cart outside the main pub. The village is built along a sharp dogleg; the church, with its magnificent landmark of a spire, is up an alley at the southern end. The lychgate originally led into the churchyard under a pair of Tudor half-timbered cottages, but only one is now standing, and a yew tree grows where its partner was.

Withyham, west of Hartfield, is hardly a village at all. In a way, it is an appendage of Knole (see p. 183), as the Sackvilles are buried in the church, the house and grounds of Buckhurst Park lie behind, and the pub is called the Dorset Arms. Buckhurst has been owned by the Sackvilles since about 1200 (the De La Warrs who live there are another branch of the family). From the stretch of grass in front of Withyham church you can see an English pastoral scene that cannot have changed since the eighteenth century, if not earlier: a pond directly below, gently undulating fields all around, and the spire of Hartfield glinting in the sun. The church is a hybrid. In 1663 it was struck by lightning, which 'came in at the steeple, melted the bells, and went up the chancel, where it tore the monuments of the Dorsets to pieces', according to an eyewitness. It was soon rebuilt, spireless, and in a homely way, with dormer windows in the roof like those of a private house. The sundial over the porch is dated 1672, the year the rebuilding was completed.

All the old monuments in the Sackville Chapel were 'turned to lime and ashes' by the lightning; but what came afterwards is impressive enough. Below the coffered ceiling painted in blue and gold, and the rows of tattered banners, is a museum of two centuries

285

of funerary carving, put there by a family who wanted nothing but the best and made sure that they got it.

The centrepiece is the memorial to Thomas Sackville, son of the fifth Earl and Countess of Dorset, who died in France aged thirteen in 1675. Carved by the Danish sculptor Caius Gabriel Cibber, it shows the boy lying on a mat and holding a skull, while his parents kneel on either side. Cibber was paid £350 for the work, a vast sum in those days, and went on to become 'sculptor in ordinary' to William III. On the north wall of the chapel are three monuments by master sculptors of their times: a composition of putti, urn and portrait of the third Duke (died 1799), by Joseph Nollekens; two women kneeling in grief for Arabella, his widow (died 1825), by Sir Francis Chantrey; and a mourning mother figure, perhaps Arabella, below a medallion of the fourth Duke, killed accidentally in Ireland in 1815, carved by John Flaxman. Yet these grand monuments have no more real dignity than the tablet which reads simply 'V. Sackville-West C.H., poet', and nothing more. On the a sle wall is a tablet to Sir David Maxwell Fyfe (died 1967), the Lord Chancellor, who lived in the village for the last decade of his life.

When E. V. Lucas visited **Crowborough**, four miles south of Withyham, in 1903, he found it plastered with posters declaring it to be 'Scotland in Sussex'. He goes on to say: 'Never was a fine remote hill so bevilla'd. The east slope is all scaffold-poles and heaps of bricks, new churches and chapels are sprouting, and the many hoardings announce that Follies, Pierrots, or conjurors are continually imminent.' Crowborough is still growing, and growing fast. It spreads over Beacon Hill, lapping against the edge of Ashdown Forest. Beacon House, at its highest point (796 feet), is the highest inhabited spot in Sussex. This house, built in 1838, is one of the oldest in the town, which shows how recent Crowborough is by Sussex standards. At the heart of Crowborough is a triangular green, with some buildings that look eighteenth-century on the south side, and on the north a dark grey stone classical church, built in 1744 and much enlarged in the 1880s. The modern town centre is at Crowborough Cross, where two main roads intersect and Edwardian gabled shops confront one another. Sir Arthur Conan Doyle lived at Crowborough for some time, as did Richard Jefferies, the keen observer and recorder of the Victorian countryside, towards the end of his life.

Maresfield is five miles south-west of Crowborough at the southern corner of the Forest. Its most notable building is the tall

Georgian Chequers Inn, built on a bluff with the ground falling away into the valley behind. Near it is a white-painted cast-iron milestone, with the figure 41 and four bells in outline surmounted by bows – one of the milestones on this road that refer punningly to the distance from Bow Bells. The church stands on the corner opposite. The Victorians sliced it right across the middle, leaving the medieval tower and west end, and adding a new chancel and transepts. It has a fine three-dimensional royal arms, carved and painted, and a Jacobean pulpit.

A mile east of Maresfield is **Buxted**, a featureless place – not surprisingly, in view of its history. For centuries it had been the ordinary English village, with parish church, villagers' houses, and the great house of Buxted Park, all close together. Then in the 1830s the owner, Lord Liverpool, decided to shift the village outside the park, to give himself more privacy. The villagers refused to budge, so the noble earl refused in his turn to repair their cottages, until they became uninhabitable. The villagers finally moved out, and were transferred to new homes near the railway. This is the reason for the church's isolation, a short way down the park drive.

It is unusually large for a medieval parish church, but when it was built about 1250 it served an enormous area, covering Uckfield, Hadlow Down to the east, and Crowborough away to the north. It has a rare dedication, to St Margaret the Queen, who was queen of Scotland in the eleventh century, and was, according to a local guide, 'the only saint who was canonized for the domestic virtues'. Three of her sons became kings of Scotland, and one of them, St David, inherited her sanctity. She is commemorated by marguerites carved on the Jacobean pulpit, and embossed on the magnificent moulded plaster ceiling of the chancel. Hop flowers decorate the sides of this ceiling, which is said to have been installed about 1600 by the rector of the day, in gratitude for a fine crop of hops. At the back of the church is an enormous chest for vestments, a good four feet high, reputedly thirteenth-century.

At the end of the churchyard a gate leads into the park. Its ancient trees – huge contorted oaks, and an avenue of vast limes, which marked the drive of the old house – were largely destroyed by the hurricane of 16 October, 1987, which also severely damaged the church. The original house was pulled down in the early eighteenth century and the lake formed on its site; the present classical **Buxted Park** was completed in 1725. In 1931 it was bought by the architect Basil Ionides, who altered it considerably, mainly after a fire in 1940 had gutted it. He removed the top storey, reconstructed the interior, and made it a magpie's nest of bits from other houses that were being demolished or had been blitzed; thus the main staircase came from Old Burlington Street, and the front door from Clumber in Nottinghamshire. In recent years it has had a wide variety of owners: it was a health hydro until 1972, when it was sold to the President of the United Arab Emirates; in 1987 it was bought by the Electrical, Electronic, Telecommunication and Plumbing Union; and it is now a luxurious country house hotel.

At the entrance to the park is the black-and-white half-timbered **Hogge House**, the home of Ralph Hogge, whose rebus (a hog and the date 1581) appears on the wall. Hogge is traditionally the first man to have cast guns in England, in 1543, according to an old rhyme which ran:

> *Master Hogge and his man John,*
> *They did cast the first Can-non.*

In 1573 Hogge, describing himself as 'the quenes Maiesties gonnestone maker of yron', made a self-righteous complaint to the Queen about the malpractices of his competitors, stating that they were overcharging for shot, and illegally exporting guns overseas. The outcome was an immediate census of all the ironmasters, and a closing of the loopholes for illegal trade. Ernest Straker, the historian of the iron industry, says that one practice was for gunmakers to export the smaller-calibre cannons for which export licences were allowed; the foreign buyer would then bore them out to take larger shot. Tudor arms dealers, like their modern successors, knew how to get round the regulations.

Maresfield is now practically joined to **Uckfield** by housing estates. Uckfield's old town centre lies round the T-junction at the top of the High Street, which slopes steeply down to a level crossing. There are some good weatherboarded and tilehung buildings, and a large bow-windowed Georgian pub, the Maiden's Head. The rest of the High Street is an assortment of unmemorable twentieth-century shop design, except for the small cinema, which proclaims itself 'The Picture House, 1916', and is still showing films – surely a record among country-town cinemas. Uckfield church, long and low, with a grey-shingled spire, was built in 1839 on the site of a medieval building. Most of the churchyard is overshadowed by a gigantic and kingly cedar. Down the High Street and over the level crossing, Uckfield spreads south along the main road, and east towards Heathfield.

Uckfield's nearest neighbour in this direction is **Framfield**, which has a church similarly long and low, reached through an approach with good tilehung houses on either side. Built in 1288 and dedicated to Becket, this church has had more than its fair share of misfortunes: in 1509 it was severely damaged by fire, and in 1667 the tower collapsed and was not rebuilt for over two centuries. According to E. V. Lucas, in 1792 Framfield offered to field a cricket eleven from among its fifteen oldest inhabitants, whose combined ages added up to over a thousand years, but could find no suitably ancient opponents.

Two main roads lead south from Uckfield, one taking you in a zigzag way to Eastbourne, the other in an arc to Lewes and Brighton. The first place of any consequence on the Eastbourne road is **East Hoathly**, at least twenty miles by road from West Hoathly. It is a compact village, and stands on what is probably the worst main-road bend in Sussex. The stocky church, up a side road, is mainly a rebuilding of 1855, but is a convincing piece of medievalism. The squat fifteenth-century tower is one of the so-called 'Pelham towers' found in the area; others are at Chiddingly and Laughton. They were built by the Pelham family, and have the Pelham family badge, a belt buckle, carved on them, usually on either side of the door. The badge was awarded to Sir John Pelham (who came from **Halland** near by) for his part in capturing King John of France at the Battle of Poitiers in 1356. There is a deep slit in the stone moulding on the right of the door, said to have been made by a bullet fired at a later Pelham, Sir Nicholas, in the seventeenth century. The would-be murderer was the Cavalier colonel Thomas Lunsford, who was fined £8,000 and outlawed. Lunsford had a wandering and adventurous life. During his exile he joined the French army, returned to England to fight for Charles I in the Civil War, emigrated to America, and died in Virginia in the 1650s. Like Sir Goddard Oxenbridge of Brede, he left behind him a reputation for cannibalism.

Though not far from the main road, **Chiddingly**, three miles south-east of East Hoathly, seems utterly remote. The tall fifteenth-century stone spire of its church, 130 feet high, looms across the fields well before you get to the village, which is hardly more than a hamlet. Inside the church there is a massive monument to Sir John Jefferay, Baron of the Exchequer under Queen Elizabeth. However, the reclining figures of Sir John and his wife are eclipsed by their daughter and son-in-law, who stand arrogantly large in niches on either side; the daughter's costume is a caricature of the Elizabethan farthingale. The drums on which they stand are said to be cheeses which they used as stepping-stones to walk from Chiddingly Place to church. At the top stand Father Time, and a gravedigger at work with his sleeves rolled up – a good near-contemporary illustration to Hamlet. The monument has lost hands and fingers, knocked off, the story goes, by infuriated locals who wrongly thought that the Jefferays were related to Judge Jeffreys of the Bloody Assize. Of their Tudor mansion, Chiddingly Place, two sections survive, one a farmhouse and the other used as a barn.

Near Halland and **Terrible Down**, which looks as though it must have been given its name by Edward Lear, is the ideal antidote to a surfeit of villages or weekend traffic – the collection of birds at the **Bentley Wildfowl and Motor Museum** (owned by the East Sussex County Council). Reached from the road between big cylindrical flint gate-piers, Bentley's original unpretentious farmhouse is flanked by modern classical-style pavilions. In the grounds about twenty-five acres have been dug with ponds, planted with trees and shrubs, and surrounded with fox-proof fences; and a hundred or so varieties of wildfowl honk, hiss, squawk, swim and flap in as near-natural conditions as a reserve of this sort can provide. Flamingos stand philosophically on one leg; black swans with their brilliant red bills launch themselves silently upon the water; and the giant whoopers beat their wings, stretch out their necks and utter their ear-splitting cries. The motor museum at Bentley consists of a constantly changing collection of elderly vehicles, nearly all in full running order, lent by private owners.

Isfield nearby is a workaday farming village, stretching along a road above the Ouse. The church, down a track and almost on the banks of the river, is worth visiting for the chapel and tombs of the Shurley family. These begin with an inscription to John Shurley, who died in 1527 and was 'Chefe clerke of the kechen' to Henry VII and cofferer or treasurer to Henry VIII, and end a century later with the vast alabaster tomb of Sir John (died 1631), who lies impartially between his two wives, with nine children dutifully kneeling below. The chapel still has its sixteenth-century linenfold panelling and pews; the modern stained glass shows the Sussex Red cattle which are bred locally.

Going west along the A272 from Maresfield, you come to the gorse, bracken and pines of **Piltdown Common**. Piltdown will always be remembered for the greatest archaeological hoax of all time; and the pub called the Piltdown Man still keeps its sign, with the famous skull on one side and a skin-clad stone-brandishing humanoid on the other. This skull, with its human braincase and ape-like jaw, bewildered the archaeologists for forty years, from the time it was 'discovered' by Charles Dawson in 1912, until the fake was unmasked by modern scientific methods in 1953. It is now known that the jaw was that of an orang-utan, and the braincase that of a medieval man whose bones had thickened by disease.

All sorts of eminent men have been suspected of perpetrating the hoax, from the theologian Teilhard de Chardin to Sir Arthur Conan Doyle; but the finger of suspicion now points reasonably unwaveringly at Dawson himself. He is known to have faked other antiquities including Roman brick-stamps and a cast-iron Roman figurine which, if it had been genuine, would have pushed the invention of cast iron back centuries to Roman times. Everyone believed in Piltdown Man because everyone wanted a 'missing link' between man and the apes. Besides, Dawson was a respectable lawyer. Still, Piltdown Man was fun while he lasted.

A mile west of Piltdown, **Newick** has expanded into a roughly oval shape along the main road and a minor one behind. It has a village green complete with long-handled pump, and a large housing estate. The church, beside a farmyard a little way out of the village, is a simple building, with porch timbers about six hundred years old, and white doves flying in and out below the eaves. The Victorian chancel is elaborately tiled, painted and gilded.

Chailey is a much smaller place, built round a tiny green. The church has a strange pyramidal spire; though basically thirteenth-century it was much altered by the Victorians, which accounts for the angular jutting woodwork of the interior. Chailey's modern offshoot, **North Chailey**, is built round an open area of land, the North Common. Nearly four hundred acres are now a local nature reserve, where wet and dry heathland and patches of rare sphagnum bog are preserved.

Shooting up over the common is another tall spire, belonging to the chapel of the **Chailey Heritage** and one of the main centres in the country for educating and rehabilitating handicapped children. It was founded in 1903 as an offshoot of a London home for boys with tuberculosis, called, in the patronising fashion of the time, 'The Guild of Brave Poor Things'. One of the founders, Dame Grace Kimmins, remained in charge for half a century and is commemorated by a tablet in the cloister. While TB no longer counts seriously as a children's disease, the Heritage has expanded to deal with disabilities like spina bifida and cerebral palsy. On the wall of the chapel is a rope from Scott's last expedition, placed there to symbolise the co-operation achieved at the Heritage.

Though **Fletching**, across the Ouse three miles to the east, was famous in the Middle Ages for making arrowheads, the name has nothing to do with the French word *flèche*, meaning arrow. It is another Saxon -ingas tribal name; fittingly, the church shows traces of Saxon work. Fletching does not sprawl: it has a beginning, a middle and an end. The L-shaped village street has several good Georgian houses, and across the road from the church is a battlemented lodge and gateway to Sheffield Park.

Below the tall broach spire the church tower is Norman, with small rounded windows. Most of the building is Early English, completed about 1230; the arch between nave and tower may be Saxon, and is decorated with Norman chevron ornament. The unusually long chancel has lancets down the sides and an east window of strangely pointed Geometrical design. The church is connected with one of the great leaders of the Middle Ages, Simon de Montfort, who spent the night before the Battle of Lewes in vigil there; after defeating Henry III he was virtually ruler of England until he was killed at Evesham the following year, in 1265.

Another man as great in his way, Edward Gibbon, author of *The Decline and Fall of the Roman Empire*, is buried in the Sheffield mausoleum behind the north transept. He was a close friend of John Baker Holroyd, the first Earl of Sheffield, and in 1794 spent the final months of his life at Sheffield Park. In the south transept is a unique brass showing not a human figure but a fashionable pair of fifteenth-century gloves. This commemorates a glover called Peter Denot, who is known to have taken part in Jack Cade's rising of 1450, but was pardoned. One of the new church bells, installed in 1949, was the gift of an insurance broker and is aptly inscribed 'I sing of heavenly assurance'.

When Gibbon stayed at **Sheffield Park**, where he wrote several chapters of his *Decline and Fall*, the gardens that Capability Brown (or Repton, the authorities differ) had laid out can hardly have grown beyond the sapling stage. Now, after two centuries, they are one of the glories of Sussex: trees and shrubs, lawns and glades around a series of four lakes, shaped like an inverted T, that lead down from John Baker Holroyd's Gothic Revival house. The house is privately

The lake and some of the magnificent trees of Sheffield Park Gardens.

1890s prosperity at Standen, near East Grinstead.

occupied and cannot be visited, but it forms the pivot of the whole design, and its battlemented front and traceried chapel window make a perfect foil to the constantly changing vistas of trees and water. The National Trust bought the gardens in 1954. At Sheffield Park the tree specialist can hunt for rarities like the coffin juniper which the Chinese grow (or grew in pre-Communist days) to be sawn into planks for coffins; while the ordinary garden-lover can stand on one of the bridges between the lakes and marvel that the word 'tree' can mean such a profusion of column, sprawl, tight sphere, or shaggy irregularity.

A century after Gibbon, so E. V. Lucas tells us, the Lord Sheffield of the day was a great patron of cricket, once even playing on his yacht at Spitzbergen, under the midnight sun. In the 1890s Australian visiting teams used to open their season with a match on the Sheffield Park pitch; while 'in the long winter of 1890–91 several cricket matches were played on one of the lakes in the park, with well-known Sussex players on both sides'.

Sheffield Park has the southern terminus of the **Bluebell Line**, a seven-mile stretch salvaged by enthusiasts from the old Lewes to East Grinstead railway, which potters gently northwards through the countryside to Kingscote Station, linked by a bus service to East Grinstead. Sheffield Park station has been restored in the turn-of-the-century style of the old London, Brighton and South Coast Railway, while Horsted Keynes station, half way up the line, is refurbished in 1930s Southern Railway style. It is hoped eventually to open the remaining mile or so of track between Kingscote and East Grinstead.

Horsted Keynes village is three miles north of Sheffield Park, off the A275 and a good mile from Horsted Keynes station. The 'Keynes' in the name derives from a Norman baron called de Cahanges. There is a pretty village green, with a couple of good pubs. The mainly Norman church, tucked away down a side road, has a tall shingled spire, round arches in the nave, and a pigmy Crusader's effigy, possibly scaled down to fit a niche in the chancel.

Back on the main road is **Chelwood Gate**, where Harold Macmillan (Lord Stockton) lived. In 1963, when Macmillan was Prime Minister, President Kennedy stayed with him here; a clump of pine trees and an inscribed stone slab commemorating the visit are on the west side of the main road, between Chelwood Gate and **Wych Cross**, where five roads meet at the heart of the Forest. Lord Stockton is buried in Horsted Keynes churchyard.

Forest Row, a couple of miles north, must be one of the few villages where the main pub – the tilehung Chequers, once a coaching inn – is older than the parish church. The church is long and low, with a shingled spire, and was built in 1836. Opposite is the large village hall, built in 1892, which takes up most of the green. A stone in the wall commemorates the visit of President Kennedy.

East of Forest Row are the ruins of the seventeenth-century **Brambletye House**; one of the corner towers, complete with roof-cap, can be seen from the East Grinstead road.

Although **East Grinstead** is now a few miles away from Ashdown Forest, its name – the 'green steading' or clearing in the woodland – dates back to a time when the Forest was vastly more extensive than it is today. Like other commuting towns, it seems at first sight to consist of little more than an accumulation of new housing estates, especially if you approach it from the Surrey side. But its nucleus is a compact Sussex market town, with a High Street consisting largely of sixteenth-century half-timbered houses, and a large parish church towering up at its highest point. In fact, almost every building on the south side of the High Street has a Tudor look about it. One shop, which looks as though it is covered in strips of cork-bark between the timbers, has a strange collection of heads carved on the beams inside, including one that has been identified as Anne Boleyn's sister.

On the corner at the eastern end of the High Street, set back a little from the road, are the sandstone walls and gables of **Sackville College**. Founded by the Earl of Dorset in 1609, it is not a college in the modern sense of the word, but a set of almshouses, now old people's flats, built round an elegant quadrangle. Over the turret at the back is the heraldic leopard of the Sackvilles, and until the 1950s the men pensioners wore cassocks and the women capes and bonnets, embroidered with the Sackville arms. An ancient 'hutch' or box, still kept in the chapel, received the fines imposed on inmates for offences that included gambling and 'secret feasting or drinking', while for smoking or keeping tobacco they could be fined five shillings – a good week's wages.

Most eminent of the wardens who have run the college since its foundation was the Rev. John Mason Neale, who took it over in 1846 when it was at a low ebb and had improved it out of all recognition when he died twenty years later. Neale's tomb, in a small memorial garden in the churchyard, describes him as 'Liturgiologist, Ecclesiologist, Church Historian, author and translator of hymns'.

The best known of his original hymns are *Good King Wenceslas* and *Jerusalem the Golden*, which he is said to have written looking down the valley to the spire of Bidborough church, ten miles away, lit up by the setting sun. Neale also appears inside the parish church, at the centre of the Oxford Movement centenary window in the north wall. He wears Byzantine vestments of green and gold, and is shown with John Keble and other leading figures in the movement for church reform.

Neale's High Church leanings got him into trouble with the authorities, to such an extent that the Bishop of Chichester forbade him to exercise his clerical functions for fifteen years; while popular feeling against his supected 'Popery' became so extreme that in 1851 rioters attacked the college and tried to set fire to the warden's lodgings. But Neale had a more frivolous side – a friend wrote that on his nightly rounds of the quadrangle he would 'take his friends out to hear the inmates snore. I shall not forget the sounds'.

The **Parish Church** stands on an ancient site, but was rebuilt to James Wyatt's designs at the end of the eighteenth century, after the old tower collapsed in 1785, making the whole building unsafe. It is a great wide place, dedicated to St Swithun, whose connection with wet weather (and hence with ducks) is commemorated in the carving on the left-hand side of the high altar. Unusually, the rood screen is complete with a figure of Christ, as in a medieval church. Outside the porch are three plain graveslabs by the path in memory of the Protestants Thomas Dunngate, Anne Tree and John Forman, burnt at the stake in the High Street in 1556.

On the other side of the High Street, the Dorset Arms, a Georgian coaching inn, lends itself to some speculation by its inscription 'For Families and Gentlemen'. Inside, if you reckon you come into either of these categories, you can find among other things a framed railway share of the East Grinstead Railway Company, valued at £25 and dated 1853.

East Grinstead is famous for the pioneer work in plastic surgery carried out at the Queen Victoria Hospital, inspired by Sir Archibald McIndoe, who worked there from the start of the Second World War until his death in 1960. The hospital is about a mile north of the High Street; the complex of buildings includes the McIndoe Burns Centre, built in the 1960s for research into the treatment of severe burns, and the Blond McIndoe Centre for Medical Research. The hospital is still the centre of the Guinea Pig Club, consisting of airmen who were severely burned or facially injured in the war, most of whom had been treated by McIndoe. There is a portrait of him in the main vestibule below the clock tower.

Standen (National Trust), on a by-road south of the town, is a comfortable country house embalmed in the prosperous glow of late-Victorian England. It was built in the 1890s by Philip Webb, the close associate of William Morris, for a wealthy London solicitor, and is the only major Webb building to survive intact. It is decorated throughout with Morris-designed wallpaper and textiles, and is full of the well-crafted furniture and twirly light fittings of the period. The south front, with its row of five handsome gables, looks across Weir Wood Reservoir to the heights of Ashdown Forest. Nearby is **Saint Hill Manor**, a dull stone eighteenth-century house, headquarters of the Scientology sect founded by the late Ron Hubbard.

Beyond Saint Hill the road curves downhill to give wide views over the **Weir Wood Reservoir**. With its wooded headlands, surrounding hills and rock outcrops, and flocks of moorhen and mallard, it is the nearest approach to the Lake District this part of England can provide. During the autumn migrations the reservoir is visited by all sorts of wildfowl; and curlews can sometimes be seen there.

South of the reservoir the road leads east to Wych Cross (see above). On the north side of the road is **Plaw Hatch Hall**, a country club owned and run by trade unionists. The gaunt stone house was built in 1874 by a banker called Arbuthnot on the site of an old manor house, and looks north across the reservoir to the hills beyond. In early summer the gardens are appropriately ablaze with red rhododendrons. Inside the walls are covered in socio-realist paintings; one vast canvas, showing every manifestation of anti-establishment protest from John Ball to CND, must have made Arbuthnot turn in his grave. Arbuthnot's motto, 'Innocent and True', is carved in stone above the front door: a good target for both bankers and trades-unionists to aim at.

West Hoathly, built on a ridge south-west of the reservoir, was a centre for smugglers, who were especially fond of the Cat Inn. The village church, with its squat tower and needle spire, and the stone manor house face each other across the street. Down the road is the fifteenth-century **Priest House**, a low half-timbered building with a roof of massive Horsham stone slabs. Before the Reformation this was the estate office for the monks of Lewes Priory, who owned the manor; it is now a small museum run by the Sussex Archaeological

Society. The collection includes old furniture, and bygones such as mantraps, and shepherds' smocks treated with oil to keep out the rain. As recently as 1905 it was a ruin; it is now the perfect country cottage. West Hoathly church was begun soon after the Conquest. The north wall of the nave, built about 1090, survives from the original building, which was altered and enlarged throughout the Middle Ages, the tower being added about 1400. Inside are some iron graveslabs of the Infield family, who were ironmasters of Gravetye. By the door is a gigantic chest, said to be twelfth-century, hollowed from a single oak log; and on the south wall nearby is a little brass to Anne Tree, one of the East Grinstead martyrs. Inscribed 'She was remembered in 1940. George Friend made this', it must surely be about the most recent portrait brass in the country.

In a combe north of West Hoathly is **Gravetye Manor**, an Elizabethan ironmaster's house, now a hotel. The road to Gravetye winds down through Forestry Commission conifer plantations, which cut off the house from the outside world. The stone house, gabled and mullioned, was built in 1598, and was greatly extended by William Robinson, who lived there for over half a century, from 1884 to 1935. Robinson was a landscape gardener who pioneered the English natural garden style at the end of the nineteenth century. Though there is a small formal garden at the back of the house, most of Robinson's plantings make use of the contours of the narrow valley, centring on a lake hidden behind tall trees and surrounded by reeds and bulrushes.

19

Crawley and Horsham

IT IS EASY to feel depressed as you first enter a New Town, and contemplate the rows of monotonous houses, varied only by texture of wall and colour of roof; the shopping precincts with their concrete tubs of geraniums and plastic shopfronts; the regulation spindly churches and sprawling schools; the general impression of a thin urban gruel, sieved through the planner's mind and slopped down over a few thousand acres of countryside. As one of the original New Towns designated after the New Towns Act of 1946, **Crawley** is open to such criticism. Nevertheless, these towns are places where people can live and work without exhausting journeys to office or factory, and where families can shop and children can play without constant danger from traffic. After half a century the 'new' housing of the early years, now surrounded by mature trees, has taken on a thoroughly established look.

Crawley is really an amalgamation of the villages of Three Bridges and Ifield with the small market town of old Crawley. In the process the ancient nuclei have been swamped but not completely submerged. Crawley has been there probably since Saxon times. After centuries of a quiet life, it woke up briefly at the end of the eighteenth century when the Prince Regent and his friends used it as a convenient stopping place on their journeys to and from Brighton, faded again when the London–Brighton railway removed most of the through traffic, and is now as prosperous as any town in the South-East. Before the New Town was started Crawley was hardly noticed; though at the turn of the century E. V. Lucas wrote of it: 'One would be hard put to it to think of a less desirable existence than that of dwelling on a dusty road and continually seeing people hurrying either from Brighton to London or from London to Brighton. Coaches, phaetons, motor cars, bicycles, pass through Crawley so numerously as almost to constitute one elongated vehicle.' The town centre is now bypassed, so it may well be quieter today than it was in the 1900s.

Crawley's wide High Street runs due north-south. If you stand by the timber-framed Old Punch Bowl Inn at the northern end and look down the street, you can still get something of the illusion of a market town. On your right is the George Hotel, a long low coaching inn, with Horsham stone slabs on the roof and a 'gallows' inn sign across the road; and on your left a row of old houses, among them the jutting gables and timbering of the former Ancient Prior's Restaurant (now offices), thought to have been built originally for the parish priest. The illusion is increased on Fridays and Saturdays, when much of the High Street is given over to an open-air market.

The sturdy little medieval church is down the narrow Church Walk; the oldest part dates from about 1290, but much is nineteenth-century rebuilding. The best thing about it is the fifteenth-century roof (contemporary with the tower), which has the panels between the beams boarded over, and an arcaded framework of strengthening timbers. An inscription in medieval English on one of the beams warns of the vanity of wealth. There is a nice Charles I pulpit, with an inscription on the ledge (visible only to the preacher) which reads 'Be brief' (Acts XX, 9). The verse in question runs: 'And there sat in the window a certain young man named Eutychus, being fallen into a deep sleep: and as Paul was long preaching, he sunk down with sleep, and fell down from the third loft, and was taken up dead.' Fortunately Paul was able to resuscitate him. Mark Lemon, the first editor of *Punch*, is commemorated by one of the north aisle windows. Lemon, who was a playwright as well as a journalist, was co-founder of *Punch* in 1841 and edited it until his death in 1870.

North and east of the church is the main shopping area, centred on Queen's Square, a wide expanse of paving, with curlicued bandstand, surrounded by 1960s shops, few more than three storeys high. The latest addition, very much of the 1990s, is the vast and sumptuous County Mall, built between the war memorial gardens and the station. Along The Boulevard are the civic buildings, among them the long low Town Hall and the tower block of Crawley College. Only a mile or so farther north, past the gleaming buildings of the factory estate, you are into the roar of **Gatwick Airport**.

Unlike **Three Bridges**, which is almost totally absorbed by Crawley's eastward spread, **Ifield** keeps some of its village character. It marks the western limit of the town: you can stand in the churchyard and look across miles of farmland. Church, pub and cottages lie down a cul-de-sac. The church is a typical thirteenth-century Sussex building, with a low tower surmounted by a shingle cap. Inside there are two fine tombs of about 1340, one on either side of the nave; the carved recumbent figures are thought to be Sir John de Ifield and his wife Lady Margaret.

From Ifield you can go by devious back roads to **Rusper**, a little village tucked away near the Surrey border. There used to be a nunnery at Rusper, and a prioress and four of the sisters are buried in the churchyard. The church has a medieval tower, but the rest of it was rebuilt in 1855 by the Broadwood family of piano manufacturers. Lucy Broadwood (1858–1929), who has a memorial tablet with a white profile medallion inside the church, was a key figure in the English folksong revival, led by Cecil Sharp. The fence on the north side of the churchyard is marked with Roman numerals, each number corresponding to a family responsible for the upkeep of that section of the fence. Rusper's forge has gone, but the two huge bellows can still be seen attached to the wall of the Star Inn, flanking the village pump. Rusper's peace is constantly shattered by the roar of jets, as it lies almost directly under the Gatwick flight path.

South of Crawley the land is still heavily wooded, with St Leonard's, Tilgate and Worth Forests forming a fairly continuous belt. **Worth** village, south-east of Crawley off the B2036, stands on the edge of the woodland, with suburbia to the north, the M23 to the east, and lakes and gnarled trees to the south. Its church is mainly Saxon, though it does not look it from a distance, as it has a Victorian tower and broach spire. Seen from close to it is monumentally solid, with thick walls and little round-arched windows high up, in pairs separated by dumpy pillars. In the north wall is an enormously tall Saxon doorway, now blocked up. Inside, the church is equally massive, with high rounded chancel arch, and lower, narrower arches to the transepts. This ponderousness is reflected in the heavy balusters of the gallery, dated 1610. Outside the south porch, the inscription to 'poor old John', the Victorian sexton, celebrates a life spent

Within the walls by Saxons reared of old,
By the stone sculptured font of antique mould,
Under the massive arches in the glow,
Tinged by dyed sunbeams passing to and fro.

Worth Abbey, a nineteenth-century tycoon's country house originally known as Paddockhurst, now a Benedictine monastery and Roman Catholic boys' public school, is a few miles away on the

B2110 to Turners Hill. From the road, you can see the battlemented brick gatehouse which was once the entrance to stables and model farm complex built by Robert Whitehead (1823–1905), a marine engineer who in the course of a much-travelled life was a friend of Garibaldi, and invented the torpedo.

In 1894 the first Lord Cowdray bought Paddockhurst from Whitehead and added greatly to it; the huge stone house lies a little below the buildings on the hill and has magnificent views towards the South Downs. Lord Cowdray had made a fortune from civil engineering works, including the Admiralty Harbour at Dover and the Blackwall Tunnel under the Thames; he left £6 million when he died in 1932. Paddockhurst was his weekend cottage – on which, when he was really working at it, he spent £10,000 a month in improvements. The house is plastered with the Cowdray crest (the unusual supporters are a diver and a Mexican peasant, symbolising harbour engineering and oilfields in Mexico), and with its richly coffered and painted ceilings and stained glass has a sumptuousness that rivals its Tudor models. The room now used as the masters' dining-room has a moulded frieze done by Walter Crane in 1896, showing the evolution of transport from Stone Age man to the Age of Steam.

After Lord Cowdray's death, Paddockhurst was bought by the Benedictines in 1933, as a dependent priory of Downside Abbey in Somerset. In 1957 it became an independent house, and since 1965, when it became Worth Abbey, many new buildings have been added. The most striking recent addition is an unusual church crowned by a drum-shaped lantern above a dome.

Turners Hill has a big landmark of a late-Victorian church, which stands at the highest point for miles and catches every wind that blows. The village climbs the steep north face of the hill, with a crossroads pub and a bogus but nice group of half-timbered houses round a lawn, on the East Grinstead road.

Three miles south of Turners Hill, off the B2028, is **Wakehurst Place**, the Tudor home of the Culpeper family whose ramifications spread through Kent and Sussex. The Culpepers got hold of Wakehurst in the fifteenth century, when two Culpeper brothers abducted two Wakehurst girls, who were carried off 'makyng grete and pittious lamentation and weping'. However, the *fait accompli* led to the respectability of marriage, and both couples settled down at Wakehurst. A descendant, Edward Culpeper, built the gabled stone house in 1590.

Down the centuries, and especially since 1900, Wakehurst's owners have built up a magnificent collection of trees and shrubs, now owned by the National Trust and run as an offshoot of Kew Gardens (gardens open every afternoon except Christmas Day). As at Kew, the trees are labelled and often marked with the date of planting. To see the gardens properly, you must be prepared to walk at least a couple of miles, as they are on a vast scale, and include every kind of scenery from an enchanted lake studded with tiny islands to a long path below a rampart of dank and mossy rock.

Nowadays **Ardingly** is chiefly famous for the showground of the South of England Agricultural Society, which holds a three-day annual show in June. The modern village is next to the showground on the main road; old Ardingly, consisting of a church and a few houses, is on the twisting back road to Balcombe. It is best approached from the Balcombe side, as you then become aware of its commanding position above Ardingly Reservoir. The church, with its stocky fifteenth-century tower, is a mixture of the medieval and the Victorian. On the chancel floor are some exceptional brasses to the Tudor Culpepers, naively portrayed, one couple with ten sons and eight daughters. There is a delicately carved fifteenth-century screen, and at the other extreme of carpentry a tower staircase of rough-hewn logs cut across the diagonal to form wedge-shaped steps. In 1643 the men of Ardingly are said to have used the churchyard wall as a defensive position against Cromwell's dragoons, who had come to expel the Royalist rector.

Ardingly College, down another back road, is one of the Rev. Nathaniel Woodard's Sussex public schools (see also Lancing and Hurstpierpoint). It is a large redbrick place, with a squat-towered chapel and huge east window as the central feature, and is set back behind lawns in a beautiful stretch of country.

Three miles south of Ardingly is **Lindfield**, a famous beauty spot and almost too done up for its own good. Nevertheless, with its wide common, used in medieval times for fairs and markets, village pond and gently sinuous High Street leading uphill to the church, it is a beautiful place, and everybody's ideal of the English village. The houses are mainly brick and tilehung; a few of them are colour-washed, more like Cornwall than Sussex. The grand Queen Anne and Georgian houses are at the top of the hill, near the church. Older and more fascinating is Old Place, down the lane behind the church. It is basically a small Elizabethan manor house, timber-framed with brick infilling; it has three gables, the central one leaning at a drunken angle. It owes its present great size to Charles Kempe, the Victorian stained-glass artist, who lived at Old Place and made it an accumulation of architectural bits and pieces. The original house is said to have been Queen Elizabeth's country cottage; similarly the pretty thatched cottage next door is said to have been Henry VII's hunting lodge.

The church is mainly thirteenth- and fourteenth-century, almost as wide as it is long, and has an enormously tall spire – a necessary landmark when the country was still heavily wooded. Inside it is not particularly interesting. The roof of the north transept, originally reached from outside, was once used as a pigeon loft. In the nineteenth century the church was famous for its band, consisting of a flute, two clarinets, bassoon, violin and cello. As in Thomas Hardy's *Under the Greenwood Tree*, the instrumentalists were made redundant when the organ was installed. Helena Hall's excellent parish guide prints several old churchyard inscriptions, now mostly illegible. An eighteenth-century one ran as follows:

> *Long was my Pain, great was my Grief*
> *Surgeons I'd many, but no relief*
> *I trust through Christ to rise with the just*
> *My leg and thigh was buried fust.*

Beside the churchyard is Church House, formerly the Tiger Inn. After the defeat of the Armada in 1588, the Tiger supplied so much strong ale to the triumphant bellringers that they broke all the ropes and cracked one of the bells. Now it is used for more sober church business.

At its southern end Lindfield links up with **Haywards Heath**, a commuting and shopping sprawl, with a mile or so of the A272 as its centre. Its prosperity is due to the fact that both Lindfield and Cuckfield refused to have a railway running through them. So it was built across a stretch of heath running between the two; a church (said to be the centre of Sussex, if a county so long and narrow can have a centre) was built in the 1860s; and the houses proliferated.

Cuckfield (pronounced Cookfield) still keeps plenty of its small country-town character. On the outskirts is a sign showing a cuckoo on a tree – a reference to one derivation of the town's name from the Saxon 'Cucufelda', a clearing full of cuckoos, Or it may mean 'land surrounded by a quickset hedge', less poetic but more probable. In

Norman times it belonged to William de Warenne, son-in-law of William the Conqueror, who had a hunting lodge and chapel there.

Cuckfield is built on the side of a hill, with a steep High Street running down to an attractively irregular group of old houses and shops, and the tall-spired church rising behind. This is a noble church on a noble site, which gives enormous views southwards over woodlands to the downs. The tower was built in stages in the thirteenth and fourteenth centuries, and the main structure was completed about 1366. The nave has a fifteenth-century wagon roof, painted in Victorian times with most medieval-looking roses and foliage. Under the tower is the old clock mechanism, dated 1667. On the other side of the road a footpath runs along the side of Cuckfield Park an Elizabethan house with a little Tudor gatehouse which can be seen through the trees. Ockenden, now a hotel, is a sixteenth-century timber-framed house, with a three-storey stone addition dated 1608. It belonged to the Burrell family, several of whom were local ironmasters, and was probably used originally as a hunting-lodge.

One member of the family, Timothy Burrell, kept a diary of his life in Cuckfield from 1683 to 1714, full of references to the lavish dinners he gave, and the chronic drunkenness of his coachman, John. A typical Burrell dinner began with soup, went on to carp, pigeon pie, leg of mutton and chicken, and proceeded via pancakes, asparagus, goose and soused mackerel to raisins in cream, calves' foot jelly, flummery pudding (custard or blancmange), cakes and 'Imperial cream'. In the intervals of gorging himself, Mr Burrell restored his digestion by drinking mineral water from a medicinal spring at Ditchling. Relics of old Cuckfield are kept in the public library (Queen's Hall) in the High Street.

Balcombe, three miles north of Cuckfield, is a largish village, with a few old houses at its compact centre. The church, buried in holly trees and conifers, is a little way to the north. It was completely restored in the nineteenth century, apart from the medieval tower with its low broach spire. Near Balcombe are two of the highlights of the London–Brighton railway – a tunnel under the forest to the north, and a viaduct over the Ouse to the south. A marvel of Victorian brickwork, its thirty-seven arches stride across the countryside for more than a quarter of a mile.

North of Balcombe you are back in the forest. The best impression of these towering miles of trees can be got from the B2110 to **Handcross**. Vast pollarded beeches have been left to shoot up to the limit of their growth, and in places the road is hemmed in by walls of self-sown rhododendrons.

Handcross itself is little more than a flyover across the Brighton road surrounded by houses; but near it are the superb National Trust gardens of **Nymans**. Nymans was bought in 1890 by Ludwig Messel, a wealthy German-born stockbroker; the house was a conventional nineteenth-century villa, which Messel extended with a vast conservatory for exotic plants and a tall Italianate tower. He was a friend of the great gardener William Robinson (see Gravetye, p. 298), and soon set about creating his own garden at Nymans. Its centrepiece is a roughly circular walled garden, laid out in a wavering symmetry. The rest of the garden is a series of outdoor 'rooms', like the heather garden, with heather shoulder high, and the sunk garden, with concentric flower beds round a tall white Byzantine urn. Ludwig died in 1915, and his son Leonard, another enthusiastic gardener, took over, increasing its stock of rarities with plants from as far afield as Tasmania and South America. In the 1920s he pulled down the Victorian villa and rebuilt the house in mock-medieval style. When Leonard died in 1953, the National Trust took over Nymans.

Much of the house was burnt down in 1947, and the empty shell of golden stone provides a hauntingly unreal backcloth to lawns and massed banks of rhododendrons. The garden suffered severely in the October 1987 hurricane, but is now well on the way to recovery. Among the new plantings is a rose garden, and the little School Copse, which was paid for by Handcross schoolchildren and planted by them on the first anniversary of the storm.

As well as the garden, what survives of the Messels' house can be visited – comfortable rooms, full of old oak furniture, wall hangings, books and paintings.

To the south is **Slaugham** (pronounced Slaffem), only half a mile from the Brighton road, but amazingly remote. It has a heathland common, with a large pond surrounded by reeds and full of birds; a neat village centre with houses on either side of a dead-end; and a church that dates from Norman times. Its strange name has been derived from various Saxon words: *sloh* for a slough or marsh, *slogu* for iron dross or slag, and *slaga* for a slayer or hunter have all been suggested. The church was greatly restored about 1860, but still keeps its thirteenth-century tower. In the south chapel is a magnificent monument to Richard Covert, who died in 1579. Seventeen little stone figures all face the east, men and boys in front,

306

women and girls behind. They have been spared the usual mutilations and knocks, and the carving is beautifully clear, down to the embroidery on the sleeves. The Coverts came from Slaugham Place, south of the church; the large lake in the grounds can be seen from the churchyard.

Warninglid is in the same quiet hinterland, a hamlet guarded by a village sign depicting a spear-brandishing Saxon, with the words 'Werna Gelad' inscribed mysteriously over his head. Hilaire Belloc cited **Lower Beeding**, a couple of miles west of Warninglid, as a typical example of a Sussex name that 'should give fools to think'. In *The Four Men* he wrote of 'the height called Lower Beeding, which means the lower place of prayer, and is set upon the very summit of a hill. Just as Upper Beeding is at the very lowest point in the whole County of Sussex, right down, down, down upon the distant marshes of Adur.' However, Ekwall, in his place-name dictionary, derives the name from the Old English 'Beadingas', meaning 'Beada's people', and thinks that in this instance 'Upper' and 'Lower' refer to the villages' importance rather than their altitude.

Lower Beeding has a solid grey Victorian church and a solid yellow ochre eighteenth-century pub. In May and June it is a Mecca for lovers of rhododendrons and azaleas, who come to see the marvellous **Leonardslee** gardens. Begun in 1889 by Sir Edmund Loder, after whom the *Loderi* rhododendron varieties are named, Leonardslee is formed in a deep valley, with a string of lakes and waterfalls along the bottom reflecting the plantings that rise on either side. The Victorian house stands on an open lawn above, from which you plunge down among huge rhododendrons, their flowers white or pink-flushed, towards the sound of running water in the valley. As a bonus, you may well spot a wallaby or two hopping about in the undergrowth, descendants of the animals introduced by Sir Edmund Loder.

Nuthurst, two miles farther west, consists of a few houses and a spindly church, worth a look for its brilliantly painted chancel and rood screen, a redecoration done in the 1940s. On the south wall is a tablet to Sir Nevile Henderson (died 1942), who came from Sedgwick Park near by. The inscription 'Blessed are the peacemakers' is an ironic epitaph for the man who, as ambassador to Germany at the time of Munich, supported the appeasement policy that made war inevitable.

You can get the best idea of **St Leonard's Forest**, east of Horsham, from the minor roads that cut across it. It gets its name from a chapel to the saint that once stood there. In the days when the trees were continuous and the gloom lay heavier, the forest was a great breeding-place for legends. St Leonard himself fought and finally conquered a dragon there; wherever the saint's blood fell on the ground, clusters of lily-of-the-valley sprang up. A later dragon was vouched for in 1614 by three locals from Faygate, on the edge of the forest. The *Harleian Miscellany* gives their account of the monster. It was 'reputed to be nine feete, or rather more, in length, and shaped almost in the forme of an axeltree of a cart, a quantitie of thicknesse in the middest, and somewhat smaller at both endes. The former part, which he shootes forth as a necke, is supposed to be an elle long; with a white ring, as it were, of scales about it.' As if that were not bad enough, the dragon could 'cast his venome about four rodde from him', and could kill at a distance; and wherever he walked he left 'a glutinous and slimie matter . . . which is very corrupt and offensive to the scent'.

Apart from the presence of dragons, the forest was famous for an absence of nightingales, after a sour-tempered hermit had banished them for disturbing his meditations.

In recent years **Horsham** has undergone a drastic and highly successful central redevelopment, integrating the ancient streets with underpasses, shopping precincts and car parks, bringing in the new without disrupting the old. Like Oxford, it has a Carfax at its centre; and like Chichester it has a sensible arrangement of North, South, East and West Streets, so that you know where you are (though North Street, with the local council offices, is some way from the other three). The Carfax is a conglomeration of shops and pubs (the King's Head is dated 1401), with a cheerful blue-and-white bandstand and tall plane trees facing the battlemented former town hall, now used for all sorts of community events.

Behind the town hall is the **Causeway**, Horsham's architectural gem – a quiet cul-de-sac of old houses leading down to the church. At the top end is the gabled fifteenth-century Causeway House, now the town museum. Big and rambling, it specialises in local material from the Horsham area, or from Sussex in general, with wheelwright's and saddler's shops, a blacksmith's forge, and displays on prehistory including bones of the Rudgwick dinosaur, found locally. There is also a small display of early editions of poems by Shelley, the region's most famous local inhabitant. Among the old prints, paintings and photographs is an extraordinary drawing of a hard-labour machine installed in Horsham Gaol – a long row of cubicles, each with a hand-operated crank connected to a vast wind vane which purposelessly beat the air. A parable on the futility of the penal system, then as now. An eighteenth-century barn, re-erected in the peaceful museum garden, displays old agricultural tools and machinery.

Opposite the museum is the old Manor House, the headquarters of the RSPCA, which moved there from London in 1973 and is due to move to new Horsham premises in the fairly near future.

The Causeway ends at the church, and the town does too. Beyond are playing fields and meadows where the Arun, still a small stream, flows by. The church has a massively buttressed tower begun in the twelfth century, crowned by a soaring, twisting spire. Inside it is basically Early English, with a vast Perpendicular seven-light window filled with garish glass. There are medieval tombs on either side of the altar: on the left an altar tomb dated 1485, which has a lute-playing angel carved on the canopy frieze; and on the right the tough-looking effigy of Thomas de Braose (died 1395), minus his nose. A tablet under the tower reads simply 'Percy Bysshe Shelley. 1792–1822'. One of his poems was the inspiration for the striking open-air fountain at the end of West Street, by the sculptor Angela Conner. Entitled *Rising Universe*, it consists of a giant globe with water flowing over and through it, and is an unusually successful example of abstract public art.

Shelley came from **Warnham**, a small well-groomed village two miles north-west of Horsham. A good many of the houses are roofed with slabs of Horsham stone, which give a feeling of antiquity, regardless of the age of the buildings they cover. The church, basically fourteenth-century, has a fine wall monument to Sir John Caryll (died 1613) and his 'sweetest and most religious wife' Lady Mary, and numerous Shelley memorials. The poet himself has no monument, though a case in the south aisle contains a copy of the entry of his baptism (on 7 September, 1792) from the parish register. His ashes are buried in Rome, and his heart is in his son's tomb in Bournemouth. He was born at Field Place outside the village, and as a boy sailed boats on a lake in what is now Warnham's nature reserve.

Three miles west of Horsham, Stane Street – the Roman road from London to Chichester, now the A29 – branches off from the A281. A couple of miles west of the junction a side road leads to **Rudgwick**, running uphill to the sturdy church on the Surrey border. The oldest part is the squat west tower, built in the thirteenth century, with huge corner buttresses; the twelfth-century font is made of Sussex marble – a stone that preserves the shells of sea creatures fossilised and clearly discernible. Back on Stane Street, for a mile or so south of the junction the road runs on top of a very obvious *agger* (raised causeway), several feet higher than the broad grass verge.

Slinfold is worth a detour down the back lanes. It has a gently curving village street, a good Victorian church with a choice of two stone-roofed lychgates, and a nicely varied collection of houses.

Itchingfield, still farther into the countryside to the south-east, is hardly a village at all. The church, down a cul-de-sac, is basically Norman, built about 1125; it has an astonishing 600-year-old belfry tower made entirely of vast beams held together by oak pegs. When Sir Gilbert Scott was restoring the interior in the 1860s, his workmen found a skull high up on one of the beams, said to have been the head of Sir Hector Maclean, executed for his part in the Old Pretender's rising of 1715. Maclean was a friend of the vicar of the time, who presumably put this macabre souvenir on the beam for safe keeping. In the churchyard is a pretty little brick-and-timber priest's house, put up in the fifteenth century as an overnight lodging for the priest who rode over from Sele Priory, at Upper Beeding (see above), to collect the church dues.

From Itchingfield you can see the tall brick tower of **Christ's Hospital** a mile to the east. The boys and girls of this ancient boarding school still wear its unique uniform of long blue topcoat, white neckbands and yellow socks, described in a school history as 'a modified survival of the ordinary dress of the Tudor period'. The yellow linings to the coats were perpetuated in the seventeenth century, following some medical myth of the time, 'to avoid vermin, by reason the white cottens is held to breed the same'.

Christ's Hospital moved from London to Horsham in 1902; E. V. Lucas, who saw it when it was brand new, called it 'a glaring red-brick settlement which the fastidiously urban ghost of Charles Lamb can now surely never visit'. Lamb – after whom one of the boarding houses is named – was at the school at the end of the eighteenth century, along with two other famous literary figures, Coleridge and Leigh Hunt. They all left reminiscences of their schooldays which are a similar mixture of pride and fascinated horror at memories of wretched food, floggings and solitary confinement. The first day of term the headmaster found Coleridge crying with homesickness, and bellowed at him 'Boy! the school is your father! Boy! the school is your mother! the school is your sister! the school is your first-cousin, and your second cousin, and all the rest of your relations! Let's have no more crying!' Fortunately, in these gentler scholastic times, such memories belong to the distant past. The school went co-educational in 1985, when two hundred girls from its sister foundation in Hertford moved down to Horsham.

It is built round a gargantuan main quadrangle, designed by Sir Aston Webb. The dining hall (at a rough pacing 150 feet long) has a vast painting by Verrio along most of one side. Painted between 1684 and 1690, it commemorates the founding of the Royal Mathematical School (an integral part of Christ's Hospital) by Charles II, who sits enthroned in the middle, gesturing expansively, with charity girls on the left and bluecoat boys on the right. Edward VI, who founded the original Christ's Hospital in the buildings of the former Greyfriars Monastery, Newgate, in 1552, has a modest little portrait on the opposite wall. The speech hall ('Big School') and chapel are huge and dull; the chapel walls are covered with large frescoes by Frank Brangwyn. In the quadrangle the boy king Edward VI surmounts a fountain, and four bluecoat boys, including Lamb and Coleridge, stand below.

Billingshurst, strung out along Stane Street, has been linked by etymologists with Billingsgate, where the Roman road entered London. Perhaps both were named after a Roman surveyor or official called Belinus. Less fancifully, it is more likely to be a Saxon *-ingas* or tribal name. The main street still has the general outline of a village, though not many of the old buildings are left. At its centre is a little sloping green leading up to the church, a sturdy building with a vastly disproportionate shingled spire. The best thing about it is the fine Tudor entrance porch below the tower, all brick and ancient timbers. Though the church stands on quite a high point, the view all around is blocked by featureless modern housing estates.

From Billingshurst the A272 ambles eastwards towards Haywards Heath, in places hardly more than a country lane, in spite of its importance as a traffic artery. Near **Coolham** a sign points down a lane to 'Blue Idol', which sounds like an exotic country club, but is in fact a Quaker meeting-house and guesthouse, remote and peaceful. Originally an Elizabethan farmhouse, one end of the building was converted at the end of the seventeenth century into a meeting-house by removing the first-floor timbers; the result is a tall, galleried room, ideal for the purpose. William Penn used to walk here from Warminghurst (see p. 332) to worship, while his wife Gulielma and their children rode over in an ox-drawn coach. The strange name has been explained in various ways. The one generally accepted is that during the nineteenth century, when the building was no longer in use or 'idle' and was colour-washed in blue, it was known as the 'blue idle meeting-house' – hence Blue Idol. The whole place is completely self-effacing: no doubt deliberately so, in view of the hounding the Quakers had to face in their early days.

A mile south of the main road, reached down leafy lanes, is **Shipley**, Hilaire Belloc's village from 1906 until his death in 1953. He lived in King's Land, a low rambling house on the outskirts of the village, and as a lover and praiser of windmills had his own mill at the end of his garden. Since his death Shipley Mill has been restored, and is now the only remaining working smock mill in West Sussex. (As a matter of terminology, a smock mill differs from a tower mill in having the top floors of wood, not of brick.) It was built as recently as 1879, the last of all the Sussex smock mills – and the biggest. On certain summer weekends, when the weather is right for milling, the great sweeps turn, sacks of wheat rise gently on the hoist to the top of the mill, and the grain drops through the shoots to the grindstones, then down the meal shoots to the bins below.

Across a field from the mill is Shipley church, a beautiful building, with a square central tower held together by iron cramps. It was built early in the twelfth century by the Knights Templars, and has fine Norman arches below the tower. Old pictures show it with a shingled pyramid cap on the tower, and minus the nineteenth-century north aisle, which destroyed its boxlike severity. In the chancel is a sumptuous monument to Sir Thomas Caryll and his wife, dated 1616. The composer John Ireland, as much a poet of Sussex as Belloc was, is buried in the churchyard. A tablet on the south wall of the church refers to his grave, 'marked by prehistoric sarsen stones to symbolise that antiquity the love of which inspired much of his music'.

West Grinstead, across the Worthing road (A24), is seventeen miles from East Grinstead as the crow flies. Whereas East Grinstead is a sizeable town, West Grinstead is hardly even a village. The big house of West Grinstead Park has been demolished, except for the battlemented stables. A medieval moat and stewponds for fish survive in the centre of the park; and one of the fine old trees is still known as 'Pope's Oak' from the tradition that the poet wrote much of *The Rape of the Lock* stretched out beneath its shade.

West Grinstead church is remote but well worth hunting out. It lies at the end of a back road, with a little bridge over the Adur just below, and is a rough-hewn place, roofed with Horsham slabs and with a broach spire that seems to rise straight from the roof. On the north wall is a patch of exposed Norman herringbone work, and round on the south side is a Norman door, shifted when the south aisle was added in the thirteenth century. The big wooden porch is fifteenth-century, and looks as though it has hardly been repaired since then. The monuments are of all shapes and sizes. In the south-west chapel are two tombs with good brasses, one to a lady who died in 1395, the other to Sir Hugh Halsham, an Agincourt veteran, and his wife charmingly named Lady Jocosa. In the south aisle is a monument to Sir Merrik Burrell, Governor of the Bank of England, portrayed in profile on a simple medallion; and another to his nephew Sir William Burrell, commemorated by an angular oddity by Flaxman. Sir William (died 1796) was an antiquarian who bequeathed his collection of Sussex documents to the British Museum. The old pews are marked with the names of the farms whose owners occupied them a century and a half ago, names as gnarled and worn as old oak trees – Freezers, Priors Bine, Sunt, Grinders, Hobshorts, Figland, Swallows Nest, White Soan, Thistleworth, and dozens more.

A fragment of the medieval **Knepp Castle**, stronghold of the Norman de Braose family, can be seen beside the Worthing road a mile south of the A272 crossroads.

The cottages in the middle of **Cowfold**, three miles east along the A272, sensibly turn their backs on the traffic and look in towards the medieval church. In the chancel is one of the most famous brasses in Sussex, to Thomas Nelond, Prior of Lewes in the 1420s. The tonsured figure is life-size, and the whole brass, with its elaborate canopy, is over ten feet long. The carpet above the brass is kept padlocked, but there is a rubbing hanging in the church.

Rising above the trees a mile south of Cowfold is the spire of one of the most astonishing places in the Weald: **St Hugh's Charterhouse (Parkminster)**, the only Carthusian monastery functioning in the British Isles – the others were destroyed by Henry VIII. (Visits by written permission only.) Thirty or so monks of this contemplative order live here, cut off from the world behind high stone walls. The order was founded in the eleventh century, but this monastery was built in the 1870s, after the English Roman Catholic hierarchy had been restored in 1850. It is currently (1999) being restored with the help of grants from the Carthusian order and English Heritage.

The vastness of its scale can only be guessed at from outside the huge and forbidding gatehouse. Once inside you cross the Court of Honour to the tall church; then through to the cloister, built on a scale that dwarfs any medieval foundation, and encloses three and a half acres of orchard. The monks' cells – small hermitages, each with its own garden and workshop – open off the cloister. The monks emerge only for services and dinner together on Sundays, and the occasional white-robed figure walking in the distance only enhances the solitude of the place. They emerged into the public eye (or ear) in 1998, when they recorded a CD of plainchant from the Night Office of their order.

The buildings, designed by a French architect, Clovis Normand of Calais, are nineteenth-century Romanesque and Gothic in style. Yet certain aspects, like the Prior's flower-filled garden, hidden below the towering walls of the church, have more of the real Middle Ages about them than the majority of piously tended monastic ruins. Most timeless of all is the small burial ground, where the monks are buried not in coffins but on wooden boards, with nameless wooden crosses above them.

20

Below the South Downs

FIVE MILES FROM Billingshurst down the dead straight line of Stane Street is **Pulborough**, which is divided into two distinct parts: the lower village, which straggles towards Storrington and has several pubs with gardens overlooking the Arun; and the upper, consisting of Georgian cottages round the church and a prosperous Queen Anne stone rectory across the road. The church stands at the top of the hill, and is a big commanding place, with two wide aisles and a clerestory, dating mainly from the early fifteenth century. Apart from a fine brass to a fifteenth-century rector, Thomas Harlyng, in the north aisle, the only other monument worth looking at is a Victorian one, showing William Hammond dying at his ease in a wing chair, with wife and children in dutiful attendance.

Heading south along the A29, it is easy to shoot past the tiny hamlet of **Hardham**; but it is worth stopping, as the whitewashed church has some of the finest medieval wall paintings in England – and some of the oldest, as they were done about 1100. Over the round chancel arch is the Lamb of God in glory; and on the walls are St George slaying the dragon and being broken on the wheel, the Magi, the Serpent tempting Adam and Eve, Eve milking an enormous cow in a homely Eden. A little to the south is Hardham Priory, now a farmhouse. Part of the cloister survives, turned into a flower garden.

Bury, three miles farther on, is a secluded village beside the Arun. The village street, hardly more than a lane, leads down to the tall-spired church, still with its fourteenth-century rood screen. The river is only a few yards away, and the remains of a jetty mark the old ferry across to Amberley. John Galsworthy, author of the *Forsyte Saga*, lived in Bury House from 1926 until his death in 1933. His ashes were scattered on the Downs.

Amberley is a dream village of thatched cottages draped with wisteria, dozing above the waters of the Arun. Even the name itself,

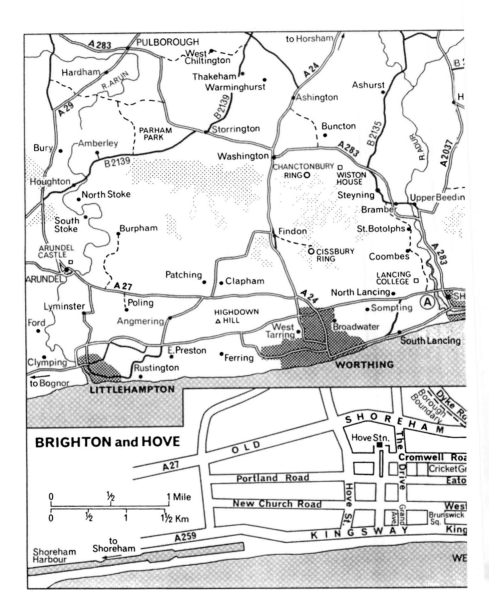

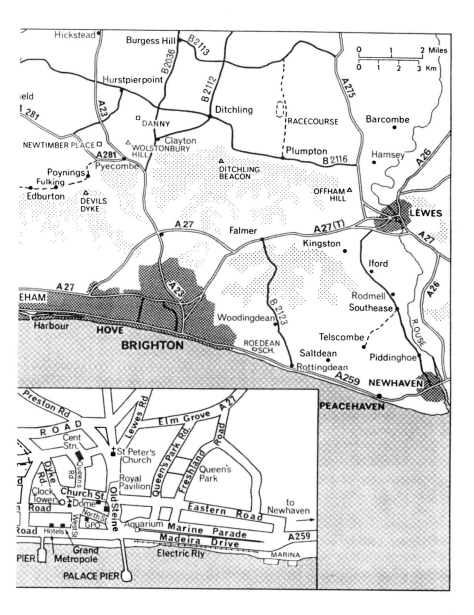

said to mean 'fields yellow with buttercups', has a drowsy feel about it; you can say it with your mouth hardly open. Yet Amberley has not always been a place of somnolent rusticity. In the troubled times of the 1370s, when the French were harrying the South Coast, Bishop Rede of Chichester found it worth his while to guard the north side of the Arun gap with a square-towered castle, enlarging Amberley's old manor house with the great curtain wall that rises sheer from the river level. According to tradition, Charles II spent a night in Amberley Castle in October 1651, on his flight to the coast and exile after the Battle of Worcester (see also Bramber, below, and Shoreham, p. 355), and his horse is said to have cast a shoe on the downs above the village. Presumably he was following, more or less, the line of the South Downs Way. Though the castle ruins belong to a hotel and cannot be visited, they can be seen well enough from the path down to the Wild Brooks, as the levels are poetically named, and over the churchyard wall; and the grouping of castle, church and village can be appreciated as a whole from the Arundel–Pulborough road. The play of light and shadow over the network of small watercourses and meadows was magically caught by John Ireland in his piano piece, *Amberley Wild Brooks*, composed in 1921.

Amberley's history goes back to the early days of Saxon England, when lands there were granted to St Wilfrid by King Cedwalla about AD 680. There would certainly have been a Saxon church on the site; the present building and the manor house were probably begun about 1100 by Luffa, Bishop of Chichester. The nave has rounded Norman windows and a tall chancel arch with multiple chevron ornament on the inner face. At the side of the arch are red ochre wall paintings of about 1200; a Calvary procession and a Crucifixion can be made out. There are also two consecration crosses on the nave walls.

Just south of the village, a huge quarry gouged from the chalk hillside is given over to the lime-kilns, forge, engine-house and other relics of a vanished industry preserved by the enthusiasts who run the **Amberley Museum**. Lime-burning at Amberley reached its height in mid-Victorian times; the lime was transported all over Sussex first by way of the Arun, and after 1863, when the line was built, by rail. On warm summer days the skies above Amberley are no longer acrid with smoke from the kilns, but bright with the multi-coloured wings of hang-gliders.

The road below the downs leads east from Amberley along the southern side of **Parham Park**. Parham, which was bought by the

Pearson family in 1922 and is now run as a family trust, is the westernmost – and the grandest – of the Elizabethan mansions built below the northern slopes of the downs. A many-gabled building of the local grey-brown stone, it keeps the downs at a distance, set in a huge park where deer graze below the ancient oaks and horse chestnuts. The approach brings you in on the east side, and the visitors' entrance is across a courtyard and up a nineteenth-century staircase at the back, neither of which give any idea of the building as a whole. The best preliminary is to go round to the south side, in the direction of the church, where you can see the E-shaped Elizabethan front with its wide wings and narrow central porch, and the tall mullioned windows that light the Great Hall. Overall, in fact, Parham is in the form of an H, as the wings project both north and south; the eastern wing is built on an earlier medieval house, which survives in the massive arches of the kitchen (now used for lunches and teas).

In medieval times the estate belonged to the Abbey of Westminster, and at the Dissolution it came into the hands of the Palmer family. As a guarantee of good luck the foundation stone of the new Parham was laid by a child (Thomas Palmer, the grandson and heir aged two and a half) 'about tenne of the clock in the forenoone' on 28 January, 1577. However, young Thomas himself was not so lucky. He served with Drake and Hawkins, and died in 1605 of smallpox. Meanwhile Parham had been bought by Thomas Bysshop, a London barrister from Henfield, whose family lived there for the next three centuries.

The Great Hall is the heart of Parham, and the first room you see. A splendid double cube, flooded with light from its lofty windows, it really looks the part. Medieval in shape and function, it is decorated in Renaissance style, with a moulded plaster ceiling, and oak screen carved in classical forms. A nineteenth-century owner of Parham, Robert Curzon, the Oriental traveller, filled the hall with suits of armour, which gave an uncanny effect described by a visitor. 'The only light came from a wood fire, so our end was all dim and ghostlike, for the fire flickered and the knights came to life and moved their helmets.' Nowadays all is clarity rather than ghostly dimness. Instead of armour, there are Elizabethan portraits round the walls – the Queen herself, her favourites Leicester and Essex, the young Edward VI, old Sir Thomas Bysshop, who bought Parham.

The big equestrian portrait of Prince Henry, the eldest son of James I, who died young leaving the throne free for Charles I, was

319

painted by the court painter Robert Peake about 1611, the year before the Prince's death. When heavy seventeenth-century overpainting was removed in 1985, the picture was transformed. Below the murky landscape background an allegorical scene was revealed, depicting 'The Prince leading Opportunity by the Forelock', Opportunity being portrayed as a bearded old man, winged and carrying the Prince's lance over his shoulder. Perhaps, in view of Henry's untimely death, the allegory was no longer considered tactful, and so Opportunity was painted out. In one corner of the Great Hall is the slender spiral of a narwhal's tusk, believed by the Elizabethans to be a unicorn's horn and a symbol of the rare and fabulous.

Parham is a treasurehouse of paintings and needlework, and the Great Parlour opening off the hall has both. The most arresting picture, over the fireplace, shows the man-of-war *Sovereign of the Seas*, launched at Chatham in 1637. Though the finest ship in the navy, she was not much use, as in all but the calmest seas her gunports were awash. A most unusual portrait of Charles I, by Mytens, shows him without his beard. Other portraits in the room are of Henrietta Maria, his future Queen, and members of their two families. The chairs have their original seventeenth-century embroidery, hardly faded with the passage of time.

Next is the Saloon, an eighteenth-century Adam-style interior. Among the paintings are two views of London painted by William James, a pupil of Canaletto, which make the Thames into something approaching the Grand Canal. Upstairs in the Great Chamber is a sumptuous four-poster bed, still with its sixteenth-century needlework coverings traditionally said to have been made by Mary Queen of Scots. (An alternative suggestion is the French queen Maria de Medici; the M monogram would fit them both.) The Tudor-looking overmantel, showing Parham's south front, a knight, a jester and assorted animals from family coats-of-arms, was in fact made by a twentieth-century plasterer, Esmond Burton, who had the true Tudor wildness about him.

The West Room is hung with 'flame-stitch' wall coverings. Over one of the doors is a periwigged old man holding a little dog. This is Henry Bysshop, who hid from the Roundheads with his dog in his arms; during the search the loyal animal made no sound, and years later this picture was painted as a tribute. After the Restoration Bysshop was postmaster-general and introduced date-stamping for letters; some early examples are shown. Opposite old Bysshop is Sir

Ralph Assheton and his wife. She ran off with a lover; Sir Ralph went after her and got her back, and on her return had himself painted with his foot placed on her dress and his hand entwined in her hair to prevent any further straying. The Green Room has lithographs of Sir Joseph Banks, the great botanist who sailed with Captain Cook, and his contemporaries. There are two pictures of Omiah, the first South Sea Islander to visit England, who came back with Banks and Cook and whose excellent table manners gave Georgian London a talking-point; and a Stubbs painting of a kangaroo, done from a skin but surprisingly full of bounce.

Finally the Long Gallery. This enormous room, stretching from end to end of the house at second-floor level, is as perfect in its own way as the Great Hall. The damaged Victorian ceiling has been raised about a foot and painted by Oliver Messel in a straggly foliage design. The gallery is full of bits and pieces, from a Roman lead cistern to James II's ornate state saddle. A little bedroom off it has a collection of naive Stuart needlework pictures, in contrast to the grandeur all around.

Parham's gardens are as varied as the house, with a four-acre walled herb garden, vegetable garden and orchard. Beyond the wall is an informal 'pleasure ground' which is full of wild flowers and includes a lake, a small brick and turf maze laid out to an Elizabethan embroidery pattern, and a lead figure of a lounging river god.

South of the house is Parham's small church, all that is left of the medieval village. The inside was remodelled in 1815–25, and a tower was added; the fireplace in the north transept shows an unusual addiction to comfort. The church still has its box pews, and there is a rare fourteenth-century lead font.

By contrast with Parham, **Storrington** outside its gates is a small town of little character. Its centre is a jumble of everything from traditional Sussex stone through Edwardian shop-fronts to horizontal concrete modern. The church lies behind, on a mound. Part of the original Norman building survives in the nave and north aisle. In earlier times the tower had a tall spire, but it was destroyed by lightning in 1731. The churchyard includes a piece of land called the Old Pillery Gardens – not, as you might think, a misspelling for Pillory, but called after the patent pink pills once dispensed by a Mr Dixon from his house near by.

Around 1900 E. V. Lucas wrote of the village of **Washington**: 'There are few better spots in the country for a modest contented man to keep a horse.' At the top of the hill is the village church, much restored, with a sturdy battlemented tower; and at the bottom a pub whose beer is good enough, though nothing like the brew Hilaire Belloc found there on his tramp through Sussex: 'nectar brewed in the waxing of the moon and of that barley which Brutus brought hither in the first founding of this land.' But he was writing before the days of pressurised keg beer.

From Washington you look up to **Chanctonbury Ring**, the most famous landmark on the South Downs. It is best to allow a good two hours for the walk to the top and back; and it is worth remembering that the steep parts of the chalk track can get extremely slippery after rain. The grove of majestic beech trees on its summit took a terrible battering in the hurricane of 16 October, 1987; the inner trees were largely blown down, though surprisingly a fringe was left round the outside. The storm brought one mystery to light – a human leg bone, revealed underneath an uprooted tree. From Chanctonbury you can see the whole of mid-Sussex spread out before you: the nearby villages of Ashington and Washington, Shipley Mill and St Hugh's Monastery in the middle distance, and far away the slopes of Leith Hill across the Surrey border. Southwards is a horizon of sea beyond Cissbury; and on a clear day you can see the bluff of Selsey Bill a good twenty miles away. Below the trees are the ditch and rampart of an Iron Age camp. Legend says that if you run seven times backwards round the Ring you can conjure up the Devil.

Chanctonbury's trees were planted about 1760 by Charles Goring, who lived at **Wiston House**, a stone Elizabethan mansion in a park below the downs. Wiston is now leased by the Foreign Office and is not open to the public; but you can still enjoy the beauty of the park and the house's faded stone façade on your way to the church. This has various memorials to the powerful de Braose family – heraldic glass to Lady Annys, a small wall tomb to the infant son of Sir John, Sir John's own brass on the floor of the south chapel. Dated 1426, it shows him in armour; the empty spaces on the brass are filled with little scrolls repeating the words 'Jesus', 'Mercy', like a Tibetan prayer wheel reciting the same words over and over.

On the windowsill in the chapel is the shattered figure of Sir Thomas Shirley, who built Wiston about 1576. His son Sir Robert, one of the greatest of Elizabethan travellers, visited the Persian court, fought for the Persians against the Turks, and married a Circassian girl; their portraits by Vandyck are at Petworth. According to Fuller's *Worthies*, on his return Sir Robert 'much affected to appear in

Looking north across the Sussex Weald from the South Downs.

forreign Vestes; and, as if his *Clothes* were his limbs, accounted himself never ready till he had something of the Persian Habit about him'. With so much oriental influence around, it is not surprising that Wiston is claimed to be the first place where coffee was drunk in England, in the first decades of the seventeenth century.

The country round Chanctonbury inspired many of the works of the composer John Ireland (see also Amberley, above). Towards the end of his life, in the 1950s, he bought Rock Mill below Chanctonbury, a converted tower mill now left high and dry on a spit of land above immense sand quarries. A plaque on the wall records that 'Dr John Ireland (1879–1962) lived his last and happiest years in this house.' He is buried a few miles away at Shipley.

The tiny church at **Buncton** is easy to miss: it lies across a miniature ravine by the back road from Chanctonbury to Ashington. You get to it by a path over a stream, and through a small wood carpeted in spring with bluebells, yellow dead-nettles and wild garlic – a magical approach. Buncton was the nearest that later generations could get to the unpronounceable Saxon 'Biohchandoune'. Hardly more than a stone barn surrounded by trees, it was built about 1150 and has a round Norman chancel arch and some rough carving, including the figure of a man lying down.

Steyning, Bramber and Upper Beeding have now more or less coalesced. **Steyning** (pronounced Stenning) is a pretty little town. The sloping High Street is filled with antique and handicraft shops, and has the clock tower of the Old Market House as its focal point. Steyning was an important place in Saxon times. It was a royal manor owned by Alfred the Great, had its own mint, and, in the days when the Adur was much wider than it is today, was a harbour town.

It also has its own saint, Cuthman, a favourite with Sussex designers of stained glass windows because of his estimable habit of trundling his old mother about in a handcart, a theme capable of endless interpretations. As a shepherd boy in the West Country, Cuthman would draw a circle on the grass with his staff, and command his sheep not to stray in the name of the Lord; and the magic circle was so powerful that the sheep stayed put. But on the death of his father Cuthman was forced to move, so he loaded his mother on to a cart and headed east. On one occasion the cord by which Cuthman pulled the cart broke while he was passing some haymakers. They roared with laughter, whereupon the saint, uttering the words 'Laugh men, weep heaven', called down a shower of rain that ruined their crop, and fell on the field in haymaking time for ever afterwards. The cart broke down irreparably at Steyning. Taking this as a sign, Cuthman built a hut for himself and his mother, and set up a small timbered church, the remote ancestor of the present splendid Norman building.

Though the solid sixteenth-century tower would look big enough attached to a normal parish church, it is quite out of scale against the tall Norman nave, topped by a high roof above round-arched clerestory windows. The nave is of cathedral-like grandeur, with powerful arcading, and a chancel arch unusually high for a Norman church. This is the only survivor of the four arches that would have supported the central tower (it is not known if this was ever built). The present chancel was added in the eighteenth century, roughly where the Norman tower would have come. Too much Norman moulding can lead to visual indigestion; but all these stone spikes and zigzags are leavened by grotesque animal and human heads at the junctions of the arches, doodles in stone by craftsmen relaxing for a moment. At the east end of the south aisle is a Romanesque capital that looks as though it has strayed from Venice or Sicily; perhaps the sculptor of these lions and tendrils had seen something similar on the Crusades. In the porch is a broken coffin lid taken from the Saxon burial ground; suggestions are that it came from the grave of Cuthman himself, or from that of King Ethelwulf, father of Alfred, who died in 857.

Church Street, which leads up from the High Street, is a harmonious undulation of timbered overhangs and Horsham stone roofs. The most substantial building is the grammar school, built in the fifteenth century as the home of a religious order and known as Brotherhood Hall. It has a good brick Tudor doorway. A plaque on the wall of a cottage up the street proclaims 'This is Sir Harry Gough's house, 1771'; it was put up there by the local MP after a tenant had refused to pay the rent. Chantry Green, where the road widens out, is a harmlessly peaceful spot today, yet it saw the burning of a Protestant martyr in Mary's reign. W. B. Yeats wrote some of his later poems in the big Queen Anne house facing the green.

High above **Bramber** towers a steep hill, with a fang of masonry at the summit. This is all that survives of the keep of the great Norman Castle (English Heritage) that once stood there, guarding the lower reaches of the Adur. The name derives from the Saxon 'Brymmburh', meaning a fortified hill; and a Saxon stronghold probably stood on the ground at the back of the castle. William the

Conqueror gave the Rape of Bramber to William de Braose, and by 1090 the castle was complete, with an outer gateway somewhere on the line of the present main road, and an approach across a deep moat to the tall square keep. The castle survived the Middle Ages, but not the Civil War, when it was held first by the Royalists and then by the Parliamentarians, who finally dismantled it. The church on the slope below was built soon after the Conquest; it was a cruciform building, but lost its chancel and transepts in the Civil War. The Norman chancel arch survives; one capital has a very Chaucerian fox carrying off Chanticleer.

St Mary's House near the river is one of the finest timber-framed houses in Sussex. It was built in the fifteenth century as a home for four monks, who were bridge wardens of the important bridge across the Adur and looked after the chapel that stood on it. Big though it is, what survives is only half of the original courtyard building, which was also a guesthouse for pilgrims on their way to Chichester or Canterbury, and for other travellers who wanted a night's rest. When the monasteries were dissolved it came into private ownership and was turned into a comfortable home; the 'Painted Room', said to have been decorated in 1585 for a visit by Queen Elizabeth, is an extraordinary piece of Tudor *trompe-l'oeil*, with illusory arches leading the eye towards tiny landscapes. An upstairs room, known as the King's Room, was very probably where Charles II stayed before escaping down to Shoreham and across to France (see p. 355). It is easy to imagine that tall swarthy figure, disguised as a groom, peering out of the window towards the bridge and slipping quietly across the river when the Roundhead patrols had passed. (The old bridge, far longer than the present one, began almost at the door of St Mary's.)

Before the 1832 Reform Bill, Bramber was a really rotten borough, returning two Members for less than a hundred inhabitants. One of its MPs was William Wilberforce, the anti-slavery campaigner. While driving through the village one day, he asked the postboy what it was called. 'Bramber,' said the boy. 'Bramber?' queried Wilberforce. 'Why, that's the place I'm the Member for!'

In the Middle Ages **Upper Beeding** had Sele Priory to counterbalance Bramber's castle. Now it has nothing much except rows of nondescript houses and a grim Scottish Baronial mansion, straight from the wilds of Aberdeen.

Because it lies behind Brighton, the range of hills east of the Adur is better known and more visited than any stretch along the whole length of the downs. It is also more liable to encroachment: a glance at the map will show the tide of houses lapping up the contours towards the crest of the London road. But so far the steep northern slopes are as empty as they have been for centuries, and the villages below consist of little more than an ancient church and a few cottages and farms. Fortunately the solitude of these peaceful slopes has been guaranteed for the foreseeable future, since in 1987 a couple of miles of escarpment above the village of Fulking was bought by the National Trust. This stretch of downland is deeply cut by the ancient tracks or 'bostals' up and down which the weatherbeaten Victorian shepherds used to drive their flocks; and the springy hill turf is a paradise for rare blue butterflies and all kinds of fragile plant life. The scrub that has invaded the sheepwalks is being cleared – one hopes with due respect paid to the witches who, according to ancient superstition, are the guardians of the elder trees, and whose permission should be sought before they are cut down.

Of the villages below the escarpment, **Edburton** is named after Edburga, grand-daughter of King Alfred, who is supposed to have built a church here in the tenth century. The present Early English building is large for a parish church. It has a Norman lead font, battered through having been taken outside and used as a horse trough in Cromwellian times. **Fulking**'s centrepiece is a pub with the good downland name of the Shepherd and Dog. Beside it, a spring bubbles out from a neat little Victorian brick-built shelter, and runs in a stream by the side of the road; in Fulking's heyday it was a sheepwash where the shepherds used to dip their flocks. **Poynings**, the largest of the three, is an up-and-down village which goes in for ironworking and stonecutting in a modest way. Its church is a big cruciform building, noble and austere inside and out, with a battlemented central tower. It was built under the will of Michael de Ponynnges, who died in 1369, and is Early Perpendicular in style. The pulpit, screen and other woodwork are Jacobean.

Above Poynings looms the bulk of Dyke Hill, an Iron Age camp with the great gash of the **Devil's Dyke** forming a natural defence along the southern side. If you want the solitude of high places you will not find it up here, as there is a large hotel right on the summit. But it is a tremendous viewpoint, with the whole central Sussex plain lying below, and to the south the high-rise flats of Brighton. It was here that the Devil stood glaring at the churches of the Weald, and swore that he would drown them by cutting through the downs between sunset and sunrise, thus letting in the sea. Taking no notice of the pleadings of St Cuthman, he set to work, hacking out great lumps of chalk and hurling them all around him. Where they fell are the round hills that stud the lower slopes of the downs.

At the last moment, when the Devil needed only a few more chops with his mattock for the sea to come pouring in, an old woman of Poynings lit a candle and looked out of her window to see what was going on. Inspired by St Cuthman, the candle gave out such a blaze that the cocks woke up and started to crow, the Devil fled with a howl of rage leaving the Dyke unfinished, and the Weald was safe for the next few thousand years. The Iron Age works are naturally puny compared with those of the Devil (or the 'Poor Man', as he used to be called locally), but the rampart and ditch are still substantial in the south-west corner of the camp.

There has been a house on the site of **Newtimber Place**, just north of Poynings, since Saxon times, and at the back the building rises sheer from the moat on medieval foundations. The bulk of the house was built in 1681; it has an unusual classical front, made of squared flints with redbrick surrounds to the windows. Its main feature is the entrance hall, painted with eighteenth-century murals in the Etruscan style, with tapestry and furniture to match, showing improbable goddesses and charioteers in terracotta colours. The murals were derived from the plates in *Greek and Roman Antiquities*, written for Sir William Hamilton and published at Naples, where he was British ambassador, in the 1760s. Behind the stables is an octagonal dovecote, with hundreds of brick-built nests perfectly preserved, but no longer any doves to fill them.

Newtimber belongs to descendants of the Buxton family, whose most famous member, Earl Buxton (1835–1934), was a leading Liberal politician and was later Governor-General of South Africa. His memorial tablet is in the church down the road, a thirteenth-century building with an absurd little tower of 1839 tacked on the end. It is filled with Buxton memorials. A gentle Epstein-like stone figure of a mother and child commemorates the Earl's daughter, who died in childbirth; a gilded St George is in memory of her brother, killed in the First World War; a St Francis window recalls a naturalist brother who died in 1911. More recent (1955) is a tablet to the Earl's wife, the maker of Newtimber's beautiful garden. **Newtimber Hill** belongs to the National Trust, as does Devil's Dyke.

Pyecombe has one of the smallest of all the downland churches. In the last century the village was renowned for its shepherd's crooks, known as 'Pyecombe hooks'. They were 'indispensable to every rightly-equipped shepherd', says Augustus Hare.

From the outside, **Clayton** church, with its patched-up walls and shingled bellcote, looks nothing out of the ordinary. But inside it is exceptional, both for its pre-Conquest chancel arch, and for its medieval wall paintings. Though their date is disputed, at some time, possibly as early as 1080, the Saxon church was plastered and painted with an overall design centred on the Christ in Judgment above the chancel arch. On the walls of the nave are processions of kings, clerics and laymen; and on the north wall can be seen the arcades of the New Jerusalem. Faded and mutilated though they are, the paintings link this remote church with the great world of hieratic religious art that stretches across Europe to the mosaics of Ravenna and Santa Sophia. In recent years the paintings have had to contend with being spattered by bat droppings, as Clayton church seems to be a magnet for all the bats of the area. So far all attempts to keep them out have proved useless.

From Byzantine-inspired sublimity you can step across the main road to the ridiculousness of the brick baronial entrance to the Clayton tunnel on the Brighton line. Between the corner towers is a small house, right over the mouth of the tunnel and rocked continually by the roar of trains passing underneath. The commuting townships of Hassocks and Burgess Hill were outlying farms of Clayton before the railway was built. On the downs above Clayton, and reached down a side road, are two windmills that can be seen for miles around, called appropriately Jack and Jill. Jill is a post mill, complete with sails, built in 1821 and hauled here by oxen across the downs from Brighton about 1850. Jack has no sails, but is just the black painted tower of a smock mill.

Ditchling Beacon is a landmark as famous as the Devil's Dyke, and a good deal higher (813 as opposed to 711 feet). However, it has no legends attached, and no restaurant for those who like refreshments to go with their views.

Plumpton is the last village in this direction before the main road to Lewes (A275). It is now known mainly for its racecourse, which lies a couple of miles north of the old village, beside the railway. Leonard Mascall, a Tudor landowner with a botanical turn of mind, lived at Plumpton Place. He was a great cultivator of apples – a tradition carried on at the Plumpton agricultural college next door. You get to the church through an orchard; like Clayton, it has frescoes of about 1100, though not nearly so well preserved.

Ditchling, at the foot of the Beacon, is the largest of these villages. In Saxon times 'Diccelingas' was the administrative centre of a vast Wealden royal estate, and there is still a good deal of pre-Conquest work in the nave of the church. This stands above the road near the village crossroads, and is a chunky building with central tower and pyramid spire. Inside there are four fine Early English arches below the tower, with foliated capitals on the arch into the chancel; and on either side of the elegant east window are the carved heads of a king and queen, possibly Henry III and Queen Eleanor. Across the road from the church is Wing's Place, a Tudor house with some intricate timbering and a fine arched brick doorway. There are plenty of smaller half-timbered houses, rubbing shoulders with Georgian symmetry in the High Street.

The nineteenth-century church school, beside the village pond, is now a museum of bygone Ditchling life, ranging from relics of a triple murderer whose body hung for years from a gibbet on Ditchling Common, to a pottery wyvern, emblem of Alfred the Great who owned the manor of Diccelingas. In the last century splinters from the gibbet, known as 'Jacob's Post' after its occupant, Jacob Harris, were carried around by the locals as a charm against toothache.

Since the turn of the century Ditchling has been a popular place for artists to live. A small art gallery keeps up the tradition by holding shows of paintings by local artists. Sir Frank Brangwyn lived there, as did Eric Gill, the sculptor and designer of lettering; and it may be due to Gill's influence that the modern tombstones in the churchyard have unusually stylish inscriptions. A secular commemoration that other places might well follow is a plaque to a well-loved local doctor on a wall in South Street.

Burgess Hill, a couple of miles north of Ditchling, is a complete contrast – an overgrown Victorian village, owing its existence to the railway. In spite of its lack of aesthetic appeal, it has carried out an ambitious central redevelopment scheme, which puts many larger but less enterprising places to shame.

Hurstpierpoint, south-west of Burgess Hill, is an unpretentious place, with a good deal of Georgian building in the High Street. The tall church, built in the 1840s by Sir Charles Barry, looms over the surrounding houses. Inside there is some good pseudo-medieval arcading, and two genuinely medieval much-battered effigies of knights, reputedly members of the Norman de Pierpoint family. A mile north an immense grey flint building dwarfs the surrounding countryside – the chapel of Hurstpierpoint public school, founded, like the schools at Lancing and Ardingly, by the Rev. Nathaniel Woodard. Murray's *Handbook* of 1893 gives the annual fees at Hurstpierpoint as 'from 25 guineas'.

The de Pierpoints' ancestral home was at **Danny**, below the smooth grass dome of Wolstonbury Hill. About 1450 the de Pierpoints had to flee for their lives from Danny, after Simon de Pierpoint deliberately burned a number of his serfs to death, and his other retainers set fire to the house in retaliation. The site stood empty until George Goring built the present splendid Elizabethan house between about 1580 and 1595. The main front is of the classic E-shape, with tall mullioned windows lighting a great hall. Goring was a fervent Royalist and forfeited Danny at the end of the Civil War. At the beginning of the eighteenth century it passed to the Campion family, who added the symmetrical Queen Anne south façade and remodelled the interior; they put in a sweeping staircase (the original Tudor staircase is at the back), and altered the great hall by lowering the ceiling and building pilastered screens at either end. The house has now been turned into flats.

Danny's moment of historical glory came at the end of the First World War, when it was rented to Lloyd George, the Prime Minister. The terms for the armistice with Germany were drawn up in the great hall; a plaque on the wall near the fireplace gives the names of the War Cabinet, including Churchill. Lloyd George used to take his state papers up **Wolstonbury Hill** when he wanted to work in peace. No doubt he climbed the steps up the hill, which were cut, says an old parish guidebook, 'by the paupers when the workhouse was kept in the village. They were marched there under the charge of the parish beadle'. One can imagine this sad little procession of the elderly, the shiftless or the simple-minded, hacking at the chalk and flints under the self-righteous eye of local officialdom.

A couple of miles to the north, beside the A23, are the grandstand and fences of the **Hickstead** show-jumping course.

Henfield, four miles west of Hurstpierpoint, has more back alleys and is easier to get lost in than any other township I have come across. The name has nothing to do with the inhabitants' fondness for chickens: it comes from the Saxon 'Hamfelde', meaning 'settlement on the open land'. The church, which stands well away from the bustle of the High Street, dates back to a charter of AD 770. It was much restored in 1870, but still has its massive Perpendicular tower and thirteenth-century arcading. In the Parham Chantry is a wall tablet to Henry Bysshop, whose portrait is at Parham (see above). A mile south of the village, the **Woods Mill Countryside Centre** is the headquarters of the Sussex Wildlife Trust, housed in a restored eighteenth-century watermill. It is the starting-point for a nature trail through woodland and wetland.

Though **Ashurst** is only a couple of miles away across the Adur from Henfield, it is a good five miles by road, through Partridge Green. But it is worth the detour, as the small flint church, set among trees miles from anywhere, is one of the hidden gems of this area. The base of the tower seems to take up about half of the building, and the interior is a single space, with a roof that covers both nave and aisle. The church was built about 1200 by the Knights Templars; during the restoration of 1877 the tower was rebuilt, leaving the spire resting in mid-air on the beams – a tribute to the solidity of Sussex oak. In a case above the north door is a vamping horn, dated 1770; this is not a musical instrument but was used as a megaphone to keep the congregation more or less in tune (there is another at Charing in Kent).

From **Ashington**, a bungaloid sprawl along the Worthing road, a lane leads to **Warminghurst**, just a remote church and a handful of houses. The village's most famous inhabitant was William Penn, who lived at Warminghurst Place and drafted the first constitution of Pennsylvania there. The hostility the Quakers had to meet is shown by an order for Penn's arrest made in January 1685, in which he was accused of being 'a factious and seditious person', given to holding 'unlawful Assemblyes and Conventicles' (see also Blue Idol, p. 311). The church is a modest building dating from about 1220, with a neat little tilehung belfry, and a wooden chancel arch painted with a large royal arms of Queen Anne. The seating looks eighteenth-century: high pews, the front ones with drawers for the squire's prayer-books; and a clerk's chair below the pulpit. There is a good Tudor brass to Edward Shelley, an ancestor of the poet, his wife, and a clutch of seven sons and three daughters.

Thakeham, only half a mile away across a field, though four miles by road, lies down a leafy lane, in an area given over to enormous glasshouses. It has plenty of pretty houses, and a big Early English church on a mound. The Perpendicular tower has a curious 'henhouse' roof on top instead of the usual pyramid cap.

At the heart of the network of lanes towards Pulborough is **West Chiltington**, a trim village built round a crossroads. The church is a rugged place, rough-rendered on the outside. Inside there is a

Norman arcade; with crudely carved capitals, and some faded medieval wall painting. The old stocks are kept by the churchyard gate.

21

Lewes and Brighton

HEMMED IN BY the South Downs and bathed in a brilliant light that springs from some interaction between the bare green hills and the nearby sea, **Lewes** has the ability to make even the most cantankerous visitor feel cheerful. When Cobbett rode over from Uckfield in the winter of 1822 for a stormy meeting at Lewes County Hall, his ill-temper was soon charmed away. 'The town itself,' he wrote, 'is a model of solidity and neatness. The buildings all substantial to the very outskirts; the pavements good and complete; the shops nice and clean; the people well-dressed; and, though last not least, the girls remarkably pretty.'

Lewes was the natural place for a Norman stronghold, strategically placed near the mouth of the Ouse, between two spurs of the downs. The **Castle** is the best place for a first acquaintance with the town, as everything can be seen at a glance from the roof of the keep. Southwards the Ouse meanders towards Newhaven, with a glimpse of the sea in the gap between the downs. Due east are the steep slopes of Malling Hill, gouged with chalk pits; half way up stands the stone obelisk to the Lewes martyrs, a total of seventeen Protestants burnt between 1555 and 1557. West is a roofscape, rising up the hill to the square tower of the prison; and to the north is Offham Hill, where in 1264 Simon de Montfort defeated King Henry III.

Lewes was an important place in Saxon times. At the Conquest William gave it to his son-in-law, William de Warenne, who was married to William's daughter Gundrada (though this parentage is now doubted). De Warenne's castle is unique in being built on two artificial mounds or mottes – the mound on which the keep stands, and the hillock called Brack Mount a hundred yards to the east across the bowling green. Much of the surviving walling dates from his time; though the magnificent barbican, or outer gatehouse, was built in the early fourteenth century. The castle was never besieged but succumbed to natural causes and a desire for building material. Most of the buildings were pulled down in 1620, when the stone was sold at fourpence a load. An eighteenth-century owner turned the keep into a summerhouse (hence the Gothic windows); and it is now owned and run by the Sussex Archaeological Society, as are the town's two museums.

The **Museum of Sussex Archaeology**, adjoining the castle, is a large town house which underwent continual alteration and improvement from the Middle Ages to the eighteenth century. It has rooms devoted to the Stone and Bronze Ages, the Romans and the Anglo-Saxons; and there is some superb pre-Christian Saxon jewellery from Alfriston, including two large brooches, gilded and square-headed, and a good collection of Saxon and Roman coins.

The main street of Lewes runs up from the river, beginning as a gentle slope and rising more steeply to the western edge of the town. The buildings are mainly Georgian, dignified brick, plain or painted, flat or bow-fronted, with the occasional half-timbered survival, like the Bull House, dated 1450. Tom Paine, the Radical and future author of *The Rights of Man*, lived at the Bull House as exciseman and tobacconist from 1768 to 1774. In the evenings he used to go down the road to the White Hart (a tall Georgian coaching inn, little altered) and debate on the burning republican topics of the day; according to E. V. Lucas he used to be a regular recipient of a copy of Homer, known as the 'Headstrong Book', sent round the next morning to the most obstinate debater.

South of the High Street run the steep little alleys which are among the delights of Lewes, some of them now closed to traffic: Keere Street, down which the Prince Regent is reputed to have driven a coach and four at full gallop, though as the gradient is about one in three I find it hard to see how he could have managed it; St Martin's Lane; and Church Twitten, which winds between high flint walls. (A twitten, according to the *Dictionary of the Sussex Dialect*, is 'a narrow path between two walls or hedges'.)

You can pick almost any of the buildings in the High Street and find something interesting about it. Thus on the wall of Castle Place is a plaque commemorating Dr Gideon A. Mantell, a nineteenth-century doctor and palaeontologist who discovered the first skeleton of an iguanodon in Tilgate Forest; below the redbrick Victorian mass of the town hall are the cellars in which the Lewes martyrs were imprisoned before being burnt in the market place (see also Warbleton, p. 233); while the Georgian frontage of Shelleys Hotel hides an Elizabethan inn called the Vine. When the Shelleys owned the house Dr Johnson visited them and left his mark on their family history by lifting one of the little daughters into a cherry tree to get away from her chatter, walking away and forgetting all about her. She was not rescued for several hours.

Lewes is a town of many churches, and the High Street has two of them. At the top, opposite Shelleys, is **St Anne's**, the oldest church in Lewes. It stood well outside the medieval town, which ended beyond the town wall in Westgate, and was originally known as 'St Mary Westoute'. It is a massively solid Norman building, with a tower built about 1150 and a late twelfth-century aisle, divided from the nave by stumpy columns. On the south side of the chancel a low window divided by a pillar looks into an anchoress's cell, where a thirteenth-century recluse lived and died in pious discomfort. Directly behind St Anne's are the large glass-panelled blocks of the East Sussex County Council's administrative buildings. Over the main entrance is a long glass-fibre abstract sculpture, domesticated by house martins nesting in the interstices. The buildings have been sited tactfully below the brow of the hill; but they block the view of the downs from the churchyard, and unduly dominate the townscape from the Lewes bypass.

The other High Street church is **St Michael's**, below the castle, a landmark with its twisting needle spire and round tower (the only other towers like it are at nearby Southease and Piddinghoe, see below). The tower is thirteenth-century; the church much-altered fourteenth. The interior is on the gloomy side, except for the monument on the north wall, which shows Sir Nicholas Pelham, his wife and children, brilliantly picked out in black, crimson and gold. In 1545 Pelham defeated a French expeditionary force which had sailed on to Seaford (then the harbour at the mouth of the Ouse) after attacking Brighthelmstone.

With the parish church, **St John's**, in Southover High Street, we are back with William de Warenne and Gundrada. While Lewes castle expressed the strength of William's arm, the priory he founded at Southover expressed his piety, or possibly his conscience for the Saxons massacred at Hastings. At any rate, about 1077 he and Gundrada pulled down the little wooden Saxon church at Southover, built a stone church there and handed it over with a large tract of land to monks from the abbey of Cluny, in Burgundy. This grew into the great Cluniac Priory of St Pancras, whose ruins can still be seen, surrounded by tennis courts and football fields, in the meadows behind

Not built for modern traffic: Keere Street, in the centre of Lewes.

Southover High Street. Though it had a church bigger than Chichester Cathedral and monastic buildings to scale, it was utterly destroyed at the Dissolution in 1537.

It was left to the railway age to bring the remains of William and Gundrada to light. In 1845 workmen on the Lewes–Brighton railway, which cut right across the priory, unearthed two lead coffins which had been buried near the high altar of the priory church, inscribed with the names William and Gundrada. The carved black marble slab from Gundrada's tomb, which had been taken to Isfield church at the Dissolution, was brought back to Lewes, and coffins, skeletons and slab now lie reunited in a side chapel of St John's church. The church itself once formed the *hospitium* or guesthouse at the gates of the priory; it was converted into the parish church when a bigger *hospitium* was built in the late thirteenth century. Externally it is notable for a solid-looking brick tower, built in the early eighteenth century to replace one that had fallen down. The splendid nineteenth-century weathervane on top is in the form of a salmon-trout, 'reminding us', says the church guide regretfully, 'that the Ouse was once a salmon river'.

By the priory ruins (reached most easily through a lane under the railway west of the church) is a rugged bronze memorial, by the sculptor Enzo Plazzotta, commemorating the 700th anniversary of the Battle of Lewes in 1264 – a helmet-like structure with a frieze illustrating the events of the battle round the top. It is put to good use by the local children, who run round it, climb up it, and shout through it.

Nearly opposite the church is **Anne of Cleves House**, a timber-framed house built about 1500, with the massive beams hidden externally by tilehanging. It is so called not because Henry VIII's 'Flanders Mare' actually lived there, but because she received the property of Lewes Priory as part-payment for granting Henry a divorce. It is now the local history museum of the Sussex Archaeological Society. Of unique interest is the collection of ironwork in one of the galleries, with its series of firebacks from the crudest sixteenth-century efforts to the ornate productions of the later ironmasters, like Richard Lenard of Brede, who portrays himself grasping a hammer and surrounded by the tools and products of his craft.

On the walls are a couple of pictures highly evocative of the town's past. One shows the 'Lewes avalanche' of December 1836, when snow hurtled down from the hills on to the suburb of Cliffe, across the river, shattering and burying several cottages. The other shows the Lewes 'bonfire boys' parading through the streets in 1853, trundling barrels of blazing tar, jumping over fire-crackers, and waving banners with anti-Papist and anti-Russian slogans (the Crimean War was only months away). Lewes is still renowned for its November 5th celebrations, though blazing barrels no longer roll through the streets, and the onlookers no longer wear spectacles of wire netting to protect themselves from the giant rockets or 'rousers', which E. V. Lucas described around 1900.

Cliffe, where the avalanche fell, is cut off from Lewes proper by the Ouse. The river is a muddy yellow, flowing by timber yards, with warehouses rising sheer from the water. In Cliffe High Street is John Harvey's brewery, founded in 1790, the last independent brewery left in East Sussex. Lewes has always been famous for its beer; and Harvey's, with its gleaming vats, rows of barrels and heady vapours, typifies not only brewing but the whole Lewes temper of individuality. The Brighton-bound traffic is now carried in a tunnel burrowed through the chalk.

Immediately north of the town, the A275 runs below the steep escarpment of **Offham Hill**, where the Battle of Lewes was fought. On the morning of 13 May, 1264, the armies of Henry III and Simon de Montfort met on the windswept summit of the downs; the previous night de Montfort had kept vigil in Fletching church, while the king and his generals had caroused in the castle and priory – one reason given by the moralists for the king's defeat. De Montfort's troops were drawn up in three divisions on three spurs of Mount Harry, facing towards Lewes; the corresponding royal divisions were led by Henry III, his son Prince Edward (later Edward I), and his brother the King of the Romans. Shouting his challenge *'Simon, je vous defye'*, Henry led his troops up the slope to the attack.

The king's downfall was really caused by Prince Edward's impetuosity. He broke the barons' left flank and chased their troops for miles over the downs, whereupon de Montfort brought up his reserves and routed the remaining two royalist divisions. King Henry fled back to the priory. The King of the Romans took refuge in a mill, and was finally captured in the evening to cries of 'Come out, you bad miller!' – which seems a remarkably polite command under the circumstances. Prince Edward returned from his pursuit to find the battle lost, and fled to the castle. Many of the king's troops tried to escape across the Ouse to Pevensey, struggling over the bridge, or picking their own way through the undrained marshland and the river, where many of them drowned. For years afterwards the bodies of knights were found in the mud, still seated on their horses with drawn swords in their hands, or so legend claims.

The Victorian church at **Offham** was built in 1859 after the old church, at Hamsey across the fields, had become almost deserted because of its inaccessibility. So **Hamsey Old Church** was spared any touch of the restorer's hand, but has been maintained just enough to prevent it from actually falling down. You get to it from Offham, across a cut which isolates it on a bend in the Ouse, through a farmyard and over a derelict railway; and there it is, the typical church of a thousand eighteenth-century engravings, with gravestones cock-eyed in the churchyard, yews growing close against the sturdy stone tower, and the sweep of the downs behind. Inside, it gives a feeling of even greater remoteness in time. Birds flutter among the worm-eaten beams; in the Norman nave ancient pews are pushed back against the wall; and the chancel is almost bare, except for an unexpected and beautifully carved canopied tomb on the north side of the altar.

Barcombe, two miles north of Offham, is a loose group of hamlets rather than a village, with a nucleus at Barcombe Cross. The unpretentious church is almost as remote as the one at Hamsey, in a pretty setting of farm buildings and large pond.

Along the western bank of the Ouse the former main road from Lewes to Newhaven runs by a string of little villages, bypassing all of them, as a French main road would do. First comes **Kingston**, with its village street petering out into a steep downland track; farm gates open directly into the street, and there is a small flint church and an old pub. Next is **Iford**, whose Norman church is unusual in having a central tower, where the chancel was, and a second chancel beyond; thus there are two chancel arches, both beautifully carved.

Rodmell is a harmony of flint houses and walls, with a Norman church reached through the school playground. The church's square tower is well seen from the garden of **Monk's House** (National Trust), where Virginia Woolf had her country retreat from the intellectual hothouse of Bloomsbury (see also Charleston, p. 277). With her husband, Leonard, she lived here from 1919 until 1941, when she committed suicide by drowning herself in the Ouse, wading into the water with her pockets weighted down by stones. In his autobiography, Leonard Woolf tells us that her body was not found for three weeks, and then only by children playing beside the river. It seems incredible that the discovery took so long – after all, the Ouse is not a big river, and there must surely have been a hue and cry after the disappearance of one of the most famous writers of her day.

Monk's House is an up-and-down sort of house, built in the early eighteenth century; it was without water, gas or electricity when the Woolfs bought it for £700, and still does not look particularly comfortable eighty years later. Down the years they filled it with books, paintings, and furniture similar to that at Charleston, decorated by Vanessa Bell and Duncan Grant. The garden, unfussy and simply laid out, gives wide-spreading views of the downs across the river. Virginia's ashes, and those of Leonard, who lived on until 1969, were scattered in the garden they had made together.

Two miles off the road, in the heart of the downs, is **Telscombe**, buried away in a hollow like an Exmoor village – just a few houses up and down the hollow, and a Norman flint church. If you go right to the top of the lane, where it turns into a number of branching tracks, you can look over the crest of the downs to the bungalow growth of Peacehaven and Saltdean nearby; but Telscombe was bequeathed to Brighton Corporation and is now run by them, so is reasonably safe from being engulfed. It used to be a centre for training racehorses.

Finally there are two villages with round-towered churches. **Southease** is just a hamlet, down a hill with a small green beyond the church. There was a church here in Saxon times, mentioned in a charter of 966; the present building is early twelfth-century. When the Normans came, Southease was a flourishing village of farmers and fishermen, being assessed in Domesday Book, apart from farm produce, for 38,500 herrings and £4 for porpoises. At **Piddinghoe** there is an unmistakable smell of the sea in the air. Boats of all shapes and sizes are drawn up on the mudflats, and the Royal Oak is full of sea angling tackle. The church, drastically restored in the last century, stands on a bluff above the Ouse; the round tower has an awkward octagonal cap, unlike Southease and St Michael's, Lewes, which have conical ones. The theory that all three towers were built at the same time as watchtowers tends to be dismissed nowadays; nevertheless they would have formed a useful series of beacon towers to give warning of raiders off the Ouse.

Augustus Hare, visiting **Newhaven** in the 1890s, found it 'an ugly, dirty, little town and smoky little port, with dangerous drinking water, and a long pier at the mouth of the Ouse, whence steamers cross to Dieppe in four and a half hours'. (They were still taking four

341

hours when the service was suspended in 1999; though the journey time has been cut by half since catamarans took over.) Newhaven was originally called Meeching; but a great storm in 1579 diverted the mouth of the Ouse from its former outlet near Seaford, and a 'new haven' grew up at the new river mouth. On the bluff above the harbour mouth, the massive defensive works of **Newhaven Fort** have been restored for use as a military museum. The brick-built fort was constructed during the 1860s, during one of the nineteenth century's periodic French invasion scares; it consists of a ring of casemates (vaulted gun emplacements) and barracks round a large inner parade ground. During the Second World War it was equipped with modern guns, and was bombed several times by the Germans.

Newhaven's vestigial old town has a steep High Street running up to the parish church perched on its hill. The church is really in two parts: Norman sanctuary and apse; and Victorian west end, with timber supports painted red and gold. From the churchyard you can look inland to Lewes Castle, or across the Ouse to the dreary acres of Newhaven's eastward expansion. The white-painted Bridge Hotel, at the foot of the hill, is dated 1623. King Louis-Philippe, deposed in the Revolution of 1848, stayed in the hotel after fleeing across the Channel, and booked in with Queen Marie Amélie as 'Mr and Mrs Smith'. He died two years later, at Claremont in Surrey.

West of Newhaven you are up and over a hill and into **Peacehaven**, that vast expanse of bungalows and small houses laid out on the grid pattern after the First World War. It was the brainchild of a wealthy businessman, Charles Neville, who bought 650 clifftop acres for a town to be called Anzac-on-Sea, in honour of the Australian and New Zealand troops who fought in the trenches; in 1918, with the ending of the First World War, it was renamed Peacehaven. In recent years it has been held up to scorn, yet it is no worse than the outlying suburbs of Brighton; what it lacks is any connection with the downs behind or the sea in front. On the clifftop a memorial to George V marks the Greenwich Meridian, which runs through Peacehaven, and lists the distances to all the outposts of Empire.

If the welcoming signs are to be believed, Brighton begins at **Saltdean**, similar to Peacehaven in its wanton engulfing of downland. Saltdean has one remarkable feature, an Art Deco lido of 1935, complete with huge open-air pool, tea terrace and sun deck. But there is still **Rottingdean** to be seen before Brighton proper begins. Built in the only gap in the cliffs between Newhaven and

Brighton, Rottingdean was naturally enough a smugglers' village. The old High Street runs inland from the shore – a street of pebble-walled houses, leading to a pretty green and village pond, with larger Georgian houses clustered round about. The artist Burne-Jones lived in a rambling house by the green for the last twenty years of his life (he died in 1898); while Kipling spent the years from 1897 to 1902 at The Elms, across the road, before moving to Bateman's inland. Lady Burne-Jones was Kipling's aunt; she virtually ran Rottingdean, and caused an uproar in 1900 by hanging an anti-Boer War banner from her window after the relief of Mafeking. At Rottingdean Kipling wrote *Kim*, the *Stalky* stories, the *Recessional* and the poem *Sussex*. **The Grange**, formerly owned by the artist Sir William Nicholson, is now a museum, with a Kipling room of handwritten letters and other relics, a room of Sussex crafts, and a collection of toys.

The **Parish Church** nearby is a Saxon foundation, with pre-Conquest work surviving in the nave and centrally placed tower. The chancel was added about 1080, and the south aisle was enlarged and restored in Victorian times. During the French raids of 1377 the villagers took refuge in the belfry. The French set fire to the church and burnt them alive; the pink and grey colour of the stone is said to be due to the enormous heat. In the chancel and tower are seven windows designed by Burne-Jones and made by William Morris. The three-light east window, given in celebration of the marriage of Burne-Jones's daughter in the church, shows three angels and 'war in heaven' – not the happiest augury for a marriage. West of Rottingdean the vast brown frontage of **Roedean** girls' school guards its pupils behind central turrets and a gatehouse.

This is much the best side from which to approach **Brighton**, as you arrive right in the middle of it all, without the miles of housing that stretch along the roads to London and Lewes. From the hill that leads down to the front you can see the whole of Brighton foreshortened into the distance: the Marina below you, the silver elegance of the Palace Pier picking its way out to sea, the long vista of hotels and houses, the skyscrapers of modern Brighton, and high on the downs the black hulk of the racecourse grandstand. The whole scene is brilliantly lit by the sun dancing on the sea.

Brighton is the ultimate touchstone by which all other seaside resorts have to be judged. What it has pre-eminently is a sense of style, the legacy of that spendthrift, dissolute, gouty, musical, changeable, loved and hated prince, who came to the fishing village of Brighthelmstone, liked what he saw, and built his fantasy palace there, away from the stuffiness of London and the whims of his mad old father.

The Prince Regent paid his first visit in 1783, but Brighton had been becoming known for thirty years previously. In 1750 Dr Richard Russell, a Lewes general practitioner, brought out a Latin treatise on the merits of sea water – for drinking, as well as for swimming in; and in 1752 the first English translation appeared. Three years later 'Brighthelmstone water' was being bottled and sold in London. Dr Russell prospered, bought property in Brighton, and gathered the nucleus of fashionable hypochondriacs needed to get a new resort off the ground. A portrait in the Brighton history galleries shows a colourless old man, in grey coat and grey wig, sunken-cheeked and shrewd-eyed. He died in 1759 and was buried at South Malling, a suburb of Lewes. On the other staircase in the same building is Sir Thomas Lawrence's coronation portrait of the Prince Regent, transmuted into George IV in 1821. Flamboyantly robed and glittering with decorations, he stands for the panache of Brighton, summed up by that extraordinary collection of buildings that has the Royal Pavilion as its centrepiece.

The **Royal Pavilion**, with its onion domes and minarets, its bizarre Oriental interiors and its general air of sumptuous extravagance, passed through all the shades of public and private disapproval before its present acceptance as one of the glories of British architecture. To William Cobbett it was a box covered in turnips and 'a considerable number of bulbs of the crown-imperial, the narcissus, the hyacinth, the tulip, the crocus, and others'; to Sydney Smith, the nineteenth-century wit, it looked as though the dome of St Paul's had come down to Brighton and pupped; and Queen Victoria (whose statue stands at the south end of Victoria Gardens) was not amused by it. It was only saved from demolition by the inhabitants of the town themselves, who in 1850 got up a petition and raised the money to buy it from the Crown, spending the then-vast sum of £53,000 for what was virtually an empty shell. Over a century of restoration has followed, and the original contents, removed by Queen Victoria, have been handed back by the present Queen. The Pavilion is once again the hub of Brighton.

It began life as a simple timber-framed farmhouse, and in its present form is the culmination of three decades of building and alteration. The first Pavilion, built by Henry Holland and completed in 1787, was a classical design, with a central rotunda and wings on

Oriental extravaganza: the Prince Regent's Brighton Pavilion.

either side, which can still be traced under the exotic trappings of the later building. In the following years the Prince was bitten by the current mania for the mysterious East. From about 1802, beginning with the inside of the building, architects succeeded each other first with chinoiserie and then with Indian-based designs, until John Nash, architect of Regent's Park and Carlton House Terrace, produced between 1815 and 1822 the strange bird of paradise we see today.

The Pavilion is permanently open to the public, and is used for Brighton celebrations of all sorts. The entrance hall leads into a long corridor, with an exquisite wall decoration of blue birds and flowers on a pink ground. At the corridor's south end is the Banqueting Room, a riot of Chinese dragons and huge chandeliers, which pass beyond mere vulgarity into some special dimension of display. Some years ago I went to a 'Regency breakfast' in this room, held as part of the annual Brighton Festival. Game pie and port, followed by kedgeree, at nine o'clock in the morning made a fairly indigestible substitute for bacon and eggs; but it all settled into place to the accompaniment of bawdy catches sung in the splendid Music Room – the kind of uninhibited social singing that George and his less reputable friends delighted in. Beyond the Banqueting Room is the kitchen, all gleaming copper pans and turning spits, with an iron hot-plate right along one end.

In back of the corridor, between the Banqueting and Music Rooms, are two galleries separated by the round Saloon; this is the classical part of the Pavilion, with tall windows opening on to the lawns. These rooms are sober enough in comparison with the rest, but full of quiet beauty, like the Saloon's domed ceiling painted as a sky lightly covered in cloud. West of the Music Room, and still on the ground floor, are the King's Apartments – anteroom, library and bedroom, the bed set in a deep recess, with a hidden door to a private spiral staircase which led to a bedroom above.

On display are some of the savage cartoons attacking George for his greed or his lechery, and above all for his unpopular marriage to Mrs Fitzherbert, whom he secretly married in 1785, when he was twenty-three. The cartoonists, for all their vitriolic portrayals, seem to have amused rather than annoyed him, as he used to keep a collection to show to visitors. It was left to a twentieth-century artist, Rex Whistler, to express that sense of slightly malicious amusement with which we contemplate the foibles of the Prince Regent. His allegorical painting *HRH the Prince Regent Awakening the Spirit of*

346

Brighton shows the swag-bellied prince, naked except for the Garter above his knee and the star of the order balanced on his backside, tiptoeing forward to unveil a drowsy-eyed and equally naked girl. This was Whistler's last work. Immediately after completing it he was killed in the D-Day landings of June 1944.

The restoration of the Pavilion suffered a devastating setback in 1975, when an arsonist set fire to the gloriously decorated Music Room. After years of repair to the carving, gilding and decorative painting, the Music Room suffered another disaster during the great storm of 16 October, 1987, when one of the minarets was dislodged by the hurricane and hurtled through the ceiling, doing untold damage to the ceiling and the sumptuous carpet, which had just been installed. Ironically enough, the minaret was knocked out of place by the roof scaffolding, put up in the course of the enormous structural renovation programme. This has now been completed, leaving the Pavilion in better shape than it has been since the days of the Prince Regent.

The same gale brought down many of the fine old trees round the Pavilion and along the Grand Parade; one fell through the roof of St Peter's Church, at the junction of the London and Lewes Roads. The afternoon after the storm I had driven to Brighton from Kent through a gale-blasted landscape, and saw the most bizarre sight of all just behind the Pavilion – two of the sturdy old red phone-boxes knocked slightly out of true by a huge tree, but supporting its weight without collapsing.

The Pavilion and the grassland of the **Old Steine** (pronounced Steen) were the centres round which all Brighton's activity revolved. The Pavilion's outbuildings have survived and been put to other uses: the stables, with their prominent glass dome on top, are now the Dome concert hall; and the vaulted riding school, known as the Corn Exchange, is a general-purpose open space for flower shows and other displays. The biggest of the exhibition rooms in the **Art Gallery** was built as an indoor tennis court. This gallery, also a museum, has some fine collections that would have appealed to the wide sympathies of the Prince Regent – old musical instruments, Greek coins, and a large group of Surrealist paintings.

While George enjoyed himself, Brighton expanded. The old Brighthelmstone was in the area bounded by North Street, West Street and East Street; thus the Pavilion lay outside the original town. Some of it still remains, notably a few of **The Lanes**, narrow alleys between the streets, now filled with antique shops.

Bartholomews, where the Town Hall stands, is named after a medieval chantry of St Bartholomew. The Town Hall is a tall white building of the 1830s, with huge double porticoes on two of the sides and a glazed central well that goes from ground to roof. It now forms an integral part of Bartholomew Square, along with the rear entrance to the Thistle Hotel, modern offices and an array of trendy boutiques.

The old **Parish Church** stands right outside the original town, a good pull up Dyke Road beyond the Victorian clock tower. Early pictures show it with open country beyond, but it has long been engulfed. Its chief treasure is a drum-shaped font of about 1170, beautifully carved with the Last Supper and scenes from the life of St Nicholas, to whom the church is dedicated. In the churchyard is a gravestone to Phoebe Hessel, who was born in 1713 and served in the infantry as a private. After a military career which included being bayoneted in the arm at Fontenoy in 1745, she retired to Brighton, where she died aged 108 in 1821.

From this small nucleus grew the squares and crescents, the colonnades and hotels. The first piece of Brighton planning was **Royal Crescent**, a discreet little row of houses half a mile east of the Old Steine, built in the late 1790s. From then on, Brighton houses were built to face the sea, instead of turning their backs on it as previously. Dwarfing all other developments on this side of the town was **Kemp Town**, laid out by Thomas Reid Kemp, one of the lords of the manor, in the 1820s. This colossal scheme, centred on **Lewes Crescent** and **Sussex Square**, is still virtually the eastern limit of Brighton. Behind the long stretch of the Marine Parade is much of Brighton's early nineteenth-century expansion, an east-west grid of streets a mile or so long.

At the same time the town was spreading along the London and Lewes roads – an expansion for which **St Peter's Church**, the parish church since 1873, was built in the 1820s. Designed by Sir Charles Barry, St Peter's stands on a green at the junction of all the main roads serving Brighton from the north. Its pinnacled tower is the first recognisably Brighton landmark as you drive into the town from this direction. Strangely, it is orientated north and south, the 'east' window pointing north. Some time ago it was renovated: Barry's work has been painted white, and the later chancel left the natural stone colour in contrast. The ceiling bosses have been picked out in brilliant colours.

Between St Peter's and the station is a run-down area of nineteenth-century Brighton, with unexpected delights here and there, like the little houses round the green of Pelham Square, or the open-air street market of Kensington Gardens, traffic-free and with shops spilling their goods on to the pavement. The side streets hereabouts are crammed with shops selling curios, antiques and exotic foods.

In Ann Street is a monumental Victorian church, **St Bartholomew's**, built in the 1870s by Father Arthur Wagner, a wealthy High Churchman who built churches all over the poorer areas of Brighton. Pevsner says of it: 'As far as East Sussex is concerned it may well be the most moving of all churches.' It is certainly the most overwhelming, built entirely of brick and with a nave roof soaring up to the fantastic height of 135 feet – over 30ft higher than the nave of Westminster Abbey. Like St Peter's it is orientated north and south, which means that the midday sun streams through the vast rose window, lightening the gloom of the tall brick arches along the nave. It was meant to have an apsidal north (altar) end, but the money ran out, and instead there is a blank brick wall, with a giant silver cross where the window should be. With its golden mosaics beside the altar, enormous baldacchino (altar canopy) and ornate silver sanctuary lamps, St Bartholomew's is as exotic in its way as the Royal Pavilion, and forms a weighty Byzantine counterpart to the Pavilion's mock-Indian frivolity.

From the station, Queens Road leads down to West Street and the front, passing modern Brighton on the way. Western Road is the main shopping centre, with the typical new-town precinct of Churchill Square, recently renovated, on its southern side. In West Street is St Paul's church (built by Arthur Wagner's father), with a prominent octagonal belfry tower; and then you are on the front again, below the blatant modernity of the Brighton Centre's jazzy roofline.

Nearby the two hotels that sum up Victorian holiday luxury stand side by side: the **Grand**, white-painted and black-balconied, built in the 1860s and by now matured into near-elegance; and the redbrick bulk of the **Metropole**, completed in 1890. In October 1984, the Grand made international headlines when an IRA bomb exploded there during the Tory party conference, killing and injuring several people, and doing an enormous amount of structural damage. By the summer of 1986 it had been completely refurbished – a recovery typical of the resilience of Brighton hoteliers. The Grand and the Metropole, like the other large hotels, are now used as much for conferences and exhibitions as for holiday visitors. The boxers, actresses and 'ladies of the Gaiety with their cavaliers' commented on by C. B. Cochran, have made way for a worthier though duller clientele.

In total contrast is the glittering **Thistle** (formerly Ramada), back towards the Palace Pier; American-inspired, it is built round a lofty atrium where trees and shrubs can flourish, sheltered from the buffeting seafront winds outside. Near by is the **Old Ship**, doyen of all the Brighton hotels. Originally a fishermen's inn, it was bought in 1671 by Captain Nicholas Tettersell, who had saved the life of Charles II twenty years before. In pre-railway days it was the town's main hotel. The violinist Paganini gave a recital there in 1831; and Thackeray stayed there a few years later while writing *Vanity Fair*, making it the setting for George and Amelia Osborne's honeymoon, and naming the licentious Lord Steyne after Brighton's most famous street.

For most people Brighton remains the front, and the strip of shingle that leads down to the sea. This was so in George's day, when Martha Gunn and Old Smoaker ruled over the bathing machines; and it is still true today, when holiday-makers are so tight-jammed that you can hardly get to the sea between them. The flourishing **Palace Pier** has all the usual attractions, from a ghost train to candyfloss kiosks; though the father of all piers, the splendid Chain Pier which stood a little east of the Palace Pier and was built in 1823, was destroyed by a storm in 1896. Built originally for the utilitarian purpose of landing passengers at Brighton without getting their feet wet, and looking like a suspension bridge that came to an end abruptly in the middle of the sea, the Chain Pier became a fashionable place for a stroll, and was used for band concerts and firework displays. In 1843 Queen Victoria landed there after crossing from France in the royal yacht; a cheerful painting in the Royal Pavilion shows the yacht surrounded by an army of small boats and smothered in flags and bunting.

Another nineteenth-century enterprise still survives at this end of the front – **Volk's Electric Railway**, whose carriages, initialled 'VR' with cunningly implied royal patronage, trundle backwards and forwards beside Madeira Drive. Magnus Volk was a great pioneer in the use of electricity, and his railway, opened in 1883, was the first electric railway in Britain. In 1896 he built an extension below the cliffs to Rottingdean. As the track was covered at high tide, he devised an extraordinary carriage on stilts, known as the 'Daddy-Longlegs', which could hold 150 people. This contraption wobbled along the coast until the turn of the century, when the Rottingdean line was abandoned.

Madeira Drive itself has a fine piece of Victorian elegance in the cast-iron arcade, painted blue and cream, which forms the backdrop for the end of the London to Brighton veteran car run. At the Drive's western end, opposite the roundabout where the Old Steine joins the front, is the most splendid cast-iron construction of all – the cathedral-like arcades of the **Brighton Sea Life Centre**, where fish of every shape, colour and size goggle at you with a solemnity fitting to the place. The aquarium was opened in 1872, and from then on no visit, royal or otherwise, was considered complete without 'a tour of the tanks'. Its marvellous cast-iron columns, decorated with fish motifs, have been painted up, and you can walk through an underwater tunnel surrounded by sharks and other large aquatic creatures.

At the eastern end of Madeira Drive, Brighton's huge **Marina** is the largest man-made harbour in Europe. Though not quite Cannes or St Tropez, its 2,000-odd berths are crammed with every sort of craft from floating gin-palaces to workaday sailing dinghies. Between the main moorings and the chalk cliffs a complete village has been built beside the inner harbour, where water fanatics can sit in their armchairs and look out of their windows at their boats moored alongside.

Along the front towards Hove is the **West Pier**, a once-elegant and popular structure now unusable after years of dereliction. It was so badly damaged in the 1987 hurricane that its landward end had to be demolished; but at the time of writing (1999) lottery money has been promised to save it, so there is once again hope for it. **Hove** itself begins with tremendous panache at the bow fronts and massive pilasters of **Brunswick Square**, built in the 1820s. Though it seems incredible nowadays, when Hove is a byword for discreet respectability, it was once a smuggling village. But any reminders of the past have long ago vanished under the relentless grid pattern of housing, with Grand Avenue as the main windswept thoroughfare up from the front. At the seaward end a green bronze statue of Victoria, enthroned above panels symbolising Empire, Education, Science and Art, and Commerce, turns her back on the feeble modern blocks of flats and gazes out to sea.

Hove church has been completely remodelled externally, but still has Norman columns inside. Sir George Everest, the Surveyor-General of India after whom Mount Everest was named, is buried in the graveyard. Brooker Hall, the home of **Hove Museum and Art Gallery** in New Church Road, has a faint echo of the Royal Pavilion's orientalism standing in the forecourt. This is the Jaipur Gateway, made of ornately carved teak and crowned with a dome, which was built for the Colonial Exhibition of 1886. Between Brunswick Square and Grand Avenue, the plan of Brighton's Kemp Town is echoed in the hour-glass-shaped layout of **Palmeira Square** and **Adelaide Crescent**, with a landscaped garden between tall houses that look as though they have strayed from South Kensington. Hove makes its own contribution to marine gaiety in the long row of bathing chalets along the pedestrian esplanade, painted blue-green, with the doors a brilliant spectrum of different colours.

On the high ground inland, Hove's monumental Victorian water-pumping station, complete with 100 foot brick chimney-stack and ponderous beam-engine, is preserved as the **British Engineerium**. On Sundays in summer the great engine is once more 'in steam', hissing and thudding as it did when it pumped Brighton and Hove's fresh water from the chalk subsoil 150 feet below. A mile to the west, standing high above Portslade beside the new dual-carriageway A27, the **Foredown Tower Countryside Centre** has one of this country's few examples of the *camera obscura*, housed in an Edwardian water tower. This forerunner of photography makes use of an ingenious system of mirrors to cast an image of the outside world on to a large horizontal surface, with every detail shown in astonishing clarity.

At their western end, Brighton and Hove merge into the industrialised landscape of Shoreham Harbour

A mile or so inland from central Brighton are two very different museums worth hunting out. The **Booth Museum of Natural History** in Dyke Road is a real curiosity – an immense and well-lit hangar built in the last century to house the enormous collection assembled by E. T. Booth, a wealthy Brighton sportsman. At the door you are faced by the enormous punt-gun with which he wreaked havoc among the wildfowl; and the cases contain everything from golden eagles at an eyrie, reconstructed down to the last stone and twig, to bramblings in a landscape of snow and artificial icicles. More conventional is **Preston Manor**, beyond the arches of the great railway viaduct across the Preston Road. Once the manor house of a village outside Brighton, it is now a museum with a fine collection of furniture from its final two centuries of private occupation. The low white classical house was built in 1738 on much

Victorian steam-power: the British Engineerium, Hove

older foundations: there are still traces of medieval work below ground level. House and contents were bequeathed to the town in 1933; strangely, it has far more of a lived-in feeling about it than many houses that are still occupied.

A couple of miles along the London Road, on the northern outskirts of Brighton, the steep village street of **Patcham** keeps the old downland atmosphere. The hilltop church has a Norman chancel arch, with remains of medieval painting above; and behind the church a great barn marks the point where Brighton ends and the country begins. On the downs to the north is the Chattri Monument, marking the spot where First World War Hindu and Sikh soldiers who died in Brighton hospitals were cremated.

Leaving Brighton along the Lewes Road, you come to the centres of higher education, first the glass box of the College of Technology, and at the very outskirts of the town **Sussex University** and the University of Brighton facing each other across the dual carriageway. Built in the beautifully undulating landscape of **Stanmer Park**, Sussex University has such an idyllic setting that you wonder how anybody gets any work done. In its design Sir Basil Spence ingeniously combined the quadrangle principle of Oxford and Cambridge with the use of brick as a building material, and added a touch of his own by incorporating reflecting sheets of water here and there. A building of arresting originality is the circular Meeting House, an interdenominational chapel, with walls built of concrete blocks alternating with coloured glass. The Gardner Centre for the Arts, designed by Sean Kenny, takes the circular idea one stage further by tacking circular studios and music rooms round the periphery of a circular central auditorium. The university has the space to build out instead of up, and so the students have a cellular village to live in rather than tower blocks. The few farms that make up Stanmer village are at the end of the long drive to **Stanmer House,** a stone classical building which looks across wide lawns to a spiky nineteenth-century church.

Near by, unseen from the main road which brings you back to Lewes four miles away, is the village of **Falmer** – flint-built houses by a muddy pond, a Victorian church with sheep grazing among the tombstones, and the open sweep of the downs behind.

22

From the Adur to the Arun

SINCE ROMAN TIMES there has been a harbour at the mouth of the Adur, where the river gives access to the hinterland north of the downs. The modern **Shoreham Harbour**, shaped like the letter T with an immensely elongated upper horizontal, runs for a good three miles, from the western end of Hove through Portslade and Southwick to the old town of Shoreham; it forms an inland lagoon protected from the sea by long spits of shingle. Shoreham is in fact the biggest commercial harbour between Southampton and Dover; and its wharves and derricks, stacks of timber and petrol storage tanks strike a harshly industrial note on this holiday coast.

At Shoreham itself you come to the yachtsman's water, where crowds of sailing dinghies cram together at the riverside. The town keeps vestiges of its seagoing past, like the High Street pub with an enormous and gaudy ship's figurehead attached to the wall. In medieval times **Shoreham** was the busiest port on the South Coast, a centre for the export of wool from England and the import of wine from France. King John landed there with an army in 1199, and in 1346 Shoreham had to raise twenty-six ships – more than Bristol or Dover – to fight the French. Its most famous historical moment came in 1651, when Charles II, fleeing from England after the Battle of Worcester, escaped to France in the coalbrig *Surprise*. Her captain, Nicholas Tettersell, is said to have been paid £60 for his part in the escape. After the Restoration the *Surprise* was renamed *The Royal Escape* and enrolled in the English fleet.

Shoreham has two magnificent Norman churches, **St Mary de Haura** or 'New' Shoreham church, right in the town, and **St Nicholas**, 'Old' Shoreham church, half a mile to the north near the Adur. They may have been built by successive members of the de Braose family, the lords of the Rape of Bramber (see p. 245). With its noble tower, centrally placed and square-cut, St Mary de Haura is a most queenly building. (The name 'de Haura' means 'of the harbour', as in the

355

French Le Havre.) It was originally far larger than it is now, with a nave that stretched to the ruined wall in the churchyard beyond the west door. One bay of the Norman nave still stands, but the most magnificent Norman work is in the four arches below the tower. In the Transitional period at the end of the twelfth century the Norman apsidal east end was replaced by the present wide choir and aisles; it has been suggested that the masons came on to Shoreham from Canterbury. after they had finished the choir there in 1184. Unusually for a parish church, there is a triforium gallery above the arcades; on the triforium arches are hook-shaped corbels of a type found mainly in France.

Roughly contemporary is the **Marlipins Museum** (Sussex Archaeological Society) in the High Street, a small building full of character. with a chequerboard stone front. The curious name, spelt in the Middle Ages Malduppine and Malapynnys, has never been properly explained. Marlipins dates from the early twelfth century, and was probably built as a customs office by the de Braose family, from Bramber Castle. The exhibits include nineteenth-century views of Shoreham, old maps and charts, and a collection of aircraft models from the early days of flight – suitably enough, as Shoreham's small airfield, opened about 1910, is one of the oldest in the country.

On the opposite side of the river mouth, the spit of land west of the harbour is covered by the seaside housing of Shoreham-by-Sea. At its tip, guarding the harbour entrance, are the remains of **Shoreham Fort,** one of the coastal forts built around 1860 at a time when fears of a French invasion were widespread. Though nothing like as impressive as Newhaven Fort, built at much the same time, its brick bastions and outer defensive wall give a good idea of the thoroughness with which the Victorians built even their minor defensive works.

Old Shoreham church, St Nicholas, is much less dramatic than St Mary's. Left stranded when the river silted up and the port moved downstream, it still has its long narrow Saxon nave; and later Norman and thirteenth-century work has not destroyed the homely scale. The nave may be earlier than AD 900. As at New Shoreham, the tower and transepts are Norman. The arches are carved in every variety of Norman ornament: the church guide lists 'chevron with pellets; cable with beads; billet, stud, lozenge and rose; wheel stud; limpet'. The wooden screen across the chancel is late thirteenth-century and one of the oldest in the country.

From Shoreham two roads lead west along the coast – the A259, which keeps close to the shoreline as far as Worthing, and thereafter runs a mile or so inland; and the more important A27 to Arundel, which gives access to the villages of the South Downs. **Worthing** is recognizably of the same family as Brighton. While hardly a poor relation, it is altogether a quieter town, without the bounce but without the brazenness either. In place of the exuberant Prince Regent to set it on its course, Worthing had his delicate younger sister, Princess Amelia, who came there for her health in 1798. Until the bathing boom of the late eighteenth century, Worthing was a fishing hamlet, an offshoot of Broadwater up the road. By about 1820 it had a Steyne, like Brighton, and smart rows of houses like Warwick Street were springing up. The oldest parts of the town are concentrated in the streets round the pier: the bow windows of Liverpool Terrace and Montague Place, and the straight frontages of Montague Street, now turned into a shopping precinct.

The spine of modern Worthing runs inland from the pier, up South Street and Chapel Road, to the neo-Georgian town hall topped by a feeble cupola. In the building next door is a first-rate local **Museum and Art Gallery**, with cases illustrating the history of an area which has been inhabited since Palaeolithic times, a children's corner full of Victorian dolls, toys and games, and costume galleries lined with dummies dressed in clothes from the nineteenth century to the present day. It has an extensive collection of Sussex painters and puts on enterprising temporary exhibitions both in its galleries and sculpture garden. Chapel Road is named from the big porticoed **St Paul's Church**, which was built in 1812 as a chapel-of-ease to Broadwater. Inside, with its white-painted galleries and flat ceiling, it is much more elegant than its ponderous outer appearance would suggest. When it was first built, the pews were sold freehold, together with the soil on which they stood – one way of making sure of a seat in church. In 1862 a pew cost between £37 and £70, according to size and position.

The most sparkling of Oscar Wilde's comedies, *The Importance of being Earnest*, may have taken some of its high spirits from the general good temper of Worthing. Wilde wrote it in three weeks while on holiday there in September 1894, and named his hero John Worthing in appreciation.

Broadwater, the parent village of Worthing, has been largely obliterated by the needs of traffic; even its large green is isolated between torrents of cars. However, there are some old village houses left in Broadwater Street East, and the splendid low-towered Norman church still rises above the trees. Inside, below the tower, are two very fine late Norman arches carved with all manner of ornamentation, including a row of beakheads. Two of the best-known nineteenth-century writers on natural history, W. H. Hudson and Richard Jefferies, are buried in Broadwater cemetery south of the green. The name of the village derives from a wide tongue of the sea that once stretched inland below the downs.

Tarring (or West Tarring, to distinguish it from Tarring Neville near Newhaven) is another village that has been engulfed by Worthing. As it is lucky enough not to be on a main road, it has kept far more of its village character than Broadwater. The narrow High Street has plenty of pretty white-painted houses; but Tarring's showpiece is a row of fifteenth-century half-timbered cottages, owned by the Sussex Archaeological Society. Nearby is what remains of a palace of the Archbishops of Canterbury, a gabled medieval building used as the village school. Though the Old Palace was built after Becket's time, there is a legend, said to be without foundation, that he stayed at Tarring and planted the first fig tree grown in this country in his garden there – Tarring is still a great place for figs. St Richard of Chichester lived at Tarring in the 1240s, and carried out a miraculous graft on a fig tree there.

Tarring's massive church has a tall spire rising above a battlemented tower. The nave was built in the thirteenth century at the same time as the Old Palace. In the chancel, it is worth upending the medieval misericord seats to look at the carvings of flowers and bearded heads on the under sides. Tarring still belongs to Canterbury and is, in ecclesiastical jargon, an 'archbishop's peculiar'.

Between Worthing and Littlehampton is a coastal strip that is a curious medley of half-smothered villages and exclusive seaside estates, guarded by barriers and notices telling you to keep out and not to park. The northern boundary is the A259, lined with market gardens, huge glasshouses and modern laboratories where mushrooms and other plants are investigated and developed.

At **Ferring** there is a unique survival on this stretch of coast: about half a mile of road which runs with the sea untrammelled on one side and fields, open and unbuilt-on, on the other. How this has escaped the developers remains a mystery. Heading eastwards, you will not find another stretch of road remotely similar (downland roads excluded) until you are almost at Bexhill, a distance of over forty miles. Ferring can be a hard place to get to, as the level-crossing gates that give access to it close with the regularity of the jaws of a feeding crocodile. Its neat little Early English church, at the heart of a recognisable village centre, is full of tablets to the Henty and Olliver families, and has the bassoon and clarinet from the old church band in a glass case inside the door.

The most famous of the Ollivers is buried on **Highdown Hill**, a little way north of the main road. This was John Olliver, whose mill once stood on the hill and who died in 1793, aged eighty-four. When he was not actually grinding corn, his thoughts seem to have dwelt on the subject of death to a most unmillerish degree. He kept his coffin under his bed, and had his tomb made thirty years before his death. 'At his funeral,' says Murray's 1893 *Handbook*, 'his coffin was carried round the field by persons dressed in white, and attended by a company of young women attired in white muslin, one of whom read a sermon over the grave.' The tomb is hidden away behind the gardens of **Highdown**, the prototype of all chalk gardens, made by Sir Frederick Stern. Where the hillside has been cut away the plants sprout happily from what appears to be a solid bed of chalk and flint rubble. Elsewhere sloping lawns look across Ferring to the sea.

East Preston, whose coastal extension is for some reason called Angmering-on-Sea, has a much-restored Early English church to which a remarkably thin tower (just over six feet wide internally) was added about 1500.

Angmering, half way between the two main roads, has managed to keep its separate identity. It is an unexpectedly hilly place, built round a small tree-shaded village green. The church stands high up on the northern side; virtually all that remains of the original building is the western tower of 1507, tacked on to the harsh stonework of a near-complete Victorian reconstruction. Inside the best thing is the Victorian font, carved with flowers and leaves of a Grinling Gibbons-like delicacy. Opposite the church is a nice little alley of stone cottages, several of them whitewashed; and up the hill on the other side of the green are some fine flint houses, including the Pigeon House, which conceals the massive timbers of a medieval hall house behind its flint and brick exterior.

The nearest village to Littlehampton is **Rustington**, which has a good many old thatched cottages, and a fine medieval church dating mainly from about 1170, among the shopping centres and bungalows. Below the church tower at ground level is the sturdy eighteenth-century mechanism that works the clock. A few minutes' walk down Sea Lane is Knightscroft House, a large red-tiled

Victorian building where the composer Sir Hubert Parry lived from 1879 until his death in 1918. He wrote his setting of Blake's *Jerusalem* there – an artistic link across the years with Blake's Felpham a few miles down the coast.

Littlehampton is the least pretentious of the South Coast resorts. Though it has no pier and no proper seafront, it makes up for these deficiencies by wide beaches, especially the expanse of dune and sand on the western side of the Arun, and the lively harbour, where power boats zip about with Mediterranean panache. Littlehampton was an important port as far back as Saxon times, and in the Middle Ages was a landing-place for the Caen stone from Normandy used in churches and secular buildings all over Sussex.

In later centuries it pottered on quietly as a small port easily accessible from France, and at the end of the eighteenth century shared some of the prosperity brought by the bathing machine. In 1808 it was visited by Lord Byron; but it never expanded to a full-scale Regency seaside resort, though South Terrace has a few elegant houses, built about 1803. Most of the hotels and boarding houses, set back behind the enormous seafront green, are redbrick Victorian and Edwardian. A few old flint houses survive well inland round the High Street and Church Street area; but even the parish church is modern – a brick rebuilding of the 1930s in a style well described by Nairn as 'eerie disembodied Gothic'. It is a simple building, full of light and surrounded by wooden galleries, to which all the monuments from the previous church have been banished. The tracery of a Decorated window was salvaged and built into the tower.

The small **Museum** in Church Street has brooches and pottery from local Roman villas, and a good assemblage of old paintings and photographs of Littlehampton. One large oil painting shows Victorians walking along the gusty promenade beside the bumps and hollows of the green, not yet levelled out when the scene was painted. In the nineteenth century Littlehampton had an extensive timber trade, which lives on in the name of Baltic Wharf beside the Arun.

The day cannot be far off when **Lyminster** links up with Littlehampton; but for the moment it is still a self-contained village, looking inland and across the watermeadows to the churches and towers of Arundel rather than southwards to the sea. At the beginning of the tenth century, the name appears in Alfred the Great's will as 'Lullyngminster', and by the early tenth century at the latest there was a Benedictine nunnery here. The church, long, tall and narrow, still keeps its Saxon form. Originally the nave was the parish church, and the chancel was set aside for the nuns. The north aisle was added about 1170, and the tower some thirty years later.

A coffin slab behind the font is said to come from the grave of a local hero, a farmer's boy called Jim Pulk, who killed a dragon that was ravaging the countryside. This dragon lived in the Knucker Hole, a circular pool among the reeds a hundred yards or so down the track that runs north of the churchyard. The Anglo-Saxon word for sea-monster is *nicor*, and this legend may be the survival of some dim folk memory of a conflict between a local Beowulf and the Lyminster Grendel. The Knucker Hole still steams with a dragon-like breath in winter; though it was plumbed some years ago and found to be about thirty feet deep, with no trace of even the smallest monster.

The direct route from Shoreham to Arundel is along the A27, which runs parallel to the coast a couple of miles inland. The A27 crosses the Adur by a dual-carriageway bridge a short way upstream from the old wooden tollbridge, which has been relegated to the status of a footbridge. It was built in 1781 by unemployed Welsh miners, from ultra-durable jarrah or mahogany gum-tree wood imported from Australia – surely one of the earliest of all imports from Down Under.

The dominating landmark of the lower Adur is the bulk of **Lancing College Chapel**, standing guard over the valley on the west side of the river. This great stone building, in a superb situation, inspired Ian Nairn to an enthusiasm rare in the *Buildings of England* series – 'a Gothic chapel as Turner might have imagined it in paint, or Mendelssohn might have personified it in music'. It is the testament of the Rev. Nathaniel Woodard, who founded Lancing (along with Ardingly and Hurstpierpoint) in the middle of the last century. Murray's *Handbook* gives the social stratifications: Lancing was 'for the education of the upper classes', Hurstpierpoint 'for sons of farmers', and Ardingly 'for sons of small traders'. The other school buildings of Lancing are typically Victorian educational, with flint walls and tall narrow gables. Though the foundation stone was laid in 1868, the west end of the chapel, with its rose window and flying buttresses, was not completed until 1978. The bronze effigy of Woodard, the instigator of this blend of Victorian practicality and Gothic make-believe, lies in a chantry below the towering vault.

361

The chapel's statistics are cathedral-like: the external height is 150 feet, on a par with Westminster Abbey, and the internal height to the nave roof is ninety feet. All the work was done by college craftsmen, using local materials and without any mechanical assistance. Behind the altar hang three enormous tapestries to scale with the building, each thirty-five feet high by ten wide, and among the largest in the world. They were designed in 1933 in an insipid medievalism, but they give a great splash of colour with their gilded figures and red backgrounds. Britten's cantata *St Nicolas* was written for Lancing's centenary in 1948, and the Estonian composer Arvo Pärt – best known for his *Cantus in Memory of Benjamin Britten* – wrote a work for the school's 150th anniversary in 1998.

North of the college the road wanders past two small medieval churches. **Coombes** is tucked away behind a tall green silage tower and reached across a field. Outside it looks hardly more than a trim stone barn, pierced with Perpendicular windows; but inside the early Norman nave and chancel arch are covered with wall paintings, perhaps done as early as 1100. Among them is a fine Lion of St Mark above the arch; and painted inside the arch is an extraordinary figure – a man with a grotesquely elongated mouth, yelling as he strains to support the masonry that bears him down. **St Botolph's** (or plain Botolph's) is a narrow Saxon building, which expanded in the Middle Ages and has since shrunk back to its original size, as a blocked arcade in the north wall shows.

North Lancing still keeps a good deal of the genuine downland feeling in its curved street. The name may be among the most ancient of all Saxon village names, deriving from Wlencing, one of the sons of Aella who led the first Saxon invasion into Sussex in AD 477. The old church is a comfortable building, typically Norman in plan with its central tower, but largely rebuilt about 1300. East of Lancing much of the land towards the sea is taken up by the hangars and buzzing light aircraft of Shoreham airport.

Continuing westwards, the village and church at **Sompting** are sundered by a dual carriageway. The village is south of the road; the church to the north is unique for its Saxon tower, built early in the eleventh century. It has a spindly look, due partly to the narrow strips of stone that run vertically up it. Each side terminates in a steep gable, and the roof is formed of four diamond-shaped surfaces meeting in a point – the 'Rhenish helm' shape found nowhere else in Britain, though common in the German Rhineland.

In 1154 the church was given to the Knights Templar, who pulled it down except for the tower and rebuilt it, leaving the Saxon arch from the tower into the nave and keeping the narrow shape of the original building. As unique as the tower is the square Templars' chapel, now turned into the south transept but originally entirely separate; the door through was cut at a later date. Below the arch into the tower is a Saxon carver's groping attempt at Ionic capitals; and other fragments of Saxon carving are attached to the walls. One, a little figure of an abbot with a book propped beside him, has all the freshness of the Saxon world, breaking here at Sompting through the world-weary crust of later centuries and more knowing cultures.

The northern suburbs of Worthing are spreading out towards **Findon**, but have not yet absorbed it. However, the village has been cut off from the church by the dual carriageway A24. The church is built at the foot of a steep wooded hill overlooking the pedimented classicism of Findon Place. It is mainly thirteenth-century, with a wide roof spanning the double nave, and a thirteenth-century oak screen. Findon village, across the main road, is a pretty place built on a network of lanes.

One of them takes you past the wide triangular green and up the hill to **Cissbury Ring** (National Trust), the Iron Age capital of this stretch of the downs. Cissbury is a really grand hill fort, surrounded by a ditch and rampart that still look defensible. The top is covered by plants of some small variety of sorrel, which wave in reddish undulations when the wind passes over them. At the western end Cissbury is gouged into hollows – the remains of flint mines dug by Neolithic man centuries before Cissbury became a fortress. Excavations in the 1950s uncovered a 4,000-year-old tragedy in one of the mines. The body of a girl was found lying where the roof had caved in on her, still holding in her hand the charred remains of the torch she had taken to light her through the galleries.

West of Findon, the A280 makes a magnificent sweep through the cornfields along the valley floor. This stretch of road is known as the **Long Furlong**; it was constructed in 1818 by a member of the Shelley family, who tried unsuccessfully to start his own coach service between London and Worthing. The coaches may have failed, but the road is spectacular.

Clapham, a mile before you get back on the A27, consists of a single narrow cul-de-sac. The church is in the depths of a wood up a stony track; at one side it overlooks an enormous farm. It is basically

Early English, much restored by Sir Gilbert Scott in the 1870s, down to such details as Victorian saints painted in outline in the window splays. The chancel is full of Shelley memorials. On the floor is a brass of 1526 to John Shelley and his wife Elizabeth, who wears a robe decorated with the three whelk shells which formed the 'canting' or punning arms of the Shelleys; and on the north wall is the recessed tomb of their son Sir William, his wife and children, crudely carved one behind the other in line-ahead formation. The hamlet of **Patching** balances Clapham on the other side of the A280; its church is likewise Early English, but in place of a pyramid cap has a tall spire, covered in green slates – eight tons of them, I was told by a man tending the graveyard.

Poling, three miles towards Arundel, is hardly a village at all. It consists of a few houses down a cul-de-sac south of the A27, and a small church almost swallowed up by farm buildings. The nave is Saxon, the south aisle of about 1200, and the chancel and tower were added at intervals of about a century. On the north wall is a plaque to Sir Harry Johnston (1858–1927), described as 'administrator, soldier, explorer, naturalist, author and painter'. An immensely able man, Johnston was largely responsible for the various treaties and annexations that added East Africa to the British Empire. He explored widely in East and West Africa, discovered the okapi, and exhibited at the Royal Academy.

Just before you reach Arundel, a cul-de-sac wanders along the eastern side of the Arun for a good three miles before coming to rest among the thatched flint-walled cottages of **Burpham** (pronounced Burfam). The cruciform church has some remarkable bits and pieces inside, notably a vaulted stone roof to the early thirteenth-century chancel, and a late Norman arch in the south arcade, carved on the transept side with grotesque heads, one human and one ape-like, and fringed with savagely spiky chevron ornament. Church cottages and creeper-covered pub form as pretty a village centre as you could hope to find.

Arundel is everyone's idea of what an ancient town should be: a steep street of old buildings rising from a peaceful river, a huge church on the crest of the hill, the soaring towers of a castle against a backcloth of park and woodland. Even when you discover that the church (in fact the Roman Catholic cathedral) is a Gothic imitation of the 1870s, and that the castle's residential buildings date from the same time, the medieval illusion is not really spoiled. Seen from a short distance away – upstream along the towpath, or from the byroad to South Stoke – Arundel blends the genuine and the Victorian harmoniously together.

Arundel first appears in history in 901, when it is mentioned in King Alfred's will. It was an important harbour town until the twentieth century, when Littlehampton at the mouth of the river grew in importance and Arundel's trade vanished. Until the eighteenth century, the name was usually spelt 'Arundell', which splits conveniently to mean 'the dell on the Arun'. Ekwall says that it derives from the Old English 'Harhun-dell', meaning 'valley of horehound' (a plant of waste ground whose juice has medicinal properties), and that the name of the River Arun is a back-formation from Arundel. A much more fanciful and attractive suggestion derives it from *hirondelle*, the French for swallow, because it is the first place where summer reaches Sussex; or – better still for so legendary a place – from a legendary horse, the swift steed Hirondelle, ridden by the giant Bevis of Southampton.

Bevis was warder of the gatehouse of **Arundel Castle** (one of the castle's Norman towers is named after him). Every week he ate a whole ox, together with enormous quantities of bread and mustard, and drank two hogsheads of beer. When he felt his death was near, he climbed to the top of his tower and hurled his huge sword, called Mongley or Morglay, far away across the park. Bevis was buried where it fell. Mongley hangs on a wall in the castle armoury – an evident impostor, as it is a quite ungigantic medieval two-handed sword, much smaller than the Chinese execution sword that hangs nearby.

The Saxons would certainly have had some kind of fortification at so strategic a spot. After the Conquest the combined Rapes of Arundel and Chichester were given to Roger de Montgomery, the most powerful of all the Norman barons, who began his stone castle soon after 1070. The inner gateway dates from his time; the square stone outer barbican was built by the Fitzalan family at the end of the thirteenth century. A little north of this entrance is the Norman keep, a circular building that fits neatly on the top of a steeply conical motte. About 1800 the eleventh Duke of Norfolk introduced a colony of North American owls into the keep. The birds were named after various friends and acquaintances. sometimes without strict regard for biological accuracy, as happened when the butler announced: 'Please, your grace, Lord Thurlow's laid an egg.' This eminent bird died in 1859, aged over a hundred. The owls had gone by 1870. 'Their privacy,' says Murray's *Handbook*, 'was destroyed by excursion trains.'

In 1135 the castle was given as her dower to Queen Adeliza, widow of Henry I, who three years later married William de Albini. From the Albinis Arundel passed to the Fitzalans – who automatically became Earls of Arundel on possessing the castle – and then in the mid sixteenth century to Philip Howard, son of the fourth Duke of Norfolk. The Norfolks, hereditary Earls Marshal and senior peers of England, have lived there ever since, except for a brief interlude in the Civil War. In 1643 the castle was besieged by Sir William Waller's Roundheads, who bombarded it, captured it and occupied it until 1649. The damage was not fully repaired until the final restoration in the 1890s.

The great baronial apartments that are open to the public have been much criticised for their ostentation – but vast vulgarity in the right place never hurt anybody, and no one could call them mean-spirited. On the right as you go in there is a large chapel, all Purbeck marble columns and striped stone vaulting; and on the left is the enormous Barons' Hall, built with impossibly high hammerbeams, and hung with tapestries and portraits. Above the dais at the far end is an endearingly absurd eighteenth-century historical composition showing Thomas, Earl of Surrey, pleading his case for clemency before Henry VII after the Battle of Bosworth Field in 1485.

The long, low picture gallery, running the whole width of the castle, is lined with the procession of Norfolks and their forebears. Though he looks shrewd, the first Duke, known as the 'Jockey of Norfolk', backed the losing side in the last phase of the Wars of the Roses. According to Shakespeare, the night before Bosworth, when he was killed fighting beside Richard III, he found pinned to his tent a note which ran 'Jockey of Norfolk, be not too bold, For Dickon thy master is bought and sold'. Norfolk died in spite of the warning. His son, the Earl of Surrey shown in the Victorian painting, was taken back into favour by Henry VII and had the dukedom restored by Henry VIII; Henry's executed queens, Anne Boleyn and Katherine Howard, were both the second Duke's grand-daughters. The clean-shaven canny face of the third Duke is that of a man destined to survive – and survive he did, outliving both Henry VIII and his own son, the Earl of Surrey.

Henry, Earl of Surrey, has the most magnificent portrait in the gallery; he stands in melancholy pose in a theatrical Renaissance setting of masks and cupids, wearing a sombre suit of dark brown and silver. Known as the 'sweetest poet' of his time, Surrey was executed in 1547, aged about thirty, on the charge of incorporating

366

the arms of Edward the Confessor with his own, regarded by Henry VIII as asserting a claim to the throne. His son, Thomas Howard, the fourth Duke, is shown as a long-faced dandy. Like his father, he aimed too high, and was executed in 1572 for plotting to marry Mary Queen of Scots. In the gallery is a portrait of his son, St Philip Howard (thirteenth Earl of Arundel), canonised by Pope Paul VI in 1970 for remaining faithful to Roman Catholicism throughout Elizabeth's reign. He was a prisoner in the Tower for eleven years, and died there in 1595.

Obviously a capacity for survival was in the genes of the Howards. But the fourteenth Earl, no doubt taking warning from the fate of his father, grandfather and great-grandfather, preferred fine art to politics and spent much of his time abroad. He was even out of the country when the castle was bombarded by Waller. A portrait of him in the Drawing-Room shows him in front of the 'Arundel Marbles', classical statues he collected on his travels in Italy. After the Restoration the dukedom was revived, and after the Catholic Emancipation Act of 1829 the Earls Marshal could get on with the peaceable business of organising coronations and other ceremonials.

Round the corner from the gallery is a suite of smaller rooms, of which far the most impressive is the Library, a wood-vaulted tunnel dating from the Regency phase of rebuilding, and lined with leather tomes behind gilded grilles. Mary Queen of Scots appears on an early portrait in the (comparatively) little Billiard Room, and several of her relics are preserved, including a rosary given to Anne Countess of Arundel, the wife of St Philip Howard, which Mary was holding as she waited for execution on the scaffold.

Medieval Arundels and more recent Norfolks lie buried in the **Fitzalan Chapel**, across the lawns west of the castle. The Catholic chapel in fact forms part of the Protestant parish church, from which it is separated by a glass screen; thus Catholic and Protestant services are held under the same roof. Chapel and church were built about 1380; at the Dissolution the chapel fell into decay, and the process of destruction was almost completed by the Roundheads, who stabled their horses among the tombs, while they bombarded the castle from the church tower. The chapel was restored in 1886 by the fifteenth Duke, who built the baronial parts of the castle; his bearded effigy, in green bronze, lies in the centre of the nave. The chief glory of the chapel is the Perpendicular seven-light east window. On either side of the altar are Arundel tombs topped by immensely elaborate stone canopies. Near by lies the battered effigy of John, the seventh Earl.

Called the 'English Achilles' for his prowess in battle, he was wounded and taken prisoner by the French in 1435, and died a few weeks later as the result of losing his leg. Below the armoured figure lies a *memento mori*, the effigy of a corpse reminding us that to this end must even heroes come.

To get into the parish church you have to go out of the castle and up the London Road. As the Fitzalan Chapel occupies the whole of the chancel, the interior of the church is very truncated. The stone-canopied pulpit is a rare pre-Reformation survival, thought to have been designed by Henry Yevele, the architect of the nave of Canterbury Cathedral. On the north wall are remains of medieval painting, including an angel in long robes that swirl like a Beardsley drawing.

In Arundel the parish church takes second place to the Catholic **Cathedral** over the road. Built by the fifteenth Duke in the 1870s, this vast building was intended to be even vaster, with a spire soaring to 280 feet, which would have made it an overwhelming landmark. It is better seen at a distance than visited, as inside, despite its apsidal east end and forest of superimposed columns, it is not particularly interesting. From this high point steep alleys of good Sussex pebble-walled cottages lead back to the town centre, and the mixture of small boats and mudflats that gives riverside Arundel its character. The **Arundel Museum**, in the High Street, sets the town's history firmly in its Sussex setting, with special emphasis on local trade and shipping.

Along the lower edge of Arundel Park a lane leads to the picnic and beauty spot of **Swanbourne Lake**, in a tree-covered combe. Between the lake and the river, the Wildfowl and Wetlands Trust has turned sixty acres of watermeadow into a splendid wildfowl reserve, where you can walk along paths, or peer from hides, to study the lifestyles of more than a thousand swans, geese and ducks, including such rarities as blue ducks from the mountains of New Zealand, which splash and preen themselves in a specially built mini-landscape of rocky roosting-holes and cascades.

After a couple of switchback miles, the lane ends at **South Stoke**, a tiny and peaceful place consisting of a few farm buildings, an old rectory, and a small stone church with a Victorian witches' hat spire perched on the narrow medieval tower. A footbridge leads over the Arun to North Stoke and the downs behind Amberley. The main road to Pulborough skirts the opposite side of the park for two miles north of Arundel.

Slindon, three miles west of Arundel, has the great advantage of a dramatic site on the slope of the downs. Two-thirds or so of its flint-and-brick cottages are owned by the National Trust. The main street runs steeply up between typical downland houses; and at the top of the hill is a miniature village square, complete with a perfect Tree of Idleness encircled by a bench. For all its Englishness, this corner of Slindon on a sunny afternoon can give you the feeling of being whisked a couple of thousand miles to the East Mediterranean – even if only for an instant.

Slindon's church has a Victorian tower, but is basically twelfth-century. In the south chapel is a wooden effigy, unique in Sussex, believed to be of Sir Anthony St Leger, who died in 1539. The crisp carving of face and hair has lasted far better than many stone effigies of the same age. (There are wooden effigies of similar date in Goudhurst church, see p. 217.) On one of the arcade columns is a tablet to Stephen Langton, who as Archbishop of Canterbury at the time of Magna Carta in 1215 lent his tremendous authority to the barons in their struggle with King John, and died at Slindon in 1228. At the bottom of the hill a path by the village pond leads into the National Trust woodlands of the Slindon Estate – 3,500 acres of wood and farmland stretching over the downs to the hills above Bignor.

Eartham is a little flint-built village, which was the home of two early nineteenth-century celebrities, William Hayley and William Huskisson. There is a tablet to Huskisson in the small Norman church, and a monument by Flaxman to William Hayley's son, who died in 1800 aged twenty, 'having borne an agonising distemper with cheerful magnanimity' says the inscription signed by Hayley himself. On the capitals of the Norman chancel arch are comical carvings of a rabbit's head and a bearded face.

Half a mile to the north are **Eartham Woods**, where **Stane Street** can be followed right up to the downs behind Bignor. For much of the way the *agger* or raised causeway of the road is perfectly preserved, sloping gently uphill with the beech trees pressing in on either side, until you come out on the open downland above Gumber Farm, and can look south to the narrow line of the sea glinting above the dark skyline of trees. As an additional bonus, the Forestry Commission have marked out a 'forest walk' through the woods.

23

Chichester and the Coast

IT WOULD BE hard to imagine two places more different than the cathedral cities of Kent and Sussex. Where Canterbury is a grand administrative and tourist centre, **Chichester** remains very much the Georgian country town. Canterbury cathedral stands, lordly and aloof, at the centre of its close, cut off from the life of the city outside; whereas Chichester cathedral is a village church writ large, almost on the pavement and opposite the main hotel of the town. Its cloisters are used as a short cut, and the paths around it are made into a display ground for the paintings of local artists. Canterbury's Bell Harry Tower demands attention, but Chichester spire steals upon your notice as you approach the city or wander through the streets.

Chichester stands in a flat plain below the downs. Its plan has the simplicity of the Roman town – a plain cross of four roads (North, South, East and West Streets), surrounded by a roughly circular wall, of which a good deal still survives. There may well have been a town of sorts here before the Roman conquest of AD 43; at any rate, the Roman name for Chichester, Noviomagus, seems to imply that it was a new successor to an older foundation. The local tribesmen (the Atrebates) were among the first of the loyal supporters of Rome, and under their ruler Cogidubnus (or Togidubnus, see Fishbourne below) they made Chichester into one of the earliest Romanised towns.

The most striking relic of this period is built into the wall of the Council House in North Street, below the brick arcade – a battered dedication stone, dug up nearby in 1723, from the Temple of Neptune and Minerva. This temple was built by the Guild of Craftsmen of Chichester, and the letters '. . GIDVBNI' are still legible. For years the inscription has been expanded to 'Cogidubni' ('of Cogidubnus'), but research into ancient Celtic names has found that whereas 'Togi-' is a known prefix, 'Cogi-' is otherwise unknown. So Togidubnus is now preferred by scholars. Important Roman finds were made during the 1960s restoration of the cathedral, which

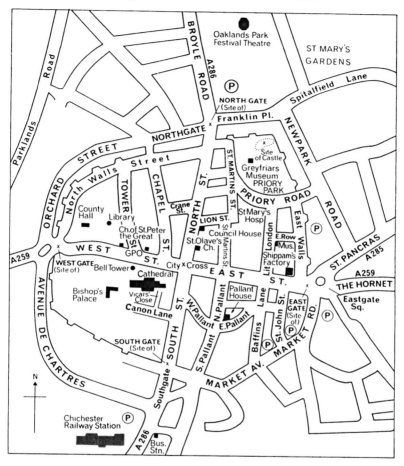

seems to have been built partly if not completely on the site of a Roman public building. Chichester gets its present name from Cissa, one of the sons of Aella, the Saxon who invaded and conquered Sussex in AD 477 – 'Cissa's Ceaster', the camp or stronghold of Cissa.

Historically speaking, Chichester has always been a backwater, apart from a brief taste of violence in the Civil War. Even the local saint, St Richard, was not a martyr or a spectacular miracle-worker, but an ordinary well-loved thirteenth-century bishop. He would find his **Cathedral** far less altered than Becket would if he returned to Canterbury. The bulk of it is still very much the Norman building

371

begun by Bishop Stigand in about 1075, when the see was transferred from Selsey to Chichester, and continued by Bishop Seffrid a hundred years later, after a great fire in 1187 had destroyed the wooden roof. Seffrid and his successors added the stone vaulting to the roof, and the external flying buttresses to take the additional outward thrust. They also built the bays of the retro-choir behind the high altar, in which the graceful pointed arches of the Transitional take the place of the dumpy rounded openings of Bishop Stigand's Romanesque, and livened up the austere columns of the nave arcades with shafts and stringcourses of black Purbeck marble.

Apart from the side chapels and Decorated windows, the only major additions to the original cathedral were the long, narrow Lady Chapel, completed about 1300, the detached campanile on the northern side, dating from about 1400, the early fifteenth-century Chapter House, and the spire, built above the central tower during the fifteenth century. This extra weight was carried by the fire-weakened Norman stones for four hundred years; then, on 21 February, 1861, while workmen who had been called in to shore up the tower were at lunch, spire and tower collapsed onto the cathedral floor. 'The beautiful airy spire,' a contemporary reporter wrote, 'sank gently below the cathedral roof, with no more noise, say observers, than that produced by the tilting of a cartload of stones in the road.' The damage was repaired with astonishing speed. Funds were raised, Sir Gilbert Scott was called in as architect, and between 1865 and 1867 the whole tower and spire were rebuilt.

Perhaps the spire had already been weakened by the fireball which struck it around the beginning of the eighteenth century, and which Daniel Defoe heard about from the locals. 'Such was the irresistible force of it, that it drove several great stones out of the steeple and carried them clear off, not from the roof of the church only, but of the adjacent houses also . . . The breach it made in the spire, though within about forty five foot of the top, was so large, that as the workmen said to me, a coach and six horses might have driven through it.'

Inside the cathedral, the most startling novelty is John Piper's huge symbolic tapestry behind the high altar. The design consists of seven tapestry strips separated by the buttresses of a sixteenth-century oak screen; the three central panels represent the Holy Trinity, and the outer pairs symbolise the four elements above and the evangelists below. They are in the tradition of art patronage established at Chichester by Bishop George Bell, who was bishop from 1929 to 1958. Other modern works in the cathedral, due to the

The calm elegance of Chichester Cathedral's spire.

initiative of the Very Rev Walter Hussey, Dean from 1955 to 1977, are the pulpit, an unobtrusive affair of concrete and cast aluminium, and matching lectern; the furnishings of the St Mary Magdalene chapel, centring on a Graham Sutherland painting of Christ appearing to St Mary after the resurrection; and a glowing window by Chagall in the retro-choir. Bell is commemorated by a portrait plaque, and by the Bell-Arundel screen at the west end of the choir, a graceful stone arcade built by Bishop Arundel about 1475, taken down by the Victorians and restored in 1961. In 1983 the centenary of Bell's birth was celebrated by the dedication of a chunky black stone font, carved by John Skelton. Still more recent is the Poussin-inspired reredos by Patrick Procktor, in the Chapel of St John the Baptist, and the furnishings of the retro-choir, once more a pilgrimage centre, as it was in the Middle Ages. Behind a simple Purbeck marble altar, designed by Robert Potter, is a dazzling semi-abstract tapestry by Ursula Benker-Schirmer, woven part in West Dean, Sussex and part in Bavaria, as a token of Anglo-German reconciliation.

An earlier patron of the arts, though a less disinterested one, was Bishop Sherburne, who in Henry VIII's time commissioned the enormous paintings on wood in the two transepts. The artist was Lambert Barnard, whose portraits of kings and bishops look remarkably like Victorian bit-part actors dressed up as kings and bishops – no doubt because they were repainted in the eighteenth century. The south transept painting shows Sherburne receiving a guarantee of the rights of the cathedral from the king. Sherburne's gilded tomb is in the south choir aisle, between the cathedral's greatest works of art – the two twelfth-century stone panels showing Christ arriving at the house of Martha and Mary, and the Raising of Lazarus. There is no feeling of joy or triumph over death on the faces of these hieratic figures, only intense concentration as Christ and the disciples arrive at the house, and intense weariness when the miracle is accomplished. The effect would surely not have been so overwhelming when the empty eye-sockets were filled with precious stones and the faces and draperies were painted.

It is only because they were behind pillars that these sculptures escaped the attention of Sir William Waller's Puritans, who captured Chichester after a brief siege in 1643. When the troops entered the cathedral, they 'ran up and down with their swords drawn, defacing the monuments of the dead, and hacking the seats and stalls'. St Richard's shrine, which stood on the dais behind the high altar, had already disappeared at the Reformation. Whether because of

Roundhead zeal or for some other reason there are remarkably few ancient memorials in the cathedral. Best are the Arundel tombs in the north aisle, one to Maud, Countess of Arundel, about 1270, and the other to Richard Fitzalan, Earl of Arundel, and his wife, lying with their right hands linked, which dates from a century later. The strange conflict of emotion roused in a modern sensibility by these calm effigies is expressed in Philip Larkin's *An Arundel Tomb* :

> *Side by side, their faces blurred,*
> *The earl and countess lie in stone,*
> *Their proper habits vaguely shown*
> *As jointed armour, stiffened pleat,*
> *And that faint hint of the absurd --*
> *The little dogs under their feet . . .*

In the south-west corner, behind the font, a Flaxman relief shows eighteenth-century poet William Collins, who was born and died in Chichester. He wrote a series of Odes, much approved of by Dr Johnson, which reacted against the fastidious classical style of Alexander Pope. His final insanity is referred to in the inscription. Two great English musicians are commemorated in the north transept. Thomas Weelkes, composer of madrigals, was organist at the beginning of the seventeenth century. Fortunately he did not live to see the outrages of the Puritans, who 'brake down the organ in the cathedral, and dashed the pipes with their pole-axes, crying in scoff, "Harke how the organs goe!" '. Below the tablet to Weelkes an inscription in the floor slabs marks the spot where the ashes of Gustav Holst are buried. The most striking of the post-Cromwellian memorials is the toga-ed figure of William Huskisson, MP for Chichester and later for Liverpool, in the north aisle. Huskisson was the first prominent rail fatality; at the grand opening of the Liverpool and Manchester Railway in 1830 he was knocked over by a train, and died from his injuries.

In the 1960s and '70s the cathedral underwent a vast programme of reconstruction. The foundations were underpinned with concrete down to bedrock, and for the restoration of the fabric stone was imported from France, as similar to the original Caen stone as possible. Thus after almost nine centuries the imperfections of the Norman builders were at last made good.

Adjoining the cathedral on the south side are the cloisters, not monastic cloisters at all, but a covered walkway round the old burial ground or 'paradise' outside the cathedral. From the cloisters a pretty alleyway, St Richard's Walk, runs down to Canon Lane, the residential heart of ecclesiastical Chichester. Canon Lane is given symmetry by a medieval gatehouse at either end, one leading to the **Bishop's Palace** and the other opening into South Street. The Palace, mainly flint with brick patchings here and there, is set back behind a wide lawn and forecourt; it evolved in a piecemeal way from the Middle Ages to the eighteenth century. Just before the South Street gateway the little houses of **Vicars' Close** lead the eye back to the spire of the cathedral. They were built in the fifteenth century as the homes of the 'vicars choral' responsible for the cathedral music. During the nineteenth century they were turned into shops. The massively beamed Vicars' Hall, at the northern end of the Close, is now used for cathedral and secular functions.

On the other side of South Street is Chichester's eighteenth-century theatre, transmuted into a shopping arcade. The area behind, known as **The Pallants**, is the purest Georgian redbrick and is a microcosm of the larger city, with its four roads, meeting at a central point, called North, South, East and West Pallant. (The area should by rights be called the Pallant in the singular, as the name derives from *palantia*, meaning a district over which the Archbishop of Canterbury had, until 1552, jurisdiction or palatine rights.) Finest of all the fine houses here is the **Pallant House Gallery**, now a combination of furnished town house and art gallery. The bewildered-looking stone birds on top of the gate piers look like dodos but are in fact ostriches, carved from written descriptions sent home by the wine merchant for whom Pallant House was built. The gallery is rich in paintings by twentieth-century British artists, among them Henry Moore, Graham Sutherland and John Piper

As splendid as the Queen Anne Pallant House is the William and Mary house in West Street, built by John Edes and used until recently as the West Sussex Record Office. Behind, by way of contrast, is the wishy-washy pseudo-Georgian of County Hall. Best of this cluster of modern buildings is the West Sussex county library, a glass and concrete drum of a place which looks exactly what it is – a highly efficient building for the swift retrieval and study of information.

On the corner of Tower Street and West Street is **St Peter's Market** (formerly a church), a Victorian building with unusually graceful arcading and a splendidly bewhiskered collection of corbel heads. It now houses a cluster of specialist shops and boutiques.

West Street ends just past the long white-painted front of the Dolphin and Anchor Hotel, a former coaching inn with cobbled central courtyard. A few yards away is the **City Cross**, the hub of Chichester. Given to the city by Bishop Story in 1501, it is an octagon, left open underneath for market traders, and surmounted by a crown of stone pinnacles and ribs rising to a central lantern.

The **Council House**, already mentioned, is the centrepiece of North Street. The main section, perched up on a brick arcade, was built in 1731; on top is a stone lion, 'in an attitude', says an old city guide, 'which is both uncomfortable and nonchalant'. This is the home of the city council, making, together with East Pallant House and County Hall, a trio of official buildings, each in a different quadrant of the town. (The fourth quadrant is of course mainly given over to the authority of the Church.) The council chamber, lined with portraits of kings and city notabilities, is directly above the arcade. Between the Council House and the market cross is **St Olave's**, the oldest of Chichester's medieval churches, still serving an ecclesiastical purpose as an SPCK bookshop; and John Nash's hefty Doric portico, leading to the Buttermarket where you can buy anything from groceries to antiques. The **Ship Hotel**, north of the Council House, is a magnificently tall redbrick Georgian house, built about 1790 for Admiral Sir George Murray, Commander-in-Chief at Portsmouth. Inside, a splendid iron-balustraded staircase soars up to the second storey, with an elaborate plaster ceiling overhead. Allied generals made the Ship their headquarters during the Second World War.

Directly behind the Ship is **Priory Park**, an open space which takes up a good third of the north-east quarter of the city. At one corner is the grassy mound where Chichester's Norman castle once stood; it was probably little more than a timber stockade, as there is no trace of stone fortifications. The park takes its name from the Greyfriars (Franciscans), who were settled in Chichester by about 1245. The choir of their church, flooded with light from the tall Decorated windows, is now a branch of the Chichester District Museum.

The main **Museum** is nearby, on the corner of East Row and Little London. Built in the eighteenth century as a corn store, it was converted with typical Chichester good sense instead of being torn down, as would have happened in so many less enlightened places. Strangest of all the local exhibits is the seventeenth-century 'municipal moon' – a vast circular lantern that was carried in front of the mayor on any official visits he had to make after dark. Outside the museum a tall pillar of Westmorland slate, carved by John Skelton into the rough shape of a pair of hands, thrusts up from the cobbles of the pavement, a modern symbol of discovery perfectly at home in its eighteenth-century setting.

At the heart of this quadrant of the city is St Martin's Square, more a widened bend in the road than a formal layout, with whitewashed houses leading up to Priory Park. **St Mary's Hospital,** on the south side of the square, is the most extraordinary building in Chichester. It was built about 1290, and consisted originally of a hall (used as an infirmary) and chapel under a single enormous roof. Towards the end of the seventeenth century, eight small flats for old people were built in the infirmary section, and apart from modern mains services they have hardly been altered in the last three hundred years. Anyone planning for the needs of the elderly should take a look at St Mary's, which nicely gauges the requirements of the inmates – a communal central corridor, semi-privacy in the kitchens which look on to the corridor through wooden grilles, and complete privacy in the bedrooms and sitting rooms at the back.

Artistic Chichester has been put on the map by the **Festival Theatre,** which runs an outstanding series of different productions throughout the summer. The theatre, in Oaklands Park, north of the old city, is a hexagonal building, built in the early 1960s on uncompromisingly functional lines. The open stage is surrounded by the audience on three sides, the upper seats are cantilevered externally to form a kind of entrance portico, and the whole paraphernalia of lights, acoustic reflectors and structural steel wires are displayed naked and unashamed above the auditorium. The complex includes a studio theatre for intimate-scale productions.

Heading west from Chichester along the A259, you come to **Fishbourne,** where a vast **Roman Palace** (Sussex Archaeological Society) was first brought to light in 1960. A workman cutting trenches found some Roman tiles and reported his find; years of intensive excavation followed, and the result, laid out in a field north of the road, is a model of research and presentation. Under a stylish hangar of wood and glass the remains of a complete wing of the palace have been uncovered. This is enormous enough, but it represents only one quarter of the whole huge quadrangle which measured five hundred feet square and continues southwards under gardens, houses and the main road. The palace was built about AD 75, probably for Cogidubnus/Togidubnus, a client king friendly to the Romans (see above), who spared no expense to make it an awe-inspiring sign of the advantages of Romanisation.

When it was built the waters of Chichester Channel came farther inland than they do today, and the southern colonnade probably looked across a terraced garden straight on to the sea. A stream ran along the eastern side, and still trickles down the ditch alongside the unexposed east wing. The main administrative wings were the eastern and western, each of which had a porticoed grand entrance; the north (conserved) wing was residential, and continued in use when the rest of the palace had fallen into decay.

A visitor coming to the palace from Chichester in, say, AD 100 would have crossed the stream to the entrance portico, walked through the entrance hall to the formal garden, then along a broad path between formal hedges and up a flight of steps to an apsidal audience chamber. (The outlines of the main features in the east wing are marked in outline in the turf.) Even the plan of the garden hedges is known at Fishbourne, as the designers of the garden dug out trenches and filled them with fertile soil; the archaeologists found the trenches, and also some of the pipes which carried water to ornamental basins and fountains. The hedges are now planted with box, and the beds with roses and acanthus – all plants the Romans are known to have used in their own gardens. Outside the palace archaeologists have found the remains of a water garden, complete with fountains and colonnades. The finest mosaic floor, a swirling composition of seahorses, scallop shells and urns around a boy riding on a dolphin, was laid in the mid second century. The owner at this time had obviously had enough of the English climate, as he put in the regulation hypocaust and flues for central heating.

At the end of the third century the palace burnt down, perhaps accidentally or perhaps in one of the pirate raids on the coast which were becoming steadily more frequent. It became a quarry for other villas and probably for the fortifications of Chichester, and at some period in the Dark Ages its ruins were used as a cemetery. The mosaics show the scars of medieval ploughing, and of the twentieth-century excavator which brought the whole thing to light.

A couple of miles west is **Bosham** (pronounced Bozzum), deservedly one of the beauty spots of the Sussex coast. A Saxon church at its centre, a broad green stretching down to the harbour, harmonious groups of brick and flint houses, a riverscape crammed with boats: no wonder that at Bosham the artists seem to outnumber the ordinary sightseers. Bosham's greatest days were in the early

379

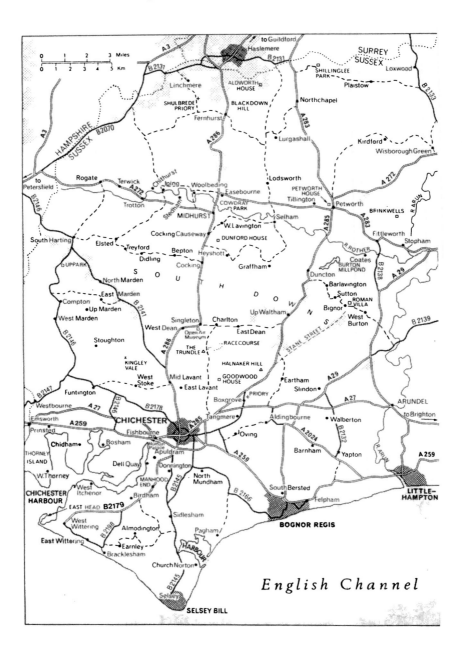

eleventh century, in the decades before the Norman Conquest. Canute had a palace there, and it was at Bosham that he rebuked his courtiers when they asked him to hold back the tide (though Southampton also claims to be the site of this story).

It was from Bosham that Harold set out in 1064 on the visit to Normandy which led to his falling into the power of William the Bastard (later the Conqueror) and precipitated the Norman Conquest. Quay Meadow, the green from which Harold embarked, now belongs to the National Trust. An early scene in the Bayeux Tapestry shows Harold, with Kitchener moustache, and hawk on wrist, riding to **Bosham Church** before his voyage. In this scene the main feature of the church is the splendid Saxon arch, which still stands at the entrance to the chancel, and rises from Roman column bases which may be from a basilica on the site. Roman tiles and bricks are built into the walls. At the foot of the arch is a tombstone to a child believed to be Canute's daughter, who died about 1020; nearly nine hundred years later, in 1906, the children of Bosham placed the stone there. About one-third of the chancel is Saxon work, as is the tower, built about 1000 as a watch-tower and defence against the Danes. It now has a sturdy shingle broach spire on top of it, a landmark in every direction. If you walk round the outside of the tower, you will be hard put to it to find a single right-angle in the wall plan.

At low tide the road below the harbour wall is uncovered, and can be followed right along. South of the inlet, the road is uncovered at all states of the tide and gives a quiet riverscape of estuary, church and waterside houses.

Bosham stands on the easternmost of the three large peninsulas that jut into Chichester Harbour, stretching from Chichester Channel to Emsworth Channel, where Sussex merges into Hampshire across the swampy shallows. This is a coast of deep-cut creeks and mudflats, where on a fine summer afternoon the sailing dinghies cover the water like flocks of sea birds, and where new marinas and moorings spring up almost overnight.

Chidham, on the central peninsula, is a remote and scattered village, the kind of place nobody goes to, because no road runs through it. **Thorney Island** is separated from the mainland by the Great Deep, and before the road was built in 1870 was reached by a 'wadeway', which was completely uncovered only at exceptionally low water, and where local inhabitants often drowned. The road comes to a dead end at **West Thorney**, in a slipway leading down to

Thorney Channel. Perched up above the channel is St Nicholas' Church, a simple flint building, with tiled roof and stumpy spire.

Westbourne, a mile north of the A27, is so nearly in Hampshire that it makes no difference: the River Ems, marking the county boundary, trickles by on the far side of the churchyard. The wide main street, opening by the church into a central space filled with a triangle of buildings, is a good village harmony of Georgian brickwork, thatched roofs and pink-washed walls. The battlemented church tower with its tall, dark-shingled spire, is a landmark across the fields. The tower is late Perpendicular, built early in the sixteenth century. At the same time the arcades were rebuilt in flat-arched Perpendicular style, giving the whole interior an open, simple effect. A splendid avenue of tall yews, planted about 1545, leads to the north door of the church.

South of Fishbourne, the deep inlet of Chichester Channel isolates the Selsey peninsula. In E. V. Lucas's day you could take a tram from Chichester out to Selsey; but a whole fleet of trams could hardly carry today's holidaymakers. **Apuldram** or **Appledram** derives its name from the Old English *apulder*, apple tree; this is still good orchard country. As at Donnington, the church lies by itself down a long path. Inside is a carved fifteenth-century oak screen in the south aisle; and the little organ, described in the church guide as 'of very sweet tone', was originally the Prince Consort's private organ at Windsor Castle, coming to this remote spot after some time in the church at Littlehampton. Near Apuldram is **Dell Quay**, a yachting centre and the port of Chichester before the canal was built.

About a mile south of Apuldram the road passes a spot marked 'Manhood End' on the Ordnance Survey map, but not in evidence on the ground. The name is a corruption of Mainwood, the vast forest which once stretched southwards from the downs to the sea, and came to be known simply as 'the Manhood'. This was an important area in English history, as it was on the coast near West Wittering that Aella landed with his Saxon followers in 477, and established the kingdom of the South Saxons that was to become Sussex.

Two centuries later, in 665, St Wilfrid was wrecked on this coast, met with a hostile reception and was lucky to escape with his life. In 681 he returned south after being expelled from his northern bishopric. The Saxons were starving after three years without rain (it seems rather hard to believe while the rain lashes down on Selsey Bill), and were so desperate that many of them were drowning themselves in the sea. The Saxon king Ethelwald agreed to be baptized by Wilfrid; and as soon as this was done the heavens opened and the famine was at an end. Wilfrid was granted lands in 'Selesea' (the island of the sea-calf or seal), and built a monastery near Church Norton. He is also credited with teaching the people of Selsey how to fish, as an alternative to drought-ridden agriculture.

Birdham lies off the main road a mile beyond the serried ranks of masts in the Chichester Yacht Basin. The churchyard contains a gigantic conifer, gnarled and contorted like the most extravagant tree in a Japanese print. **West Itchenor,** another yachting village, lies down a dead end on the way to West Wittering; the road ends with a row of cottages. a yacht club and a shingle foreshore. The little thirteenth-century church stands about half a mile up the hill from the harbour. Its most notable external feature is a great flint arch supporting the bell turret, added in the nineteenth century.

West Wittering village lies well back from the beach and the sea resort. The walls are mainly flint and rounded stones from the beach, typical of the whole of this stretch of coast. The church is a fine jumble, consisting of a twelfth-century core, with thirteenth-century chancel, and a tower with louvred belfry tacked on the north side. Inside there are many treasures. The tub-shaped font is probably Saxon; and there is a stone carved with a Saxon cross on each side on the wall in a glass case. This may have been the original gable cross of about AD 740, from the earliest days of Christianity here, thrown down when the Danes harried this coast about 1000, and then set up again with a new cross on the other side in the more settled times of Canute (1016–35).

West Wittering resort is a private estate, with the usual row of seaside houses built behind the shingle bank. It has a magnificent area of sand at low tide. The sickle-shaped **East Head** (on the east of the entrance to Chichester harbour, though the westernmost point of the Selsey peninsula), belongs to the National Trust, who have done a lot of planting of marram grass to stop these acres of dunes and saltings from being washed away by the sea. There is also danger from sheer weight of footwear, as on summer weekends East Head is crowded with people sunning themselves. The strait between East Head and Hayling Island is dangerous for swimmers.

As a resort, **East Wittering** is larger than West Wittering, with caravans, bungalows and a holiday camp. It merges into Bracklesham, which gives its name to the geologist's 'Bracklesham beds', rich in fossils which can still be found on the shore. There is no road along Bracklesham Bay to Selsey, though by zigzagging inland through hamlets like Earnley (with a midget church on a triangular green) and Almodington you can stay fairly close to the coast and join the Selsey road at **Sidlesham**. Sidlesham has a nucleus of picture-postcard thatched houses, and a harbour a mile south of the village, on a creek of Pagham Harbour.

Of all the lonely spots on this coast **Church Norton**, at the end of the road on the south side of Pagham Harbour, is among the loneliest. An avenue of great trees ends abruptly at a little chapel in a graveyard, with mudflats. Just over the wall, on the right, a path leads down beside a ditch and mound covered in undergrowth to the seabird-haunted saltings of the Pagham Harbour nature reserve. The chapel (St Wilfrid's) was formerly the chancel of Selsey church. The rest of the building was transported bodily two miles down the road in 1865 to a new site as the parish church of the growing village of Selsey. Old Selsey lies under the sea off Church Norton; there is a legend that the bells of Selsey Cathedral can still be heard pealing under the waters on stormy nights. On the north wall of the chapel is a quaint little Tudor monument to John Lewis and his wife, kneeling to face each other. He wears armoured gauntlets like enormous mittens; she might have been the model for Tenniel's Ugly Duchess.

Selsey consists of a busy main street running down to the foreshore, with roads of seaside housing to left and right. Though the raw materials of its transported church are so old, the Victorians managed to make it look very Victorian, with its enormous tiled roof and slit windows. Vast sea walls have been built to absorb the pounding force of the sea, and there is no seafront to drive along. In January 1998 Selsey fell victim to a freak tornado, which tore through the town at 100 mph and damaged more than a thousand buildings. **Selsey Bill** itself is not obvious, but is marked by Bill House – a large holiday home with a coastguard lookout perched in its weird green-tiled tower. Among the many ships that have foundered off Selsey Bill is the Navy's first submarine, called simply HMS *A1*. Launched in 1902, she must be the only submarine to have sunk twice – first in 1904, when she collided with another vessel and went down, drowning her crew, and secondly in 1911, when she sank for good off the Bill, luckily when no one was on board.

From Church Norton to Pagham, on the far side of **Pagham Harbour**, is hardly more than a mile as the seagull flies; but it is a good ten miles by road, involving a detour almost back to Chichester. It is now a harbour only in name, though you can still see sailing dinghies nosing through its channels. But in the Middle Ages Pagham was prosperous; and certainly the big church implies a much larger population than the few houses that make up the place today. By the nineteenth century the harbour had become choked, and the land was reclaimed for agriculture in 1870: but in 1910 a great storm broke the retaining wall and turned the harbour into its present combination of nature reserve and yachting basin.

You can get down to the harbour along the old metalled road which starts from the church. It is a breezy walk right along the harbour wall, with creeks towards the sea, and inland the wind shaking the tall grasses. The Sussex River Authority runs a complex system of sluices here to keep the land well drained. A notice warns the unwary of the dangers of being cut off by a fast-rising tide, even when large areas of the mudflats are still uncovered by water; in this lonely spot there would be little chance of rescue. Pagham church is dedicated to St Thomas Becket, and was probably built within a few decades of his murder in 1170. In the west wall is an unusual rose window, with glowing dark blue glass surrounding the royal arms; it commemorates the recovery of King George V in 1928 after a long illness at Craigweil House, two miles west of Bognor (the recovery that gained Bognor the title 'Regis').

Seaside Pagham consists of featureless acres of bungalows new and not-so-new – the western end of a continuous belt of housing from Pagham to Bognor, culminating in the gentility of the Aldwick Bay Estate, with its fantasies of bulging roof-tiles, sculpted thatch and bogus half-timbering (all roads strictly private).

Bognor Regis is a friendly jumble of a resort, making a virtue of the compactness of its seafront (only a mile and a half long), and with none of the urban grandeur of the terraces at places like Hove; Queen Victoria called it, rather patronisingly perhaps, her 'dear little Bognor'. Its biggest piece of development is Waterloo Square, where nineteenth-century seaside houses decked out with wrought-iron canopies rub shoulders with new houses and shops. A little farther west is the impressive white stucco of the Royal Norfolk Hotel, with gilded arms on the pediment.

Bognor owes its beginnings as a resort to Sir Richard Hotham, a wealthy London hatter who bought up 1,600 acres in the area at the end of the eighteenth century, intending to rival Bath with a resort called 'Hothampton'. Dome House, now a teachers' training college, was built in the hope that either George III or the Prince Regent would come there; but Hotham had to be content with Princess

Charlotte, the youngest daughter of the king, who came to Bognor to regain her health. Though Hotham left at his death only £8,000 out of a vast fortune, Dome House and the green spaces of Hotham Park are no bad memorial.

Like nearly all the South Coast resorts, Bognor developed from an inland village – in this case **South Bersted**, which still has a tall-spired medieval church, much Victorianised, and the occasional thatched cottage. Much of old Bognor lies under the sea. Throughout the nineteenth century storms washed away the coast, in the days before sea walls; and somewhere under the sands lie houses and a barracks used during the Napoleonic wars. At the eastern end of the seafront, the large and once-forbidding Butlin's holiday camp has received a major facelift and the new title of 'South Coast World'.

Next door to Bognor is **Felpham**, a village swallowed up in holiday housing. Felpham's chief claim to fame is the fact that William Blake lived there from 1800 to 1803; his white-walled thatched cottage is in Blake's Road. Blake came down to Felpham to do some engraving for William Hayley (1745–1820), one of the prize bores of the period, who lived in a large house in the village. Though Hayley's patronising attitude eventually turned Blake's admiration to near-pathological hatred, at the beginning he was delighted with the change from the 'desart' of London and with Felpham's 'sweet air & the voices of winds, trees & birds, & the odours of the happy ground'. He even saw a fairy's funeral in his garden – 'a procession of creatures, of the size and colour of green and grey grasshoppers, bearing a body laid out on a rose-leaf, which they buried with songs, and then disappeared'. Inside the rather dark church, up the road from Blake's cottage, is a tablet on the north wall of the chancel to Hayley, commemorating his liberality to artists.

Climping (or Clymping), four miles along the road to Littlehampton, is best known for its sandy beach, reached down a pretty country lane. The church is north of the main road, next door to the wire of Ford prison. An old saying refers to 'Bosham for antiquity, Boxgrove for beauty, and Clymping for perfection'; the main part of the church is a single unaltered Early English design, with lancet windows complete in nave, transepts and chancel. It was almost certainly built by John de Clymping, who was vicar of the church from 1220 until he became Bishop of Chichester in 1253. The tower, linked to the church by the south transept but virtually separate from it, is a fortress-like structure built about 1170; its main

386

door is richly carved with Norman ornament. On the floor of the north transept is a thirteenth-century chest, reputedly for offerings to help Crusaders get to the Holy Land.

As its name suggests, **Ford** was originally a crossing-point of the Arun. Now it is taken up by the buildings of Ford airfield (a Battle of Britain centre) converted to prison use, and a Continental-looking campsite beside the river. The little church (usually locked) is isolated in the middle of a field. Mainly Saxon and Norman, it stands forlorn among the trees, while the paint of its white bellcote peels and the medieval murals inside fade slowly into indecipherability.

Heading back towards Chichester, **Yapton** seems to be embedded in glasshouses. The twelfth-century church has a squat tower that leans at an alarming angle, an ancient wood-framed porch, and crudely rustic carvings on the arcade capitals. The modern sprawl of **Barnham** hardly looks like a fishing village, yet in the Middle Ages Barnham stood on a tidal creek, centring on the simple little Early English church which looks across the fields at the end of a side road. In more recent times the short-lived Arundel–Chichester canal ran just below the church; opened in 1820, it was made obsolete by the railway, and went out of use about 1880. **Walberton** is a cosily enclosed place; the dark church, down a side road, is on a Saxon site and still has a Saxon tub-shaped font. The north porch, built in the thirteenth century, is unusually large, with three trefoil-headed windows on each side.

Boxgrove, just north of the A27, is a nice village in its own right; but it is completely eclipsed by the magnificent priory church, which looks across open country on the east side of the village street. **Boxgrove Priory** was founded within a few decades of the Conquest, about 1117, and what remains of the church is a superb compendium of architectural styles, culminating in the lucid precision of the Early English choir. The church has a double dedication, to St Mary, and to St Blaise, the patron saint of the wool trade. Blaise was Bishop of Cappadocia in Asia Minor, about AD 300; during the persecutions under the emperor Diocletian he was tortured by being scraped with wool-combs, and was finally beheaded.

The church looks impressive enough at first glance, but what is left gives a slightly unbalanced effect, as practically the whole of the nave has disappeared. This was the end built for the parishioners; the monastic half survives. Inside the church some idea of the original appearance can be got from the Norman transepts, though they have been split horizontally by sweeping wooden galleries added in the fifteenth century. Only the extreme eastern end of the nave is still standing; this was built a little later in the twelfth century, in the Transitional style incorporating the pointed arch.

All this earlier work is hardly more than a background to the astonishing choir, built about 1210. The arcade, with each pair of pointed arches coupled by a wide semicircle of stone, the vaulting, organised into double bays, and the tall lancet windows have a consistency and exactitude utterly different to the stocky Norman and Transitional work. The arcade piers show an almost experimental attitude to variety. At the west end they start with thin and thick octagonal stone; then, like an organist changing registration, comes a round pair in Purbeck marble, followed at the east end by pairs which combine a stone centre with marble outer shafts. The vaulting was painted in the sixteenth century with a design of stylised fruit and foliage, by Lambert Barnard (see Chichester Cathedral, above). All this is matched in miniature by the De La Warr chantry, in the southern arcade – a fanciful Tudor chapel, painted and gilded, supported on columns alive with human figures, birds, flowers and grotesques.

In 1993 a gravel pit at Boxgrove was the scene of one of the most spectacular archaeological discoveries of recent years, when animal remains and flint tools were found dating back half a million years to the Palaeolithic (Old Stone) Age. Among the bones was a human shinbone – the oldest human remains yet found in Britain – thought to be that of a powerfully built man almost six feet tall. Marks of a wolf's teeth were found on the bone; perhaps 'Boxgrove Man', as he was immediately christened, had been killed by wolves, or he had died of natural causes and the bone had been gnawed subsequently. Two years later a tooth was found at the site, even older than the shinbone. Its owner must have suffered from toothache, as it was affected by tartar and had root damage.

On the top of **Halnaker** (pronounced Hannacker) **Hill,** a couple of miles north of Boxgrove above the A285 to Petworth, is Halnaker Mill, celebrated by Hilaire Belloc in one of his most famous poems. An eighteenth-century tower mill with white cap and sails, it is a tremendous landmark from the flat lands to the south.

South of Boxgrove, **Tangmere** has an Early English church down a side turning, with a shingled belfry carried on a massive timber framework inside the nave. But it is better known for modern heroism than medieval piety, since during the Second World War

RAF Tangmere was a front-line fighter airfield in the Battle of Britain, and later was the base from which SOE agents set out on their dangerous missions into occupied France. It was closed down in 1970; but its great days are recalled in the **Military Aviation Museum**, which has hangars with old fighter aircraft and a flight simulator for children who want to get a feeling for the air.

Oving's big cruciform church, with its set of Early English lancet windows virtually complete, looms up across the fields. Behind it is a mushroom-growing establishment. **Aldingbourne** is one of the largest and oldest parishes in England, first appearing in the records at the end of the seventh century, when a monastery was established there. The village sprawls round an enormous field; the church was greatly restored in the 1860s, though a Norman door and twelfth-century arcading survives. An ancient photograph in the porch shows a pretty interior before restoration, all box pews, and beams painted with biblical texts.

24

The Western Approaches

THE NORTH-WEST CORNER of Sussex, bordered by Hampshire and Surrey, has something of the flavour of both these two counties. On one side is the broad spaciousness of the downs, opening out into the uplands that spread beyond Winchester to Salisbury Plain; and on the other is the heavily wooded cosiness of the hills and combes south of Haslemere. Between woodland and downland is the broad valley of the Rother, dawdling gently along until it meets the Arun near Pulborough, and lined by little villages on roads that lead to nowhere, each with its vintage medieval bridge. The vast parks of Cowdray, Petworth and Goodwood give the final touch of romantic feudalism to a stretch of countryside as unspoilt as any within fifty miles of London.

Petworth is a main-road junction, but is quite unfitted to be one. It still has all the elements of feudalism about it – the old town, the great house, and the high wall dividing the two, especially noticeable if you come in from the north. But Petworth House is not aloof. Its outbuildings open right on to the street, and its upper windows overlook the town, which must sometimes have given the townsmen the uncomfortable feeling that the Percys or Egremonts knew everything that was going on. Daniel Defoe put it in a nutshell: 'the house', he wrote, 'stands as it were with its elbows to the town'.

The town is compact and small-scale. At its centre is the market place, with a stone town hall built by the third Earl of Egremont at the end of the eighteenth century. Lombard Street is the prettiest bit of the town, gently curved and gently sloping as old streets should be; while the finest individual buildings are in East Street, notably the stylish Georgian of Daintrey House and other town houses nearby.

The church is a most peculiar building. Its brick tower with shallow pyramid cap is quite a landmark as you approach the town from the south and east; but it used to be even more prominent, as it had a tall spire built by Sir Charles Barry in 1827, which was condemned as unsafe in 1947 and demolished. Inside, virtually all that is left of the fourteenth-century church are the arches on the north side of the nave. It is a big, untidy place, with no kind of unity. At the back of the north aisle is a seated figure of the third Earl of Egremont, by Edward Hodges Baily, sculptor of the statue on top of Nelson's Column; and in the baptistry below the tower a communal monument to all the Percy family, in the form of a draped figure carrying a cross, put up by the Earl to his dead ancestors in 1837, the year of his own death.

The Percy connection with Petworth goes back to the twelfth century. The first Percy, William, came over with the Conqueror, married the daughter of the Saxon Earl of Northumberland, and founded the Northumberland dynasty. Petworth had been bequeathed by Henry I to his widow, Queen Adeliza, and she in turn gave it to her brother Joscelyn on his marriage to Lady Agnes, the Percy heiress; it must have made a welcome southern addition to the dour fastnesses in the north. The chapel and wine cellar survive of the Percys' medieval manor house, as does a spiral staircase and stone window tracery, discovered by workmen in 1998. This was the home of the eleven Earls of Northumberland, from the end of the fourteenth century until the direct line died out in 1670. Shakespeare's Harry Hotspur was typical of this hard-living family, many of whom came to a violent end in battle, by execution or plain murder.

But such things seem far away from the huge bland front of **Petworth House** (National Trust), sprawling comfortably at the edge of magnificent parkland. The house was the first product of a new age at Petworth. The eleventh Earl was succeeded by his daughter, Elizabeth, who in 1682 married Charles Seymour, the sixth Duke of Somerset; and between 1688 and 1696 the Percy fortune was applied to the rebuilding of Petworth.

To see the house as a whole, you should go into the park and look back at it from down by the lake. This, the west front, is the true aspect of Petworth – a simple enough three-storeyed building, over a hundred yards long and only two rooms wide, looking more like a French château than an English country house (various architects, both French and English, have been suggested), with close-cropped turf stretching uninterrupted to the foot of the walls. Its restraint used to be taken for dullness, or worse; indeed, Murray's 1893 *Handbook* likened it to 'a strip from an indifferent London terrace'. There is a complete and harmonious integration between house and park, well brought out by Turner in his Petworth paintings.

The endless rooms opening one into the other make Petworth an ideal art gallery, which is largely its present function. (The best days to go there are on weekdays, April-October, when extra rooms are shown.) The Oak Hall was redecorated in 1997 and lined with blue-and-white wallpaper, returning it to its nineteenth-century appearance.

At the centre of the west front is the wide, cool Marble Hall, overlooking the park. This room was the scene of one of Petworth's few forays into history, when in 1814 Egremont received the Prince Regent, the Tsar of Russia and other sovereigns of the anti-Napoleonic alliance. A painting in the North Gallery shows the rulers and their attendants entering from the park. South of the Marble Hall is the Beauty Room, so called because of the identical-looking vapid ladies of Queen Anne's court whose portraits hang round the walls; Anne herself is over the fireplace. The Grand Staircase opening off the Beauty Room is an unexpected piece of Baroque exuberance after so much staidness. Painted from top to bottom with murals by Louis Laguerre, it shows the triumph of the Duchess of Somerset and her family (after all, she had supplied the money for building Petworth), below a riot of Olympian gods and goddesses on the ceiling.

South of the Beauty Room is the White and Gold Room, a fanciful mid-eighteenth-century interior, and beyond it the White Library lined with the book collection started by Henry Percy, the ninth Earl of Northumberland. Nicknamed the 'Wizard Earl' for his interest in science and alchemy, he was suspected of involvement in the Gunpowder Plot and was imprisoned in the Tower for sixteen years. In 1621 he was released on payment of the then-enormous sum of £11,000. This room contains one of the Petworth Turners, and a portrait of the Duke of Somerset, the builder of the house. He had such an overweening sense of his own importance and that of his family that he was known as the 'Proud Duke'. On one occasion, after a quarrel with George I, he threw his royal liveries into a dustcart and told his servants to deposit the 'rubbish' in front of St James's Palace. (Both these rooms are open on Mondays only.)

One of Somerset's inspirations was to commission Grinling Gibbons to decorate the Carved Room, the largest state room at Petworth. This room has its own splendid paintings, notably a formidable portrait of Henry VIII over the fireplace; but they are all driven into the shade by the virtuosity of the limewood carvings of fruit and flowers, dead game, trophies of war and musical instruments that cascade down the walls. With the Red Room we are in the golden age of Petworth as a centre of art patronage, under the long and benevolent sway of the third Earl of Egremont, who from about 1770 until his death in 1837 set the existing collections in order and greatly added to them. The T-shaped North Gallery is his creation. Crammed with statues and lined with pictures by Turner, Gainsborough, Reynolds and their contemporaries, it is an amazing medley of the antique and the up-to-date, in terms of the taste of the day.

There are plenty of portraits of the third Earl at Petworth, beakily distinguished, like a kindly Duke of Wellington. He let the title die out by default, only marrying 'Mrs Wyndham' after six children had been born. Turner was the perfect choice to paint Petworth and its park. He delighted in the sunset slanting across the grass and outlining the trees and deer in a hazy glow, and in the calm reflections of the lake. More prosaically, he liked to fish there, and also got on extremely well with old Lord Egremont, an eccentric like himself, who told him 'I want a picture when you have time, but remember, none of your damned nonsense'.

From the gallery you go past the Percy chapel, redecorated by Somerset and oddly theatrical with its dark woodwork and its heraldic painting in the blocked thirteenth-century windows. Visitors to Petworth can experience life below stairs in the Servants' Quarters, which include the old kitchens.

The park painted by Turner was badly damaged in the hurricane of October 1987, but a vast replanting programme has now put it well on the road to recovery.

Tillington is very much outside the walls of Petworth Park. Besides the houses on the main road, there is a second peaceful village street running parallel at a higher level. Tillington's landmark is its unusual church tower topped by stone pinnacles and a 'crown' that looks like the bottom stage of the Eiffel Tower. It was built in 1810, and has been attributed without much conviction to Turner.

The main road north from Petworth runs for miles beside the park; in fact, there is no road to the west before the lane that leads to **Lurgashall** five miles to the north. The centre of Lurgashall is the broad green, rather than the houses that are scattered round it. The church, tucked away in a corner, is largely Norman and Early English, though hardly recognisable as such. West of the tower, where you would expect an aisle, is a wooden lean-to porch or narthex, which has been variously explained as a shelter for travellers coming to the service from a long distance, as a meeting place, and as a school.

A couple of miles to the north is the nearest approach to a mountain in these parts – **Blackdown**, over nine hundred feet high and shaggily coated in trees like one of the foothills of the Jura. The National Trust owns a large area of woodland on the southern slopes. Tennyson spent the last two decades of his life up here, in **Aldworth House**, which he built in 1869. The house (not on view) is unpretentious, the only unusual thing about it being the quantity of little stone carvings that decorate it; but the view from the garden terrace is breathtaking, across miles of rolling countryside towards the sea. The poet's bust gazes reflectively at the garden, where he wrote much of the *Idylls of the King* and his later poems.

East of the main road to Petworth, **Kirdford** is a large open village. Its tree-shaded street leads down to the powerful church, which consists of Norman nave, thirteenth-century north aisle, and fifteenth-century west tower and chancel. For centuries Kirdford was a centre of industry – glassmaking from 1300 to 1600 and ironworking from 1550 to 1650 – which may account for the prosperity of the church, The village sign incorporates diamonds of locally made glass. A painted sign entitled 'Degradation of Drunkenness', set into the old vicarage wall, reminds us that drunkenness 'is the shame of nature, the extinguisher of reason, the shipwreck of chastity, and the murderer of conscience'.

Wisborough Green, a couple of miles to the east on the A272, is a perfect Sussex village, built round a smooth rectangle of grass surrounded by chestnut trees. The tall-spired church, standing a little to one side of the main village, is an architectural problem. Before the Early English chancel was added in the thirteenth century, it was a simple Norman rectangle. But why were the walls at the west end four and a half feet thick, and why were the north and south doors built thirteen feet high – tall enough to admit a mounted man? The suggestion has been made that it was originally a keep, later enlarged into a church; though Nairn thinks it was an Anglo-Saxon nave-tower, with vaulting over. The rough-hewn stone altar may be pre-Norman, perhaps a pagan sacrificial stone. In the Middle Ages the church was a centre of pilgrimage, as it had numerous relics including a crucifix incorporating a drop of the Virgin's milk set in crystal.

Half a mile west of Wisborough Green a narrow road branches off the A272 to Fittleworth. In the middle of the woodlands here is **Brinkwells**, the thatched cottage where Edward Elgar lived for a few years from 1917, writing his cello concerto and other major works. He returned there for the last time in 1921, and heralded the end of his creative life in a letter to a friend: 'I feel like these woods – all aglow – a spark wd. start a flame – but no human spark comes.' **Fittleworth** is a pretty little place, built round a central tree-covered triangle. The church, by itself on a knoll, was well and truly filleted by the Victorians, who rebuilt everything between the Early English tower and chancel. Its clock has a most musical chime.

Church, manor house and a handful of cottages make up **Stopham**, a few hundred yards off the A283 towards Pulborough. The church has a wide low tower, a Norman south doorway so rough that it could well be Saxon, and a Norman chancel arch. Stopham bridge, across the Arun, has been called by Nairn 'easily the best of the medieval bridges in Sussex'. It is incredible to think that a bridge built in 1423 can still carry modern traffic.

South of Fittleworth you cross the Rother and come again to the villages below the South Downs. **Coates**, immediately above the river, consists of a few large stone farmhouses and a tiny Norman church, with a vast cedar in a corner of the churchyard. Behind Coates is magnificent wood and heathland. Near by is the reed-lined sweep of Burton millpond, with a millrace of ten steps cascading down on the opposite side of the road. Part of the woods is a nature reserve.

The downland villages proper begin at **West Burton**, an up-and-down, buried kind of place, on the other side of the A29 from Bury. A mile or so away is **Bignor Roman Villa**, discovered when a mosaic pavement was ploughed up in 1811, and a tourist draw ever since. Bignor's thatched protecting huts were first built about 1814. The villa was built towards the end of the second century AD, on a site with splendid open views of the downs, and close to Stane Street. The first house was a modest timber-framed affair, and was not extended to the present enormous courtyard structure until early in the fourth century.

As the administrative centre of an estate of about two thousand acres, Bignor was the home of an important magnate – possibly a Romano-British wool merchant – who decorated his villa with some of the finest mosaics surviving in Britain. These display all the variety of the mosaicist's invention, from simple geometrical designs to Ganymede carried off by the eagle, a head of Venus flanked by pheasants and surrounded by a complex decorated frame, and a frieze of cupids in gladiatorial combat – a typically Roman combination of the whimsical and the sadistic. Best of all is the grave-faced head of Winter, wearing a hooded cloak of British type against the biting downland winds. The racy subjects of some of the mosaics have led some scholars to speculate that the villa was a high-class brothel. Its end was not violent: it was abandoned probably in the fifth century, and mouldered gently into the ground.

Bignor itself is a pretty village, with one unbelievably picturesque timber-framed house fronting the road, and an Early English church with a tiled roof sweeping low over narrow aisles. Inside there is a Norman chancel arch. A very steep narrow lane south of the village leads up to a National Trust car-park high on the downs. From here you can walk along one of the finest sections of the Roman Stane Street, striding south-west down to Chichester.

From Bignor a narrow lane zigzags westwards through the hamlets of Sutton and Barlavington to the main Chichester road, which makes a sharp bend to avoid sending the traffic between the tall flint-and-stone chequered gate piers at the entrance to Seaford College. **Duncton**, towards Petworth, is a nice enough village, with a blatant Victorian church on the hillside above. It is worth going down the drive of St Michael's girls' school to glance at the overbearing classical front of Burton Park, now the main building of the school, and look into the small church beside it. The little building hardly seems to have been touched for centuries; the timber rood beam still shows traces of red paint, and on the wall are painted the royal arms of Charles I, dated 1636 – the only pre-1660 example I have seen in the two counties.

Graffham, three miles west of Duncton, has a sign stating that it is the best-kept village in West Sussex. This is hardly surprising, as its sinuous main street, lined with typical downland flint and brick houses, obviously has affection lavished on it. Beyond the Victorianised flint church the road fades away into a hill track; and above are the steep slopes of the downs, covered in trees rising wave on wave to the skyline. **Selham**, a couple of miles to the north, is a leafy hamlet, with a tiny church looking like a Welsh chapel which is in fact Saxon. Inside is a surprise for such an unimposing building – a capital on the chancel arch carved with serpents devouring their own tails, the Scandinavian symbol of eternity, miles from anywhere in the English fields.

Stopham's sturdily rugged medieval bridge across the Arun.

Across the Rother and the A272 is **Lodsworth**, a largish village, whose main street jumbles up the old and the new in a satisfactory way. So does the simple whitewashed church at the edge of the village, which reconciles a Victorian biblical oil painting with a broad new window made of brilliant chunks of stained glass.

Though **Midhurst** is also at the junction of two main roads, it is not torn apart by traffic in the same way as Petworth. It has a feeling of spaciousness, brought about partly by the wide eighteenth-century layout of North Street, and still more by the huge expanse of marshy land between the road and the ruins of Cowdray, whose towered gatehouse forms the backcloth to this end of the town. North Street, with its shops, Georgian façades and elegant Angel Hotel, is the real heart of Midhurst. The original town centre, round the market square and church, is a backwater, though a very attractive one. From North Street the oddly-named Knockhundred Row swings round into Red Lion Street, where half-timbered and Georgian houses draw widely apart round the Swan and the old timbered market house on their island sites. In South Street the Spread Eagle, a huge old coaching inn with a sign that claims the date of 1430, sums up the town in its sprawling combination of two separate parts, brick and half-timbered.

For most visitors, the chief attraction of Midhurst is **Cowdray Park**, a superb place for picnicking, watching polo, or strolling about under the immense oak trees. The A272 runs through the centre of the park, past the polo ground. In the south-west corner of the park, behind the polo ground and looking on to the cricket pitch, are the Cowdray ruins. They are best approached along the causeway from North Street, though you cannot walk straight up to the gatehouse but have to make a detour to one side. The first great house at Midhurst was the medieval castle of the de Bohuns, built on St Ann's Hill behind the Market Square. About 1300 the de Bohuns left their hilltop and moved to a level site by the river – a *coudrier* or hazel coppice, from which the name Cowdray derived. From the de Bohuns this medieval Cowdray passed by marriage to Sir David Owen, natural son of Owen Glendower, in the 1490s; and from then until his death in 1535 Sir David set about building a grand courtyard house in the high Tudor tradition.

Owing to money difficulties, Owen had already sold Cowdray to Sir William Fitzwilliam in 1529. A leading figure at Henry VIII's court, Fitzwilliam was Lord Keeper of the Privy Seal and Lord High Admiral, and was created the first Earl of Southampton. He was largely responsible for the completion of Cowdray, and the finishing touches were added by his half-brother Sir Anthony Browne, who elsewhere brought down on himself the curse that his line would end by fire and water (see Battle, p. 251). In 1554 Sir Anthony's son was made the first Viscount Montague, and the Montagues succeeded one another at Cowdray until in 1793 the young eighth Viscount drowned while trying to shoot the Laufenburg Falls on the Rhine. The same year Cowdray caught fire and was reduced to the ruin we see today.

The most impressive of the remains is the tall gatehouse, which still stands to its full height, flanked by the burnt-out shell of much of the western range of buildings. The north and south sides of the great quadrangle are now marked only by foundations; but enough is left of the eastern side, where Cowdray's state apartments were, to give an idea of the splendour that has vanished. The lofty stone mullions that lit the hall and parlour are blackened by smoke, and the roofs, floors, ceilings and panelling have gone.

You go in through a low porch, where the fan-vaulting survives. The hall beyond towered the full height of the building, up to an elaborate hammerbeam roof; it was known as Buck Hall, from eleven life-sized wooden figures of buck placed on brackets round the room. Behind is the chapel, almost as large as the hall, with scraps of seventeenth-century plasterwork still clinging to the walls and the remains of a lofty altarpiece. It was here, early in the eighteenth century, that the fifth Viscount shot the family priest (the Montagues were Catholic) for beginning mass without him. After this crime he is said to have hidden away in a secret chamber, coming out at night to roam round the park, and inevitably being taken for a ghost. The hexagonal kitchen at the south-east corner was not harmed by the fire and has survived almost intact. Everything is still in place, from the great butcher's block by one of the Tudor chimneys to the iron hotplates, hardly changed since Edward VI came to Cowdray in 1552 and was 'marvelously, yea rather excessively, banketted'.

Easebourne, which links Midhurst with Cowdray Park, has some superb half-timbered houses, and a much-restored parish church which was the priory church of a thirteenth-century Augustinian convent. **West Lavington**, Midhurst's southern suburb, is a strung-out tree-filled place, with a Victorian church in a churchyard engulfed by enormous conifers. Beside the path is a large granite slab to Richard Cobden (1804–65), the Victorian politician and prophet of Free Trade, who lived near by at **Dunford House** (can occasionally be seen by prior arrangement). This pink-washed building, buried away at the end of a long drive, is now owned and run by the YMCA as a conference centre. Cobden built the house round the small Sussex farmhouse where he was born; inside you can see an anteroom with a large bust of Cobden, and his own library, full of nineteenth-century copies of *Hansard*, signed photographs of Garibaldi, and vast tomes on the Great Exhibition of 1851, of which Cobden was a chief instigator. His principles are stated bluntly on a sandstone obelisk on the hillside: 'Free Trade, Peace, Goodwill among Nations'.

Cocking village, a mile down the Chichester road, has a tiny pebbledashed church below the downs; on the splay of a Norman window is a wall painting of a red-robed shepherd from a vanished Nativity scene. **Heyshott** near by was Cobden's village; it is a flat, spread-out place, not hemmed in by the downs but keeping them clearly in view. The village hall proclaims itself the 'Cobden Club Hall', and there is a tablet in the church commemorating Cobden, put up by his daughter Jane.

Back to Midhurst again, and heading north along the main road to Haslemere (A286), you come to **Fernhurst**, the only sizeable village in an area of woodland hamlets, and a comfortable, unassuming kind of place. Half a mile to the south is **Verdley House**, a large Victorian mansion now divided into residential units. Until recently, it was the headquarters of ICI's (now Zeneca's) international agrochemicals business. Built in the 1870s to designs by Anthony Salvin, who lived in Fernhurst, it is a fascinatingly varied house, part stone-built, part tilehung, and with a steep pyramidal spire as its centrepiece. Nearby are Zeneca's up-to-date offices and conference centre; surrounded by lawns shaved to a scientific precision of jewelled uniformity, they add a flavour of unobtrusive commercialism to the lush countryside.

Along a lane two miles west of Fernhurst is **Shulbrede Priory**, like Michelham an Augustinian priory founded about 1190, but much less of a showplace, and altogether on a smaller scale (visits by special arrangement; also open to the public on some Bank Holiday weekends). The church, which stood on the north side of the cloister, has vanished; what remains is a vaulted parlour and buttery downstairs, and the prior's chamber upstairs.

At the Dissolution the Priory became a farmhouse, and the chamber was decorated with Tudor murals. One of them is unique in illustrating the medieval legend that on Christmas Day animals herald Christ's Nativity in words that correspond to their calls. The cock crows *'Christus natus est'* (Christ is born); the duck quacks *'Quando, quando?'* (When, When?); the rook caws *'In hac nocte'* (Tonight); the ox bellows *'Ubi ubi?'* (Where, Where?); and the sheep bleats *'In Bethlem'*. A suitable country conceit for this idyllic spot. At Shulbrede there is a small exhibition of memorabilia of the composer Sir Hubert Parry, whose daughter and son-in-law lived there. Parry wrote a suite of piano pieces called *Shulbrede Tunes*, inspired by the house and its surroundings.

North of Shulbrede the road shoots steeply up to **Linchmere**, a scattered farming village, green and open, which stands five hundred feet up at the edge of the Haslemere ridge. Its spindly little church is an odd building, with a narrow eleventh-century nave on the south side and a double north aisle, added in successive stages in the nineteenth and twentieth centuries. On the north wall is a bas-relief of the Seven Deadly Sins, said to be Italian work of about 1300, carved with white marble faces leering and smirking from monks' cowls and niches of grey volcanic rock. The little organ is decorated with seventeenth-century carved wooden cherubs, gilt and playing musical instruments. The village's most famous twentieth-century inhabitant was Richard Dimbleby, the television commentator, who died in 1965 and is buried in the churchyard.

The astonishing thing about **Trotton**, three miles west of Midhurst, is that its medieval bridge over the Rother manages to take the continuous pounding of today's traffic. There is no village to speak of, apart from a few cottages, the church and Trotton Place over the churchyard wall; but the church, built about 1300, is worth looking inside for two of the finest brasses in Sussex and the murals on the west wall. On the nave floor is the brass of Margaret de Camoys, who died about 1310. It shows her in tight-stretched wimple; the shields and lettering have been gouged from the brass by an earlier generation of mutilators. The other brass, far larger and more stylised, spreads across the top of the table tomb in the centre of the chancel. It shows later members of the Camoys family – Thomas, Lord Camoys, who commanded the left wing at Agincourt and died in 1419, and his second wife Elizabeth Mortimer, widow of Sir Henry Percy, 'Harry Hotspur' (see Petworth above). Thomas, in full armour, wears the Garter below his left knee and clasps his wife's right hand in his own. The murals, painted in the late fourteenth century, cover the whole of the west wall. In the middle

Christ in judgment sits above Moses and the Tablets of the Law; on the right the Good Man stands fully clad surrounded by lively medallions of Good Deeds, such as giving drink to the stranger; and on the left is the Evil Man, naked among the Seven Deadly Sins, which include giving far too much drink to himself.

The Restoration dramatist Thomas Otway, born at Trotton in 1652, is commemorated by a tablet on the south wall of the chancel. The taste of Charles II's court ran more to salacious comedy than to Otway's outmoded brand of heroic tragedy, and so he died in poverty in 1685. The story goes that he choked on a roll given to him when he was starving.

Between Midhurst and Trotton, just north of the A272, are four little villages on the Rother, each hardly more than half a mile apart as the crow flies, but far more as the river meanders or the road twists. The road along the north side of the river is in places hardly wider than a cart track. **Woolbeding**'s church has the vertical stone strips of a Saxon exterior jutting from the pebbledashed walls. **Stedham** is the biggest of the four villages, straggling from the common on the main road down to the Rother. The church, a little way above the river, is mainly nineteenth-century. Beside it is a vast yew tree, bound round with hawsers to stop it falling apart. At **Iping** the river widens out into a pond, with weir and derelict mill beside it; the church is dull Victorian, partnered by a noble tiled roof which runs the whole length of the churchyard on the riverside. **Chithurst**, though so near the main road, feels unbelievably remote, lost among the riverside undergrowth. The midget church, eleventh-century with a crude Saxon chancel arch, has hardly been touched since Domesday. It stands on an artificial-looking mound, a few yards away from a stone and timber manor house.

Rogate, the last Sussex village on the A272, is built compactly round a crossroads; a good many of the houses are of the soft-coloured yellowy-brown stone so frequently found hereabouts. The church, with its low shingled belfry and spire, is not particularly interesting from the outside; but inside the arches show the change from Norman to Transitional, as though the masons were evolving their craft as they went along. Below the belfry is a massive medieval timber framework, hidden from outside by the later stonework of the tower and moved bodily westward one bay when the church was enlarged in the nineteenth century. Deer no longer abound round Rogate, though the name is said to derive from the gate into the forest where the roe deer passed through.

Outside Rogate is the tiny Norman church of **Terwick**, known as the 'church in the field', impeccably restored and maintained. One suggestion for the building's remoteness is that it is on the site of an old burial ground, well away from any village for superstitious or hygienic reasons.

Roughly parallel to the A272, and about three miles to the south, a narrow road along the foot of the downs twists and jinks through a string of villages built on the gentle slopes below the steep northern escarpment. **Bepton**'s church, on a mound looking across to the downs, has a massive Norman tower as wide as the main building. In the chancel is a niche of 'Easter sepulchre' type, with flames of stone rising from the triangular canopy; and below it in the floor a tombstone carved with a great sword, and an inscription in Norman French to Rado de la Hedol. He must have been a gigantic warrior, as the stone is seven feet long. The simple Early English church at **Didling** has rough-hewn pews made in the fifteenth century, if not earlier, and is said to be haunted by the ghost of a singing choirboy. At **Elsted** the little church, virtually in a farmyard, has a Saxon nave, a Norman chancel arch, and an Early English chancel.

The westernmost and by far the finest of these villages is **South Harting**, in whose street Belloc left his travelling companions of *The Four Men* and turned back towards his home, 'by the nearest spur, on to the grass and into the loneliness of the high Downs that are my brothers and my repose'. An earlier and greater author lived in Harting: Anthony Trollope, whose paperknife, pen and letter scales are kept in a case in the church, along with local antiquities. Harting's long main street has more redbrick Georgian houses than most of the villages in the neighbourhood. The cruciform church, raised high on a mound above the road, is unusually large; its centrally placed tower is capped by a broach spire of brilliant green copper. Inside, it has a spectacular Elizabethan roof, a complex structure of squared beams and turned uprights, put in after the fourteenth-century church was gutted by fire in 1576; at the same time a strange supporting or 'crutch' arch was added below the chancel arch, giving the whole thing an unfocused look. In the chancel old Sir Harry Fetherstonhaugh of Uppark (see below) is commemorated by a sentimental relief of a grieving woman and a drooping spaniel.

Uppark (National Trust), a mile to the south, is a magnificent house in a magnificent position, on the crest of the downs at the top of a hill so steep that when the house was offered to the Duke of

Wellington after the Napoleonic Wars, he is said to have declined the gift because of the constant replacement of horses that would be needed as the slope wore them out. Uppark stands foursquare like an enormous redbrick dolls' house, overlooking a huge sweep of hills and farmland. Apart from a couple of pylons in the middle distance, the view can hardly have changed since the house was built in the late 1680s.

In 1989 Uppark was gutted by fire, which broke out on an August afternoon. Fortunately it was open at the time, and so a human chain of the staff and visitors managed to save nine-tenths of the ground-floor contents, handed out to them by the Fire Brigade, though the upper floors were totally destroyed. Throughout much of the 1990s the interior was reconstructed to the state it was in 'before the fire'. The National Trust got together a team of woodcarvers, plasterers, gilders and other specialists from all over the country, who meticulously restored every detail from the charred fragments that remained, amplified by photographs, documentary records and personal memories. In 1997 Uppark was re-opened to the public, back to its former glory.

It was built for Forde, Lord Grey of Werke, a dubious intriguer, who was one of the instigators of the Duke of Monmouth's rebellion of 1685. He was a hopeless cavalry commander at the Battle of Sedgemoor and was taken prisoner. Luckier than Monmouth, he was let off with a heavy fine, and retired to the country to build his house in the latest Dutch style, probably to the designs of William Talman. Grey lived down his past so successfully that William III appointed him Lord Privy Seal and created him Earl of Tankerville. Apart from its modernity of appearance, Uppark was a technological novelty as well. The site was only made possible for building by a water pump invented by Lord Tankerville's grandfather, which brought water to the top of the hill from a low-lying spring.

Tankerville provided the external seventeenth-century setting; while Sir Matthew Fetherstonhaugh, who bought Uppark in 1747, turned the interior into a treasurehouse of eighteenth-century taste, cramming it with rare carpets and furniture, and the paintings and *objets d'art* that the wealthy brought back by the boatload from the Grand Tour. He died in 1774, leaving the estate to his twenty-year-old son Sir Harry, who brought wilder times to Uppark. In 1780 he brought the beautiful Emma Hart, then only fifteen, down from London as his mistress. After a year or so he got rid of her, leaving her to future glories as wife of Sir William Hamilton and Nelson's

Doll's-house symmetry: Uppark, high on the Downs above Chichester.

mistress; in later life, when Emma had fallen on hard times, Sir Harry helped her out. For the next quarter of a century he was one of the Prince Regent's closest friends, racing and gambling with him.

When he finally fell out with the prince about 1810 he gave up his social life entirely, coming to life once more to brave the snobbery of West Sussex and marry his head dairymaid Mary Ann when he was over seventy. He died in 1846 aged ninety-two; and Mary Ann, succeeded by her sister Frances, kept Uppark as it had been in Sir Harry's time until 1895, when Frances died. Thus Sir Harry's reign, either in the flesh or from the grave, lasted for over 120 years. A witness of the final period of this immense span was H. G. Wells, whose mother was housekeeper at Uppark, and who spent part of his boyhood there kissing the maids and getting a self-taught education from Uppark's well-stocked bookshelves. The Meade-Fetherstonhaugh family still lives there.

Visitors make a circuit of the ground-floor rooms, beginning at the Dining-Room, whose endlessly reflecting mirrors look down on the long table where Emma danced for Sir Harry and his guests. Through the Stone Hall, the original entrance hall of the house, and the Little Parlour you come to the double-cube Saloon, the centrepiece of the house, decorated in greyish-white and gold and designed to house pictures like the big portraits of George III and Queen Charlotte at either end. Then comes the magnificent Red Drawing Room, with its Chippendale furniture and Grand Tour portraits by the Italian artist Pompeo Batoni. The Staircase Hall has views of the house and downs by Tillemans, showing it as it was soon after it was built, and portraits of Sir Matthew and his wife, and the young Sir Harry.

Downstairs the huge basement shows that the servants – or at least the butler and housekeeper – lived far more comfortable lives than social historians would often have us believe. The Steward's Hall, where the upper servants would have dined, now houses an enormous dolls' house made for Sarah Lethieullier, the future wife of Sir Matthew – a perfect Queen Anne microcosm of the world of Uppark.

A few miles south a circuit of small villages give you the quintessence of the West Sussex downs – Compton, the four Mardens and Stoughton. **Compton** is a well-tended place, typically brick and flint. The church, right under the steep slope of Telegraph Hill, is mainly Victorian. One perfect October day I had to stop for a herd of fallow deer stumbling across the road to Uppark.

North Marden has a combination of farm and midget church – a simple apsidal Norman chapel. The surrounds of the small arched windows are carved with pencil-thin columns, like full-size Norman windows seen through the wrong end of a telescope. **East Marden** is the most cosily village-like of the four. At the centre is a small green, with rustic thatched well-house, rope and bucket. Above the well is a notice reading 'Rest and be Thankful But do not Wreck me', which has fortunately so far been heeded. There are beehives in the churchyard, and in the church is a prettily gilded chamber organ, which came originally from St James's Palace, and was reputedly played by Prince Albert. **Up Marden** is the remotest of all, but it is far from desolate. The minute Early English church is hidden behind farm buildings; the bare, peaceful interior is candle-lit, and has an odd triangular chancel arch, possibly Saxon stonework re-used. On the chancel floor is an ancient bell inscribed 'GOD IS MY HOPE 1620'. **West Marden** consists of a single little street at right-angles to the main road, and is a landscape artist's delight of tiled and thatched roofs, and tree-covered slopes behind.

Stoughton, two miles to the south, is a placid village, lying at ease in a wide valley. The church stands commandingly on a slope above; the low, massive slate-roofed tower was added in the fourteenth century above the south transept of a Saxon church. The most notable thing about the interior is the lofty Saxon chancel arch, roll-moulded above triple-shafted columns. Stoughton was the birthplace of the most demoniac of early nineteenth-century bowlers, George Brown, whose delivery was so fast that he needed two long-stops, the front one protected by straw padding. A ball bowled by Brown went right through a coat held out to stop it and killed a dog standing on the other side. And this was presumably underarm!

Three miles to the west, the Sussex-Hampshire border bulges to take in the ancient groves of Stansted Forest, with **Stansted Park** (now preserved as a charitable foundation) at its eastern edge. The first building on the site was a medieval hunting lodge, where the chapel now stands. A large country house was built about 1688; burnt down in 1900, it was rebuilt three years later in sumptuous Christopher Wren style, complete with colonnaded portico, roof balustrades and a cupola perched on top.

Stansted's most fascinating feature is the chapel – a strange but delightful mixture of fifteenth-century brickwork, Regency Gothic windows and twentieth-century painted decoration in red, blue and gold. It owes its appearance largely to Lewis Way, who bought

Stansted in 1804 and whose main goal in life was the conversion of Jews to Christianity and their restoration to Palestine. The east window in the sanctuary, designed by Way, is the only window in a Christian place of worship which is wholly Jewish in symbolism, showing the Ark of the Covenant and the *menorah* (seven-branched candlestick). John Keats attended the consecration of the chapel in 1819 and described the window in *The Eve of Saint Mark* (not one of his most inspired poems):

> *Moses' breastplate and the seven*
> *Candlesticks John saw in heaven,*
> *The winged Lion of St Mark,*
> *And the Covenantal Ark.*

Back on the B2146 south of Stoughton, **Funtington** is a typical village of the Chichester plain, set in a flat and featureless countryside, with a wide main street and a number of good Georgian houses. **West Stoke** two miles to the east is by comparison hardly a village at all – just a white-painted Georgian manor house over the wall from a tiny medieval church.

West Stoke is the starting point for a walk up **Kingley Vale**, a steep combe rising to a downland ridge, owned by English Nature and run as a national nature reserve. Kingley Vale is famous for its yew woods, which grow thickly up the valley and fan out along the ridge. Most extraordinary and sinister are the gigantic trees towards the bottom of the valley, which form dark caves and tunnels as the branches bend down to the ground, take root, and send out fresh reinforcements of banyan-like growth. On the downs above are barrows said to be the tombs of warriors killed in battle against the Danes; and a stone which commemorates Sir Arthur Tansley, the first chairman of the Nature Conservancy (English Nature's predecessor).

Two miles east are the Lavants. **Mid Lavant** is largely a roadside sprawl; but **East Lavant** is a prettily undulating village, with the River Lavant running beside the road. The small medieval church has a Norman west door, and a seventeenth-century brick tower stuck on the south side. **West Dean College**, a couple of miles up the valley towards Midhurst, is a vast stone battlemented mansion mainly built in 1804 by James Wyatt. Set in superb gardens, it holds adult residential courses in traditional country crafts, ranging from cookery to the craft of the armourer, and from drystone walling to the study of fairground art.

Singleton is built compactly like a miniature town in a fold of the downs. The church has a big Saxon west tower and a nave which is probably Saxon as well. It is thought that it was originally built with a long room over the nave, lit by the window above the chancel arch and reached by the Saxon doorway half way up the tower. Outside Singleton is the **Weald and Downland Open Air Museum**, where houses, barns and workshops, typical of the traditional buildings of the South-East, have been saved from the effects of time or the developer and reconstructed on a gently sloping parkland site, covering over forty acres. Among the fascinating and carefully researched reconstructions are a sixteenth-century market hall from Titchfield, across the border in Hampshire; medieval Kentish farmhouses rescued when the Bough Beech reservoir in Kent was under construction; and a watermill from Lurgashall (see above). As well as saving buildings, Singleton revives dead or dying country crafts; as in a Thomas Hardy novel, you stroll through the woodland and suddenly come across a charcoal kiln and charcoal burner's turf-covered hut. Craftsmen can stay at Singleton to learn the specialist skills involved in preserving old buildings, while children can spend the weekend there getting to grips with bricklaying and basket-making.

Heading east into the downs from Singleton, you come to **Charlton** and **East Dean,** flint-walled villages in the valley where the Lavant rises. East Dean's small cruciform church dates from about 1150. Like the Deans near Seaford it claims a connection with an earlier church built by King Alfred. You can carry on east to the Petworth road near **Up Waltham,** high on the downs – just a couple of large farms, and a tiny apsidal Norman church in the middle of a field.

Southwards towards Chichester the country is dominated by **Goodwood,** the vast estate of the Dukes of Richmond. Goodwood Park runs right up to the crest of the downs, to the famous racecourse, which looks north towards Charlton across a spacious amphitheatre of downland. Beside the racecourse is the rounded hill known as the **Trundle,** which the Iron Age inhabitants of West Sussex fortified and made their capital city; it is now topped by radio masts, and used as an enclosure for watching the races.

Goodwood House lies well down below the ridge, where the steep rise levels out. The central porticoed wing and the right-hand side wing, flint-built and linked by green-domed towers, were designed by James Wyatt for the third Duke of Richmond at the end of the eighteenth century. Goodwood is a most confusing house, largely because of its odd angles. The key to its structure lies behind the main façades, in the old house which juts out at right-angles to the rest, and is in fact the main block of a much earlier Jacobean house, adapted down the years and finally incorporated into Wyatt's scheme.

This was the house that the first Duke bought as a hunting lodge in 1697. Born in 1672, he was the son of one of Charles II's favourite mistresses, Louise de Keroualle, who had the most adventurous career of any of them. She was sent over to England by Louis XIV to spy on the king, but inevitably spying took second place to more personal considerations, and Louise ended up as Duchess of Portsmouth. A Kneller portrait of her at Goodwood shows one of the typical plump, sultry beauties of the Restoration court. To Charles she was 'my dearest dearest fubs', as he calls her in a letter in the Goodwood archive ('Fub' or 'Fubs', says the *Oxford Dictionary*, is 'a small chubby person, a term of endearment').

A Lely portrait in the gilded splendour of the vast Ballroom shows Frances Stuart ('La Belle Stuart', see also Cobham, p. 141), who managed to ward off Charles's attentions; this picture shows her in see-through négligée grasping the spear of the goddess Minerva, and was used as the model for Britannia on the British coinage. Also in the Ballroom are the Vandycks which form the showpieces of the Goodwood collection, notably the enormous painting of Charles I, Henrietta Maria and their children. Among the dozens of other pictures, collected mainly by the third Duke, are two Canalettos of London in the Long Hall, the original hall of the Jacobean hunting lodge. In the Front Hall are three Stubbs racehorse pictures, painted around 1760 when the artist was at the outset of his career.

In 1996–98 the strange-looking Egyptian State Dining Room was completely restored to Wyatt's original design, incorporating black and gold Egyptian gods, crocodiles, scarabs and other motifs in the antiquarian style popular in the years round 1800. In 1998 there was another very different restoration – the reopening of the Goodwood Motor Circuit on the perimeter track of Westhampnett airfield. The circuit was founded in 1948 by the ninth Duke (1904–89), himself a noted racing driver. Closed since 1966, it was reopened on its fiftieth anniversary as the only circuit in the world devoted entirely to historic car racing.

Devotees of modern art should not miss **Sculpture at Goodwood**, on the byroad to East Dean about a mile and a half from Goodwood

410

racecourse. This open-air exhibition, in a twenty-acre wood, displays a constantly changing selection of works by modern sculptors both famous and lesser-known. As each work is sold, another is commissioned from the sculptor who created it – an unusual form of patronage for works which can cost anything from a few thousand to half a million pounds. The backdrop of woodland and open glades suits their often monumental scale far better than the normal art gallery; while the glint of sea in the distance beyond Littlehampton, and a glimpse of the spire of Chichester Cathedral away to the south-west, set the sculptures firmly in the superb West Sussex landscape.

Appendices

Opening Times of Houses, Gardens, Museums, Historic Buildings etc.

As the opening times of many places change from year to year, with few exceptions they have not been given in the text. The most comprehensive list of opening times, entrance fees and facilities can be found in *Hundreds of Places to Visit in the South East*, covering East and West Sussex, Kent and Surrey, and revised annually (available from South East England Tourist Board, 1 Warwick Park, Tunbridge Wells, Kent TN2 5TA).

Details of National Trust properties are given in the Trust's annual *Handbook for Members and Visitors*, available at many NT properties (regional offices: for Kent and East Sussex, Estate Office, Scotney Castle, Lamberhurst, Kent TN3 8JN; for West Sussex, Polesden Lacey, Dorking, Surrey RH5 6BD).

Similarly, English Heritage produce their own regularly updated *Guide* to historic buildings and monuments throughout the country (English Heritage, 23 Savile Row, London W1X 2HE). Standard EH opening times are: mid-March to mid-October, 9.30–18.30 Mon–Sat, 14.00–18.30 Sun; mid-October to mid-March, 9.30–16.00 Mon–Sat, 14.00–16.00 Sun. However, there are a good many non-standard properties, so it is worth checking beforehand.

By no means all the houses mentioned are open to the public, though many of them open their gardens during the summer. As far as churches are concerned, an increasing number are now kept locked because of vandalism and theft. Keys are normally kept in a local shop or post office, by the vicar, or by a keyholder living in a house near by.

415

Bibliography

Armstrong, J. R. *A History of Sussex*
Barton, Margaret. *Tunbridge Wells*
Batcheller, W. *A New History of Dover* (1828)
Belloc, Hilaire. *The Four Men*
Christian, Garth. *Ashdown Forest*
Church, Richard. *Kent*
Cobb, Richard. *Still Life* (a Tunbridge Wells childhood)
Cobbett, William. *Rural Rides*
Crouch, Marcus. *Kent*
Defoe, Daniel. *A Tour through the Whole Island of Great Britain*
Dinkel, John. *The Royal Pavilion, Brighton*
Egerton, John Coker. *Sussex Folk and Sussex Ways*
Ekwall, Eilert. *The Concise Oxford Dictionary of English Place-Names*
Fiennes, Celia. *The Journeys of Celia Fiennes*
Gostling, William. *A Walk in and About the City of Canterbury* (1796)
Hammond, Reginald J. W. (ed.). *The Kent Coast, The East Sussex Coast, The West Sussex Coast* (Ward Lock Red Guides)
Handbook for Travellers in Sussex (Murray's Handbook, 1893)
Hare, Augustus. *Sussex*
Hasted, Edward. *The History and Topographical Survey of the County of Kent* (1797)
Hogarth, William. *Hogarth's Peregrination*
Hughes, Pennethorne. *Kent* (Shell Guide)
Jerrold, Walter. *Highways and Byways in Kent*
Jessup, Frank W. *A History of Kent*
Lambarde, William. *A Perambulation of Kent* (1576)
Lucas, E. V. *Highways and Byways in Sussex* (1912)
Margary, I. D. *Roman Ways in the Weald*
Nairn, Ian, and Pevsner, Nikolaus. *Sussex* (The Buildings of England)
Newman, John. *North East and East Kent* (The Buildings of England)

416

Bibliography

Newman, John. *West Kent and the Weald* (The Buildings of England)

Ogley, Bob. *In the Wake of the Hurricane* (the great storm of 16 October, 1987)

Oswald, Arthur. *Country Houses of Kent*

Parish, Rev. W. D., and Hall, Helena. *A Dictionary of the Sussex Dialect*

Piper, John. *Romney Marsh*

Sackville-West, Victoria. *Knole and the Sackvilles*

Straker, Ernest. *Wealden Iron*

Victoria County History of Kent

Victoria County History of Sussex

Wooldridge, S. W., and Goldring, Frederick. *The Weald* (New Naturalist series)

417

Index

Entries in bold type refer to illustrations

Index

Index